The Torah: Myths, Metaphors, and Modern Meaning

By Professor Michael Lubatkin

Copyright 2014 by Michael Lubatkin

First edition: All Rights reserved

No part of this book may be reproduced or transmitted in any form or by any means, electronic or mechanical, including photocopy, recording, or any informational storage or retrieval system, except for brief passages in connection with a critical review without permission in writing from the author.

Dedication

To Rabbi Alan Ullman, who taught me so much over the past 20 years and from whom I continue to learn.

To my many friends who I have studied with in Rabbi Ullman's classes.

To Hanna Sherman and Daniel Sheff whose teachings extended my understanding of Torah.

And to my wife, Christa, who with Rabbi Ullman and Hanna Sherman, created, organized, and then led thirteen seven-day hiking/Torah-study trips under the name "Alpine Footsteps" between the years 1999 and 2013 to such inspirational locations as the French, Swiss, Italian, and Austrian Alps, the Canadian Rockies, Sedona Arizona, The Sierra Nevada mountains of Andalusia, and the Judean and Negev deserts of Israel.

Table of Contents

Preface 8

Chapter 1: What is the Torah Really About? 12

Chapter 2: The Early Stories – From Creation to the Babel Tower (Genesis 1 – 11) 22

Chapter 3: Abraham, Sarah, and Their Two Sons (Genesis 12 – 24) 55

Chapter 4: Jacob, Leah, Rachel, and Sons (Genesis 25 – 36) 93

Chapter 5: Joseph and His Brothers (Genesis 37 – 50) 120

Chapter 6: Israel in Egypt (Exodus 1 – 11) 148

Chapter 7: Israel in the Wilderness (Exodus 12 – 18) 193

Chapter 8: Revelation at Sinai (Exodus 19 – 20: 14) 219

Chapter 9: Receiving the Covenant (Exodus 20:15 – 40) 245

Chapter 10: The Book of Leviticus (Leviticus 1 – 27) 276

Chapter 11: The Final Preparations (Numbers 1 – 10) 307

Chapter 12: The Tales of Rebellion (Numbers 11 – 20:13) 325

Chapter 13: Preparations for Battle (Numbers 20:14 – 25) 349

Chapter 14: The Last Days in the Wilderness (Numbers 26 – 36) 369

Chapter 15: Revisiting the First Forty Years (Deuteronomy 1 – 11) 387

Chapter 16: Extending and Clarifying the Covenant Code (Deuteronomy 12 – 30) 412

Chapter 17: The On-Going Journey (Deuteronomy 31 - 33) 431

Preface

The stories from the Torah (also known as the Pentateuch, Old Testament, and the Five Books of Moses) that many of us grew up with pose questions that either challenge our sense of reason or make us moderns uneasy. Consider a few examples from the Book of Genesis: Are we to believe that Noah was 600 years old when he built the ark, that Sarah gave birth to Isaac at age ninety, and that Abraham lived to be 175? Why should Abraham be revered as the father of three religions; after all, didn't he banish Hagar and her son Ishmael to the parched-dry wilderness with only a small supply of food and water? Surely he must have suspected that Hagar and Ishmael were likely to die as a result. Did God really ask Abraham to do what no father should ever be asked to do: sacrifice his son? Wouldn't the staging of this sacrifice likely cause long-term psychological trauma to the boy? Might there have been a more subtle, gentler way to convey the message that child sacrifice is unacceptable? Speaking of Isaac, why is he portrayed in his middle-age as so old and feeble that he couldn't even distinguish between his two very different-looking sons, Esau and Jacob? Couldn't a nobler person than Jacob have been selected as one of the three patriarchs? His deceitful actions suggest a person who cannot be trusted; even his name translates from Hebrew as "heel-thief!"

Critical questions like these resonate even louder in the Book of Exodus, whose listing of the Ten Commandments have made it a foundational work in Western culture. For example, we read of the time when Moses, as a young man, kills an Egyptian task-master after seeing that person strike a Hebrew. Did the task-master's punishment fit the crime? Might a court of law today convict Moses of man-slaughter? Later in the story, why does God harden Pharaoh's heart and then punish him and all those living in Egypt with Ten Plagues? If God is all-powerful, why doesn't God instead soften Pharaoh's heart? By doing the opposite, isn't God acting more as an accomplice in crime than a savior? What about the vast number of Egyptian soldiers who drowned when the sea waters closed around them; did the nation of Israel have to be born on the backs of so many deaths? Staying on the subject of death, why does God call for the complete extermination of the Amalekites? Isn't extermination another word for genocide?

The Books of Leviticus, Numbers, and Deuteronomy continue this dire tone. Did God really have to consume Aaron's two eldest sons in a flash-fire, simply because of a minor infraction in the way that they administered over their first public ritual? How can God expect us to have compassion while showing so little? While on the subject of compassion (or lack of such), how are we to interpret God's warning in these three books that if we don't obey the commandments, we run the risk of being publicly stoned to death and made to "eat the flesh of your sons and daughters"? (You read correctly; this quote comes directly from verse 29 of the twenty-sixth chapter of the Book of Leviticus.)

Simply put, is there more to the Torah than we might glean from these questions and other similar ones? As explained in *The Torah: Myths, Metaphors, and Modern Meanings*, my answer to this question is a definite "yes." My reason for writing this book is to make the Torah more accessible to those of us who, as contemporary thinkers, find its stories primitive and problematic.

To that end, I use a literary-critical lens and knowledge of the Hebrew language. I say "literary" rather than literal, because I do not view the biblical stories in the Torah as necessarily depicting historically accurate happenings. Instead, I regard them as symbolic works in which the characters and events can be best understood as representing deeper meanings, often within a moral and spiritual context.

My choice of the word "literary" also reflects my religiously neutral focus: I try neither to discredit nor promote any particular religion. Rather, I view the five books of the Torah as more philosophical than religious (philosophy raises questions that cannot be answered with certainty, while religion offers answers that cannot be questioned). By doing so, I hope to provide many readers with a wealth of fresh insights.

Included among those insights are:

- That women played prominent roles in the biblical stories, at least on par with that of the leading men.
- That there is no mention of the word "sin" in the Garden of Eden saga about Adam and Eve, nor is it used in reference to their sexual awakening. (The word first appears in regards to Cain's killing of his brother, Abel.)
- That the Ten Plagues weren't "plagues," nor were the Ten Commandments "commandments." Moreover, these two lists of "ten" are related.

- That it wasn't just the Israelites who left Egypt during the exodus.
- That the Promised Land and the Land of Canaan are not perfect correlates.
- That laying at the very center of the Torah scroll is the verse "Be loving to your neighbor (as one) like yourself", which is often referred to as the Golden Rule.
- That Satan appears in Numbers 22 not as a fallen angel, lord of all evil and enemy of God, but rather as one of God's loyal messengers.

The book also looks at other points of interest, including:
- Why Adam and Eve did not die the moment that they ate the fruit from the tree, as God had promised they would.
- The ages given for Abraham and Sarah, why they were chosen to be the "parents of a multitude," and why Abraham was told to sacrifice his son.
- The symbolic meanings of certain numbers (e.g., 2, 3, 4, 7, 10, 12, and 40); of words and phrases (e.g., Chosen People, Israel, barrenness, matzo, Egypt, the Wilderness, and the Promised Land); and of Joseph's name and his two dreams.
- Why the Book of Exodus conjugates God's name as a verb.
- The making sense of the excessive cruelty depicted in some of the later stories.

My other goal in writing this book is to suggest a method for teaching the Biblical stories. Specifically, I follow a question-driven approach, modeled after the teaching style that I adopted during my three decades as a professor at the University of Connecticut. First, I summarize the scenario depicted in each of the Torah's many chapters. I then identify a few key "discussion" questions that may come to mind with each one. I use these questions to direct my commentary. I make no claim that the questions or the commentary that I offer are entirely original or exhaustive. My intent is simply to provide a springboard for which the readers can form their own opinions. The questions and the associated analysis provide a logical basis for a self-directed study, should one decide to tackle the Torah on his/her own or in small discussion groups. They also can serve as an instructor's guide for teaching basic courses on each or all of the Torah's five books.

All told, *The Torah: Myths, Metaphors, and Modern Meanings* introduces the layperson to a new way to read, question, and interpret the Torah. The book should help readers appreciate that the Torah is more than an expression of an ancient culture's religious beliefs and superstitions. It is a compilation of practical lessons -- universally relevant across time and culture -- which were written between two and three thousand years ago by authors already skilled in some astonishingly sophisticated literary techniques. I begin by addressing the question, "What is the Torah Really About?"

Chapter 1: What is the Torah Really About?

The Torah, which includes the books of Genesis, Exodus, Leviticus, Numbers, and Deuteronomy, has presented a special challenge to translators because it was written in ancient Hebrew, without punctuation marks and without vowels. In attempts to make sense of various portions of the text, translators have added their own interpretations. These interpretive insertions include, among many others, such familiar images as --- Eve handing an apple to Adam (the Torah does not state what the forbidden fruit is, nor does it state that women are forever cursed because of her eating that fruit); the building of the Egyptian pyramids by the enslaved Israelites (the Torah makes no mention of building pyramids); and Moses leading the Israelites across the Red Sea (neither he nor the people are said to have crossed this sea).

The problem with these and other such alterations is that they can change the original meaning, often to reflect the translator's own religious leanings. Consider the phrase, "eye for an eye, tooth for a tooth," which is taken from Exodus 21, verses 23 through 27. Many have interpreted this phrase to mean that the God of the Torah is unforgiving and condones acts of barbaric revenge. However, Hillel[1] - one of the most important figures in Jewish history, who was believed to be born about the time of Jesus – pointed out that the context in which this phrase appears suggests something very different: Should an individual cause bodily harm to another due to acts of negligence or intent, the perpetrator is obliged to pay the victim the monetary equivalent of what the lost eye – or any other body part -was worth. Taken in this light, the phrase is not about revenge, but rather represents a basis for civil law that is still relevant in today's courts.

Consider also the misunderstood expression, "The Chosen People." Some read this expression into Exodus 19:5, but there is no mention of it in the original Hebrew text. Translated

---

1

Born in Babylon around 110 BCE and coming to Jerusalem at the age of forty, Hillel is associated with the development of the Talmud, consisting of the Mishnah and the Gomorrah, both being commentaries on the Torah. One of his most famous sayings, recorded in Pirkei Avot ("Ethics of the Fathers," a tractate of the Mishnah), is "If I am not for myself, then who will be for me? And if I am only for myself, then what am I? And if not now, when?"

directly from the Hebrew, this verse reads: "If you will hearken, yes, hearken to my voice and keep my covenant, you shall be to me a special treasure from among all people." As such, this verse does not imply that God is "choosing" a specific group of people to the exclusion of all others. Rather, the if/then structure of the verse suggests that it is *we* who must do the choosing to hearken to God's voice and keep God's covenant.

Moreover, this verse implies that anyone – Jew or otherwise – who actively and willingly keeps God's commandments becomes one of the "chosen." The message of inclusiveness is reinforced throughout the Torah. For example, Exodus 12: 38 describes those who left Egypt as not only Jews, but a "mixed multitude." This message of inclusiveness is also one of the core teachings of the Jonah story, which is read on Yom Kippur, the most holy day of the Jewish calendar.

In my attempt to stay true to the original meaning of the Torah, while avoiding such interpretive insertions as the "Chosen People," I will rely primarily on Everett Fox's translations as they appear in his recently published book, "The Five Books of Moses," because his translations are believed by many biblical scholars to be the closest to the original text.

I will also take the position that the Torah is first and foremost a theological document; the stories that it tells are primarily concerned with conveying spiritual and ethical teachings and not necessarily historical happenings. Marc Brettler, in his 2005 book, "How to Read the Bible," similarly argues that while the Torah's stories may contain references to specific historical events, they were never written with the intent of historical accuracy. For example, while the Hebrews were said to have spent four centuries as slaves in Egypt, no artifacts have been found in Israel after the time of the exodus that reflect an earlier Egyptian influence. Similarly, although it is stated in Exodus 12: 37 that about six hundred thousand men left Egypt to wander for forty years in the relatively small region of the Sinai, no evidence whatsoever has been found in Sinai to suggest that such a mass exodus (which had to also include women and children), ever took place. Finally, while it is true that Mount Sodom is made from salt (and gypsum) most would agree that the mountain's composition has nothing to do with Lot's wife.

Rather than read the text as a book of history, I will approach the Torah as a collection of mythologies, folklores, and metaphors, all intended to convey philosophical and practical wisdoms for living a meaningful and socially-just life. After all, the word "Torah" means "teachings." My intent is to bring to light many of the Torah's meaningful "teachings" that are embedded in each biblical story.

There is another reason that I will not take an overly literal view of the Torah: The text contains too many inconsistencies to be taken literally. The first plague described in the Book of Exodus provides one such example. While most of the plagues are associated with starting and ending dates, the first plague, which is about all the water in Egypt turning to blood, is only given a starting date. If taken literally, this would mean that every person in this arid land would have died within a few days; from Pharaoh and his royal magicians to each slave, including Moses, all would be dead, as would be the story – no one would be alive to endure the other nine plagues! There would be no Exodus from Egypt, no revelation at Sinai - - and no Torah.

This inconsistency as well as the many others found in Torah should not be viewed as evidence of sloppy writing or poor editing, but rather as constant reminders not to literalize that which is intended to represent allegory. Baruch Spinoza, the famous seventeenth century Jewish philosopher from Holland, argued a similar point. He noted that the Torah should be interpreted like any piece of literature – its meaning and relevance dependent on the historical context of the reader. Similarly, Moses Maimonides, a revered Biblical scholar and physician, stated almost a millennium ago that if our literal reading of the scripture suggests something that is clearly contrary to reason, we must interpret what we read as metaphor for, he pointed out, the Torah often speaks "figuratively and allegorically." More recently, Yair Zakovitch, dean of humanities at the Hebrew University, said, "The thing to remember about the Bible is that the events and characters are just there to convey messages… not so much to tell us what really happened."[2] Our challenge will be to try to understand what messages the writers (without or with a capital "W" to represent God) might have had in mind by inserting inconsistencies.

---

[2] Professor Zakovitch's quote appears on page 85 of Bruce Fieler's 2005 book, "Where God was Born."

Indeed, what makes the Torah as meaningful today as it was when it was written three thousand some years ago, during the Bronze Age, is that its questions are timeless, though how we might think about them changes with our life experiences. As such, the Torah is more a book of philosophy (which raises questions that cannot be answered with certainty) than it is a book of religion (which offers answers that cannot be questioned). In my attempt to make meaningful, twenty-first century philosophical sense of the Torah, I will focus on identifying and discussing some of its timeless questions.

For example, did God write the Torah? Many have puzzled over who or what is God, and whether the Torah was written by God, by enlightened people, or by those who were spoken to by God. Few terms evoke such strong emotions, opinions, and definitions as does the term, "God." Some, like Hanna (her story appears in the Book of Samuel, and is read on Rosh Hashanah), understood God as the internal voice that can be heard during times of meditation, silent prayer, and introspection. This story teaches us that by looking inward and listening intensely to our inner voice, we can become more aware of who we are and what we need to do.

Israel ben Eliezer, the founder of Hassidism (also known as the *Bal Shem Tov*, or "The Master of the Good Name"), held a somewhat different view. In his "religion of the heart," he envisioned God as being present everywhere - even in the smallest of actions, objects, and situations, and in the "smallest of still voices" (the latter phrase appearing in I Kings 19:11-12 and in the story about Elijah). He taught that God's ubiquitous nature makes God's presence difficult to perceive unless we willingly open our hearts and awaken all of our senses to that which we are experiencing in the moment we are experiencing it. Contemporary spiritualist John Cabot Zinn refers to a very similar awakened state as "mindfulness" and Eckhart Tolle as "The Power of Now."

Others, like Albert Einstein, conceptualized God in rational, external terms: the marvelous order and lawfulness that are revealed in nature and in the world of thought, arts and science. Einstein described his feelings of awe as "Cosmic Religious Feelings" that seem to transcend one's own being.

Still others, like Martin Buber and Rabbi Mordecai Kaplan view God as an unknowable force. Buber argued that God can be found in the force that attracts us to others, which he called the "I-Thou" relationship.[3] In such relationships we demonstrate the capacity to understand others' identity deeply enough to give them what they need in real time and, as well, we come to understand our own identity ("I" only becomes an "I" in relation to a Thou"). To be bonded in such "I-thou" relationships is to feel grace, love, compassion, insight, and awe, and each bond offers us the opportunity to glimpse through to the eternal Thou. Kaplan, a founder of Reconstructionist Judaism, envisions God as a moral compass, a force that drives us to do the right things for ourselves, others, and the planet.

These various understandings of God all deal with how we experience God. They do not define who or what God is. In this regard, the Torah is not helpful. While God is clearly the single most important figure in the Torah -- no one, not even Abraham or Moses, is said to have advanced on their respective personal and spiritual journeys and their quest for a more meaningful life, without the complete support of God -- yet the concept of God remains abstract. Or, as Maimonides lamented in "The Guide to the Perplexed," our knowledge of God consists in knowing that we are unable to comprehend God.

Even God's name, *Ehyeh asher ehyeh,* ("I will be whatever I will be" or "I will be present whenever and wherever I will be present"), as it was revealed to Moses at the Burning Bush, gives no hint as to who or what God is. In point of fact, God's name, often stated as *Adonai*, is unlike all the other names in the Torah, which reveal core aspects of personality. (For example, Isaac's Hebrew name, Yitzhak, is derived from the Hebrew word for "laughter," for he brought laughter to his parents in their old age, while Jacob's Hebrew name, Jacob, means "heel-sneak" or "deceiver," because he tricked his brother and father in his quest to receive the family's birthright.) In contrast, God's name isn't so much a name - in the sense that names are nouns -

---

[3] In 1923, Buber wrote his famous essay on existence, *Ich und Du* (later translated into English as *I and Thou*). In it, he pointed out that we can either relate to people as *objects*, for the sole purpose of advancing our own agenda, or as *subjects*, wherein our foremost concern is for their needs and feelings. He referred to the first relationship as "I-It" and to the second as "I-Thou." The cultivation of "I-Thou" relationships, he said, represents the highest and most noble purpose in life.

but instead is a verb, conjugated in the first person, imperfect tense to signify a yet-to-be completed action. The construction of God's name suggests an ongoing two-way movement between the distant past and an unbounded, ever-unfolding future - - an unknowable force of infinite oneness, residing without limits (*ein sof*) outside of time, form and space, and for which there is no other (*ein ode*). [4]

Perhaps the writers of the Torah conceptualized God by this abstraction to affirm that God is beyond our ability to understand, define, predict, or influence. The instant that we say something specific about God or think that we know what God would want (as the prophet Elijah was said to have done in I Kings 19), we violate the Name. It is interesting to note that this conceptualization lies in stark contrast to the image of God that many of us grew up with: the all-wise and all-powerful parent figure who intervenes in our lives when we are at risk, rewards us when we do the right things, and punishes us when we don't. Freud described this personified parental view of God as "immature," while Einstein similarly described it as "childlike." In her book, "A History of God," Christian theologian Karen Armstrong notes that any humanized view of God can readily become idol-like, carved in *our* own image. And Rabbi Harold Kushner, in "When Bad Things Happen to Good People," points out that believing in a "parental" God can engender feelings of arrogance, intolerance, anger, guilt, and betrayal, depending on whether or not our prayers are answered to our satisfaction.

Perhaps by keeping the concept of God abstract, the writers may also be saying that there are many ways to experience God. Depending on where we are in any given moment of life, we might be looking inward or outward, in the relationship that we develop with our self, with

---

[4]

On page 84 of Maria Prager's book, "Path of Blessings", she writes that YHVH's name can be thought of as representing the three temporal tenses of the Hebrew verb "to be" -- "was" (*hayah*), "is" (*haveh*) and "will be" *(yihyeh)* - - which flow simultaneously in all directions to create an eternal sense of oneness that she refers to as "iswaswillbe" or "pastpresentfuture".

others, and with nature. The Torah is also implying that we should be wary of those who hold an anthropomorphic, humanized vision of God, of those who claim to speak or act in God's behalf, and of those who assign meaning to interpret God's actions as if they know what God is. To avoid these errors as well as the strong emotions and opinions that the term invokes, I will refer to God in this book in its most mystical, abstract way, as "YHVH", which is an acronym for *Ehyeh asher ehyeh* and is pronounced as an exhaled breath. (Those who are reluctant to speak the four letters substitute for them the word *Adonay*, meaning "to be" or "The Eternal.")

Some will be surprised to learn that the word "God" does not appear in the Torah, nor is there an equivalent Hebrew word for it. "God" - - and the personified image of the divine that this word evokes -- originated with early interpretations of the Torah, done by, among others, Greek philosophers and Catholic theologians, the latter of whom introduced the word "Gott" and a way of thinking about the divinity that is distinctly not "Torah." Closest in Torah to a "God-concept" is the word "*Elohim*", which is conjugated in the plural form and is understood to represent an infinite number of manifestations of YHVH; that is, every aspect of reality that we might encounter. For example, in the first chapter of Genesis, *Elohim* appears as a voice, while in the Book of Deuteronomy, where it states "YHVH your Elohim", the term is referring to the full set of ethical beliefs contained in the Torah. [5]

---

[5]
El Shaddai is another God-term used in Torah, specifically in Exodus 6:2, 3, where it is stated as the name by which YHVH was known to Abraham, Isaac and Jacob. Often interpreted to mean "Almighty", it, like *Elohim,* is used in Torah to capture an infinitely small aspect of YHVH's hidden essence. The word "*El*" comes from the root word meaning "might or power", while *Shaddai* comes from the root word meaning "sufficient." Shaddai is also thought to be an acronym for the phrase *Shomer daltot Yisrael* - "Guardian of the doors of Israel" – which is abbreviated as the letter Shin on most *mezuzote* (the small casing that observant Jews attach to the doorposts of their homes).

Finally, a fair question to ask before advancing to the next chapter is this: If YHVH is as unknowable as the Torah claims, then why does YHVH appear in the Torah? Might we be able to derive the same teachings from the Torah without making any mention of YHVH? For the moment, I leave this as an open question for the reader to consider. However, I will return to it in the book's concluding chapter, once we all have had time to reflect on the various teachings from the Torah.

And, what exactly are the Torah teachings? As we will discover, the Torah offers many lessons, but at its core the teachings they all have to do with how we can be more human, appreciate life before death, and participate in the ongoing process of creation. These teachings have nothing to do with what we are to believe, how fervently we believe, or our religious affiliation, but instead they provide guidance about how to transform our consciousness to more life-enhancing levels of awareness, even during mundane or trying times. "All else is commentary," Hillel might have said to this, so let's proceed with some commentary. [6]

Chapter 2 will do so on the early stories: Creation, Adam and Eve, Cain and Abel, Noah, and the Babel Tower. The third chapter offers commentary about the lives of Abraham, Sarah and their two sons, Ishmael and Isaac. Chapter 4 does the same for the lives of Jacob, his two wives, Leah and Rachel, and Jacob's many sons, including Joseph. The fifth chapter looks more deeply into the life of Joseph and his interactions with his many brothers. Chapter 6 examines core teachings from the Book of Exodus, beginning with the early life of Moses in Egypt and continuing through the Ten Plagues. The seventh chapter comments on the events that took place during the first three months in the wilderness. Chapter 8 offers fresh insights into the meaning

---

[6]

In "Saying from the Fathers" (1:14), Hillel summarized the meaning of the Torah in one sentence "What is hateful to you, do not do to your fellow [or, "Do not do to others as you would not have done to you."]. This is the whole of the Torah. The rest is commentary." The prophet Micah similarly summarized the Torah in one sentence: "Do justice, love mercy, and walk humbly with your God." The origin of these two variations of the "Golden Rule" comes from Leviticus 19:18, "You shall love your neighbor as yourself."

of each of the Ten Commandments. The ninth chapter addresses the events leading up to and immediately following the building of the Golden Calf. The tenth chapter tries to make sense of the many priestly instructions detailed in the Book of Leviticus. Chapter 11 addresses the remaining details that require attention before the people are ready to leave the Wilderness of Sinai and start their journey to the Promised Land. Chapter 12, "Tales of Rebellion" describes the thirty-eight years of wandering until the arrival at Moab, and the six mutinous attempts by the people to abandon their journey. Chapter 13, "Preparations for Battle" details the steps taken by the people, as they ready themselves to enter the land of Canaan and Chapter 14 describes the early conquests. Chapters 15, 16 and 17 examine the stories from the Book of Deuteronomy.

Chapter 2: The Early Stories – From Creation to the Babel Tower

Introduction: The early stories about creation - the Garden of Eden, the Tower of Babel, and the Flood- were borrowed from the more ancient folklore of the surrounding Mesopotamian cultures, but in their adaptation they reveal a core difference: Whereas the older stories describe the life of the early humans as being driven entirely by the arbitrary whims of the gods and having no possibility of affecting their destiny, the Torah depicts an orderly world, created by a transcendent God to promote life, and governed by explicit laws of morality that allow humans to choose how they will live. As such, while the early stories in the Torah appear almost like nursery tales, where serpents speak and humans live for hundreds of years, these stories nevertheless convey profound practical, philosophical, and spiritual teachings on which the later chapters of the Torah are grounded.

➢ The Creation Story: Genesis 1:1 through Genesis 2:4

Background: The Creation story is one of the most familiar stories in Genesis, yet one of the least understood. For many, it is an attempt to explain the origin of time and space, but an attempt that fails because of what we have learned from recent advances in cosmology, geology, chemistry, and evolutionary biology. It is not surprising, therefore, that we are inclined to skim over the story's many verses. For today, however, let's try to read these verses with a different lens, viewing them not as a story of science or history, but as a story that contains a number of core concepts that will enhance our understanding of all subsequent stories in Genesis.

Summary: *In the beginning, when the earth was unformed and void (that is, "wild and waste" or in Hebrew: "toe-hoo v'voe-hoo"), there was darkness over the face of the Ocean and the rushing wind-spirit of YHVH hovering over the face of the waters, YHVH said, "Let there be light" and saw that the light was good. YHVH then separated the light from the darkness, and called the light Day and the darkness Night. There was setting, there was dawning, the **first day**. YHVH spoke and in so doing separated the waters from the heavens, and it was so. There was setting, there was dawning, the **second day**. YHVH spoke again and the dry land separated from the waters, and it was so. YHVH said "Let the earth sprout forth with plants that yield seeds and* *fruit, and it was so. And the earth did as YHVH spoke and YHVH saw that it was good. There was setting, there was dawning, the* **third day**. *Then, YHVH spoke for there to be lights in the dome of the heavens to provide light on the earth and to separate day from night, so that they may be signs – for set-times, for days and years – and it was so. YHVH then created two great lights, the greater one for the ruling of the day, and the smaller light for the ruling of the night, along with the stars. And, YHVH saw that it was good. There was setting, there was dawning, the* **fourth day**. *YHVH spoke to let the waters swarm with living beings and the fowl fly above the earth. And, YHVH saw that it was good. There was setting, there was dawning, the* **fifth day**. *Then, YHVH spoke to let the earth bring forth all forms of wildlife, and it was so. And the wildlife made wildlife after their kind, and YHVH saw that it was good. YHVH then said "Let us make humankind, in our image, according to our likeness." So, YHVH created humankind, male and female and blessed them to "Bear fruit and be many and fill the earth" and for their eating, granted them dominion over the fish in the sea, the fowl of the heavens, all the animals and crawling things upon the earth, and all green plants. It was so. YHVH saw all that YHVH had made, and it was exceedingly good! There was setting, there was dawning, the* **sixth day**. *On the* **seventh day**, *YHVH ceased from all work, blessed the day and hallowed it.*

Discussion Questions: These verses provoke a number of interesting questions, including: What existed before Day 1? How is YHVH depicted in the story? How was Day 1 created? What is the "light" that YHVH saw then and how does it differ from the light seen in Day 4? Why does YHVH follow six acts of creation with the words "it was so" and six other acts as "good," or, in the case of the sixth day, "exceedingly good"? Who is the "us" in the words, "Let us make humankind in our image"? What is special about the seventh day; and, what does "seven" symbolize?

- **What existed before Day 1?** The writers carefully avoided the imponderable questions about "first cause" that plague cosmologists to this day (e.g., "What preceded the 'Big Bang'?"), other than to say that "in the beginning" there was YHVH and a primal disorder, using the words *tohu va-vohu*; i.e., unformed and void. (Torah, written in Hebrew without vowels, can be deliciously ambiguous. For example, its opening word, *b'ray-sheet*, which is commonly translated as "in the beginning", could also mean "at a beginning", implying an infinite number of beginnings.) Accordingly, the Torah simply states that the beginning began when YHVH spoke the world into being.

- **How is God depicted?** In Genesis 1, YHVH is introduced to the narrative as *elohim* ("*el*" simply means "deity") and is described as a wind-spirit (*ru'akh elohim*) or "God's breath" that hovers (as, in being fluid or always moving) over the dark face of the waters of pre-creation. The text is likening YHVH to something that lacks form and substance yet can be observed in the things that it touches - like a bush or a field of wheat. Thus, the Torah introduces the notion that we can experience YHVH, but never know YHVH nor any of YHVH's attributes because *Ehyeh asher ehyeh;* "YHVH will be whatever YHVH will be."

  In the Garden of Eden story, the wind-spirit metaphor comes to represent a person's soul *(nesh-ee-mah)*, first as YHVH "blew into Adam's nostrils the breath of life and the human became a living being" (Genesis 2:7), and again at the very end of Deuteronomy 34:5, where "Moses dies at the mouth of YHVH" (often interpreted as YHVH withdrawing Moses's breath).

  As we will see in later portions of the text, YHVH is referred to by other names and described by different metaphors, but all will signify an unknowable abstraction. For example, in Exodus 14:19, YHVH is depicted as a "Pillar of Cloud." Of course, clouds are not heavy, but instead are light and airy. And their shape is nebulous, never taking a discrete geometric form like a pillar. Juxtaposing "pillar" and "cloud," therefore, suggests a counter-intuitive opposite intended to transcend our logic.

- **How was Day 1 created?** Like the other six days of Creation, the first day in the Creation story is said to be formed by the separation of opposing states. On Day 1, the duality is light and darkness: YHVH created the first day by separating light from the darkness through the act of speech. The notion of separation plays an important role throughout Torah. Indeed, the word, *kadosh*, which is used when referring to Shabbat and is traditionally defined as "holy," shares the same *shoresh* (three-letter linguistic root) as does the verb "to separate" or "to set apart."

As an interesting aside, the Hebrew language uses these three-letter linguistic roots, or *shoresh'im,* to construct many of its words and to signify their conceptual similarity. For example, "Torah" shares the same *sho-resh* as does *mo'reh*, the former meaning "teaching" and the latter meaning "teacher".

Regarding the idea that YHVH created through the act of speech, it is interesting to note that in pre-biblical times, local cultures recognized the power of the spoken word that, once uttered, cannot be withdrawn, implying that the spoken word can change things forever. Consider, for example, marriages that have been destroyed by words spoken in anger. There is an Aramaic phrase that we are all familiar with that captures this wisdom: "*abra-ka-dabra.*" It means "I create as I speak." (As an aside, Aramaic is a sister language to Hebrew, spoken during biblical times by many, including Jesus and the apostles, and it is used in the chanting of the *Kaddish*, the Mourners' Prayer, in synagogues to this day.)

- **What is the "light" that YHVH saw on the first day?** How many times have we read the verse "Let there be light" without asking ourselves why light is created on the first day and then again on the fourth day? The light that is being referred to in the third verse of this story cannot be referring to light as we know it. The reason is simple: The Torah tells us that YHVH didn't create physical light until the fourth day, only after the sun and the moon are created! This delicious conundrum may have been introduced into the first few verses of text to signal to the reader that the Torah requires our full attention. And, more importantly, embedded in its resolution are at least three foundational thoughts on which the rest of the Torah is based.

First, the light seen on the first day is intended to represent spiritual light: the dawn of awareness and the source of enlightenment. As we will soon discover, the distinction between the physical and the spiritual is fundamental to decoding many of the teachings in the Torah. For example, death, as it is characterized in many of the later stories, often refers not to the end of physical existence, but rather to the movement away from spiritual ideals, as in "the death of one's spirit" or a loss of intimacy with self, other, or YHVH. Thinking of death in this way may change entirely the way that we have always thought about the ninth plague (Darkness) and the tenth plague (Death to the First Born). But, more about the plagues in a later chapter.

Second, the Torah has "day" being created twice, on the first day ("*There was setting, there was dawning, the first day*") and on the fourth day. However, the "day" that is separated from night on the fourth day is done so specifically to establish time ("*so that they may be signs – for set-times, for days and years*"). Here the Torah may be saying that YHVH and the first three days of creation transcend time in that they existed before time, or at least our understanding of what time is. The Torah may also be saying that while Creation is described in the text as taking place over seven days, this measure should not be taken literally, since the first three days do not conform to a twenty-four hour interval. This recognition that "time" in the Torah may sometimes mean something different than clock-time will have a bearing in the discussion about the meaning of Shabbat, to appear shortly.

Third, through separation, the Torah may be saying that YHVH changed the nature of darkness. Whereas there was spiritual light within the darkness that existed before Day 1, the darkness that YHVH created in Day 1 represents the *absence* of spiritual light. And, while spiritual darkness is obviously not the desired state, it was created to allow humans a degree of free will: We can choose to move closer to the light, or choose to move as far away from the light as is imaginable, as Eli Wiesel depicted in his book "Night," about the Holocaust.

Also, spiritual darkness was not created to house or give birth to a "prince of darkness." Indeed, the concept of a devil is totally foreign to the Torah. Although there are a few stories that make mention of Satan (e.g., Numbers 22:2-35; I Kings 5:11-12; and the Book of Job), Satan is never presented as a character with demonic transcendent powers, but rather as a being who argues an opposing point of view, not against YHVH, but against a person who is about to go against YHVH's wishes. In Numbers, that person is Bil'am, and in I Kings 5 that person is Solomon. Consistent with that literary role, Satan's name means simply the "opponent" or "adversary."

It is important to understand that, for its time, the notion that free will is embedded in creation was a pretty radical thought. What we know about the ancients is that they tended to believe that life was predetermined by the Great Wheel, or what some called "the Mandala." Like the moon, tides, and the farming seasons, all of life was understood to move in a never-changing and inescapable cycle of birth, growth, and death. With each turn of the wheel, every person, place, and thing that was, will forever again be. Said simply, the Mandala, unlike the Torah, has no provisions for free will, and thus there is no hope of breaking free from this deterministic wheel.

- **Why does YHVH follow six acts of creation with the words "it was so" and six other acts with "good" (*tov*), with the last being "exceedingly good"?** Carefully read each reference and you will see that "it is so" (i.e., "it is yes") is used for those acts which engender the potential to bring forth the life that is embedded within them by creation, while "good" is used for those acts where that potential is realized. Understanding this definition of "good" will soon help us decipher what the Tree of Knowing Good and Evil is intended to mean. "Exceedingly good" refers to the Sabbath, that day when YHVH was said to have separated the physical world from the spiritual world. (See the soon-to-follow commentary about "What is special about the Seventh day?")

- **The expression, "Let us make humankind, in our image, according to our likeness!" suggests that YHVH is not alone. Who is "us" and what might be the teaching?** Some have argued that the implied "others" refers to angels in the heavenly court. Fox notes that the English word, "angel," stems from the Greek word *angelos* (in Hebrew, *ma'lakh*), which means "messenger." In the context of Torah, messengers may represent another manifestation of YHVH. For example, messengers appear in Genesis 18 in the form of three men who come to Abraham's tent and announce to him that his wife will have a son. They also appear in Jacob's dream about a ladder that reaches the heavens, and "messengers of God were going up and down on it" (Genesis 28:12). And they appear when Moses saw "YHVH's messenger in the flame of a fire out of the midst of a bush" (Exodus, 3:2).

Of course, like most verses in the Torah, the verse "Let us make humankind, in our image, according to our likeness!" is open to many interpretations. Here, I would like to mention two that are ecologically friendly.

"Us" may be referring not only to YHVH, but to all of the life that YHVH had created in the sea, sky, and land on the fifth and sixth days, including *us* humans. We were all created by the same creator, evolved from the same primitive single cell, drew life from the same carefully balanced ecosystem, and have been given by YHVH the capacity to create something good (tov), that is, to realize our potential to bring forth life. As such, the Torah may have wanted to teach that we are all "one" (*ekh'ad*) and that our existence is inextricably linked to the existence of the life forms that preceded us.

"Us" may also be referring to the "land" that was created on the third day, for it too is treated in Torah as a living entity: It changes over time and has the capacity to give birth to other forms of life (e.g., *And the earth did as YHVH spoke and YHVH saw that it was good*). As we will read in Genesis 2, Adam's name comes from the Hebrew word, *a-da-ma*, which means "earth"; thus his name means "from the earth." And, like other living things, the land will lose the capacity to bring forth life and will die if not properly cared for. For example, in Leviticus 25, YHVH tells Moses that, just as humans deserve the Sabbath, so too does the land: Every seventh year it should be left fallow and whatever grows that year, even if self-propagated, should be neither harvested nor eaten by anyone other than the poor.

In sum, the Torah may have inserted "us" to remind humans that we are not separate from other life forms; we are but one part of a larger creative whole. In Martin Buber's terms, our challenge is to maintain an "I-Thou" relationship with all living things, including the land, for by destroying other acts of creation, we ultimately destroy ourselves. Put in another Buber-like way, we need to be careful not to relate to all of creation as objects whose sole purpose is to advance our own agenda.

- **What is special about the seventh day?** YHVH created the physical world during the first six days through a process of separation, or "setting apart." This process continues on the seventh day, the Sabbath (or *Shabbat),* when YHVH separates the physical world from the spiritual world.

Shabbat, which comes from the root, *shin-beit-tav*, means "to stop" and not, as it is more commonly translated, "to rest." The passage, "On the seventh day, God stopped from all labor," implies that stopping is woven into the fabric of creation; it is a fundamental part of creation, just as was the creation of the land, wildlife, and humans. Moreover, by observing the Sabbath, we are perhaps being told that we can actively participate in the creative process - if we learn how to inhabit the stopping and free ourselves from the familiar and sometimes nerve-racking constraints that time places on us, so that we can see the extraordinary in the ordinary, as Moses did when he saw the bush burning, but not being consumed.

This sounds pretty lofty, so let's try to bring this teaching down to something easier to relate to. Most of us live in a work-centric world, where we spend much of our waking hours occupying our minds and bodies with those tasks, responsibilities, and ambitions that we hope will increase our security, prosperity, and status. Yet, many of us yearn for something more from life than "building pyramids in Egypt seven days a week for someone else." Perhaps we sense that our lives are somehow incomplete; we may feel alienated from our true identity or desire to feel more whole. Within each of us lies a spiritual side with questions that want to be heard-- questions like "who am I?, why am I?, and what is my real purpose?"

Shabbat is about taking the time to listen, and then to discover personally meaningful answers to those questions. It is a time of introspection and meditation, when we try to quiet our mind of its labor-centric dialogues, listening instead to the voices of our heart (what some refer to as our "inner teachings") and being fully present in the moment. Shabbat is about stopping what we are doing long enough to build a relationship with ourselves. Drawing from Rabbi Alan Lew's book, "Be Still and Get Going," it is a time of meditation when we can move from "unconsciousness to awareness, from tension to relaxation, from being scattered to being centered, from sleep to wakefulness" (2005: 12). In other words, it is a time when we can gain self-knowledge and learn to better appreciate our own lives.

Shabbat is not about a long list of restrictions - of do's and don'ts that have no basis in Torah and which can remove us from life and from ourselves. Instead, we should feel free on Shabbat to do the things that enhance our spiritual development, engaging in activities for which we have a passion – activities that "speak to us." Gardening (or jogging, carpentry, and so on) may be work for some, but for others it represents a labor of love that brings inner peace and relaxation. In point of fact, the Torah doesn't prohibit all work on the Sabbath, but only *melachah*, i.e., those activities which we do to gain control over our physical environment for our own material gain.

In short, Shabbat is a time when we can renew our spirit, nourish our soul, and be transformed by what we learn from the experience. Only by better knowing who we are can we begin to shape our labor to the contour of our soul, rather than the other way around. By living closer to our inner-teachings, we can feel more fulfilled, insightful, and joyful - more able to actively participate in the creation process by doing what is truly *tov* ("good" - that is, those acts that serve to realize the potential to bring forth life that is embedded in creation by YHVH), even when we are actively engaged in our labor.

When is Shabbat? The Creation Story clearly states that it comes on the seventh day. As I previously mentioned, the problem with this literal take is that the seven days of creation were not necessarily intended to conform to clock-time, but instead are presented as allegory. Remember that the separation of day from night was not mentioned until the fourth day.

I like to think that Shabbat is *any* time that we allow ourselves the freedom to separate (*kadosh*) from the temptations, values, and priorities of our labor-centric lives. Some may find it best to take a Shabbat every seventh day, others every seventh hour, or once a day, in twenty minute intervals twice a day, or whenever. The point is that Shabbat teaches us that we - and not our labor or even our traditions - should be the masters of our time. By knowing who we are, we can better decide when and how to observe Shabbat in a way that is meaningful to us - - in a way that allows each of us to better connect to the transcendent, every day of our lives.

- **Why the number "7"; what does this number symbolize?**

In the Torah, certain numbers (like 2, 3, 4, 10, 12, 40, and 400) carry with them special meaning. Consistent with the seven days of creation, the number "7" in Torah is a metaphor for a completed cycle of creation, involving both the potential for bringing forth life and the actualization of that potential.

Interestingly, while most calendars mark time based on physical realities, such as the movement of the planet around the sun, the Hebrew calendar and its associated Jewish holidays are organized around the notion of spiritual time. As detailed in Leviticus 23, the first holiday mentioned in Torah is the Sabbath. Passover comes on the fourteenth day, or the second Shabbat of the New Year, and lasts seven days (eight days outside of Israel). *Shavuot* comes seven weeks after Passover, on the first Shabbat of the seventh month, which is called the "sabbatical month." Sukkot represents the seven-day harvest festival that begins on the first full-moon of the seventh month. The *Shavuot* that comes every seventh year is called the "sabbatical year," and the *Shavuot* that comes after seven cycles of seven years is called in Leviticus 25:23 the "Jubilee Year." The reason for the Jubilee Year is to remind us that the Land does not belong to us – we are only sojourners and resident settlers on it.

➢ **Garden of Eden: Genesis 2:5- 3:24**

Introduction: Perhaps the best-known of all the stories of Torah, the Garden Story reflects a Sumerian epic and retains some of the original Sumerian references, such as the names of two rivers, the Tigris and the Euphrates, the location of which archeologists have called the "cradle of civilization." A summary of the story goes as follows:

Summary: *YHVH formed the human out of dust from the soil and blew into his nostrils the breath of life and the human became a living being. YHVH then planted a garden in Eden in the east, including in it the Tree of Life and the Tree of Knowing Good and Evil, and four rivers, including the Tigris and the Euphrates. YHVH told the human to work it, watch over it [or, "guard it"], and eat from any tree other than the Tree of Knowing, for on the day that you eat from that tree, you must die. Then YHVH formed from the soil every living thing, but none corresponded to the human. So, YHVH caused the human to fall into a deep slumber and drew from him a rib, which YHVH built into a woman and said, "Therefore a man leaves his parents and clings to his wife." And, both were naked, but not ashamed.*

Now, among all the living-things of the field, a snake was the shrewdest. It said to the woman to eat from the fruit of the tree in the midst of the Garden. She said that we are not to eat nor touch it, lest we die. The snake then replied that we will not die, but instead we will have our eyes opened and we will become like the God, knowing good and evil. So, she ate from the tree's fruit, and gave it to her husband who also ate it. Their eyes became opened (enlightened) and they became aware of their nudity and covered themselves with fig leaves and loincloths.

They then heard YHVH and hid themselves from YHVH's face. YHVH called out, "Where are you?" The man said, "I hid because I was nude." YHVH asked, "Who told you that you are nude; was it from the tree that I commanded you not to eat?" The man answered, "The woman whom you gave to me, gave me from the tree and so I ate." YHVH asked the woman, "What have you done?" She replied: "The snake enticed me and so I ate." YHVH said to the snake, "Because of this, you will be damned and crawl on your belly all of the days of your life. To the woman, YHVH said, "I will multiply your pain from pregnancy and you will lust after your husband, though he will rule over you." And to Adam: "Because you listened to your wife, and not to My commandment, only by the sweat of your brow shall you eat until you return to the soil, for you are dust and to dust you will return." The human called his wife, Havva, and she became the mother of all the living. YHVH then made Adam and his wife coats of skins and clothed them. YHVH drove them from the garden to work the soil east of Eden, saying that "the human has become like one of us, knowing good and evil, so lest he take from the Tree of Life and eat and live forever..." YHVH then placed Cherubim and flashing, ever-turning swords to watch over the Tree of Life.

Background: The Torah states that "YHVH planted a garden in Eden in the east." Eden literally means "delight," and "east" is translated from the Hebrew word *mi-kedem*. *Mi-k*edem has many meanings. It can refer to a direction ("from the east") or to a time ("from the beginning of time"), or to a verb ("moving forward" or "advancing"). Accordingly, we can translate the verse as "From the east, YHVH planted a garden of delight that is advancing forward from the beginning of time." Eve's name (in Hebrew, *Havva or Khai'ah*) translates as "mother of life" or "life-giver." Adam's name comes from the Hebrew word *a-da-ma*, which means "from the land." Thus, when YHVH tells Adam, the human formed from the land, to "work, watch and guard the land" from which humans are formed, the Torah is introducing a teaching that lies at its core. Said succinctly, we are to "love our neighbors as ourselves."

The story also introduces the idea that God's breath represents a person's soul (*neshemah*), as YHVH "blew into Adam's nostrils the breath of life." And, while the story appears to be simple and straightforward, mainstream Jewish and Christian theologians have held starkly different views about its underlying message, which has to do with what it means to be human.

Discussion Questions: What do the two trees symbolize? Who is the serpent? Why didn't Adam and Eve die, as God had promised they would if they ate from the tree; that is, what is the meaning in the Torah of death? What are the Cherubim and why are they guarding the Garden against entry? Why did Adam and Eve have to leave the Garden? And, is the Torah preaching male dominance?

- **What do the two trees symbolize?** Did you notice that the text refers to one tree as the "tree of knowing good and evil" and to the other as the "tree of life," but it gives no clue as to how we are to differentiate the two? Some have argued that this is because the two trees are one and the same, but that its nature differs depending on where we are in our personal/spiritual journey when we approach it.

For example, we can better understand the Tree of Life and its questions - "who we are, why we are, and what is our purpose" - by struggling with the questions about which of our actions are good. Recall from the Creation Story that "good" (*tov*) means that which advances life - that is, any action that helps to realize life's potential. In turn, we can better advance our knowledge of good and evil, and more consistently choose good actions when we struggle with our "tree of life" questions, for it is through that struggle that we gain the requisite inspiration and direction to make better choices.

The philosophical teaching is clear: We will feel most alive (i.e., alert and aware), and best able to advance our journey when we concurrently struggle with the "good/evil" and "life" questions, because the answers to these questions are interdependent and self-reinforcing.

How is the Torah defining "evil"? It follows that if good are those actions which realize life's potential, then evil refers to those actions that inhibit or destroy that potential.

- **Who is the serpent?** In Near Eastern stories, like the Gilgamesh Epic which predates the Torah, serpents represented sources of immorality and death. The Garden Story builds on this metaphor by referring to the serpent as the shrewdest of all living things. What makes this reference interesting is that the text could have also said that the serpent was the most "naked" of all living things, for the Hebrew word *arum* has two meanings, shrewd and naked. This word-play illustrates a teaching: "Naked" symbolizes that time in our lives, soon after birth, when our conscience is undeveloped, when we have no knowledge to differentiate what is good from what is evil.

The story tells us that Adam, Eve, and the serpent were all naked and therefore all naïve, but of the three, the serpent was the shrewdest: While each was tempted by the prospects of being more "God-like" or enlightened (have our eyes opened and become like God, knowing good and evil, and able to see the Day 1 light of Creation), only the serpent thought that he understood how to get there. Taken in this light, we might think of the serpent as representing an internal metaphor - - the voice of ambition in each of us that desires autonomy, power, and enlightened understanding. Put in modern terms, the serpent may represent our ego.

As most of us know, our ego can cause us to choose badly. Of course, in the case of the serpent and Adam and Eve, there was nothing inherently wrong with their desire to be enlightened. What was wrong, from the perspective of Torah, is how they went about it. Specifically, they tried to take direct control over their own destiny, symbolically illustrated in the text by their eating the forbidden fruit from the Tree of Knowing. Being naked and thus naïve, they imagined that they could attain gratification instantly and without struggle. Having not yet learned the teachings from the Tree of Life, they over-reached by trying to be more God-like. We will soon see others in the Torah trying to do similarly - including Cain (*Kayin*), the builders of the infamous "Babel" tower, and Avram (Abraham) and Sarai (Sarah) in the story about Sarai's Egyptian servant, Hagar.

Said more generally, we can bring about problems for ourselves and for those around us when we over-reach, thinking that we can control that which we cannot control. The Torah is thus reminding us that there is much about our lives that we are not in control of, and the sooner we understand this, the sooner we can deal with life's traumas and disappointments, and find inner peace and wholeness.

This basic teaching about control is repeated in the stories about Abraham and Sarah. As we will read in Chapter 3, their personal and spiritual journey, from the time they leave their homeland in Ur of Chaldees until the time of their death, tells of their struggles to free themselves from the control of their past, while at the same time trying to stop controlling that which they cannot control, their future.

- **What is the meaning in Torah of death?** YHVH states that *"on the day that you eat from that tree, you must die."* But not only do they not die on that day, YHVH even gives them going-away presents (*coats of skins*). We are accustomed to think of death in physical terms, but when trying to interpret the Torah, we must remind ourselves that it is first and foremost a theological document and, as such, is focused more on conveying spiritual and ethical teachings than on explaining physical realities.

    Interpreted thus, Adam and Eve suffered a spiritual death by virtue of having been driven out of the Garden. From the perspective of Torah, this means that they moved away from the close relationship that they had with YHVH, away from their spiritual ideals, and towards a place where the "light" from the first day of creation shines less brightly. The Torah will treat death in this spiritual (non-physical) way throughout the text.

- **What are the Cherubim and why are they watching over the Tree of Life?** In Mesopotamian temples, these sculptured mythical figures, sometimes described as winged-sphinxes, served as guardians. The Torah borrowed this imagery in the Garden Story and again in Exodus 25:18 when Cherubim will "protect" the Ark (Tabernacle) that was built to house the tablets from Sinai. Currently, we find such figures in most synagogues perched on the outside of the ark *(aron kodesh)* that houses the Torah. In the context of the Garden Story, it is interesting to note that the Torah is referred to as "the Tree of Life" *(etz chaim)* in the Shabbat prayer that immediately precedes the opening of the ark that houses it.

    An obvious question: Why does Torah make the garden and the tablets so inaccessible (guarded) and hard to understand? The simple answer is that spiritual growth (a higher level of awareness; a connection with that which is eternal) is a part of the human condition. It is something that we all desire, even though our actions sometimes suggest otherwise. Most traditions - like Islam, Christianity, and Buddhism - recognize this, but also recognize that enlightenment does not come easy, nor is it intended to come easy. For example, the need to suffer is paramount in Buddhism, for suffering helps to promote the development of our consciousness and teaches us lessons of tolerance and humility.[7]

In a similar vein, the need to struggle is central to the teachings of Torah. To advance our understanding of good, evil, and the meaning of life requires that we struggle with the questions posed by each of the two "trees." Indeed, struggle is fundamental to being like *Israel*, which is defined in Genesis 35 as the willingness to commit to a lifetime journey of struggling with things both divine and mortal, with the knowledge that we, like all of Creation, are works-in-progress. As such, the writers of the Torah may be saying that our need to struggle and our desire to be more enlightened are woven into the very fabric of Creation.

- **Why did Adam and Eve have to leave the Garden?**
We can view the story of Adam and Eve as a coming-of-age story. At the beginning, we, like they, are naïve children with unbridled desires and undeveloped consciences, who live in the comfort and safety of our parent's home. There comes a time, however, when each of us desires to know more. For Adam and Eve, that time began with the first bite of the "forbidden" fruit. From the perspective of Torah, it is the wise parents who recognize this transformation and allow their children the freedom to leave the safe confines of the home and begin their personal and spiritual journey to find out what their lives are about. Their journey is not intended to be easy; it will entail pain and sweat, suffering and struggle, but it will also contain moments of love, joy, and opportunities to learn more about the meaning of good, evil, and life. Such,

---

[7] In Buddhism, suffering refers to the deep sadness that we feel when we discover that nothing in life is permanent – not our possessions, health, friendships, and so on. Even mountains that appear permanent will eventually erode and disappear. Suffering also comes from the awareness that we are not able to control the attainment and retention of what we value, because everything around us and everything that once existed is interconnected in a long and complex set of cause/effect associations, such that everything arises "dependently."

according to Torah, is the human experience. We will expand on this teaching when we address the story about Abraham at the moment when he is about to sacrifice his son, Isaac.

The challenge that the Torah poses to each of us is to find our way back to the Garden, which in principle we can do by mastering the teachings from the two trees and acting consistently on that knowledge.

The writers also draw implicit comparisons between Torah's depiction of the Garden and that of the "Promised Land," which we will address in a later chapter. Suffice to say here that the Promised Land represents a state of mind, an awakened state of being where we find both milk (symbolic of nourishment) and honey (symbolic of sweetness and joy), even during mundane or troubled times. In Torah, only Joshua (whose name means "salvation") and Caleb (whose name means "like the heart") are said to have entered the Promised Land (the Land of Promise) among the generation of those who left Egypt.

It is interesting to note that the Garden Story is understood very differently by some orthodox Christian theologians. For example, St. Augustine in the fifth century C.E. noted that eviction from the Garden was punishment, not only for Adam and Eve but for all humanity. In brief, his thesis was that by eating from the forbidden fruit, Adam and Eve gained carnal knowledge and, with that, spontaneous sexual desire. He argued that because we are all descendants of the two of them, we are all corrupted by their seed. Augustine thus viewed sexual desire as the universal original sin. Said differently, because Adam and Eve misused God's gift of moral freedom, we are all exiled into a world of struggling and death.

Jesus preached a more positive view based on the Garden Story: People are capable of an "angelic life," and "celibacy" should be embraced "for the sake of the kingdom of Heaven" (Matthew 19:10-12). Clement of Alexandria (180 C.E.) argued that Adam's sin was not sexual indulgence but disobedience to God, such that the theme of the Garden Story is about moral freedom and moral responsibility. For more about the various traditional Christian interpretations of the Garden story, I refer the interested reader to Elaine Pagel's book, "Adam, Eve and the Serpent."

- **Is the Torah preaching male dominance?** One of the most controversial lines in Torah is the one that states, *"You will lust after your husband, though he will rule over you."* I will delay my comments on this line until we fully explore the role that women play in the Torah, except to say that this text appears to present a very different notion of women than what is depicted in the later stories of Genesis, where the matriarchs' role turns out to be at least as important as the patriarchs', particularly when regarding the all-important family decisions about the selection of the family's spiritual heirs.

➢ Cain and Abel: Genesis 4

Introduction: This story is the first of many stories in Genesis to address parent-child and sibling relationships. It is also the first illustration of humans living outside the Garden and contains the first biblical reference to "sin." It is also here that we encounter the notion of a religious experience, for it is in this narrative that brothers independently express the need to enter into a relationship with God through offering to show their appreciation for their bounty.

Summary: *Adam knew Havva (Eve or "Life-Giver") and she bore Kayin (Cain), saying, "I have gained a gift from YHWH!" To Cain, she added Hevel (Abel), his brother. Cain became a worker of the soil, and Abel, a shepherd. As a gift to YHVH, Cain brought fruits from the soil and Abel brought the choicest parts of the first born of his flock. Cain became exceedingly upset, because YHVH had no regard for Cain's gift. YHVH asked Cain why he was so upset, saying that "if you intend good, bear it aloft, but if you do not intend good, at the entrance is sin, a crouching-demon, toward you his lust, but you can rule over him."*

Cain rose up and killed his brother when they were out in the field. YHVH asked, "Where is your brother?" and he replied, "Am I the watcher over my brother?" YHVH then said, "What have you done! The sound of your brother's cries comes to me from the soil. Damned be you from the soil; it will no longer give its strength to you." Cain replied, "My iniquity is too great to be borne. You drive me away from the face of the soil, to wander the earth. Those who come upon me will kill me!" YHVH said, "No- whoever does so, sevenfold will it be avenged." So, YHVH set a sign for Cain, so that whoever came upon him would not strike him. And Cain went from the face of YHVH to settle in the land of Wandering, east of Eden. Meanwhile, Adam and Eve had a third son, Shet (or Seth), meaning the "Granted-One" for as Eve said, "God granted another seed in place of Abel."

Background: Eve appeared much more excited when she bore Cain, referring to her first-born son as "a gift from God!" than she did when she bore Abel, referring to Abel almost matter-of-factly as "Cain's brother" or that which was "added" to Cain. Cain worked the fields, which in ancient times involved tasks generally reserved for women, while Abel became a shepherd. It seems that even at the time of this ancient story, these two professions were in conflict over the use of land, with the farmers wanting protected fields and the ranchers wanting open ranges

Discussion Questions: How does Torah define "sin"? Who are Abel and Cain? Why did Cain kill his brother? Is Cain his brother's keeper? Why did Cain have to leave home? Who is Seth and why are we told about him?

- **How does the Torah define "sin"?** Many readers will be surprised to learn that "sin" is not mentioned in the Garden Story, not when Adam and Eve eat from the forbidden fruit, nor when they become sexually aware, nor when they become sexually active. Moreover, there is no "original sin" in Torah. Instead, "sin" first appears in reference to the gift that Cain offered to YHVH. What was sinful about his gift? The story says that Abel offered the choicest parts of the first-born from his flock (suggesting that his offering was an expression of deep gratitude - a generous gift given from the heart; recognition that it never really belonged to Abel, but to YHVH). In contrast, the text hints that Cain's gift is half-hearted - nothing extraordinary, just some fruit collected from the soil. Indeed, what Cain was offering was not what he himself had nurtured. Rather, it was something which he "acquired" from the land that YHVH had created on the third day, when YHVH said, *"Let the earth sprout forth with plants that yield seeds and fruit."*

What is the teaching from this episode? To begin with, the writers are making a distinction between "sin" and "evil." Recall that in the Creation story "good" represents the actualizing of the potential to create life, while in the Garden tale, "evil" represents the opposite of good; i.e., that which negates, destroys, or kills the actualization of good. As such, *evil* is understood in Torah as an offense against God or, in other words, about breaking a divine law.

Sin, on the other hand, refers to a missed opportunity to realize our potential. It is about missing our personal target or mark and denying our potential. From the perspective of Torah, then, we – who are made in the image and likeness of YHVH - sin when we fail to actualize our potential. As Rabbi Harold Kushner writes in his book, "To Life," sin is an offense to our self and our community - a missed opportunity to choose something that is truly life-advancing.

- **Who is Abel?** Abel's Hebrew name is *Hevel*, which translates as "vapor" (or its synonyms, haze, clouds, steam, mist, spray, and breath). Keeping in mind that names in Torah are intended to reveal core aspects of the character's personality, what might the writer(s) have wanted to convey by naming this character "Vapor"? Put another way, what are the properties of vapor that can help us better understand who Abel is?

Abel is a metaphor for life: Vapor consists of air and water, the two fundamental ingredients necessary for the creation of life. Drawing on what we learned from the Genesis 1, Abel's vaporous name would imply that he was born with the potential to bring forth life that was embedded by YHVH in the Creation when the Creation brought it forth. It is this kind of potential that YHVH referred to in Genesis 1 as "it was so." Recall that YHVH extended this designation to six such acts during Creation's first seven days. It follows that Abel's birth represents the seventh such "it was so" act, and the first to come after the completion of the first full cycle of Creation.

Abel is also a metaphor for relationships: For there to be vapor, the moisture in the air has to be separated from the air, but not as completely as it was separated on the second day of Creation. Rather, vapor requires that the moisture remain in close contact with the air, indeed suspended by the air, as if the two elements are interacting within a relationship. So it is with Abel's relationship with his brother, Cain, and so it will be with many of the stories in Torah. True to form, the Torah is never about the individual, per se, but about the individual in relationship with others, be it between parents (e.g., Abraham and Sarah), parents and children (Abraham/Sarah and their two sons, Ishmael and Isaac), siblings (Jacob and his brothers), relatives (Jacob and his uncle Laban), and friends (David and Jonathan; Naomi and Ruth), to name a few.

Each pairing represents a case study from which we can abstract lessons on how to better treat others as we would want them to treat us. By putting these teachings into practice, we become active participants in Creation. That is, we can help to actualize Vapor's potential, by transforming it, which is "so", into something that is good (*tov*).

Abel's name also implies something transitory or fleeting: Abel's life was short-lived, as his name suggests. The Torah may be using the Cain/Able story to begin a dialogue on the concept of impermanence, defined by the awareness that nothing in life is permanent – not our possessions, health, friendships, and so on. This awareness inspired Koheleth (Ecclesiastes) to write: *"Temporary, temporary, all is temporary! What real value is there for a man in all the gains he makes beneath the sun? . - - There is nothing new beneath the sun!"* (Most of us know this phrase as "Vanity, vanity, all is vanity", but vanity is not a close translation of "hevel".) Koheleth concluded that our real value is not measured by how much we gained or accomplished, but by how we lived our lives. Whether a pauper or a king, all that matters in the end is whether we observed God's commandments. Rabbi Harold Kushner offered a modernized view of this wisdom in his book "Living with a Life that Matters." His thesis is that it is not death that frightens most people, but the fear of having lived a meaningless life, leaving behind no mark. He argued that our key to immortality is to be remembered for leaving the world a little better than it was before we arrived.

In summary, to say that Abel is about life, relationships, and fleeting moments is to suggest that he may be something other than a physical being. He represents each person's spiritual side – that which tries to be fully present in the moment, yearns for enlightenment and inner wholeness (*shalem*), and searches for personally meaningful answers to life's questions. Therefore, it is no surprise that when it came to showing his appreciation for his bounty in life, Abel brought "*the choicest parts of the first born of his flock.*" It wasn't so much what he gave that caught YHVH's attention, but the sincere intentionality in which he gave it, without any external prompting or ulterior motives.

As a heads-up, the theme of offering-up the "first and the choicest" is revisited in Genesis 22 when YHVH asks Abraham to sacrifice his son Isaac; in Genesis XX when *Israel* tells his son Joseph, the one who he loves, to tend to the wholeness of his brothers; in I Samuel XX when Hanna makes good on her promise by giving up her first born, Samuel, to the priesthood.

- **Who is Cain?** Cain's name (in Hebrew, Kayen) means "to acquire or gain" because his mother, Eve (the "Life-Giver") said at the time of his birth "I have gained a man." What might a name like "Gain" symbolize in this story? Cain embodies that which Abel is not. Whereas Abel represents the spiritual side of humans, Cain epitomizes the material, physical side. His offering to YHVH was not from the heart, but instead one of *melachah;* that is, an activity done to "gain" control over ones lot in life, improve one's material well- being, or gain favor with others. Moreover, while Abel seemed fully present and alert to the few transitory moments that defined his life, Cain did not. Instead, he appeared preoccupied with unresolved issues from the past ("*exceedingly upset that YHVH had no regard for Cain's gift*") and anxious about the possible consequences of his past blunders ("*Those who come upon me will kill me!*"). And, whereas Abel was honest and pure with his intentions, Cain was self-serving and deceitful (*"Am I the watcher over my brother?"*). As we will see in greater detail in later Genesis chapters, Cain is like Jacob during Jacob's youthful years when he was the "Heal-Sneak", while Abel is more like *Israel,* the more enlightened Jacob, the one who proved himself willing and able to struggle with things both divine and human.

- **Why did Cain kill his brother?** This is the first of many stories in Genesis that pertains to parenting. One teaching from the story is that if we become too involved in the lives of our children, we can cause them to hold unrealistic images of themselves. Cain may have enjoyed his first-born "favorite son" status, causing him to take for granted the privileges that came with it. Feeling entitled and absorbed in his self-worth, he failed to hear YHVH's message to him and, instead, out of jealousy and without conscience, killed his brother.

  But, did he really kill his brother? It is interesting to note that the text does not refer to Cain's murderous act as "evil" (that which negates, destroys, or kills the actualization of good), but instead as a sin ("*if you do not intend good, the entrance is sin, a crouching-demon, towards you his lust – but you can rule over him.*"). Said simply, no one died in this story. Playing with Abel's name and all that it implies, what Cain killed wasn't a another person, but his own spiritual side, the side that his mother said at the time of Abel's birth "added" to Cain. What he may have killed was his capacity to mindfully appreciate every fleeting transitory moment, the possibility for living a life that matters, and his ability to live in harmonious relationship with others. What he killed was opportunity actualize his potential. As it is with most sins, he will likely be afforded another chance sometime in the future, once he has learned the errors in his ways.

  As we will soon discover in the stories about the patriarchs, Abraham, Isaac, and Jacob, and matriarchs, Sarah, Rebecca, Leah, and Rachel, the notion of living in the present in peaceful relationship with others represents one of the Torah's core teachings.

- **Is Cain his brother's keeper?** YHVH asked Cain the whereabouts of his brother. Like the question, "Where are you?" that YHVH had asked of Adam and Eve after they ate the fruit, YHVH's question to Cain was a test, which Cain , like his parents before him, promptly failed. His response ("Am I the watcher of my brother?")

represents the third time in this short story when he fails to be all that he could be – his meager gift to YHVH and his inability to inhabit the moment being his other two "sins" or instances when he missed his mark. Interestingly, this question about being his brother's keeper is a key question in the Book of Genesis, one that is left unanswered until the end of the Joseph story.

- **Why did Cain have to leave his home?** Like the Garden Story, this story can be interpreted as a coming-of-age story. Up until the killing of his brother, Cain had lived a privileged life – his mother notably excited when she bore Cain ("a gift from God!"), and the soil readily giving him its strength (*sprouted forth with plants that yield seeds and fruit*). No longer would this be the case. Like his parents, Cain had to leave the struggle-free confines of his upbringing and start to learn about good, evil, and the meaning of life. Whether he wanted to or not, the time had come for him to wander in search of his Promised Land. As such, the writers of this story, like the Garden Story, are exploring central issues in the human condition, especially those that play out in our youth.

- **Who is Shet?** Without the birth of Adam and Eve's third son, we could readily conclude from the story that we are all descendants of a murderer. Shet (Seth) gives us another option.

➤ The Flood Story: Genesis 5 through Genesis 10

Introduction: As with the Creation and Garden Stories, the Flood Story has its origin in Mesopotamian literature and, particularly, the Gilgamesh epic. However, whereas the gods in the Gilgamesh flood planned the destruction of the world almost as a whim and without a clear rationale, YHVH in Torah planned the destruction because humans were engaged in evil pursuits, undoing the good that YHVH had created and causing an orderly universe to revert to its chaotic beginnings. Only Noah - whose name shares the same *shoresh*, or linguistic root, with the Hebrew word that means "rest" or "comfort" - remained *tam*, or unblemished and uncorrupted by the evil around him.

As I previously mentioned, the names of people in Torah give us insight into their character. Noah's name tells us that he was a man at peace with himself and with those around him. As such, he had the capacity to bring others to shelter and comfort from the impending storm.

As an interesting aside, during the pre-rabbinic period, *tam* referred to a sacrificial animal that was unblemished, beyond reproach, and therefore acceptable to God. In Modern Hebrew, *tam* means "full of integrity" and "wholeheartedness". In all of the biblical writings, only Noah, Job, and the simple son of the Passover Seder are referred to as *tam*.

Most of us are familiar with the story. YHVH asks Noah, then 600 years old, to build an ark [8] and establishes a covenant with him: *Come into the ark that I asked you to make, you and your wife and your sons (Shem, Ham, and Yefet) and their wives, and from all living things a male and female of each to keep seed alive - - for never again shall the waters become a deluge.*

In the story we find that the number "seven" appears several times: in Genesis 7:4, *"For yet in seven days – I will make it rain upon the earth"*; in Genesis 8:4, *"And the ark came to rest in the seventh new-moon – upon the mountains of Ararat"*; and again in Genesis 8:10 and 8:12, *"Then he waited another seven days."* The deluge lasted forty days and forty nights. Only Noah, his family, and the other living things that were sheltered on the ark remained alive to begin the world anew. For this reason, some view Noah, the first man born after the death of Adam, as a kind of second Adam, from whom we are all descendants.

---

8 The word "ark" next appears in Exodus, when Moses's mother builds one for Moses, in an attempt to save him from Pharaoh's proclamation that all newborn Hebrew boys be killed.

Did you know that by closely following the genealogy depicted in the early chapters from Adam to Noah and from Noah to Abraham, that Noah was ten generations separated from both Adam and Abraham? Later in this book, we will try to decipher the symbolic meaning of the number "10." Also, the names of Noah's three sons are *Shem, Ham,* and *Yefet,* which when translated into English, mean Name or Essence; Hot or Passion; and Pretty or Simplicity.

Discussion Questions: Was Noah really 600 years old at the time that he built the ark? By flooding the planet, is YHVH admitting that the first six days of creation were flawed? Why does the number "seven" appear multiple times? What might the flood symbolize? It rains for forty days and forty nights - what does the number "forty" symbolize?

- **Was Noah 600 years old?** The early stories contain a number of individuals who lived far into their hundreds, including Adam (930 years), Shet (912 years), and Metushelah (969 years). How can this be? The answer may reside in the fact that many of the early stories were adapted from the Mesopotamian Empire that marked time by the cycles of the moon. Divide the above ages by twelve, and we get a much more believable result.

- **By flooding the planet, is YHVH admitting that the first six days of creation were flawed?** Or, might the writers be reminding us that we were created with the capacity and free will to enhance life or destroy it. Removed from the Garden, the choice between good and evil rests squarely with each of us. We are all aware of the consequences to creation when we choose evil - - - the Holocaust, global warming, the extinction of numerous living species, the polluting of the land and waters with hazardous waste, and so on and so on.

- **Why does the number "seven" appear multiple times?** Recall from the Creation Story that the Torah uses the number seven as a metaphor for a completed cycle of creation, which entails not only the potential to bring forth life but also the actualization of that potential. On the surface, this life-enhancing message seems totally inconsistent with the physical reality of the flood. But remember that the stories from the Torah are primarily concerned with conveying spiritual and ethical teachings. Taken in this light, the repeated references to the number seven may be the writers' way of signaling to the reader that the Flood Story is not about physical destruction but, rather, about cleansing, forgiveness, spiritual renewal, and the opportunity to start over.

- **What might the flood symbolize?** The Flood Story's message is similar to the message of the holiday of Yom Kippur, which occurs "On the tenth day of the seventh month" (Leviticus 23: 26-32). That is, the flood is about giving humans the opportunity to cleanse ourselves of our sins (those times that we missed our mark) and our evil (life- destroying) choices, to repent and receive another chance to choose correctly. The rite of baptism, wherein a person is cleansed of original sin, has its roots in the Flood Story, as does the ritual at the Passover Seder of dipping twice. The first dipping represents the crossing of the Reed Sea, when we left behind our enslaved lives; the second dipping represents the crossing of the Jordan River on our way to the Promised Land.

- **It rains for forty days and forty nights. What does "forty" symbolize?** Forty is sometimes used as a gestational metaphor signifying "birth," for the normal period of human gestation is forty weeks. An open question is whether the writers of the Torah around the year 1,000 B.C.E. were aware of this biological fact when choosing this number to signify a transformational, or a born-again experience? I say "born-again" because as we will see, a "forty" experience in Torah always represents the birth of a fundamentally new understanding about the meaning of life, and therefore the death of what we once had held to be true. Put another way, "forty" symbolically represents moments of revelation when the protagonist crosses-over into a closer relationship with self, with others, and with YHVH. How clever is it that this number appears forty times in Torah, signifying that those who complete the Torah each year (the tradition is to complete it on the holiday of *Simkhas Torah)* are ready to start reading it again with a new point of view gained from the past year's reading and experiences!

➢ Tower of Babel: Genesis 11:1-11.9

Background: This is the first story in the Torah that deals with a community and not with a single individual or family, foreshadowing the progression from the book of Genesis (which is about individuals and families) to the book of Exodus (which is about community). The context of this familiar story is interesting. It takes place as the human race is about to begin again, a second time, this time with all descending from Noah. And it appears just before the story about Avram from Ur of Chaldees, one of the great Babylonian metropolitan centers. As it was with Adam and Eve and the forbidden fruit, the humans in the Babel story are trying to reach for the divine; here, by building a tower to reach up to the heavens.

Summary: Verses 1-4: *All the earth was one language and one set of words. They [those who survived the flood] migrated to the east and settled in the valley of Shinar, where they said, "Let us bake bricks and build ourselves a tower, its top in the heavens. And, let us make ourselves a name, lest we be scattered over the face of all the earth!"* From these four short verses come the following questions:

- **Why did they migrate to the east?** Recall that the Hebrew word used for "east" in the early stories is *mi-kedem*, which means "advancing from the beginning of time." The Garden was said to be located in the east. Adam and Eve were driven from the Garden to work the soil "east" of the Garden. And Cain was exiled to the "east" of the Garden. As the early stories advance in calendar time, humans seem to keep returning to the beginning of spiritual time and "starting over." We witness this again in the Tower Story: Those who survived the flood learned little from that experience, and they quickly returned to sin (again, sin in the Torah means not being all that you could be; that is, missing your mark). Rather than struggle with the questions of good, evil, and the meaning of life (recall the two trees in the center of the Garden), they gave in to the temptations of autonomy and power. From the perspective of Torah, they, like

Adam, Eve, and Cain before them, over-reached; i.e., they tried to be more God-like, seeking to control their destiny on their own, and without the spiritual support of God.

- **Why choose the valley of Shinar to begin the construction of the tower?** The name, *Shinar,* is built on the root, *"na-ar,"* which means "youth." The name is likely used as a metaphor to represent that fleeting time in each of our lives when we seek to establish ourselves, seek our fame and fortune, and try to make a name for ourselves. It is also a time in life when we are prone to being egotistical and short-sighted: How audacious it was for them to choose a *valley* to begin the construction of a tower that was intended to reach the heavens!

Carl Jung once wrote that Act One in a young person's life is the story of setting out to conquer the world, while Act Two is the story of that person after realizing that the world is not about to be conquered by the likes of him or her. What we witnessed in the early stories appears to be largely scenes from Act One. In a later chapter we will contrast the Tower Story with the story of Jacob's "Act Two" dream (Genesis 28:12), in which he envisioned *"a ladder that was set up on the earth, its top reaching the heavens."*

- **How do we make a name for ourselves?** This question is revisited throughout the Book of Genesis. For example, it is addressed in the stories about Avram (later to be re-named Abraham) and Sarai (later to be re-named Sarah) when YHVH promises to make their names great, and again in the story about Jacob when YHVH's "man" blesses Jacob by re-naming him *Israel.* From the perspective of Torah, we cannot make a name for ourselves by power, wealth, or such achievements in the physical world as tower -building, but rather by struggling to become more aware (again, of what is good and evil and what is the meaning of life) and acting on that awareness.

Said differently, the writers tell us that we can make a name for ourselves by being *like- Israel.* As we will read in Genesis 35, *Israel* is more than a person or a place; it refers to anyone who shows the willingness and ability to pursue his or her personal and spiritual journeys, that is, to commit to a lifetime of struggle with things both mortal (such as relationships , demands on our time, competing priorities, and our physical well-being) and divine (such as our spiritual well-being, the mysteries of our existence and purpose), while surrendering to that in our lives which we cannot control, own, or understand.

The philosophy that is being conveyed is that during the times when we are like *Israel*, we will feel a sense of wholeness, or *shalem* - a deep sense of oneness and peace with *who* we are (with no internal conflicts) and *where* we are (in the world around us).

As a quick aside, *shalem* is similar in meaning to the word "yoga," which means "to unite." Shalem shares the same 3-letter root as does the word *Shalom*, which most of us know to mean "peace." During *shalem* moments, our heart opens and all of our senses come alive. We become like Buddha (Buddha means the "Awakened One"). We are able to inhabit the present without distractions, while holding a memory of the past and a vision of the future. During these enlightened moments, we are also like *Israel*, able to inhabit the "Promised Land" and to find both milk (nourishment) and honey (sweetness) in life, even during mundane or troubled times. Paraphrasing from the Book of Ecclesiastes, during these moments we realize that "all else is vanity."

Ever felt this? Sure - we all have. Maybe it was at the early stage of a romance, when we felt at one with our loved one and believed that that person understood us completely and forever. Those are times of high energy, when we feel no limits to what we can do; when the unresolved issues from the past and the anxieties of the future no longer occupy our present; when even the mundane feels special; and when we think that we have perfect clarity about who we are, why we are and where we are going - the times we feel we are the luckiest person in the world.

There are also other times when we sense that the "Promised Land" is nearby. Some experience it in nature, when we are feeling at one with all that surrounds us, when we sense that we and all that we see are family, and that even the trees carry our name. Others know it after seeing an inspiring Broadway play, attending a rock concert, experiencing a "runner's high." The problem is that while we may know what this spiritual high feels like, we rarely are able to retain it.

Buddhism offers a similar teaching. In Jack Kornfield's book, *"After the Ecstasy, The Laundry*," he writes that enlightenment - -and our sudden and unexplained ability to awaken and see clearly the reality of the world - - doesn't last. It may transform us for a moment into a higher consciousness, but we inevitably return to struggle with our day-to-day shortcomings.

- **Why do the survivors of the Flood fear being scattered?** To be scattered is to be in exile, vulnerable, and disconnected from God, the land, community, family, and our authentic self. To be scattered is to be cursed. The Hebrew word for "curse" is *clah-la*, meaning to be so light as to be easily blown away without leaving a trace. To live a cursed life, therefore, is to live a life that does not matter to anyone, such that when we are gone, no one will remember us or our names.

In his book, *A Life that Matters*, Rabbi Harold Kushner writes that it is not death that frightens most people, but rather the fear of living a meaningless life, a life that leaves no mark on the world - a life that does not matter to those whom we have encountered. He argues that the key to immortality is to leave the world a little better off.

- **What might the bricks for the Tower symbolize?** Bricks may be a symbolic representation of the choices we must make in our lives. Bricks can represent an enslaved life, like the bricks that were made without straw to build the cities for the Egyptian Pharaoh. Or they can be like the substance of the heavens in purity, symbolic for an existential moment of infinite beauty, that Moses and the seventy elders saw beneath their feet, *"something like the work of sapphire brick"* (Exodus 24:10).

In summary, the soul-searching question that is implicit in verses 1-4 is, "Are we trying to make a name for ourselves by making bricks for Pharaoh, or are we willing to walk on the same bricks as did Moses, by living a life that is meaningful to ourselves and others?" Interestingly, the Hebrew word for "to labor" or "to build" that is used in the Tower Story shares the same three-letter root (*ayin, bet, dalit*) as the Hebrew words for work, worship, slave, and service. The story, thus, is asking us to think about who and what we are working for and why.

Summary: Verses 5-9: *YHWH looked down at the tower and said, "Here are one people with one language, and this is merely the first of their doings – there is no barrier in all that they scheme to do! Let us baffle their language so that no one will understand the language of their neighbor." So, YHVH scattered them over the face of the earth and they had to stop building the tower, which was called Babble.*

- **Why was YHVH concerned about "one language, one set of words"?** The power of speech was revealed in Genesis 1 when YHVH spoke creation into being. The "Tower" people were trying to use this power to reach for the divine: trying to be that which they cannot be and trying to control that which they cannot control (their own destiny). The Torah is once again reminding us that there is much about our lives that we are not in control of, and the sooner we understand this, the sooner we can deal with life's traumas and disappointments, advance in our struggles, and find inner peace and wholeness.

Interestingly, verses 5-9 do not necessarily imply that YHVH created a multitude of languages. An alternative explanation is that YHVH created a multitude of points of view. As we all know, it is hard enough to fully understand what others are saying, even when they speak our language.

- **Where did the name "Babel" come from?** Some have said that the unfinished tower was an attempt to make fun of the mighty and prosperous empire, Babylon, where Abraham and Sarah were raised and which they left to start a new beginning. Interestingly, the Hebrew word, "*l'valbel*", which means "to confuse," is built on the same three letter root (*shoresh*) as is the word "Babel."

Chapter 3: Abraham, Sarah, and Their Two Sons

Introduction: Avram and Sarai (their names will later be transformed to "Abraham" and "Sarah") were born in Ur of Chaldees, a prosperous city-state in the Babylonian Empire. Like most names in the Torah, Avram's name reveals an important aspect of his essence, for *av* means father *and ham* means multitude; that is, he will become the "father of a multitude." Sarai's name refers to a woman of high rank, like a princess. Their story begins with Chapter 12 of Genesis, *Lekh lekha*, verses 1 through 5, and ends with the death of Sarah (Chapter 23) and then of Abraham (Chapter 24).

> ➢ **Genesis 12:** *Lekh Lekha* – Go Forth From Your Land

Summary: *YHVH said to Avram, "Go forth from your land and from your father's house, to the land that I will let you see. I will make a great nation of you and make your name great. And, Avram, who was seventy-five at the time when YHVH spoke to him, went, as did his wife, Sarai, and his nephew, Lot, and all the property they had accumulated, and all the persons whom they had made their own.*

Discussion Questions: Why were Avram and Sarai willing to trade the comfort, familiarity, and security of their prosperous city-state for the uncertainties of a land unknown to them? Why were they chosen to become the forebears of Israel? Why not, say, Noah, who (cf., Genesis 6) had remained *tam*, or uncorrupted, even in the midst of evil? Why did Avram and Sarai bring along all of the property that they had accumulated? Was Avram really seventy-five years old when he and Sarai began their journey? And, were they real people; that is, did they really exist?

- **Why were they willing to leave their home for the unknown?** Their reasons for leaving draw interesting parallels to the story of the Exodus from Egypt, which is said to have taken place around the year 1,400 B.C.E, and with the story of the return from the Babylonian exile around the year 520 B.C.E. At the time of each of these departures, the land that was being left was a center of prosperity. I will hold off from commenting about the reasons for leaving Exodus and Babylonia until we examine the possible symbolic meaning behind the ten plagues. However, I will say here that, from the perspective of the Torah, it is hard to make a name for ourselves (recall the discussion that accompanied the Tower of Babel Story) - let alone a "great name" - when we are reaping the benefits of life in a prosperous community.

This is not to say that prosperity is intrinsically bad. However, it does have an insidious way of causing us to define our lives in terms of its pursuit. A core teaching from the Torah is that our well-being is not derived from how much we have, but whether we are seeking *shalem* (wholeness) by trying to be like *Israel* (both willing and able to struggle with personal and spiritual matters). Put another way, Torah is about moving forward to a closer relationship with ourselves and with others. The writers will repeat this teaching throughout the Torah and the later books, like the Book of Ecclesiastes.

Historians hold a complementary view about prosperity's dark side when they explain the rise and fall of civilizations. In brief, they argue that great nations start out focused and committed. Over time, this can lead to wealth and power, which can lead to affluence and luxury, which can lead to decadence, corruption, and decline. In a similar vein, John Adams, in a letter to Thomas Jefferson, wrote: "Human nature, in no form of it, could ever bear prosperity."

Rabbi Alan Lew, in his book "Be Still and Get Going: A Jewish Meditation," points to another reason that Avram and Sarai left home: They left because they felt a compelling inner need to leave. They understood that they could not advance on their personal and spiritual journeys as long as they remained where they were, for revelation rarely happens in the safe confines of the familiar.

Said more generally, the longer we stay in the familiar, the more firmly entrenched do we become in our habitual ways of interacting with our environment and with those around us. These habitual ways will dull our senses and our ability to process our reality. On the other hand, leaving allows us to become more alert, to see things more vividly and feel things more freshly. Leaving allows the present moment a greater chance of flowing through us. It forces us to struggle with insecurities and uncertainties, which can awaken us to our spiritual path and provide us with a clearer vision of who we really are.

The importance of "leaving" represents a fundamental teaching of Torah. It not only plays a critical role in the development of Avram and Sarai, but also in the lives of Adam, Eve, Cain, Ishmael, Hagar, Isaac, Jacob, Joseph, and Moses. What distinguishes Avram and Sarai's leaving, however, is that Avram and Sarai were the only ones who left voluntarily. Each of the others had different motives for leaving, but the effect was the same: Leaving served to transform each of them, enabling each to "move forward."

The importance of leaving is also recognized in other religions. For example, Jesus went by himself into the wilderness for forty days and forty nights, only to return with a new testament. And Muhammad fled Mecca for Medina, deep in the Arabian Desert, where the prophesy that served as the basis for Islam was revealed to him.

- **Why were Avram and Sarai chosen to be the "parents of a multitude"?** Thomas Cahill, in his book, *The Gift of the Jews,* offers an interesting explanation. His thesis is that what distinguished Avram and Sarai from those who preceded them was the fact that they were transformational individuals. They changed the way that people thought about time and history by suggesting that there is more to life than what is predetermined by the Great Wheel, or what some call the "Mandala." According to the pre-Abrahamic view of the world, life progressed in cyclical terms. Like the moon, tides, and the farming seasons, all of life was understood to move in a never-changing cycle of birth, growth, and death. With each turn of the wheel, every person, place, and thing that ever was, will again be. The Mandala has no provisions for free will, and thus there is no hope of breaking free from this deterministic wheel.

By choosing to leave their home to make a name for themselves, Avram and Sarai demonstrated that it is possible to break free of the Mandela. They were also the first to actively question YHVH, as Avram did when he successfully challenged YHVH's plan for dealing with the inhabitants of Sodom and Gomorrah in Genesis 18. As such, their behavior contrasts with that of Adam, Cain, and Noah toward YHVH. By that I mean that conversations with those earlier figures were largely one-way, as a parent might speak to a child. The behavior of Avram and Sarai, on the other hand, promotes the message that biblical faith in Torah should be based on understanding and not on blind acceptance. Consistent with this message, the word "*amen*" means "I confirm" or "I agree", and not as it is more commonly understood, "I believe."

Avram and Sarai, therefore, may have been selected to be the parents of *Israel* because they had advanced beyond childhood on their personal/spiritual journey, and they could enter into a student-teacher relationship with YHVH. Indeed, the stories about them contain a number of tests that YHVH posed, the first being whether they would leave their home for the unknown, and the last – and most controversial – being the story in which YHVH commands Abraham to sacrifice his son, Isaac.

With their passing of each test, they proved themselves more able to contribute to YHVH's ongoing process of creation, more able to behave in *tov* ways that enhanced life. As such, they earned the distinction of being not only the biological parents of their grandson, Jacob (later renamed *Israel*), but also the spiritual parents of all who yearn to be like-*Israel*.

I recognize that this conjecture may appear to be a bit abstract, but I think it will become clearer in the ensuing commentary. Suffice to say here that Avram and Sarai were the first characters in Torah to have "made a name for themselves," as was symbolically represented by YHVH adding the Hebrew letter '*hey*' from YHVH's name to their names. Names in Torah are purposefully given to reveal key aspects of a person's essence. By adding part of the name of God to their names, their names changed to Abraham and Sarah, symbolizing a fundamental transformation in their identities. But we are getting ahead of ourselves – they still have a ways to go on their journey before they are ready to have their names changed. Till then, I will continue to refer to them as does the Torah, as Avram and Sarai.

- **Why did they bring all their property with them?** The Torah teaches us that the best way to inhabit the present is to separate ourselves from the past assumptions, values, opinions, and behaviors that we had previously used to define ourselves. Put another way, we are best equipped to move forward (*lekh lekha*, or "go forth") to a sense of *shalem* when our past stops determining our present. By enacting this "separation" (recall the fundamental role that separation, or *kadosh*, played in the Creation Story), the writers are implying that we are actively participating in the on-going creation process.

    Regarding Avram and Sarai, by leaving their home with the intent of making a name for themselves, they showed that it is possible to break free from the past. However, as we read in the story, their break was not entirely clean, for they felt the need to bring with them lots of baggage, symbolizing their past. As their story unfolds, this baggage will end up impeding their ability to move as far forward as Jacob, Joseph, and Moses will.

- **Was Avram really seventy-five years old when he started his journey?** Rosh Hashanah celebrates the New Year in the Jewish calendar, while Passover falls in the first month of the Hebrew calendar; it comes at springtime, a time of nature's re-birth. I make reference to this calendar because there is evidence that during biblical times people viewed each of these holidays as a celebration of a new year. As such, each year as we measure it may have represented two years to them. If that is the case, then Avram left home when he was at a much more realistic age of 37.5, Sarai gave birth to Isaac when she was 45, and Moses died at the age of 60.

- **Did Avram and Sarai really exist?** Nobody knows, and quite likely will never know. If they had once lived, it would have been about 4,500 years ago, or about 1,500 years before the oral stories about them were likely to have been written. (Many biblical scholars estimate that the Torah was written down around the time of Solomon's Temple, or 1,000 B.C.E.) Thus, even if Avram and Sarai were real people, the stories about them were likely embellished into folklore, as tends to be the case with oral traditions. Any lack of historical accuracy, however, should not diminish the value of these stories, for the Torah, in the opinion of many, was never intended to be read as a book of history, but as a collection of mythologies, folklores, and metaphors, all presented to convey teachings.

➤ Genesis 13 (1-18): The Story about Lot

Summary: Avram, his family, and all their belongings arrived in the Negev, where a quarrel broke out between Avram's and Lot's herdsmen, for the land could not support both of their herds. Avram came up with a solution to keep family peace. He said to Lot: *If you look left, then I will take my herds and go to the right and if you look right, then I will go left. Lot, seeing how well-watered the plains of the Jordan were, like YHVH's gardens, like the land of Egypt, chose to journey east, pitching his tent near Sedom, while Avram journeyed to the land of Canaan. YHVH had not yet brought ruin upon Sedom and Amora, but the men living there were extremely sinful. Once Lot parted from Avram, YHVH told Avram to lift up his eyes and everything that you see to the north, the Negev (south), the east, and the sea (west) I give to you and your descendants for the ages. I will make your seed as plentiful as the dust of the ground.*

Discussion Questions: Who is Lot and what does he symbolize? What was Avram really "seeing"? What does the number "4" represent?

- **Who is Lot?** Lot may have physically left the prosperity of his homeland in Ur of Chaldees, but his acquisitive spirit did not leave with him. When given the choice of where to settle, he chose the resource-rich lands of the east (*mi-kedem*). In Torah terms, he yearned to return to his beginning. Rather than moving forward, however, he let his past dictate his present set of assumptions, values, and behaviors. Looking east, he mistakes YHVH's gardens (Eden) for Egypt (in Hebrew, *Mitz-rayim*, which we will learn in the Book of Exodus means a "narrow place" - a place where we give more attention to our material pursuits than we do to the questions of good, evil, and life.)

As we will soon read, Lot's backward spiritual view will twice lead him into harm's way and twice require rescue by his uncle, Avram. First, by settling in Sodom, Lot puts himself and his extended family at immediate risk (Genesis 14). Second, rather than take responsibility for his actions, he puts his family's future at risk as well. Specifically, he dimwittedly allows his two daughters to get him drunk on consecutive nights – so drunk that each daughter could "lay with him" and become pregnant by him – so drunk that he "claims" to have known nothing about the illicit encounters (Genesis 19). (Really, could he be that mindless – his senses of hearing, sight, smell, and touch so deadened to the world – as to not know or remember what happened!). As it turned out, the two sons born to Lot's daughters became the tribal leaders of the two great enemies of the descendants of Avram and Sarai, the Moabites (Moab meaning "from the father") and the Ammonites. The Torah is using these stories about Lot to remind us of what can happen when we move backward by letting the past shape our present.

That said, Moab holds some interesting ties with Israel. For example, Ruth, the great-great grandmother of King David was a Moabite (see the Book of Ruth, a story that is said to take place in Moab around the year 1070 B.C.E, or about 130 years after the Hebrews left Sinai and came to the "Promised Land."). And, Moab was the site of Moses' final resting place (Deuteronomy 34:1-9).

- **What was Avram seeing?** In the last chapter (Genesis 12) YHVH told Avram to *"Go forth from your land and from your father's house, to the land that I will let you see."* In this chapter we are told what Avram could see in 360 degrees - that is, long distances in all four directions. Given where he was standing, however, this is not physically possible. This is the Torah's signal to the reader to interpret the coming event in spiritual terms.

Let's try to do this: Recall that a fundamental Torah teaching, from Genesis 12, is that we can best inhabit the present by separating ourselves from the past. Lot, what he stood for, and all the property that he and Avram had brought with them from Ur of Chaldees were not only a part of Avram's past but also were inhabiting Avram's present, making him less able to fully experience the wholeness of the moment. When Lot departed, Avram momentarily perceived that wholeness, a vision of connectedness, not only with the geography, but with the promise of a future for his descendants. He was experiencing his future in the present tense.

We can imagine that at that moment, Avram felt an experience that was so vast - so deeply penetrating, so filled with clarity and awe - that it seemed to reside not so much inside of him, as he inside of it. Those who study Kabala and its mystical view of the Torah refer to these moments as *ein sof* (without limits, endless) experiences – where we encounter the divine powers and feel a sense of enlightenment.

The Torah describes a few other such *ein sof* experiences, such as Moses at the sighting of the burning bush (Exodus 3), the again Moses in Deuteronomy 34: 1-4, as he is standing east of the Jordan River, saddened by the knowledge that he will not be allowed to enter the Promised Land. From where he is standing, the mountains of Judea and Samaria are blocking his view, yet YHVH intervenes and lets him see not only the Promised Land in all directions, but even the areas where the Tribes will eventually settle, hundreds of years in the future. We will spend a lot more time discussing Moses and the teachings that we can derive by examining how he lived his life when we begin discussion of the Exodus story.

- **What was Avram really seeing?** Let's examine more closely what Avram was said to have been seeing. The traditional English translation of Verse 14 of Genesis 13 is that Avram "lifted up his eyes from the place that he was to see the north, the south, the east, and the west."

In its original Hebrew, however, the verse says something quite different. Rather than pointing to the four geographical coordinates, and what many on the religious and political right consider to be a real-estate deed (Leviticus 25:23 makes it clear that we can be sojourners and resident settlers on the land, but it does not belong to us), the verse points to the four sacred coordinates. Avram was said to be seeing to the *tzafona,* which means "towards the hidden"; to the n*egba,* or "the parched dry"; to k*edem,* or "eastward towards the beginning"; and to the *yama,* or "towards the sea."

What does it mean, "To see the *tzafona*/hidden"? Some have argued that it refers to those moments when we glimpse the eternal. It is about having the capacity to see the extraordinary in the ordinary, like a bush that is burning but is not being consumed. It is about the revelations that we have yet to receive. It is about appreciating the wonders of creation and our lives, even in the smallest of actions and objects, even during mundane or troubled times. It is about that which is *hidden in plain sight*, which for most of us defines our spiritual reality.

At the Passover Seder, "that which is hidden" is represented by the piece of *matza* referred to as the *afi-komen*. It remains hidden until all of the dinner is eaten except for the dessert, which is the *afi-komen*. At that time, the children, symbolizing our future, are asked to find it and return it to the dinner table. The Seder closes with the eating of the *afi-komen*, symbolizing our successful departure from the enslavements of Egypt and the start of our children's journey toward the Promised Land.

What does it mean, "To see the N*egba*/the parched dry"? Some have noted that this vision refers to the capacity to see life's potential and resiliency. It is about understanding that even something as desolate as parched earth can spring forth with life if it is given the requisite attention and sustenance. It is also about seeing aspects of ourselves that are troubled, not feeling "whole" (*shalem*), not being "well-watered."

Interestingly, *Negba* shares the same root as the desert known as the *Negev*, but it does not mean "wilderness" (*midbar*). The *Negba* is a physical wasteland where, without sustenance, one can quickly succumb to the elements, while the wilderness in Torah is a spiritual place where one can hear God speak (*da'ber*). This distinction is key to understanding the teaching from Genesis 21, which tells of the time when Avram banishes Hagar and her son, Ishmael, to the Negev, seemingly to die.

Looks can be deceiving. Consider that "*Lot, seeing how well-watered the plains of the Jordan were, like YHVH's gardens, like the land of Egypt, chose to journey east, pitching his tent near Sedom.*" The Torah is using metaphor to make a point: Drive to Sedom along Route 90 in the Judean Desert. You will find few places on this planet that are more parched dry than it.

Consider also the Passover story: Egypt may have appeared to some who were living at that time to be well-watered, for it offered its inhabitants jobs, food, housing, and protection from warring nations. Yet, for those who wanted more out of their lives than building pyramids for somebody else, Egypt looked "parched dry." *Matza*, on the other hand, looks and tastes parched dry; yet when seen through the right pair of eyes, it symbolizes a portal into the hidden Promised Land.

Of course there is much more to say about the Passover story, including why matza symbolizes a Promised Land portal, but it will have to wait until we complete our reading of the book of Genesis and begin our reading of the book of Exodus. Suffice it to say here, however, that Avram and Moses were many years on their personal and spiritual journeys before they were able to get a glimpse into the hidden and to distinguish it from that which is parched dry.

Why "*Kedem*"? Kedem ("advancing eastward toward the beginning") symbolizes that place which exists outside of time and space. Torah mentions two such eternal places, the Garden of Eden (Delight) and the Promised Land. To see towards Kedem is to glimpse the light that was said to be created on Day 1 (Genesis 1:3), three days before the sun and moon were created to provide physical light.

Why "*yama*"? On the fifth day of Creation (Genesis 1:20), the story states that the yam (sea) was "swarming with life." Yama is thus a symbol for that which is good (*tov*); that is, it has the capacity to actualize Creation's potential to bring forth life.

But, why was Avram asked to look at four things? The answer may reside in Genesis 2, verses 10 through 14, where the second reference to the number 4 appears. These verses tell of the river which goes out of Eden to water the garden – and from there it divides into four rivers. The first is Pishon; it circles through all of the land where the gold is that is "good." The second is Gihon; it circles all the land of Cush. The third is the Tigris, which goes to the east of Assyria. And the fourth is the Euphrates.

Let's try to connect this reference of "4" to that of Genesis 13. Pishon is said to be good (*tov*), signifying the capacity to see the extraordinary in the ordinary, like a bush that is burning but not consumed. The gold of Pishon is all around us, but if we lack this capacity, it remains for most of us to be *Tzafone*, or hidden in plain sight.

Gihon, which circles the parched dry land of Cush, is said to include the areas of the Arabian Peninsula, Egypt, and Ethiopia. The Tigris points to *me-kedem*, or "towards the beginning" (also translated as "from the east"). The Tigris runs through Iraq, flowing east to Assyria. And the Euphrates is the longest and, historically, one of the most important rivers of southwest Asia. Together with the Tigris, it is one of the two defining rivers of Mesopotamia, literally "teaming with life".

- **Why "4"?** From the perspective of Genesis 2, it takes the water from these four rivers to "water the Garden." That is, to truly experience Eden (which means "delight"), we need to embrace at one-and-the-same-time the mysteries of the tzafone, the dryness of the negba, Day 1's spiritual light (Kedem), and the goodness (teaming with life) of the yam. Put another way, to advance ourselves on our personal and spiritual journeys, we have to learn to see the big picture rather than to focus separately on each of the four directional coordinates. We have to experience the *oneness* (wholeness/shalem) that existed before the river from Eden divided.

We have already observed that numbers in the Torah are often used to represent spiritual concepts. For example, "2" is used to convey the act of separation that drove Creation; "3" signals an impending revelation; "7" represents a completed cycle of creation; and "40" in the Flood Story (and thirty-nine other places in Torah) is used to point out a transformation: the birth of a fundamentally new understanding about the meaning of life, and therefore the death of what we once had held to be true. What then might the number "4" symbolize? From Genesis 2 and 13, it appears that "4" represents a spiritual way of seeing that can get us back to the Garden.

This usage of the "4" symbol appears many times in the text. Consider the Passover story of the four sons, each with his point of view, and the four questions that are asked at the Passover Seder. Consider also the four species that are waived during the celebration of Sukkot; that is, the Lulav (a ripe, green, closed frond from a date palm tree); Hadass (boughs with leaves from the myrtle tree); Aravah (branches with leaves from the willow tree) and the Etrog (the fruit of a citron tree). Consider the four levels on which the Torah can be read: *Psha*t, the literal understanding of the text's story line; *Remish*, dealing with what the text is hinting at; *Drash*, or the ethical teachings of the text; and *Sode*, the mystical teachings of the text. And, consider Kabbalah's four levels of visions of reality: *Asiyah (*the realm of our senses where we detect distinct objects*); Yetzirah (*the realm of thinking where we distinguish between the dualities that we detected in Assiyah); *Briah* (the realm of abstract conceptualization where we see commonalities and oneness); and *Atzilut (*the realm of pure spiritual emancipation*)*. And consider the four fringes of a *tallit*, or prayer shawl, that remind us of the four dimensions of reality.

Perhaps the most interesting use of the number "4" appears the first time that it is used. I am referring to the "fourth" day of Creation (Genesis 1: 14): *YHVH said, "Let there be lights in the dome of the heavens, to separate the day from the night, that they may be for signs – for set-times, for days and years."*

As it happens, the Biblical word used for "set-times," *mo'adim*, also means "festivals." According to the Hebrew calendar, which is organized around spiritual time and uses as its base the number "seven" to symbolize the completion of a cycle of creation, there are "four" primary festivals that are detailed in Leviticus 23: *Shabbat*, which falls on the "seventh" day of creation; and the three pilgrimage festivals: *Passover*, which comes on the "fourteenth" day, or the second Shabbat of the new year; *Shavuot* which comes "seven" weeks after Passover; and *Sukkot*, which falls on the seventh month of the Hebrew Calendar.

As we did with the four rivers, we can connect these four primary festivals to what Avram was seeing in the order that he was asked to look. *Shabbat* is about stopping, as Moses did at the burning bush, for it was only by stopping that he was able to see that which was otherwise hidden (*tzafonah*). *Passover* is about draining out (parched dry, or *negba*) the impurities (symbolized by *khumatz*) in our attempt to get in touch with our authentic self (our essence, symbolized by the *matza* that we eat). It is only by seeing ourselves stripped of all our impurities and faulty assumptions that we can begin to know what we need to do. *Shavuot* marks the time when we received the Torah at Sinai. It is through the Torah that we can return towards the light of the first day (*Kedem*). And *Sukkot* is the time of harvest, a time of *yama*, a time teaming with life.

Let's try to summarize: The number "four" in Torah represents the components of spiritual wholeness and is a portal into the infinite. A teaching from Genesis 13 tells us that it is not so much "what" we see, but "how" we see it. Like Avram, we cannot move forward and truly walk the land until we first learn how to "see" it as YHVH sees it. Only when we are guided by that vision do we have the capacity to transform the land into *"YHVH's gardens."*

➢ Genesis 14: A Meaningful Tangent

Background: In both content and structure, the battle-story depicted in this chapter doesn't seem to fit with the context that preceded it and what will follow. Yet as we delve deeper, we will see how the story does, in fact, fit.

Summary: The first thirteen verses of this chapter tell of a distant battle - between a number of kings, over the cities of Sodom and Amora - that seemingly has nothing whatsoever to do with the story of Avram. As the battle comes to a conclusion, however, we learn that Lot and all of his property have been captured. Upon hearing of his nephew's plight, Avram mobilizes his forces, which totaled 316 men, and marches in to rescue Lot, whom Avram refers to as his "brother."

Because of Avram's actions, Malki-Tzedek, king of Shalem and priest of God Most-High offers Avram bread and wine, and blesses him. Meanwhile, Bera, the king of Sodom, makes Avram an offer: Return to Bera all the prisoners and in exchange Bera will give to Avram all of the captured property. To Bera, Avram responds: *"I raise my hand in the presence of YHVH, God Most-High"* that I will not take anything that is yours, so that you should not say, *"I made Avram rich."*

Discussion Questions: Who are the kings Malki-Tzedek and Bera? Why does Avram refer to his nephew as his "brother"? And why is this story included in the book of Genesis?

- **Who are the aforementioned kings?** *Malki*-means "my king," *tzedek means* "righteous," *shalem* means "wholeness ," that is, a deep sense of oneness and peace with who we are (with no internal conflicts) and where we are (in the world around us); and high priest means a descendent* of the Co'hen'im. Putting these puzzle pieces together, Malki-Tzedek is "my righteous king and high priest of wholeness."

  It gets more interesting: The High Priest is a descendent of Aaron (Moses's brother) who comes from the tribe of Levi, who was one of the twelve sons of Jacob, who in turn was the son of Isaac - - and Isaac, who is the son of Abraham, is yet to be born!. In other words, the writers are telling us that Malki-Tzedek comes from the distant future.

  Bera's name is also symbolic, for it consists of two syllables, "*beh*", which means "in" and "*ra*", which means "evil." In Torah "evil" is the opposite of *tov* (good). Accordingly, Bera's name means: that which inhibits or destroys the actualization of the potential of life that is embedded in the creation.

- **Why call Lot Avram's "brother"?** Recall that the question about being one's brother's keeper is a key question in the Book of Genesis. It was first asked by Cain, but was left unanswered. While the answer to this question will be more formally developed in the Joseph Story, Avram's answer to it, by virtue of his actions to risk all to save his misguided "brother," is a resounding "yes."

- **Why is this story included in Genesis?** The story appears to indiscriminately blend aspects from the future (e.g., High-Priest) with that of the present (Lot's capture). Added to this, the two kings' names are laden with symbolic meaning, suggesting that the Torah is once again presenting a "teaching" rather than a historical event. Specifically, having just been taught to "see" the land, Avram is now being tested as to which vision will guide his walking of the land. Will he sacrifice the future for the rewards of the present? Will he choose Malki-Tzedek's righteous, life- enhancing path or Bera's evil, life-destroying path?

Fascinatingly, Avram, in making his choice, invokes the name of *YHVH*. What makes his announcement so striking is that it is not until the third chapter of Exodus, in the story of Moses and the burning bush, that God's name is explicitly revealed. Perhaps the writers are conveying the point that Avram, when tested, was able to put into practice his "seeing" lesson. That is, by accepting the high-priest's blessing rather than Bera's material wealth, Avram was already displayed the understanding that the God which is now shepherding his life "will be whatever God will be." As we will soon read, none of his immediate descendants, neither Ishmael, Isaac, Esau, Jacob, nor any of the twelve sons of Jacob including Joseph, will demonstrate this fundamental level of spiritual awareness.

➢ Genesis 16: Hagar and Ishmael

Background: In the events leading up to Genesis 16 in Genesis 15, Avram expresses serious concern that he will die childless. YHVH tries to comfort him, saying that Avram's seed will be as many as the stars in the heavens. YHVH also tells more of Avram's future, saying that his descendants will journey to a land not theirs where they will be enslaved for four hundred years. For the moment, Avram trusts that YHVH will keep YHVH's promise. Sarai, on the other hand, considering their respective ages, is less trusting. Her concerns become Avram's concerns.

Summary: *Ten years after settling in the Land, Sarai said to Avram, YHVH has obstructed me from bearing. Come to my maid, Hagar the Egyptian; let me be built up with sons through her. When Sarai saw that Hagar was pregnant, however, she complained that Hagar is viewing her with less esteem. She cries out to Avram that "the wrong done to me is upon you!" He replies that "your maid is in your hand, deal with her however seems good in your eyes." So, Sarai made life difficult for Hagar, causing her to flee.*

A messenger found Hagar by a spring in the wilderness and asked, "From where do you come and where are you going?" Hagar answers, "I am fleeing from Sarai." The messenger replies, "Return to her and let yourself be afflicted by her - - I will make your seed be more than you can count. Your son will be named Ishmael [which means 'God hears'] and he will be a wild-ass of a man, his hand against all, hand of all against him, yet in the presence of his brothers shall he dwell." And, Hagar called the name of YHVH, the one who was speaking to her: You God of seeing!" Hagar returned and bore Avram a son, Ishmael. At the time, Avram was already eighty-six years old.

Discussion Questions: By foretelling what lies in store for Avram's descendants over the next four hundred plus years, is the Torah suggesting that we lack free will? Sarai is just one of many women in the Torah and the later books who are said to struggle with being barren; what might this recurring theme mean? Who is Hagar, really, and what does she represent in the Torah? Why does the messenger tell her to return to Sarai and to let Sarai continue to mistreat her? And, how might we interpret the words, "a wild ass of a man"?

- **Is the Torah suggesting that we don't have free will?** On the one hand, a fundamental Torah tenet, which the writers introduced in the Garden story, is that we have the freedom to choose between good and evil. Without this freedom, there would be no need for us to struggle and, consequently, no opportunities for personal and spiritual growth. Without this freedom, Adam and Eve would never have left the Garden, which would have caused Creation to have ceased on the sixth day, instead of being an ongoing process. And, without free will, we would not be "created according to YHVH's likeness and name" ("I will be what I will be") because we would never be able "to be what we will be."

On the other hand, the writers pose a conundrum, for how can there be free will if YHVH can foretell the future? Many biblical scholars have puzzled over this seeming inconsistency. I will not be so presumptuous as to offer resolution where others before us have not, other than to say that the writers of Torah conceptualize YHVH as an abstraction, beyond our ability to understand, define, predict, or influence. All that we might know from their depiction of the first three days of Creation is that YHVH exists outside of our linear understanding of time, in some uncharted dimension where the past doesn't necessarily precede the present, nor does the present necessarily precede the future. Did this commentary shed any light on the question of free will? Probably not, but from the perspective of Torah and the imponderable way that it conceptualizes YHVH, I did not expect that it would – not for you, and certainly not for me.

Why did the writers make the concept of YHVH so inaccessible? Some have argued that by presenting YHVH as an imponderable abstraction, the writers are telling us that our purpose in life is to seek *shalem*/wholeness by struggling with things both mortal and divine. We cannot hold true to our purpose, however, if we give in to the temptation to define that which is indefinable. Doing so leads us down an unproductive path - of anthropomorphizing YHVH's image, claiming to speak or act in YHVH's behalf, or assigning meaning to YHVH's actions as if we know what "I will be what I will be" is. This point will be explained further when we explore the meaning behind the Second and Third Commandments.

- **What might barrenness mean in the context of Torah?** Many women in Torah and in the later books of the Tanakh are said to suffer from this affliction - including Sarai, Rachel (later to be the mother of Joseph), and Hanna (later to be the mother of Samuel). Why this strange preoccupation with a woman's inability to conceive? Like other puzzles in Torah, "barren" is referring to something spiritual, not physical. Women in Torah are said to be barren during the time in their lives when they *and* their husbands are not yet ready to "create" something that is truly good (*tov*, or life sustaining and life enhancing), and not yet ready to raise their offspring so that they will yearn to be like *Israel* (willing and able to struggle with things both human and divine).

The writers are not saying that the couple cannot have children, nor are they implying that these children will grow up to be socially maladjusted. But they are saying that the children that a couple has during their time of barrenness will grow up to be less spiritually aware and thus less able to participate in the ongoing process of creation.

From the perspective of Torah, couples will remain barren until they have truly struggled with questions emanating from the Tree of Knowing Good and Evil (" Which actions are truly *tov*?") and the Tree of Life (" Who am I and what is my purpose in life?"), so that they can pass on what they have learned to the next generation. Said differently, spiritual barrenness ends when couples are able to live their lives by the meaning of the twenty-third Psalm ("The Lord is my shepherd").

By turning to Hagar to "build up with sons," Avram and Sarai continued their barren ways. Like some deterministic Mandala wheel, they allowed their past to "shepherd" their present, and thus they were stuck, unable to move forward. Recall that YHVH repeatedly promised Avram and Sarai that they would have a rightful heir, but did not specify when. Like the builders of the Tower, who attempted to reach up to the heavens rather than wait for the heavens to come down to meet them (as it will in Jacob's dream in a later chapter of Genesis), Avram and Sarai grew impatient and tried to take control of the situation.

- **Who is Hagar, really?** We are told that she is Sarai's maidservant, someone Avram and Sarai brought with them from Egypt after briefly travelling to that prosperous nation. "Hagar" means "the stranger," and the Hebrew word *mitz-ra-yim* (i.e., Egypt) is built on the three letter root *"tz-a-r,"* which means a "narrow place" - a place where we tend to give more attention to our material pursuits than we do to the questions of good, evil, and life.

Putting these puzzle pieces together, "Hagar the Egyptian maidservant" becomes "the enslaved stranger who came from a narrow place." The writers are telling us that at the time of her pregnancy, Hagar (like Sarai) is still defining herself by her past and thus not yet free to choose a better (truly *tov*) life for herself and her child.

This is not to say that she was in any way flawed; indeed, it is she, and not Sarai, who is the first female after Eve that YHVH speaks to. The writers are once again reminding us that you don't have to be Jewish to hear YHVH. It is not about our status or position in life - - even an Egyptian female maid-servant can hear YHVH.

Hagar also represents Avram's and Sarai's past. Coming from a prosperous nation, she is like the property that Avram and Sarai felt compelled to bring with them when they left their home in Ur of Chaldees, believing that these possessions would bring them comfort and security.

And Hagar represents a portal to the future of Avram's and Sarai's descendants. In Genesis 15:13 we read that YHVH tells Avram that his "seed will be sojourners in a land not theirs; they will put them in servitude and afflict them for four hundred years." Of course, YHVH is referring to Mitz-rayim, a "narrow place."

The writers are being very clever by suggesting through subtle association that the descendants of Avram and Sarai who settle in Egypt will be like Hagar – "enslaved strangers from a narrow place." Hagar is thus inadvertently giving Avram and Sarai the opportunity to "walk in her shoes," and with that opportunity the possibility to learn the meaning of compassion. Unfortunately, the two of them may still have been too "barren" - too influenced by their past ways of thinking and behaving - to fully inhabit the moment and thereby gain a glimpse into their distant future.

- **Why does the "messenger" tell Hagar to return to Sarai?** The messenger (YHVH) is telling Hagar that she cannot run away from her struggles with Sarai, nor should she. Up to this point in their relationship, Sarai has treated Hagar as an object, , what Martin Buber referred to as an "I-It" relationship. That is, her interactions with Hagar were solely for the purpose of advancing Sarai's own agenda. On the other hand, Hagar allowed herself to be treated as an "It." For her to move her life forward, she needs to break free from her past, stop seeing herself as nothing more than Sarai's maidservant, stop allowing others to treat her like a victim. If she does not make this transformation, she will remain forever enslaved and incomplete (not whole).

In his book, "*A Road Less Traveled*," Scott Peck notes that life is a series of struggles. Confronting them may be painful but doing so gives new meaning to our lives, allowing us to grow mentally, emotionally, and spiritually. Hagar has to start confronting her struggles.

- **What is a "wild ass of a man"?** On the surface, the term does not appear to be complimentary. For example, we see "wild" in the Book of Job 39: 5-8 describing those who live a wandering, lawless life. Yet, Jacob refers to his favorite son and chosen heir, Joseph, using this same word in Genesis 49:22 as a compliment. The prophet Jeremiah is also referred to as a "wild ass." Clearly there is more to this expression than meets the mind. But I will hold back on offering further commentary on this expression until we come across it again in the Joseph Story, other than to say that "wild-ass of a man" can be interpreted as someone who lives in opposition to us, as a prophet or an opponent might.

➢ Genesis 17-20: The Covenant and the Birth of Yitzhak(Isaac)

Summary: *Thirteen years have passed since the birth of Ishmael in Genesis 16. Avram is now 99 years old (or, if you prefer, 49.5 years old), and once again YHVH promises him that he will have a long and plentiful line of descendants and that he will become the father of many nations. This time, however, YHVH's promise comes in the form of a formal Covenant, in which YHVH gives the land of Canaan to Avram and his descendants forever, while asking in return that all newborn males be circumcised eight days after their birth, as a sign of the covenant.[9]*

Ishmael was thirteen years old when he was circumcised, along with Avram and all the men of Avram's household. YHVH then transforms Avram's and Sarai's names to Abraham and Sarah, saying that "I have known them – they shall keep the way of YHVH and do what is right and just." YHVH tells them that Sarah will soon give Abraham a son. Upon hearing this, Abraham "fell on his face and laughed – shall ninety-year old Sarah give birth?" YHVH answers by saying that the child's name shall be Isaac (Yitzhak) – which literally means "he laughs."

YHVH repeats the promise in Genesis 18, when three messengers mysteriously appear at Abraham's tent. Seeing them, Abraham begs them to stay and places before them a generous portion of freshly prepared bread, cakes, meat, milk, and cream. One of them tells Sarah that she will have a son, which makes her laugh. Suddenly YHVH is heard asking why she laughs and then says, "Is anything beyond YHVH?"

---

9 This is the second covenant mentioned in Torah, the first being when YHVH said to Noah, "I will establish a covenant with you that all flesh will never be cut off again by the waters of the deluge" (Genesis 8: 11).

Discussion Questions: Why circumcision; what might it represent? Why and how were Avram and Sarai's names "transformed"? What does the acceptance of the "Covenant" entail? Who were the three men and why "three"? What might the number three symbolize? Why is the Torah telling us that the meal that Abraham and Sarah are sharing with the three men consists of an un-kosher combination of milk and meat?

- **What does circumcision represent?** Everett Fox notes that circumcision is an ancient ritual, usually done in primitive cultures at the time of puberty and/or marriage. As we have already noticed in other passages, physical acts in Torah often have a spiritual counterpart, and circumcision is no exception. The Torah uses it to symbolize a lifelong commitment to living in accordance with the Covenant.

    This interpretation is subtle and is not clarified until the fifth book of the Torah, Deuteronomy 30:6 when Moses, in his farewell address to the people, tells them that "YHVH will circumcise your heart and the heart of your seed, to love YHVH with all your heart and with all of your being in order that you may live."

    Moses was likely referring to the Second Commandment: *"You are not to have any other gods before my presence [or, "on my face"]. You are not to make yourselves carved-images or any figure"* (Exodus 20). YHVH recognized that we are tempted to accept false gods that blur our vision of YHVH. The gods that Moses was referring to included not only tangible images and material pursuits, but also those emotions – pride, anger, envy, jealousy, and hatred - that serve to close our hearts, take control of our thoughts and behaviors, and undermine our ability to experience *shalem*.

    These emotions emanate from unresolved experiences from our past or from attempts to control our future. They can be destructive to our well-being and to those around us because they impede our ability to ascertain reality as it is, blurring the gap between the way things appear to be and the way they are, and impairing our judgments and our reactions. As such, these emotions come between us and the face of YHVH. What Moses may have been saying, therefore, is that by "cutting off" (circumcising) these emotions from our hearts, we are better able to experience compassion, kindness, empathy, love, and life - - more able to be in YHVH's presence.

- **Why and how were Avram's and Sarai's names transformed?** As previously mentioned, YHVH added the letter '*hey*' from YHVH's name to signify the transformation of their character. This was an acknowledgement of their willingness to enter into a Covenant with YHVH. In other words, YHVH did not choose them but, rather, offered them the Covenant, which they chose to accept. Tradition has it that because they accepted, they became the first "chosen people."

- **What does choosing to live by YHVH's Covenant mean?** The passages about the Covenant give no clue as to what "living by the Covenant" entails, or even what its terms and conditions are. All it says is that we will receive a lot of Land in the future if all the males in the community are circumcised.

However, we can glean the intention of the Covenant by reflecting on the theological teachings that we drew from earlier stories in the Torah. For example, living by the Covenant can mean seeking *shalem* by trying to be like *Israel*; that is, by showing willingness and ability to struggle on a daily basis with things both human and divine, and, in turn, with questions about good, evil, and the meaning of life. It can also mean trying to fully inhabit the present by giving up control of that which doesn't belong to us, and by living our lives according to the Twenty-third Psalm ("The Lord is my shepherd"). It is also about helping future generations to cross-over into a closer relationship with themselves, with others, and with YHVH. Said simply, living by the Covenant is about learning how to be more human, to appreciate life before death, and to participate in the ongoing process of creation.

What makes the Covenant remarkable is that it is as meaningful today as it was when it was written three thousand years ago, at a time we now call the Bronze Age.

An interesting aside : The Hebrew word for "Hebrew" is "*Ivri,*" which means "cross-over" (*ah-ber*) when used in the context of a "closer relationship with YHVH." *Ivri* and *ah-ber* share the same three-letter root (*alef- bet- resh*).

- **Who were the three men and what might the number "three" symbolize?** Of the three messengers who came to visit Abraham and Sarah in Genesis 18, only one revealed their future - the one who told them that he would return next year when their son will be born. We can assume that the other two messengers represented their past, when they were still barren, and their present ; only these two would visit Lot (Genesis 19) to warn him of the ruin that is about to befall Sodom. In Sodom there is no need for the "future" messenger, because Sodom has no future.

The concept of "three" appears many other times in the Torah. It was on the third day of creation that life first appeared on the dry land, one day before the sun and the moon were formed. Three messengers mysteriously appeared at the tent of Abraham and Sarah, one year before their son Isaac was born. It was also on the third day of the journey in which Abraham takes his son Isaac from their home to be sacrificed that Abraham looks up and sees Mount *Mor'iah*, the "Mountain of Teaching." Similarly, it was on the third new moon following the exodus from Egypt that Moses comes to Mount Sinai. And the Ninth Plague (Darkness) lasted three days. The number "3" also appears throughout the Christian Bible; e.g., the coming of the three wise men to the manger where Jesus was born, and the concept of the Holy Trinity, where the Holy Ghost represents the future, the Father the past, and the Son the present.

In all of these examples, the writers are using the number three to symbolize the impending arrival of a revelation, at the moment when our mind, heart, and body are fully present and alert to appreciate it. It is that extra-perceptual moment when we are able to glimpse our inner truths (e.g., who we are and what we are about) and find clarity, wholeness, and unity (*shalem*). Said differently, revelation is that transformational moment when we realize that the emotional baggage that we've accumulated from past encounters is finally behind us, so that we can now fully inhabit the present and move on, less encumbered, to a more enlightened future.

Most of us have experienced revelations – maybe not on the grand scale experienced by Abraham, Sarah, and Moses – but revelations just the same. They are those "ah-ha" moments, or sudden insights about ourselves that cause us to change our ways, allowing us to better "hit our marks" (not sin) and be all that we can be.

- **Why did the Torah reveal that the "Parents of Israel" served a non-kosher meal?** Just as we viewed the early stories (Adam and Eve, Cain and Abel, the Flood, and the Tower of Babel) as coming-of-age stories, we can view the three generations of patriarchs and matriarchs as representing stages in personal and spiritual development, beginning with Abraham and Sarah, and then advancing with the ensuing generations. This point should become clearer once we read about the generations of Isaac, Jacob, Joseph, and Moses.

Suffice to say here that the dietary laws that require a clear separation of milk and meat did not appear in Torah until the later stories of Moses. Perhaps it took someone as spiritually advanced as Moses to realize that it is not only morally offensive to eat a calf along with its mother's milk, but also disrespectful to the various forms of life that appeared on the fifth day of Creation and that YHVH saw as "good." By specifying the menu served by Abraham and Sarah, the writers may be reminding us of what is realistic to expect from those of us just starting the journey.

➢ Genesis 21: The Banishment of Hagar and Ishmael

Summary: *Sarah bore Abraham a son at the set time that YHVH had spoken of and the boy was circumcised on his eighth day. One day Sarah saw Ishmael laughing at Isaac. She said to Abraham to drive out Ishmael and this slave-woman, for Ishmael shall not share inheritance with Isaac. This was exceedingly upsetting to Abraham, but YHVH said to hearken to her voice, for while "I will make Ishmael, your son, a nation of him - - it is through Isaac that your seed will be called by your name." Abraham started early in the morning, and gave bread and water to Hagar and sent them away to roam in the wilderness of Be'er Sheva. And, when they ran out of water, she cast her son under one of the bushes, and went a distance away, for she did not want to see her child die. YHVH heard the voice of the lad, and called out to Hagar from the heavens, saying "What is the matter with you? Do not be afraid; open your eyes and see a well* *of water." YHVH was with Ishmael as he grew up. He settled in the wilderness, became an archer, and his mother took him a wife from the land of Egypt.*

Background: In most cultures, particularly during the time of the Patriarchs, inheritance was based on primogeniture, with the family's resources passed primarily to the first born, regardless of merit. The writers of Torah, however, are suggesting that when it comes to the family birthright, merit is everything. We see this in each of the three key birthright decisions described in Genesis: Isaac is selected over his older brother Ishmael, Jacob over his older brother Esau, and Joseph over his many older brothers.

Discussion Questions: Why does YHVH side with Sarah in her dispute with Abraham regarding Hagar and Ishmael? By sending Hagar and Ishmael into the wilderness with little water, were they being sacrificed? And, why is this Torah portion read on the first day of Rosh Hashanah?

- **Why does YHVH side with Sarah?** Sarah, more so than Abraham, seemed to understand the responsibility that goes with choosing to accept YHVH's Covenant. At this point in Torah, it should be obvious that the inheritance that she is concerned about has nothing to do with the family's net worth or family business. Torah is never about the material well-being of its key figures and always about their spiritual well-being.

  It follows that the inheritance that concerns Sarah has to do with the family's spiritual birthright: Which son, Ishmael or Isaac, is more worthy of receiving this birthright? Which of the two demonstrates the wisdom to understand the Covenant and pass that knowledge to the next generation? Which one yearns to be like *Israel* and therefore has the greater capacity to contribute to the ongoing process of Creation for the family and for the community?

  We might ask, "Why choose one when we can choose both?" I suspect that by forcing the parents to choose, the writers are conveying the message that choosing to live by the Covenant often exacts a price. When it comes to decisions that affect one's spiritual future, there is no room for compromise, rationalization, and emotions. The story leads us to believe that Abraham could not have made this decision, given how upset he became when he heard Sarah's directive.

But why choose Isaac over Ishmael? Up to this point, the text has told us almost nothing about the two that would enable us to judge them on their merits, other than the fact that they were borne to different mothers. Ishmael was born to three barren parents - Avram, Sarai, and Hagar – barren, not necessarily in a physical sense, but in a spiritual sense: Not yet ready to "create" something that is truly good (*tov*), and not yet ready to raise their offspring so that they will yearn to be like *Israel*. In the case of Avram and Sarai, they, like the builders of the Babel tower, acted in a barren way by seeking to control their own destiny. They turned to Hagar, a stranger who came from a narrow place, rather than trusting the promise that YHVH had made to them that they would have children; and in the case of Hagar, she, like Lot, acted in a barren way by defining herself by her past. This parentage suggests that Ishmael's spiritual development may have been stunted from birth.

In contrast, by the time that Isaac was born, his parents, Abraham and Sarah, had already been transformed by their willingness to adhere as best they could to the Covenant. Remember that the teachings from the Torah are all about how to move forward on our journeys into closer relationships with ourselves, others, and ultimately with YHVH. We can imagine that Isaac, being born and raised by more enlightened parents, is better able to pass his parent's *Israel*-like wisdom on to the next generation than Ishmael, and therefore is more deserving of the birthright.

- **Were Ishmael and Hager being sacrificed?** By banishing the two of them to roam in the wilderness of *Be'er Sheva* with only a small supply of food and water, was Abraham and Sarah's behavior consistent with those who have chosen to live by the Covenant? Since the answer to this question appears to be an emphatic "no," what might the writers have wanted to teach in telling this story?

Perhaps Abraham and Sarah may have sent the two of them off into the wilderness for Abraham's and Sarah's own sake. Ishmael and Hagar represented some of the last major vestiges of their unenlightened past in the Ur of Chaldees, from which they needed to separate in order to better inhabit their present and move forward to their future.

On the other hand, the answer to the above question may in fact be "yes." To begin with, Abraham and Sarah were not sending them off into the wilderness to die. To understand this point, it is important to know that the Hebrew word for wilderness, *mid-bar*, shares the same *shoresh* as does the Hebrew word, *da-ber*, which means "to speak." At first glance, these two words would seem to share nothing, conceptually, but this is misleading. Indeed, those who have had the good fortune to spend time alone in Israel's wilderness areas quickly observe that the area is profoundly silent. Yet this is the area where many of the key characters in the Hebrew and Christian Bibles find inspiration and prophecy.

Quoting from Bruce Feiler's book, *Walking the Bible*, "Spend enough time in the desert and you begin to see that nothing is quite what it seems to be. Water becomes wisdom. Food becomes salvation. And sandstorms become poetry. Everything, in other words, becomes grist for allegory…. By its sheer demands – thirst, hunger, and misery – the desert asks a simple question: What is in your heart; in what do you believe?" (pp. 278-279).

From the perspective of Torah, therefore, the wilderness is where we will hear YHVH speak (*da-ber*). This holds true not only for key characters, but also for "enslaved female strangers from a narrow place." We read that YHVH spoke to Hagar twice, both times while she was in the wilderness, the first being in Genesis 16 and the second in Genesis 21.

Recall also from our discussion of Genesis 13 ("What really was Avram seeing?") that while the wilderness in Torah is a spiritual place where one can hear God speak (*da'ber*), the *negba* is a physical wasteland where without sustenance one can quickly succumb to the elements. This distinction is key to understanding Genesis 16: When Avram sent away Hagar and her son Ishmael, he was not sending them into the Negev to die, but instead into the *midbar*, where they would have the opportunity to find a more personally meaningful answer to their lives.

More to the point, the name of the wilderness to which Abraham and Sarah sent them is *Be'er Sheva*, which translates as "seven wells" - not the kind of place where a resourceful person would die of thirst or hunger. In other words, the story is saying that Ishmael and Hagar were sent into a "land of plenty where you will hear YHVH speak" – a land bountiful in nourishment for both the body and the spirit – a land where "*YHVH was with Ishmael as he grew up.*"

Moreover, Abraham and Sarah were also sending Ishmael and Hagar off into the wilderness for Ishmael's and Hagar's sake. Like their counterparts in the Exodus story (i.e., the mixed multitude who left *Mitz-ra-yim*), these two "enslaved strangers from a narrow place" also need to break free from their past, leave their enslaved ways, and go to the wilderness where they will hear YHVH. And Hagar needs to stop defining herself as someone else's servant; she needs to "open her eyes and see a well of water" and start taking responsibility for herself and her child. Simply put, she needs to move forward and begin her own personal and spiritual journey so that she can start the process of discovering her authentic self.

- **Why is this story read on the first day of Rosh Hashanah?** The literal translation of *Rosh Hashanah* is "the head of the year." It represents the beginning of the year and symbolizes the opportunity for a new beginning. This message applies to Hagar, for if she does not begin her journey now, she will put her life and that of her future (i.e., Ishmael and his descendants) in jeopardy. The message also symbolically applies to Abraham and Sarah who, by separating themselves from the last vestiges of their barren past, can now better inhabit the present. Finally, on this important holiday, the story reminds us that YHVH speaks to all people, even enslaved females who come from narrow places. This message of inclusion is repeated during the holiday of Yom Kippur with the reading of the Jonah story.

> **Genesis 22: The Sacrifice of Isaac**

Summary: *God tested Abraham, saying to him: "Abraham!" And, he answered, "Here I am." YHVH then said, "Take your son, your only one, whom you love, Isaac, and go forth (lekh lekha) to Mount Mor'iah and offer him up there as an offering-up." Abraham started early in the morning, taking with him his donkey, two serving lads, split wood, and Isaac. On the third day he lifted his eyes and saw the place from afar. He told his lads to stay here with the donkey and 'I and the lad will go yonder and then return to you.'" Abraham took the wood, the fire, and a knife and went together with his son.*

Isaac said, "Father!" and Abraham replied, "Here I am." Isaac said, "Where is the lamb for the offering?" and Abraham said, "God will select for himself/Himself the lamb." Thus, the two of them went on together.

They came to the place that God had told Abraham. He built a slaughter site, arranged the wood, and bound his son. He then took the knife to slay his son, but then a messenger called from the heaven, saying "Abraham." And he replied, "Here I am." And the messenger said, "Do not do anything to harm him, for now I know that you are in awe of God."

Abraham lifted up his eyes and saw a ram caught in the thicket. He took that ram and offered it up. He called the place "YHVH sees."

YHVH's messenger called him a second time, saying, "I will bless you and make your seed many, and all nations of the earth will enjoy blessing through your seed." Abraham returned to his lads and they went together back to Be'er Sheva.

Background: Perhaps no story in Torah is more problematic for readers than this one (also known as the *Akedah*, meaning "the Binding"), for it appears that YHVH is not only putting Abraham to a test that no father should ever be put to, but also running the risk of causing long-term psychological trauma to the son. The traditional explanation is that the story is about Israel's rejection of the widely practiced ritual of child sacrifice, but clearly there are more humane ways of getting this message across. Like many of the stories in Torah, we will see that here too there is more than what meets the literal eye.

To begin to unravel a more humane teaching of this story, we can note its similarities with the banishment story. In both stories, Abraham is said to "start early in the morning," with little awareness of what he is going to be asked to do or why. In both, one of his sons is placed in mortal danger, and in both stories God's messenger intervenes.

The similarities make the differences starker and more interesting. For example, the news that Ishmael will be sent away was *"exceedingly upsetting to Abraham"* (Genesis 21), yet he expresses no emotion whatsoever when learning that he is to sacrifice his son, his "only one, whom you love, Isaac," the son that YHVH had repeatedly promised to him, the son whom he understood from the Covenant would be the first in a long and plentiful line of descendants. As Everett Fox points out, what makes Abraham's passivity here so out-of-character is the fact that he rarely accepted his fate as a given. Unlike those who accepted the notion that life was predetermined by the Great Wheel (Mandala), Abraham stood his ground with relatives (e.g., Lot in Genesis 13), with local princes (in Genesis 20), and even God (in Genesis 18). Yet, in the *Akedah* story, with his most precious possession at risk, he remains strangely and silently compliant.

Discussion Questions: Why was Abraham so passive? "Here I am" appears three times in this story – what might this expression mean? And, the expression, *Lekh lekha,* appears here for only the second (and last) time in Torah – what might it be symbolizing? Why is this Torah portion read on the second day of Rosh Hashanah?

- **Why was Abraham so passively compliant?** The story opens with the line, *"God tested Abraham."* This is the only story in the Torah where the reader is being explicitly told that what is about to transpire in the story is a test (as in "not the real thing"), suggesting that Isaac's life is not going to be placed at risk. Of course, words like "sacrifice" and "offering-up" generally suggest real physical risk, but not so in the Torah, which tends to use worldly phenomena and objects as metaphors for things spiritual. In Torah, words like "sacrifice" are used to symbolize the giving up of control of that which doesn't belong to us.

  Recall that the "banishment" of Ishmael and Hagar symbolized Abraham's giving up the control that his past held over him. With the sacrifice of Isaac, Abraham is being asked to stop trying to control his future and that of his son. The teaching is that when we are no longer preoccupied by illusions of control or shepherded by memory and anticipation, we are finally ready to fully inhabit the present.

There is more: Most of us hold the image of Isaac as being a small child. He is not – at the time of this story he is thirty-seven years old, still living at home, and given his passive obedience in the story as he walks with his father to the altar, probably still subservient to his parents' control.

Why do I say that Isaac was thirty-seven? According to the Torah, Sarah was 90 when she was said to have conceived Isaac (Genesis 17:17) and she was 127 years old when she died (Genesis 23:1). Because her death is mentioned in the opening sentence of the chapter that immediately follows after *Akedah* chapter, we can assume that she died soon after this event - - and perhaps because of it. By subtracting 90 from 127, we get 37.

The writers do a beautifully poetic job of making this point with their use of three symbols, a lamb, a ram, and the thicket. Once like a lamb (*"God will select for himself the lamb"*), Isaac has grown to become a ram (an adult lamb) that happens to be caught in a thicket. For Isaac, the thicket may represent the web of influence that his parents still hold over him which keeps him entrapped and unable to move forward with his own life.

Recall one of the teachings from the Cain and Abel story: If we become too involved in the lives of our children, as Eve did with her son Cain in Genesis 4, we can cause them to hold unrealistic images of themselves. Recall also one of the teachings of the Adam and Eve story: It is the wise parents who allow their children the freedom to leave the safe confines of home and begin the journey to find out what their lives are about. Or, as Khahil Gilbran wrote: "Children may come from you, but they don't belong to you." Abraham is about to learn a similar teaching about effective parenting, on Mount *Mor'iah,* or the "Mountain of {God's} Teaching". (The Hebrew word for teacher, "*mor-eh*", is built on the same the same 3-letter linguistic root – *mem, resh, hey* - as is Mor'iah.)

The time for Isaac to leave his home and start his personal and spiritual journey is well overdue. He has been too precious to Abraham and Sarah, not only for who he is but also because he represents their future and the ultimate fulfillment of the Covenant. In the terms of the Second Commandment ("You are to have no other gods before my face"), he has become like an idol to his parents, "a god before YHVH," who has kept them from fully perceiving YHVH.

Isaac needs to be set free, but at this late date in his life extreme measures may be required: Abraham needs to "sacrifice" his relationship with his son, the one who is his "first and his choicest", as painful as that will be. The writers give us a clue that this, in fact, is what happened, when they note that *Abraham returned to his lads and they went together back to Be'er Sheva.* The verse makes no mention of Isaac. Indeed, the two of them appear to have permanently parted ways following the messenger's intervention and are never mentioned together again in the Torah until the time when Isaac and Ishmael return home to bury their father.

So, why was Abraham so passively compliant? Perhaps he knew deep in his heart that this was only a test; YHVH would never put the life of his son at risk. Remember that for the better part of his life, Abraham has "walked" with YHVH, listened to YHVH's promises, and learned to trust YHVH's words. For YHVH to suddenly ask Abraham to sacrifice his son would undermine the bond that had been built and violate the core terms and conditions of the Covenant. There could be nothing *tov* about this. It would totally contravene every interaction that YHVH has had with Abraham. Moreover, surely Abraham must expect that if YHVH is telling him in the second verse to *take your son - - and go forth to Mount Mor'iah,* that he is about to learn something of great importance. What else could happen at the "Mountain of God's Teaching" other than a revelation (e.g., give up trying to control your future), that will bring him closer to his authentic self and to YHVH.

Unfortunately for Isaac, this revelation may have come a bit late. The writers give numerous clues in the later portions of Genesis to suggest that Isaac struggled with separating himself from the influences of his past and consequently never advanced on his journey as far as did his parents or his son, Yaakov (Jacob). For example, we read in in Genesis 26 that Isaac is following much too closely in his father's footsteps: He encounters the same Avimelekh that his father encountered in Genesis 21, uses the same excuse to protect himself against Avimelekh (referring to Rebecca as his sister, just as Avram had referred to Sarai as his sister), and then is seen digging up the same wells as did his father, even to the point of calling them by the same names. Interestingly, it is only with the last well, which Isaac called *Rehovot* (or "space"), did he finally dig his own well and feel at peace with himself.

Isaac's inability to spiritually advance himself is symbolically represented by the fact that, unlike his parents and his son, Isaac's name is never transformed by adding the letter *hey* to it. We will come across other such clues as we move into the Isaac stories.

- **What does the expression "Here I am" represent?** *Hee-nay-nee*, or "Here I am" appears for the first time in the Torah in the *Akedah* story. It is heard again in a few other stories in Torah, but only at life-altering moments, as when Moses heard YHVH's voice calling him from the midst of the burning bush in Exodus 3:4. When Abraham answered "Here I am," as he did twice in this story – once when addressing YHVH and once to his son - he was saying that he was totally present, not knowing what was about to be asked of him but nevertheless ready to respond without hesitation. He was saying that his heart was entirely open and all of his senses were fully awake to fully inhabit the present.

It is interesting to note that in Genesis 12 Abraham did not answer "Here I am" when YHVH said to him, *"Lekh lekha – Go you forth from your land – to the land that I will let you see."* While this *Lekh lekha* request, like the one that YHVH asked of Abraham in the *Akedah* story *("Take your son ... and go forth to Mount Mor'iah")* represents a life-altering moment, Abraham only answered *hee-nay-nee* to the second *Lech lekha* request. The writers may be saying that the kind of "mindfulness" demonstrated by Abraham in the second *Lekh lekha* comes only after years of struggling with one's personal and spiritual development – only after one is transformed.

- **What is the meaning of *Lekh lekha* ?** The expression appears only twice in the Torah, once in Genesis 12, when Abraham is asked to go forward and to leave his past behind, and then again in the *Akedah* story (Genesis 22), when Abraham is asked to relinquish his attempts to control his future. In other words, the *lekh lekha* is all about moving forward in a spiritual sense to better inhabit our present for, as the Torah teaches, only in the present can we experience YHVH.

  But, what does inhabiting the present entail? To Hanna in the Book of Samuel, it means being able to hear her inner voice during times of meditation, silent prayer, and introspection. To the *Baal Shem Tov*, it means being able to appreciate the wonder of even the smallest of actions, objects, and situations and in the "smallest of still voices." To Einstein, it means feeling a sense of awe for the marvelous order and lawfulness that is revealed in nature and in the world of thought, arts, and science. And to Martin Buber, it means being aware of that unknowable force that attracts us to others. In short, inhabiting the present means feeling a deeply penetrating sense of *shalem*.

- **Why do we read the Sacrifice story on Rosh Hashanah?** This story is read on the second day of Rosh Hashanah (the New Year). The teaching of the Hagar and Ishmael story, which we read on the first day, is that we risk our lives and our future if we continue to let our old ways control our present. The teaching of the Sacrifice story is that we also risk our lives and our ability to inhabit the present if we try to control our future. Together, the two stories serve to remind us of where and on what we should be focusing our attention. Or, as is chanted at a traditional Rosh Hashanah service: "Awake, awake, you sleepers from your sleep; examine your deeds, return in repentance, remember your Creator; those of you who forget the truth and go astray the whole year in vanity and emptiness that neither profits nor saves, look to your souls."

One final thought: Abraham had to learn the lesson that Abel (Genesis 4) understood without having to be taught; that is, we all have to be willing to offer up our "first and our choicest" to its rightful owner in order to fully mindful of the present. As we will later read in Chapter 5, *Israel,* the more enlightened side of Jacob, the one who proved himself willing and able to struggle with things both divine and human, showed that willingness when he sent Joseph to look after the *shalem* (wholeness) of Joseph's brothers.

➢ Genesis 23- 25:20: Conclusion of the Abraham and Sarah Stories

Summary: *Sarah died at the age of 127 years, in a town near Hebron. Abraham then purchased title to a choice burial site for her at the Cave of Makhpela. Following her burial, he asked his servant to go to the land of his kindred and bring back a wife for his son, Isaac. He also told his servant, in no uncertain terms, that he did not want Isaac himself to go to that land.*

The servant took ten camels with him and ventured to the land, stopping by a spring of water as the women of the town went out to draw water. His plan was to approach one of them and say, "Pray, lower your pitcher that I may drink." And if she responded, "Drink, and I will also give your camels to drink," then he would know that she is the one for Isaac.

The woman he approached was Rivka (Rebecca), a niece to Abraham. She not only generously responded to his request for water, but she and her brother, Lavan, offered him and his camels hospitality for the night. After telling Lavan the story of why the servant had come (though diplomatically leaving out Abraham's warning against Isaac going back to that land), of his plan at the well and how Rebecca had responded, he asked Rebecca if she would go with him. Without hesitation, she responded, "I will go," and they made the long trek back to the Negev, where Isaac had settled. As she approached him, their eyes met. She became his wife and he loved her. He was forty years old at the time of their marriage.

Abraham died at the age of 175 years. Isaac and Ishmael buried him in the Cave of Makhpela. Ishmael then settled near Egypt, had twelve sons, and died at the age of 137.

Discussion Questions: Why did Abraham not want Isaac to marry a local woman nor return to the land of his kindred? By initiating a search for his son's wife, is Abraham still trying to control the future? Why does the text tell us that Isaac "loved her"? Why are we told that he was forty years old at the time of his marriage and that Ishmael had twelve sons?

- **Why did Abraham not want Isaac to marry a local woman nor return to the land of his kindred?** The Abraham and Sarah stories are about *lekh lekha*, the struggle to move forward in a personal and spiritual sense towards *shalem* by following the teachings of YHVH. In contrast, the population around them (the eleven tribes of the Canaanite nation, including the Hittites) held a very different, polytheistic or "pagan" belief structure which, as you will recall, Abraham in his younger days had rejected. Simply put, to marry a local woman would be to marry outside of the faith. From the perspective of Abraham and Sarah, this would have represented a move backward, a move from which they and all of their descendants might never recover.

  Returning to the land of his kindred represented a different kind of "moving forward" challenge. On the one hand, some in that land, like Lavan, apparently knew of YHVH. But if Isaac were to go back to that prosperous land at a time when he was only beginning his journey, he might never return. Abraham certainly must have remembered the attraction that prosperity holds, the number of years it took him to break free of its hold (he was said to have been seventy-five when he finally left), and how it affected his nephew Lot's choice of where to settle. And, as we will read in Genesis 31, Lavan and his family may have known YHVH but they apparently also worshipped other gods. Perhaps Abraham felt that his son had not yet "moved forward" enough to face up to this challenge.

- **Is Abraham still trying to control the future?** It sure seems that way. It is one thing to learn the lessons from *Mount Mor'iah* (the Mountain of God's Teaching) and quite another to act on them. That, so it is said, is the difference between knowledge and wisdom. In this way, Abraham is like all of us.

- **Why does the text tell us that Isaac "loved" Rebecca?** This is the first time in Torah that the word "love" appears to describe a relationship between husband and wife. Perhaps the writers wanted to tell us that while Abraham tried to arrange the marriage, it wasn't *his* actions that brought the two together, but instead it was their immediate attraction for each other.

- **What do the numbers "forty" and "twelve" symbolize?** Recall from the commentary about the Flood Story (Chapter 2) that "forty" was used as a gestational metaphor, signifying "birth." In Torah the number represents the birth of a fundamentally new understanding about the meaning of life and, therefore, the death of what we once had held to be true. By saying that Isaac was forty years old at the time that he married Rebecca, the writers may have been saying that he was no longer under the influence of his father, but instead was ready to cross-over into a closer relationship- with himself, with others, and with YHVH.

  As for being told that Ishmael had twelve sons: We are told in a later chapter of Genesis that Jacob also had twelve sons. The writers may have been drawing our attention to the parallel between YHVH's promises to Hagar (Genesis 17: 20: "He [Ishmael] will beget twelve tribal leaders, and I will make a great nation of him"); and to Abraham (also Genesis 17:5) "You will have a long and plentiful line of descendants and that you will become the father of many nations".

➢ **Addendum: Isaac and Rebecca**

Summary: *Isaac may have received the family birthright, but as we will read, he plays a relatively minor role in the Genesis stories, particularly when compared to his parents, his son Jacob, and his wife, Rebecca (Rebecca). Moreover, we will never learn much about who he is, about his dreams and his struggles. Indeed, "there hardly exists a story about him in which he is anything but a son and heir, a husband, or a father" (Everett Fox, p. 111). Unlike his parents, his name does not get transformed by adding the letter "hey" from YHVH's name, suggesting that he never advanced far enough on his personal and spiritual journey to willingly enter into a Covenant with YHVH. And in Genesis 27, only two chapters after his father dies, he appears in the Text as old, almost feeble, and nearly blind, at least in a spiritual sense. Soon thereafter, he is not mentioned again in the text until the time of his death, many years later.*

A far more important character to Isaac's generation turns out to be his wife, Rebecca, the third women that YHVH speaks to, Eve and Hagar being the first two. Like Sarah, Rebecca seemed to understand better than her husband the importance of the birthright decision for the fulfillment of the Covenant. And, while there is no mention in the text of her name being transformed, it didn't need to be - for her name (spelled resh, bet, koof, hey) already contained the letter hey.

Chapter 4: Jacob, Leah, Rachel, and Sons

Introduction: More is written in the Torah about Jacob than about the two other Patriarchs, and so we get to know him more intimately than we do even Abraham . We read about his failings, struggles, dreams, fears, and growth. His birth name is hardly flattering; it means the heel-sneak, deceiver, or trickster, and in his youthful years he certainly lived up to his name. His self-serving interactions with his father and brothers in his youth make us feel uneasy – we naturally expect more from someone designated to be a Patriarch. We will also find it interesting to watch him as his personal and spiritual struggles transform him into a more enlightened person. In the end, it is he, and not Abraham, who attains the status of being the first "*Israel.*"

> ### ➢ Genesis 25 - 27: Jacob, Esau, and the Blessing

Summary: *Rebecca was pregnant and aware that she was carrying twins, for the two almost crushed one another inside of her. In pain and despair, she cries out to YHVH, who tells her that "there are two nations in your body and that the elder will be a servant to the younger." The elder came out ruddy, like a hairy mantle, and so they called his name Esau, meaning the rough-one (or, hairy-one). Then came the younger, his hand grasping Esau's heel, and so they called his name Jacob, the heel-holder (or, heel-sneak) Isaac was sixty years old at the time of their birth. He grew to love Esau, for he hunted-game for his mouth, but Rebecca loved Jacob.*

One day when Jacob was boiling stew, Esau came wearily from the field and said, "Pray, give me a gulp of the red-stuff," to which Jacob replied, "I will do so if you sell me your firstborn-right here- and - now." Esau said, "I am on my way to dying, so what good to me is a firstborn-right?" So, he sold his birthright to Jacob and in return Jacob gave him bread and boiled lentils. "Thus did Esau belittle his firstborn-right."

Esau was forty when he married a Hittite woman, and "there was a bitterness to the spirit of Isaac and Rebecca."

Now, Isaac was old and his eyes had become dim. He called Esau and said, "My son," to which Esau replied, "Here I am." Isaac said, "Pick up your weapons and hunt me some game and make me a delicacy that I love so that I may give you my own blessing before I die."

Rebecca was listening and so when Esau went off to the field, she told Jacob to go to the flock and take two fine goat kids. "I will make them into a delicacy which your father loves so that he may give you the blessing." Jacob replied that Esau is a hairy man; perhaps my father will feel me – "then I will be like a trickster in his eyes and I will bring a curse and not a blessing on myself." But his mother said, "Let your curse be on me!" While Jacob went to the flock, she took garments from Esau and clothed Jacob, covering his hands and the smooth part of his neck with the skins of goat kids.

Carrying the delicacy that Rebecca prepared, Jacob came to his father and said, "Father," to which he replied, "Here I am. Which one are you, my son?" Jacob answered, "I am Esau, your firstborn." Isaac asked, "How did you prepare the delicacy so hastily?" Jacob answered, "YHVH your God made it happen for me." Then Isaac said, "Come closer that I may feel whether you are really my son Esau or not." Jacob moved closer. Isaac said, "The voice is Jacob's voice, but the hands are Esau's hands- are you my son Esau?" And Jacob said, "I am."

As Isaac ate the delicacy, he smelled the smell of Esau's garments that Jacob wore and said, "The smell of my son is like the smell of the field." And Isaac blessed Jacob, saying "May tribes bow down to you, may your mother's sons bow down to you, those who damn you be damned and those who bless you be blessed."

Soon after Jacob left his father's tent, Esau returned from his hunt and offered his father the delicacy that he had prepared. Confused, his father asked, "Which son are you?" He replied, "I am Esau, your firstborn." Trembling, Isaac said, "Who was it that I blessed? Now blessed, he must remain!"

When hearing his father's words, Esau cried a bitter cry and said, "Bless me also, father!" But Isaac replied, "Your brother came with deceit and took away your blessing." Esau cried, "Is that why his name is Jacob/Heel-Sneak? He has now sneaked against me twice: My firstborn-right he took and now my blessing. Haven't you reserved a blessing for me?" Isaac said, "You will live by the sword and will serve your brother, but you will eventually tear his yoke from your neck."

And Esau held a grudge against Jacob. He said in his heart: "Let the day of mourning for my father draw near, and then I will kill Jacob my brother." After Rebecca was told the words of

Esau, she sent for Jacob and said, "Arise and flee to Lavan my brother in Haran and stay with him some days until Esau's anger turns away and he forgets what you did to him."

Discussion Questions: The number "forty" seems to mean something different in this story. What? Why does Isaac love Esau more than he does Jacob? Why is Isaac made out to be old and feeble when he still has almost half of his life to live? Why can't Isaac withdraw the blessing that he mistakenly gave to Jacob? And, how is Rebecca's handling of the birthright decision different than Sarah's?

- **What might "forty" symbolize in this story?** As we have already observed, "forty" was used in earlier stories to signify a transformational moment - the birth of a fundamentally new understanding about the meaning of life – and the death of a less meaningful understanding. The story about Esau, however, offers no evidence whatsoever that Esau was changed or enlightened when he turned forty. All that we are told is that at this age he married a pagan woman (where "pagan" refers to those who believe in more than one god), which greatly upset his parents. From their perspective, the marriage represented a move backward in regard to the spiritual well-being of their descendants. By marrying a Hittite woman, Esau demonstrated the same disregard for his birthright that he had in his younger days when he belittled his birthright by choosing a bowl of soup over it. Again, the birthright in Torah has nothing to do with the family's material possessions or net worth. Instead, it grants two other treasures: first, the responsibility to live one's life in accordance with the Covenant so that the current and future generations can "move forward" into a closer relationship with each other (our personal challenge) and with YHVH (our spiritual challenge); and second, the choice to accept the offered responsibility.

Interestingly, as Esau's twin brother, Jacob also turned forty, but the text makes no mention of this. Why? As we will read in later chapters of Genesis, Jacob is on a very different journey than his brother, one in which he actively struggles with questions about good, evil, and the meaning of life. Given how he behaved in Genesis chapters 25 through 27, however, it appears as if he has not yet made any serious progress on this journey. From the perspective of Torah, he is years away from turning forty.

Suffice to say here that the story offers an important clue to understanding the symbolic meaning of "forty." For some, like Esau, it refers to biological time, while for others, like Jacob, it takes on a more spiritual metric.

- **Why does Isaac love Esau more than he does Jacob?** The story leaves us to guess the answer to this question. Some have noted that Isaac and Esau share a common past. Each was said to be forty at the time he married, and neither had the letter *hey* added to his name, meaning that neither had advanced far enough on personal and spiritual journeys to experience revelation. Others have said that they both shared a hunger for food, whether a bowl of lentil soup or some delicacy prepared from the hunt.

    I like the explanation that Isaac prefers Esau because Esau reminds him of his brother, Ishmael (a "wild ass of a man"), who had been banished from the family. This episode may have left an indelible impression on Isaac, who at a young age was unlikely to have understood his parents' actions. Is Isaac subconsciously trying to correct what he perceived to be the sins of his parents by now showing favoritism to Esau? Or, might Isaac be showing favoritism to Esau because he somehow feels responsible for the banishment of his brother, as children often feel when their parents separate?

    Rabbi Alan Lew wrote that "forgiveness means giving up the hope for a better past."[10] This may sound a bit strange, but he explains that many of us refuse to give up on our version of the past, and so find it impossible to forgive ourselves or others, and in turn find it impossible to act in the present. Is Isaac unable to forgive himself and his parents?

- **Why is Isaac made out to be so old and feeble?** We were told that Isaac was sixty years old when Rebecca gave birth to their two sons, who at the time of their blessing

---

[10] Alan Lew (2005) "Be Still and Get Going: A Jewish Meditation Practice for Real Life," Little Brown and Company.

were both forty. This makes Isaac about the same age that his father was when Isaac was born. Recall from Genesis 22 that Abraham was still young enough, thirty-seven years after Isaac's birth, to take his son on a three-day walk to Mount Mor'iah. And Isaac is not even close to being on his deathbed for, as we will read, he will live another eighty years. Bear in mind the evidence that during biblical times each year was comprised of two new years, meaning that at the time that Isaac was described as being old and feeble, he was likely to have been only fifty. As we have seen in many of the preceding stories, therefore, this description of an old and feeble Isaac is difficult to take literally.

We can draw clues by observing that Isaac is favoring the senses of taste, smell, and touch, while not trusting sight and sound. This is particularly interesting because the latter two senses in Torah are much more commonly associated with moments of revelation, while the former three are not. For example, Abraham , Sarah, and Hagar were all said to have *heard* YHVH's voice. And, Avram was said, in Genesis 13, to have *seen* long distances in all four directions, as did Moses in Deuteronomy 34. The importance of sight will be mentioned again in the discussion of the Ninth Plague, the plague of darkness "when a man cannot see the face of his brother." The darkness that this plague refers to is not due to the absence of physical light, but rather the absence of spiritual light, the light that was separated from darkness on the first day of creation. (More about the symbolic meaning of each of the ten plague will be presented in Chapter 6.)

Taken as a whole, these clues suggest that Isaac's spiritual light was fading. He must have known that Jacob was the rightful heir to the family birthright, if only because YHVH had told this to Rebecca at the time of her pregnancy; that is, *"there are two nations in your body and that the elder will be a servant to the younger."* And surely Rebecca, as Isaac's loving wife, would have relayed this message to him. Yet, Isaac, with his spiritual light fading, denies the message, denies what he sees and hears, and denies the fact that Esau had actively belittled his firstborn birthright. Rather than experiencing a sense of clarity and wholeness that comes when the mind, heart, and body are fully present and alert, enabling a glimpse at our inner truths, Isaac is experiencing discord and internal conflict. He trusts what he wants to trust, and he seems to love his son Esau.

- **Why can't Isaac withdraw his blessing to Jacob?** Some have said that Isaac was not as old and feeble as he was making himself out to be, but was acting this way because he was testing just how far Jacob, the heel-holder and deceiver, would go with his charade. After all, many of the lessons that Jacob will later learn on his journey might not have been learned had he not done so poorly on this test. Others have said that deep in his heart, Isaac knew that Jacob was the rightful heir to the family birthright, but had too much difficulty admitting it to himself. Perhaps by saying that he could not withdraw his blessing, Isaac was taking the easy way out. Finally, some have said that during biblical times people understood the power of language differently than we do today (as, for example in the Creation story, when YHVH speaks the world into existence), that once uttered, the words can never be withdrawn. Or, as the Aramaic phrase *abra-ka-dabra* tells us, "I create as I speak."

- **How is Rebecca handling the birthright decision differently than Sarah did?** Recall that during her barren years, Sarai grew impatient with YHVH's promise and tried to take control of that which cannot be controlled, as she did when she tried to bear a child for Avram through Hagar. However, once she chose to adhere to the Covenant, she was transformed, bearing a son "*at the set time that YHVH had spoken.*" As Sarah, she understood the importance of the birthright and the difficult decision that would have to be made to ensure that the family birthright would be passed on to its rightful heir. Only after she made this decision did YHVH speak, telling Abraham to "hearken to her voice."

Rebecca handled the matter of the birthright differently, more like Sarai than like Sarah. YHVH told her during her pregnancy that Jacob would be the rightful heir. However, like Sarai, she worried that YHVH's prophesy was not enough to make it happen, and so she deceived her husband and made Jacob an accomplice. Like Sarai, she acted and spoke on YHVH's behalf. Like Sarai, she allowed the ends to justify her means. And, like Sarai, she sinned (i.e., missed her mark) by acting self-righteously.

We can draw another interesting teaching from her actions. Earlier, I wrote that no mention in the text is made about Rebecca being transformed. I said that she didn't need to be because her name (spelled *resh, bet, koof, hey*) already contained the letter *hey*. If this is the case, we might then ask, "Why did she act in a '*Sarai*' kind of way?" Perhaps the Torah is telling us that we are all born with the potential to be transformed or enlightened. The struggle we all face is to convert that potential into reality. This conversion is analogous to what we read in the Creation story, when YHVH transformed the "and it was so" (defined as the potential to bring forth life) into something "*tov*" (acts that realize that potential).

➢ Genesis 28: Jacob's Ladder

Summary: *Isaac tells Jacob not to take a Canaanite wife and, instead, to go to the country of Aram, to the home of Lavan, his mother's brother, and take a wife from there. So, Jacob left Be'er Sheva and rested in Haran where he spent the night. Placing a stone at his head, he dreamt: A ladder was set up on the earth, its top reaching the heavens, and messengers of God were going up and down on it. And here, YHVH was standing over him, saying, "I am YHVH, the God of Abraham your father and the God of Isaac. I will give to you and your descendants the land on which you lie, and will not leave you until I have done what I have spoken to you."*

Jacob awoke and was awe-struck, saying, "I did not know that YHVH is in this place. This place is the house of God and the gate to heaven." And he called the place "Bet-El" and said, "If YHVH will be with me, and watch over me as I go, and will give me food to eat and garment to wear, and if I come back in peace to my father's house, then YHVH shall be God to me, and everything that You give to me, I shall tithe it to you."

Discussion questions: What is the meaning of the ladder in Jacob's dream? Why does YHVH refer to Abraham as Jacob's father, and not Isaac? Why did Isaac tell Jacob to go to the land that Isaac was told not to go to?

- **What is the meaning of Jacob's ladder?** Picture the scene: It is Jacob's first night away from his home and he is feeling vulnerable, fearing for his life. We can imagine his conscience working on overdrive, questioning his past behaviors, wondering why he chose deception over honesty, and worried about the consequences. Clearly this is not yet the person whom we had been told in previous chapters would be the rightful heir to the family's spiritual birthright, the person who will move the family forward. Indeed, we have yet to read anything about him to suggest that he will be a worthy heir.

    This begins to change with the revelation which he is about to receive in his dream, where he sees, perhaps for the first time in his life, the possibility that his life can have purpose and meaning. He realizes that while he may be physically separated from his family, he is spiritually connected to them, as well as to his ancestors and his descendants. He may not be ready to understand the full meaning of this revelation, for he is only beginning to "move forward" on his journey and the ladder in his dream is exceedingly long. The good news is that he doesn't have to reach the top. As he moves up the ladder, there will be messengers coming down to him.

    Why was Jacob awe-struck by his dream? Perhaps he was asking himself "Why me? After all the bad things that I have done, why did YHVH reveal this vision to me?"

    An aside: The message conveyed by the story of Jacob's dream reworks the message of the Babel Tower story. In the Tower Story, the people tried to erect a building to reach the heavens, while in Jacob's dream, the ladder descended from the heavens to reach the earth. There is a meaningful difference. The Tower story tells of those who over-reached by trying to be more God-like, seeking to control their destiny, seeking to control that which they cannot control. In contrast, the Dream Story's message is that no one is in control of where, when, or for whom the ladder will appear.

The Dream Story is also telling us that the ladder is there for everyone, even a "heel-sneak." However, to perceive it and begin our climb requires that we have at least a rudimentary awareness of what had been our good and evil behaviors, and the willingness to act on that knowledge. For Jacob, dreaming of the ladder represented a moment of revelation - an awakening to a new direction in his life, and recognition that much that he had held to be true about himself was no longer meaningful.

That said, the revelation seemed to last but a brief moment for Jacob, for soon after realizing that YHVH was "in this place," he returns to his conniving ways by dictating a litany of conditions that he says YHVH must meet if Jacob is to accept YHVH as his God. In fairness to Jacob, his reluctance to surrender control over his own destiny might be expected from someone who is just beginning his personal and spiritual journeys. The Book of Exodus will describe similar doubting behaviors among all who begin their journeys away from their enslavements in Egypt.

- **Why does YHVH refer to Abraham, but not Isaac, as Jacob's father?** The Torah is once again making the distinction between our physical and spiritual realities. Isaac was Jacob's biological father but, as we have read, Isaac's spiritual light never burned very brightly and then started to fade at an early age, in contrast to his father, Abraham, and ultimately to Jacob himself. And, while Jacob is clearly biologically linked to Abraham, from the perspective of Torah, one's spiritual heir can come from outside the family lineage. Many of the stories convey this perspective, including the David Story where David refers to Saul as his father and Saul refers to him as "my son."

- **Why did Isaac tell Jacob to go to a land that Isaac was told not to go to?** Perhaps Isaac perceived Jacob to be better able than he, Isaac, was to meet the challenge that prosperity holds. Perhaps Isaac resented his father's wishes and did not want to micro-manage his son's life in the same over-bearing way that his father had managed him. Perhaps Isaac heard from Rebecca such wonderful things about her homeland that he wanted his son to go there. Or, perhaps Isaac's light had grown so faint that he was unable to grasp the risks.

➢ Genesis 29: Rachel and Leah

Summary: *Jacob continued on his journey east until he came to a well, where he saw Rachel, Lavan's daughter, with her father's sheep. And Jacob told her that he was the son of her father's sister, Rebecca. Rachel ran to tell her father, who came and welcomed Jacob and gave him shelter.*

After a month's time, Lavan said to Jacob, "Just because you are my relative, should you serve me for nothing? Tell me, what shall your wage be?" Now, Lavan had two daughters, the older being Leah, whose eyes were delicate, but Jacob fell in love with Rachel. He replied, "I will serve you seven years for Rachel."

And when his years of labor were fulfilled, he came to Lavan, who gathered everyone to have a drinking feast. Unbeknownst to Jacob, Lavan gave him Leah. Jacob awoke the next morning to discover that he had slept with Leah, and went to Lavan, saying "Why have you deceived me?" Lavan replied that in this place, the younger is never given away before the firstborn. " Serve me another seven years and you shall have Rachel as well." So, Jacob worked another seven years, after which Lavan gave him Rachel.

Discussion Questions: Why did Jacob suggest that seven years was fair wage for Rachel? Who is Lavan (aside from being Jacob's uncle)?

- **Why "seven" years?** Recall from the Creation story that the number "seven" is a metaphor for a completed cycle of creation, involving both the potential for bringing forth life and the actualization of that potential. As such, the number is used to symbolize the spiritual reality of life. It follows that by saying that he would work seven years for Rachel, Jacob was saying that his attraction for Rachel was more than just physical. He was envisioning his relationship with her as a "spiritual union," something that would be truly good (*tov*), or life-enhancing.

- **Who is Lavan?** Lavan is what Jacob was: a deceiver. If there is a difference, it is that Lavan appears to be more polished in the art of deception. It is one thing to trick your aging father into believing that you are really his other son, and quite another to trick a young man into believing that he is sleeping with the woman of his dreams, when in fact it is her sister. In Lavan, Jacob finally gets to see himself as others may have seen him. Lavan might represent the person that Jacob might have become if not for the "revelational" ladder dream.

➢ Jacob's Eleven Sons: Genesis 29-31

Summary: *When YHVH saw that Jacob loved Rachel but Leah was unloved, YHVH opened Leah's womb while Rachel remained barren. And Leah bore Jacob a son, Re'uven, and said, " YHVH has seen my being afflicted, but now with this son, Jacob will love me." And she became pregnant again, and bore Jacob a second son, Shim'on, saying that YHVH has heard that I am unloved. She became pregnant again and bore a third son, Levi, for "now this time my husband will be joined to me for I have borne him three sons." She became pregnant again and bore Jacob a fourth son, Yehuda, saying, "This time I will give thanks to YHVH." Then she stopped giving birth. Rachel envied her sister, saying to Jacob, "Come now, give me children!" Jacob replied in anger, "Am I in place of God, who denied you fruit from your body?" So Rachel gave Jacob her maid, Bilha, so that Rachel could "build-up-with-sons through her." Bilha became pregnant and bore him a son, Dan, and Rachel said, "God has done me justice and heard my voice." And Bilha bore Jacob a second son, Naftali, and Rachel said that she had struggled with God and with her sister, and "Yes, I have prevailed."*

Leah, who saw that she had stopped giving birth, gave her maid, Zilpa, to Jacob. She bore him a son, Gad, and Leah said "What fortune!" Then, Zilpa bore him a second son, Asher, and Leah said, "What happiness!"

During the days of the wheat harvest, Re'uven found some love apples (aphrodisiacs) and brought them to his mother, Leah. When Rachel saw them, she asked to have some, to which Leah replied, "Is your taking away my husband such a small thing that you would now take away my son's love apples?" Rachel responded, "Very well, he may lie with you tonight in exchange for your son's love apples."

So, when Leah saw Jacob returning from the fields, she said, "Come to me, for I have hired you for my son's love apples." She became pregnant and bore Jacob a fifth son, Yissakhar, for "God has given me hired wages." And she became pregnant again, bearing a sixth son, Zevulun, saying "this time my husband will exalt me."

But God kept Rachel in mind, and she became pregnant and bore a son, Joseph (Yosef), for "YHVH has added another son to me."

Discussion Questions: Who is Rachel and who is Joseph?

* **Who is Rachel?** Perhaps no character in Torah is as interestingly complex as Rachel, who embodies aspects of Sarai, Rebecca, *Israel*, and Esau. Like Sarai, Rachel offers her maid to her husband in the attempt to deal with their barrenness, but doing so only reaffirms the reasons why she and Jacob were said to be barren. Recall from the Sarai and Avram stories that "barren" can be used symbolically to represent something spiritual rather than physical. When women in Torah are said to be barren, it means that they and their husbands, as a pair, have not yet chosen to live by the Covenant. As our commentary from Genesis chapters 17-20 mentioned, living by the Covenant entails the willingness and ability to struggle with things both mortal (such as relationships and competing priorities) and divine (such as our spiritual well-being and the mysteries of our existence and purpose), while also surrendering those things in our lives which we cannot control or understand. Living by the Covenant also means struggling with questions about good, evil, and the meaning of life. It means trying to fully inhabit the present by giving up control of that which doesn't belong to us, and by living our lives according to the Twenty-third Psalm ("The Lord is my shepherd"). And, it is about helping future generations to cross-over into a closer relationship with themselves, with others, and with YHVH. Said simply, living by the Covenant is about learning how to be more human, to appreciate life before death, and to participate in the ongoing process of creation. As we will read in Genesis 35, living by the Covenant is to be like *Israel*.

When Rachel offered her maid to Jacob and he accepted the maid, Rachel and Jacob proved themselves not yet able to live by the Covenant and therefore ill-prepared to "create" something truly good (*tov*) like, for example, a Joseph. As we have just read, Joseph's name means "YHVH has added."

Rachel was also like Rebecca. Both tried to control that which humans cannot control. In Rebecca's case, she tried to take matters into her own hands, when she helped Jacob steal his father's blessing; and, in Rachel's, by offering her maid to Jacob.

Rachel also bears similarity to *Israel*, but with interesting differences. As we will read in Genesis 35, *Israel* is more than a person or a place; the term refers to anyone who shows the willingness and ability to live by the precepts of the Covenant, and to commit to a lifetime of struggle with things both human and divine. Like Israel, Rachel recognized the importance of struggling with things both moral and divine when she said "A struggle with God have I struggled with my sister; yes, I have prevailed!" However, to be like *Israel* is to commit oneself to a lifetime of struggles, and not, as she does, proclaim an early victory ("I have prevailed!").

Finally, Rachel embodies aspects of Esau, as both allowed themselves to give up something deeply meaningful in their attempts to satisfy a momentary hunger. Esau, for his part, belittled his first-born rights by trading them for a bowl of his brother's lentil soup ; while Rachel belittled her marriage by allowing her sister to "lie with" her husband in exchange for some love apples. But make no mistake: Jacob was not an innocent bystander in this exchange, but instead willingly participated, with gusto - for, from the transaction, Leah bore him two more children.

And so it was that Rachel and Jacob continued to behave as a barren couple.

- **Who is Joseph?** At this point in the book of Genesis, we don't know much other than he is the only offspring of Rachel and he is Jacob's eleventh son. However, we can draw some interesting inferences about who Joseph might be. To begin with, aside from being Jacob's eleventh son, Joseph is also Jacob's "seventh" son -- if we count only those sons born to his wives and not the four sons born to Leah's and Rachel's maids. As we already know, the number "seven" is used in the Torah as a metaphor for a completed cycle of creation, involving both the potential for bringing forth life and the actualization of that potential.

Some might say that the association between Joseph's birth order, when excluding the sons born out of wedlock, and the importance ascribed to the number seven is a quirky coincidence, but there are few meaningless coincidences in the Torah. Moreover, we are told in Genesis 31 that Joseph's name means "YHVH has added." Let's put these two puzzle pieces together. By virtue of being the seventh son and having a name "YHVH has added," the Torah may be suggesting that through Joseph, God will be "adding" to a new cycle of creation. We will further explore the meaning of Joseph's name and the importance that he plays in Torah in Chapter 5 of this book. Suffice to say here that while Joseph is not considered to be a "patriarch," as are Abraham, Isaac, and Jacob, he nevertheless rivals them in terms of being spiritually advanced.

Finally, we can assume that for Jacob and Rachel to have given birth to a "Joseph," they must have lost their barrenness. The text, however, gives us no clue as to when or how.

➢ The Tale of the Two Deceivers : Genesis 30:25 through Genesis 31

Summary: *Once Rachel bore Joseph, Jacob said to Lavan, "Send me free, that I may go back to my land - - for you know that I have served you." Lavan replied, "YHVH has blessed me on account of you and I have become wealthy. Tell me what I owe you and I will give you payment." Jacob said, "You are not to give me anything, only do this one thing for me: Let me go over your flock and keep every blemished lamb and goat." Lavan agreed, but then proceeded to remove all the blemished lambs and goats from Jacob's flock. Realizing that Lavan was once again trying to trick him, Jacob then used a breeding trick on Lavan's flock to make a special herd of robust blemished flock-animals for himself, while leaving Lavan with a herd of feeble animals. Lavan's sons tell their father that Jacob has plotted to take away Lavan's wealth, which naturally angered Lavan.*

YHVH tells Jacob to return to the land of his fathers and "I will be with you." Jacob, in turn, tells Rachel and Leah, saying, "You know that I have served your father with all my might, but he cheated me and changed my wages ten times over." Jacob then tells his wives that YHVH came to him in a dream and told him that all the animals would bear blemished offspring, for YHVH had seen what Lavan has done to him. And so "God has snatched away from your father's livestock and given them to me." Rachel and Leah listen and agree that what God snatched for them rightly belongs to them, and they tell Jacob to do whatever God tells him to do. As Jacob readies his family and all of the property that he gained in Aram, Rachel steals terafim (a household idol) from her father. Without telling Lavan that they are about to flee, Jacob starts the journey homeward.

Three days later, Lavan hears that Jacob has fled. With his tribal brothers, he pursues Jacob, catching up to him in the hill country of Gil'ad, a seven-day journey. God comes to Lavan in a dream, warning him not to speak ill to Jacob. The next day Lavan says to Jacob, "Why did you trick me and then lead my daughters away like captives, without telling me? Why did you not even allow me to kiss my grandchildren and my daughters? It lies in my hand's power to do all of you ill." Jacob did not know that Rachel had stolen the terafim and hid them in her camel's saddle basket when he said, "With whomever you find your gods – he shall not live." Lavan searched the tents and camels, but did not find anything.

Jacob became upset: "What is my sin that you have dashed hotly after me and felt through all my wares?" I have been under you for twenty years and have never stolen from you. ... I served you fourteen years for your two daughters and six years for your animals, and you have changed my wages ten times. ... Indeed, if you had your way, you would have sent me off empty-handed."

Lavan said --- everything that you have and see is mine, but because of my daughters, let us cut a covenant. So they collected stones and built a mound. Lavan said, "I will not cross over this mound to you, and you will not cross over this mound to me, for ill!" And Lavan started early in the morning, kissed his grandchildren and daughters, and returned to his home.

Discussion Questions: Have Jacob and Rachel "moved forward" in how they deal with people? What is the meaning of the numbers three (as in "3 days later"), seven (as in a "7-day journey") and ten (as in "he changed my wages 10 times")?

- **Have Jacob and Rachel "moved forward"?** Remember that the teachings from the Torah are all about moving forward on our journeys into closer relationships with ourselves, others, and ultimately with YHVH. That is to say, the teachings are about "going forth" (*lekh lekha*) to a sense of *shalem,* the point when our past stops determining our present. On the one hand, the fact that they gave birth to a "Joseph," someone born with the spiritual capacity to begin a new cycle of creation, is proof positive that they had moved forward. That is to say that, from the perspective of Torah, children like Joseph are not born to barren parents.

On the other hand, the text gives us no clear evidence that Jacob has abandoned his trickster ways. He may have gotten a first glimpse at what it means to "go forth" during his ladder dream, but here we see that his past ways are continuing to "shepherd" his present, in spite of what might have been revealed to him in his "ladder dream." If there has been a change at all, it is that Jacob has gotten better at the art of deception. I say this because Lavan represented a formidable opponent, yet Jacob was able to out-wit him (and do so without the help of his mother, who - as you will recall - helped him trick his aging and weak father).

The text provides other clues to suggest that Jacob is struggling with the next step. First, like Avram and Lot, Jacob is leaving Aram and taking with him all the property that he had gained during his twenty-year stay there - and then some - suggesting that he, like his ancestors, was still having difficulties making a clean break with his past. Recall in Genesis 13 how the inability of Lot to accept the uncertainties of the present for the certainties of the past ended up costing his family its future.

And second, when explaining to Rachel and Leah his reasons for taking their father's livestock, Jacob spoke as if his words came directly from YHVH. By doing so, Jacob seemed to be acting in the same self-righteous manner as did his mother, Rebecca, who invoked YHVH's name when arguing that Jacob, and not Esau, should be the recipient of the family's birthright.

As for Rachel, by stealing the terafim, she was also struggling with taking the next step. (Terafim are thought to be small figurines, either representing pagan gods or ancestors. The word may have come from the Hittite word, *tarpi*.)

- **What are the meanings of the numbers "7," "3," and "10" in this story?** We have observed that numbers in Torah are not casually selected, but rather are used either as metaphors for various spiritual conditions, or to point out the absence of those conditions. For example, from the Creation Story in Genesis 1, we observed that the number "seven" refers to the completion of one cycle of creation. The fact that the text tells us that Jacob willingly worked *seven* years for both Leah and Rachel, therefore, suggests that there is something about their unions that are, or will be, life-enhancing. For the union with Leah, that something turns out to be the birth of Levi, from whom Moses descended. And for the union with Rachel, that something turns out to be the birth of Joseph, who later becomes instrumental in protecting the family from the drought and famine that will afflict their homeland.

We see this again when the text uses the number "three." Recall that "three" has been used to signal the impending arrival of a revelation, a divine moment when we realize that we have separated from our past, but know in the present what will be in our future and what we need to do to get there. For example, we read in Genesis 17-20 about the three men who mysteriously appear at the tent of Abraham and Sarah, announcing to Sarah that she will bear a son. We also read in the *Akeda* Story that Abraham looked up on the *third* day of his journey with Isaac and saw Mount *Mor'iah*, or the "Mountain of Teaching."

And we see this again with the text's use of the number "ten." It appears in this chapter when Jacob says that Lavan "changed my wages ten times over." Like the other key numbers, this number appears many times in the text: Think the Ten Plagues and Ten Commandments. Think also the Ten Days of Awe between Rosh

Hashanah through Yom Kippur, the ten generations that separated Adam from Noah and Noah from Abraham, and the custom of "tithing" (see Genesis 14:20 and 28:22). In Genesis 16, Sarai says to Avram *ten* years after being in the Land, that "YHVH has obstructed me from bearing." And in Genesis 23, the story tells us that Abraham's servant took *ten* camels with him when venturing to find a bride for Isaac. In these and other references,[11] the number is signifying a sufficient amount to capture one's attention and strike one's spirit. For example, if ten plagues are not enough to cause the Hebrews to leave Egypt, an eleventh won't do it. Similarly, if we cannot find forgiveness during the .ten days of awe, we won't find it on the eleventh day. And, like the plagues, ten is the number of times that Lavan will have to change Jacob's wages before Jacob finally says, "Enough," and begins his preparation to leave.

That said, numbers in the Torah are sometimes used to symbolize the *absence* of a spiritual condition. We observed this in an earlier passage (Genesis 26:34) where it was stated that Esau turned forty, but without any hint of a revelation, a transformational experience that would have caused him to cross-over into a closer relationship with himself, with others, and with YHVH; a moment when he would have been able to move forward to a more enlightened future by leaving behind the emotional baggage of the past.

The same non-spiritual connotation can be seen in the current portion of the text, which says that it took seven days for Lavan to catch up to Jacob. Clearly, "seven," as used here, would seem to have nothing to do with the completion of a cycle of creation. The same can be said about the number "three," when (three days later)

---

11 For example, In Deuteronomy 26:12, the Torah commands Jews to give one-tenth of their produce to the poor (Maasei Ani). From this verse and from an earlier verse (Deut. 14:22) there derives a practice for Jews to give one-tenth of all earnings to the poor. Also, in Jewish liturgy Ten Martyrs are singled out as a group. There are said to be Ten Lost Tribes of Israel (those other than Judah and Benjamin). There are Ten Sephirot in the Kabbalistic Tree of Life. In Judaism, ten adults (a *minyan*) are the required quorum for prayer services.

"God comes to Lavan in a dream" and tells him in no uncertain terms "not to speak ill to Jacob" - not the kind of message that can be thought of as a precursor to a revelation.

The Torah (which means "teaching") appears to follow sound pedagogical principals by asking its readers to remain actively engaged in the text; here by challenging us to differentiate those times when numbers have spiritual connotations from those times when they do not.

➢ Genesis 32: On Becoming Israel

Background: In this pivotal chapter, the Torah is telling us that that our struggles, painful as they may be, can be our best teachers. It is through struggling that our true self – our identity and purpose, the essence of who we are - is revealed. But as we will read in later chapters, enlightenment does not come from one grand revelation. Rather, it is approached through a willingness to engage in perpetual struggle, for situations change, as do people. What worked yesterday may not hold true today.

Summary: *As Jacob was journeying home, he was encountered by messengers of God. Jacob sent them ahead to Esau, telling them to say "It is me, Jacob, your servant." The messengers returned, telling Jacob that Esau, along with four hundred men, is coming to meet him. Upon hearing the news, Jacob was exceedingly afraid and distressed. He divided the people and animals with him into two camps, saying that if Esau attacks one camp, then the other camp will escape.*

He then prayed to the God of his fathers, Abraham and Isaac, asking YHVH to remember His promise and to save him, his wives and his children.

He then sent his servants to Esau bearing a generous gift of many livestock and the plea that "I, Jacob, will wipe the anger from your face, that you will be gracious to me."

Later, once the servants had left, he arose during the night and took his two wives, his two maids, and his eleven children to cross the Yabbok River. And Jacob was left alone.

A man wrestled with him until the coming of dawn. And when the man saw that he could not prevail against him, the man touched the socket of Jacob's thigh that had been dislocated as he wrestled with him. The man then said, "Let me go for dawn has come up!" But Jacob said, "I will not let you go until you bless me."

The man said, "What is your name," to which Jacob replied, "Jacob/heel-sneak." The man said, henceforth your name will be Yisrael/ God-Fighter, for you have fought with God and men and have prevailed."

Then Jacob asked, "Tell me your name," to which the man replied, "Why do you ask my name?" And the man gave him a farewell blessing. And Jacob limped away.

Discussion Questions: What is the meaning of the number "400"? Has Jacob's recent experience with Lavan caused him to "move forward"? Who is the "man"? Why did the "man" ask Jacob's name? Why was Jacob's hip injured? Why did the "man" not reveal his name?

- **What is the meaning of the number "400"?** Esau was said to have an army of four hundred men. Seeing how this number is used here and then again later in the Book of Exodus, where it says that the Hebrews spent four hundred years as slaves in Egypt, it appears that this number is used to symbolize a formidable amount. Thus, by stating that four hundred of Esau's men were coming to meet Jacob, the text is implying that enough men were coming to strike Jacob with fear.

- **Has Jacob "moved forward"?** When we addressed this same question in the previous Genesis chapter, we found no evidence that Jacob had made much progress. He was still, as his name suggests, Jacob/the deceiving "heel-holder." That is to say that he may have received a revelation about himself during his "ladder dream," but he is having difficulty acting on its insights.

  Until the appearance of the mysterious "man" in verse 25 of the current chapter, we still see no substantive evidence. On the one hand, we find Jacob pleading to YHVH for protection. On the other hand, his pleas appear to me more calculating than sincere. I say this because just before making his impassioned appeal, he tries to take matters into his own hands by strategically dividing his people and livestock into two camps in the attempt to save at least half of his belongings. Then, right after his pleading, he again tries to control his destiny, this time through diplomacy, by sending his servants to Esau with a large and valuable "peace offering." Clearly, he continues to put his trust in his own wits at least as much as he does in YHVH.

- **Who is the mysterious "man"?** The text depicts a powerfully reflective scene. As he was in the Ladder Story, Jacob is feeling vulnerable, only this time his attempts to control his fate through deception have put at risk not only his own life, but also the lives of his family and everything that he had worked for in the past twenty years. He is acutely aware that Lavan is behind him and that Esau is blocking his way forward. In Torah terms, Jacob is trying to run from his past, yet is reluctant to face the future. He is feeling that the reality of who he has been is closing in on him. It is night time, he is totally alone, stripped of all his possessions, beside himself with fear, unable to sleep, with a mind that is working overtime.

   Suddenly a man appears. Who is the man? Might he be a messenger from God? I think not. I say this because when messengers have appeared in the Torah (as in Genesis 11, 16, 22, and Exodus 3), they are referred to as "messengers." In this story, however, the man is referred to as "the man" (in Hebrew, "*eesh*"). Moreover, the text states that Jacob was left alone. This is no small remark, as it is the only time that the Torah refers to a person being left alone.

   So, who is this man who wrestled with Jacob at a time and place where the only one present is Jacob? Might the man be Jacob himself; and might Jacob's wrestling opponent be his conscience? For the second time in the story of Jacob, he is looking deeply inward, soul searching, struggling to come to terms with who he really is, as opposed to who he thought he was or had to be.

- **Why is the man asking Jacob what his name is?** Jacob is being tested. Recall that his father twice asked Jacob his name and twice he answered "Esau." His answer may have reflected his felt need to be someone other than the person he was. But now, answering with his true name, Jacob is finally recognizing that he is no longer the person who he thought he was; that the blessing that he received from his father was received under false pretense; that he has the capacity to be more than a deceiver and a heel-sneak. At this spiritually charged moment, Jacob is sensing that he is about to receive a revelation. Said differently, by removing the burdens of his past desires and values, he is finally able to "move forward." Jacob is ready to receive a blessing as "Jacob" and therefore feels empowered to ask for one.

The man, in turn, acknowledges Jacob's transformation with the blessing that he gives, "Your name shall no longer be Jacob, but Israel, *"for you have fought with God and men and have prevailed."* Recall that names in Torah are purposefully given to reveal key aspects of a person's essence. By having his name changed from Jacob to *Israel*, the Torah is confirming that fundamental transformation has taken place in Jacob's identity. Recall also, *Israel* refers to more than a person or a place. As the mysterious man said, one becomes Israel by fighting with God and men and prevailing. Put another way, to be *Israel* is to show a willingness and ability to live by the precepts of the Covenant, to commit to a lifetime of struggle with things both mortal and divine.

* **Why the hip?** Why did the man *"touch the socket of Jacob's thigh that had been dislocated as he wrestled with him"*? Like many other worldly phenomena mentioned in the Torah, the "hip" is likely to symbolize something spiritual. Let's try to decode the meaning of "hip" by starting with the observation that the text places a premium on movement. For example, repeated reference is made to the importance of "leaving" (*lekh lecha*), "moving forward," "walking with God," and "crossing over into a new relationship with oneself, others, and with YHVH." For example, in verse 2 of Genesis 17, Avram is told by God to "walk yourself to My face" (Written in the reflexive tense, the expression can be restated as "mindfully move to My presence"; that is, make conscious that which is otherwise is done automatically.") And, the Hebrew word for rituals, *halakhah*, shares the same three letter root (*shoresh*) as does the word, *holech*, which means "walk." Even God's name, *Ehyeh asher ehyeh,* or

YHVH, ("I will be what I will be," or "I will be present whenever and wherever I will be present"), isn't so much a name in the sense that names are nouns, but instead it appears as a verb, conjugated in the imperfect tense to signify a fluid, ongoing, in-motion, process.

Consistent with this theme of movement, Jacob, the "heel-sneak" – someone who walks through the early years of his life with someone else's identity until his moment of revelation - asks to be blessed. The Hebrew word for "blessing" happens to share the same *shoresh* as the word *berekh*, which means "knee," used to signify movement, as in "to bend or humble one's self."

In the process of wrestling with "the man," Jacob's hip is displaced, evidence that his struggle was real. This will cause him to walk differently, with a limp. From the perspective of Torah, however, it will cause him to walk better (closer to himself, others, and YHVH), for his limp will forever serve to remind him of the person he has the capacity to become.

➢ Genesis Chapters 33-36. The Conclusion of the Jacob Stories

Summary: *Jacob lifted up his eyes and saw Esau coming with four hundred men. Advancing ahead of his family, he bowed to the ground seven times, until he came close to his brother. Esau ran to meet him, embraced him, and kissed him. The two wept. Esau then saw Jacob's family and each bowed to him. He then saw the large sheep herd and said to Jacob, "What to you is all this camp?" and Jacob replied, "To find favor in your eyes." Esau responded, "I have plenty, my brother, let what is yours remain yours." Jacob then said, "Pray take my token of a blessing, for God has shown me favor, for I have everything" and so Esau took it and promised Jacob safe passage.*

Jacob traveled to the city of Shekhem, in the land of Canaa. It was there where Dina, Leah's daughter, went out to see the woman of the land, was raped by Shekhem, son of Hamor. This pained Jacob's son, who said that Shekhem had disgraced them. Hamor tried to appease the sons, saying that his son loved Dina and wanted to marry her. The sons replied that they would agree to this marriage only if every male among you were circumcised. Hamor and Shekhem agreed. On the third day after all were circumcised and hurting, two of Jacob's sons, Shim'on and Levi, who, like Dina, were borne by Leah, came to the city and killed all the males, before taking Dina back to Jacob's home. However, when Jacob heard what they had done, he said, "You haves stirred up trouble for me, making me reek among the settled-folk of the land, the Canaanites and the Perizzites, for I have menfolk few in numbers; they will band together against me and destroy me and my household. But they said, "Should our sister then be treated like a whore?" Jacob traveled to the home of his father, Isaac, in the city of Hebron. On the way, and soon after giving birth to Binyamin, Jacob's twelfth son and Rachel's second, she died and was buried in Bethlehem. Isaac was 180 years old when he died. He was buried by his two sons, Esau and Jacob.

These were the twelve sons of Jacob, all born to him in the country of Aram [except Binyamin]; From Leah, Jacob's first born, Re'uven, Shim'on, Levi, Yehuda, Yissakhar and Zevulun. From Rachel, Yosef and Binyamin; from Bilha, Rachel's maid, Dan and Naftali; and from Zilpa, Leah's maid, Gad and Asher.

Esau, the tribal leader of Edom, took his wives, children, and all the persons in his household, as well as all of his livestock and acquisitions that he had gained in the land of Canaan, and went to another land, for his property and that of Jacob's was too much for one land to accommodate.

Discussion Questions: Wasn't Jacob's name changed - - why is he again referred to as Jacob? More than half of Isaac's life has passed since he was last mentioned – why is the Torah silent about his life for this eighty-year span? Jacob is said to have twelve sons – what is the meaning of the number twelve? Who is Esau?

- **Why is Jacob not being referred to as "Israel"?** In "After the Ecstasy, the Laundry," noted Buddhist theologian, Jack Kornfield, writes that enlightenment - - and our sudden and unexplained ability to awaken and see clearly the reality of the world - - doesn't last. It may transform us for a moment into a higher consciousness, but we invariably return to struggle with our day-to-day shortcomings. Times of great wisdom and deep compassion alternate with times of fear, confusion, and struggle.

Of course Kornfield wasn't commenting specifically on the Jacob story, but his insights seem to apply nicely. Jacob may have had his spiritual side revealed to him, but - as we should understand by now - revelation is one thing, and living up to one's spiritual ideal is quite another. In later stories we will witness Jacob continuing to struggle with being *Israel*. During those moments when he succeeds, the text will refer to him as "*Israel*." And, during those "laundry" moments when he is enmeshed in the mundane and the minutia of everyday, human life, but not in a divine manner, the text will refer to him as "Jacob." By now it should be apparent that Jacob is a lot like us, and his struggles to be Israel are a lot like ours.

- **Why is the Torah silent about most of Isaac's life?** Isaac's contribution to the family's spiritual movement forward apparently came to an end when he mistakenly blessed Jacob. From the perspective of Torah, his role in the story had played out. With his inability to take the next step, the attention naturally shifted to Jacob, his spiritual heir and the inheritor of the family birthright..

- **What is the meaning of the number twelve?** Recall YHVH's promise to Avram in Genesis 12: "*I will make a great nation of you.*" The nation that YHVH was referring to would be made up of "twelve" tribes, each tribe a descendent of one of Jacob's "twelve sons." Thus, the number twelve appears to represent that which is necessary but not necessarily sufficient to make a nation great. To be both necessary *and* sufficient requires the transformation of twelve distinct and sometimes fractured points of view into a state of wholeness (*shalem*) and "oneness" (*ekhad*), such that its whole will be greater than the sum of its twelve individual parts, as it became during the time of David.

It is important to note here that the number "twelve" is used sparingly in the Torah. The only other context that I am aware of is in Genesis 25, where we are told that Jacob's uncle, Ishmael, had twelve sons. Recall that YHVH's promise to Hagar in

Genesis 21 was that "I will make Ishmael, your son, a nation of him." From these two references, we might conclude that Ishmael's descendants would be of the necessary size and diversity for national greatness, but lacking in wholeness and oneness to be sufficient.

Of course, we should not take these references literally or use them to make condescending remarks against those who see themselves as the true descendants of Ishmael, but rather to decode the symbols used in Torah and the teachings that we can draw from them.

- **Who is Esau?** As with Hagar's son, Ishmael, various commentaries in the Talmud try to make Esau out to be a troublemaker, yet there is nothing in the text to support this dark-sided view. True, in his youth Esau married pagan women and showed disregard for his birthright; but in fairness to him, we must note that his twin brother Jacob, prior to his struggle with the "man," was hardly a bastion of spiritual enlightenment. And while the text is silent about Esau's middle years, we witness him in Genesis 33-36 as someone who is forgiving, understanding, and still respectful of his father - - his anger against his brother apparently having long since dissipated. The grandson of the Baal Shem Tov might concur. He saw the simple goodness in Esau when he said that the "Messiah will come when the tears of Esau have dried." I take this to mean that we will all walk closer with YHVH when we can show the same compassion to Esau that Esau showed to Jacob.

Chapter 5: Joseph and His Brothers

More is written about Joseph (whose name means "God has added") than about any of the Patriarchs and Matriarchs. As Everett Fox points out, the story stands well on its own as a novella, with characters that express more emotional depth than did those in Genesis's previous chapters. However, the Joseph story is best understood in the context of those chapters, for the story revisits and offers resolution to two reoccurring themes in Genesis that have to do with parent-child relationships and sibling rivalry. The Joseph story also draws close comparison to the Jacob story for, like Jacob, Joseph encounters deception, sibling hatred, exile, and dreams. And, playing off of the meaning of Joseph's name, the story finally addresses the question, "What is Joseph's presence adding?"

An interesting sub-plot to the Joseph story deals with his brothers: What is it like to be them, knowing full well that they will never be loved by their father, *Israel* (Jacob's spiritual dimension) as much as Joseph is loved by *Israel*? How did the brothers deal with life's disappointments - - and, put in a similar situation, how would we? A core teaching that comes out of this sub-plot is that until we can make peace with our past, our ability to inhabit the present and move forward into the future is limited.

Because almost every verse offers meaningful discussion points, I will follow a different format for commenting on the Joseph story than I did with the previous stories, at times going verse by verse.

- **Genesis 37: Joseph and His Two Dreams**

Verse 1: *Yaakov settled in the land of his father's sojourning, in the land of Canaan.*

> A more literal translation of "his father's sojourning" is "where his father (Isaac) was a resident alien." A resident alien? The text is implying that Isaac may have been born, lived, and died in the land of Canaan, but he never really inhabited it.

> Let's try to decode this point. The "land" in the first verse undoubtedly refers to the "Promised Land," that place where a person is able to receive both milk (sustenance) and

honey (sweetness and joy), during bad as well as good times. It is a place defined not by some physical coordinates, but rather by a state of mind.

What distinguishes those who inhabit this Land from those who simply journey through it is that the inhibitors have "crossed over" into closer relationships with themselves, with others, and ultimately with YHVH. Said differently, you know that you are in the "Promised Land" when you are able to struggle with life's problems without experiencing a loss of sustenance, sweetness, and joy.

Isaac remained an alien in the Land because he never was able to make that "crossing." For example, we are told in Genesis 26 that even after Isaac left his parents' home (following the *Akedah* story), he never developed an identity distinct from them. Instead, he followed closely in their footsteps, digging up the same wells even to the point of calling them by the same names. We are also told in Genesis 27 that Isaac had grown feeble and his eyes had grown weak, while he was still very much in the middle years of his life.

Unlike Isaac, both Abraham and Jacob "crossed over." As you will recall, the Torah symbolically marks this transformational moment with a name change. This is not to say that Isaac didn't have close relationships; he did (e.g., with his wife, Rebecca, and his son, Esau), but none that transformed him.

It is also of practical interest to note that those who inhabit the Promised Land are not expected to remain there 24/7. This teaching was represented in the Jacob story by noting that he was in his Jacob-state at least as many times as he was in his *Israel*-state. Or, as Jack Kornfield writes in his book, "After the Ecstasy, the Laundry," enlightenment- -our sudden and unexplained ability to awaken and see clearly the reality of the world - - doesn't last. It may transform us for a moment into a higher consciousness, but we inevitably return to struggle with our day-to-day challenges and shortcomings.

Verse 2: *"These are the generations of Jacob, Joseph being seventeen years old. And Joseph brought to his father an ill-report on his brothers."*

From the story's opening lines, we can see how it departs from previous stories. Whenever we came across the expression "these are the generations of," it was followed by a long list of generations and "begots." Not so here; only Joseph's name is mentioned, leaving us no doubt as to who will receive the family's birthright. But why was Joseph Jacob's favorite son? Perhaps Jacob saw a little bit of himself in Joseph, but more about this as the story unfolds.

Verse 3: *"Now Israel loved Joseph more than all of his sons, so he made him an ornamented coat."*

This verse complements the "favorite son" message of the previous verse, but puts it on a higher plane, for in verse 3 it is not only *Jacob* who loves Joseph, but also *Israel,* Jacob's spiritual side. It was this side which may have seen Joseph as a kindred spirit and "soul mate," having the capacity to struggle with things both human and divine, advance the family on its personal and spiritual journey, and – as Joseph's name signifies, "add" to the family's well-being. This is not to say that *Israel* didn't love his other sons, for as we will read in verses 12 to 14, he puts Joseph at risk for the sake of *Israel's* other sons. As such, Joseph is to Israel as Isaac is to Abraham (see Genesis 22 and the story of the Akidah). Both sons are also to their fathers as the "first and choicest" offering was to Abel in Genesis 4.

But, why might *Israel* have been so forthcoming and blatant in singling Joseph out to be the heir apparent to the family's birthright? Might it be because *Israel* remembers how his father, Isaac, mishandled his succession plans by waiting until the last minute to name his successor? As we previously read in the Jacob stories, this caused a jealous rift between Jacob and Esau which nearly cost Jacob his life. Perhaps because of this rift, *Israel* felt it best to announce his intentions as early as possible so that there would be no confusion or false expectations among the other siblings as to who would be the chosen son.

Interestingly, this is the first birthright decision in the book of Genesis that is made by the family patriarch. You will recall that Abraham's decision was largely made by his wife, Sarah, and Isaac's decision was largely masterminded by his wife, Rebecca.

Another interesting point about the birthright decision: As it was with Isaac, who received the family birthright over his older brother Ishmael, and Jacob who received the family birthright over his older brother Esau, so too will it be for younger brother Joseph. By seemingly going out of its way to select the youngest offspring as the heir apparent, the Torah is again challenging the estate transfer custom of choosing the first born that characterizes many cultures, even to this day. The Torah is suggesting that at least when it comes to the spiritual well-being of the family, the birthright should go to the offspring who shows the greatest capacity to move the family members "forward" to a closer relationship with themselves, with others, and with YHVH.

And, why the "coat" - - what might it symbolize? Might it be connecting Joseph's situation to that time when Jacob wore a sheepskin coat to deceive his father into receiving the birthright?

Verse 4: *"and when his brothers saw that their father loved Joseph above all his brothers, they hated him and could not speak to him in peace."*

We learn from this verse that being spiritually enlightened does not necessarily ensure good outcomes. In spite of *Israel*'s best intentions, his succession plans had unintended consequences. It did not bring peace and wholeness to the family, as Jacob had hoped. Joseph will now have to struggle with sibling jealousy, just as his father struggled with Esau, and his grandfather Isaac struggled with Ishmael. If you haven't already noticed, family discord is a recurring theme in Genesis, dating all the way back to Cain and Abel!

Verses 5-8: *Joseph dreamt a dream, and told it to his brothers – and from then on they hated him still more. He said to them: "Here we were binding sheaf-bundles out in the field and my sheaf arose and stood upright, and your sheaves circled around my sheaf and bowed down to it." His brothers replied, "Would you be king over us? Would you really rule us?" From then on they hated him more – for his dreams and for his words.*

Dreams had played an important role in Jacob's spiritual development (e.g., the "Ladder" and "Wrestling" dreams). Like Jacob, Joseph will have two dreams. But, why does Joseph feel the need to tell his dream to his brothers? By modern standards, he appears to be acting arrogantly, but this was not the case during biblical times. Dreams were understood then as prophetic statements from God that the receiver was compelled to share. In Genesis 42 we will learn that Joseph's "wheat dream" does indeed foretell the future – the brothers will indeed be bowing down to Joseph – but for very different reasons than that which they had interpreted from Joseph's dream.

Verses 9 -11: *But he dreamt still another dream and recounted it to his father and brothers: "Here the sun and the moon and eleven stars were bowing down to me!" And his father rebuked him, saying, "What kind of dream is this that you have dreamt? Shall we – your mother and your brothers – come to bow down to you to the ground?" His brothers envied him while his father kept the matter in mind.*

What makes this dream different from the first dream? What does it "add"? (Again, Joseph's name means "God has added.") Unlike the first dream, where Joseph appears as a sheath of wheat, no mention is made in the second dream of Joseph's physical appearance. This, plus the dream's celestial references, suggests that the second dream is not so much about Joseph, but rather about something spiritual. Not surprisingly, his brothers again feel threatened and insulted, but once again they are interpreting Joseph's dream incorrectly. In fairness to them, Joseph also doesn't understand the true meaning of the dreams and won't until Genesis 50:16-21, when he is reunited with his brothers in Egypt.

The substance of the second dream suggests that Joseph's father knows there is something very important in the dream, but he does not yet understand what it might be. What we don't know, however, is who is keeping "matters in mind." We know that it is Joseph's father, but the text is deliciously vague as to whether Joseph's father is, in this case, Jacob or his spiritual counterpart, *Israel*.

Verses 12-14: *Israel said to Joseph, "Go to your brothers in Shekhem," and Joseph replied, "Hee-nay-nee." Jacob then said, "Look into the well-being of your brothers and their sheep and bring me back word."*

The word, *hee-nay-nee*, or "Here I am," first appears in the Akedah story of the near-sacrifice of Isaac (Genesis 22). It is heard again in a few other stories in Torah, but like the Genesis 22 story, only at life-altering moments, such as when Moses hears YHVH's voice calling him from the midst of the burning bush. Like Abraham before him and Moses afterward, Joseph, by saying *hee-nay-nee*, is saying that he is totally present and ready to embark on a life-transforming experience, whatever it might be and however threatening. He is mindful of the fact that it is *Israel* who is calling him, not Jacob. It is *Israel* who is inviting Joseph on a sacred mission: to safeguard the wholeness (*shalem*) of his brothers, in spite of the obvious risks to Joseph of doing so. As such, *Israel* is showing the willingness to offer up his "first and choicest", the one on whom he had been banking his legacy, the son whom he loves above all others and to whom he intends to pass the family's birthright. Recall that the ritual of "offering up the first and choicest" and the meaning behind it was introduced in the story of Cain and Abel (Genesis 4) and then revisited in the *Akedah* story when Abraham was about to sacrifice his son Isaac (Genesis 22).

And, by saying "Look into the well-being of your brothers," *Israel* is answering the question, "*Am I my brother's keeper?*" that has remained unanswered since it was first asked by Cain, way back in Genesis 4. Said more broadly, the Torah is leaving us with the message that every sibling has the responsibility to attend to the *shalem* of his or her family, for the cost of sibling rivalry is very high. It resulted in the murder of Abel, the exile of Ishmael, and a death threat to Jacob – and it will soon put Joseph's life at risk.

Verses 15-17: *And Joseph went. On his journey, a man who came upon him said, "Who do you seek?" Joseph replied, "My brothers; pray tell me where they are tending sheep." The man answered, "I heard them say, 'Let's go to Dotan.'" Joseph went after his brothers and came upon them in Dotan.*

Who might this man be who just happens to be wandering the fields, happens to know that Joseph is searching for someone, and happens to know where that someone is? Might this man be like that mysterious person Jacob wrestled with? Might he be Joseph's inner voice, his intuition, a dream vision?

And, where is Dotan? Its location remains to this day unknown. Moreover, it show up only one other time in biblical literature, in II Kings 6: 13. The writer of that story likely was drawing a subtle connection between it and the Joseph story. Whereas the Joseph story is about relationships within families, the II Kings story is about relationships between communities.

Verses: 18-21: *Joseph's brothers saw his coming from afar and conspired to slay this dreamer, throw him into a pit and say that an evil beast devoured him. "We will see what becomes of his dreams!"*

The brothers' incorrect interpretation of Joseph's dreams pointed them to a future that they obviously do not want to inhabit. Not surprisingly, they therefore took measures to try to prevent it from happening. However, their attempts go against a core teaching in Torah - that, to be truly present, we must surrender to the life forces over which we have no understanding or control. Like the builders of the Tower of Babel, the brothers were guilty of "over-reaching" into that which is in YHVH's domain.

Verses 22- 24: *Reuben said, "Do not shed his blood but, instead, strip him of his ornamented coat and drop him into a dry pit (cistern)," which they did, and then sat down to eat bread.*

They celebrated because they thought that they had freed themselves of the dreamer and the dictates of his dreams.

Verses 25 – 27: *The brothers lifted up their eyes and saw a caravan of Yishmaelites coming to them, carrying balm, balsam, and laudanum, on their trading route down to Egypt, to Mizrayim. Yehuda said, "What gain is there if we kill our brother. Let us sell him to the Yishmaelites and let not our hand be upon him, for he is our brother, our flesh." And the brothers agreed.*

Notice how this story cleverly weaves together the past (Ishmael being the exiled son of Avram), present (Joseph about to become the exiled son of Jacob), and future (the communal exile in Egypt).

About the cargo carried by the Ishmaelites: Balm is used to deaden pain; balsa is a glue used to hold things together; and laudanum is an opiate to numb the mind. Why does the text bring to our attention these three things? Some have posited that the Ishmaelites, as the exiled descendants of Avram, remained stuck in the past, still bitter about the injustice that they felt was done to them. Balm, balsa, and laudanum are what they used to try to cope with their pain.

Verse 28: *Meanwhile a group of Midianite merchants passed by, hauled Joseph out of the pit, and then sold him for twenty pieces of silver to the Ishmaelites, who then brought Joseph to Egypt.*

Why does the text state "twenty pieces" of silver? Might this number symbolize a connection between past and present? Recall that the last time that the number "twenty" appears in the text, it referred to the number of years that Joseph's father labored for Lavan before summoning up the courage to leave. Here, the same number is used to mark a return to bondage.

The reference to the Midianite merchants might be a literary attempt to link the present with the future. As we will read in the Exodus stories, Moses escaped from Egypt and ran into the wilderness where he was befriended and mentored by a Midianite priest, Jethro, who later became Moses' father-in-law.

Verses 29 – 36: *When Reuben discovered that his brother was not in the pit, he rent his clothes, overwrought with guilt. The brothers then dipped Joseph's coat in the blood of a goat, and returned to their father saying, "This is what we found and we know not if it is your son's coat or not." Jacob recognized the coat and said, "My son's coat! An ill-tempered beast has devoured him!" Jacob rent his clothes and mourned for his son for many days. All of his sons and daughters arose to comfort him, but he refused to be comforted. Meanwhile the Midianites sold him into Egypt to Potifar, Pharaoh's court official, Chief of the Palace Guard.*

Notice that the brothers said "your son" and not "our brother." Of course it is Joseph's coat! Are the brothers trying to trick their father with almost the same prop that their father had used to trick his father, Isaac? Can Jacob be so blind to the truth, just as his father was when Jacob had tried a similar deceit?

What should have made Jacob even more suspicious was the fact that his sons showed no remorse, nor did they refer to the coat as belonging to their brother. It is hard to imagine Jacob, a trickster himself in his younger days, never suspecting that it was the brothers – and not some beast - who had killed Joseph.

Jacob is thus facing a dilemma: Should he punish all of his sons, or simply live out his days stuck in the past in a state of bitter denial?

We can imagine that Jacob must also be wracked with guilt for having sent Joseph to report on his brothers. He might have known that the brothers' hatred ran deep enough to jeopardize Joseph's life. Perhaps he is holding himself at least as responsible for Joseph's fate as are his sons.

And, did you notice that the story presents a puzzle within a puzzle. First, who sold Joseph to Egypt? Verse 36 states that it was the Midianites, but according to verse 28, the Midianites sold Joseph to the Ishmaelites, and it was they brought Joseph into Egypt, a claim reaffirmed in Genesis 39:1. As if this question of "who" isn't baffling enough, why does such a glaring inconsistency appear in the Torah? Usually this kind of inconsistency appears to point the reader to some spiritually meaningful teaching.

Let's try: The almost interchangeable usage of the two tribes suggests that the Midianites and the Ishmaelites are virtually indistinguishable, as would be close tribes of the same family. This allows us to once again witness an ironic convergence of past, present, and future. Specifically, whereas Avram and Sarai banished Ishmael and his mother, Hagar, an Egyptian slave, it will be the descendants of Ishmael who will banish Joseph to bondage in Egypt. Also, while Avram and Sarai tried to protect their blood line from Ishmael and his descendants, their offspring will again converge through Moses, by virtue of his close relationship with Jethro, a Midianite, and his daughter, whom Moses marries.

What "teaching" can we draw from these ironic turn of events? Might the Torah again be reminding us to not do as Avram and Sarai did; that is, stop trying take control over that which we have no understanding or control?

- **Genesis 38: Yehuda (Judah) and Tamar**

Summary: *About the time that Judah left his brothers - - he saw a Canaanite woman named Shua, whom he married and who bore him three sons. For his first son, Er, Judah got a wife, Tamar, but Er died soon after. As was the custom then, Judah told his second son, Onan, to do his duty as a brother-in-law and provide offspring for Er by marrying Tamar, but he too soon died. Afraid for the life of his third son, Shelah, Judah told Tamar to remain a widow in her father's house until Shelah would be old enough to marry, a promise he had no intention of keeping.*

A long time later, Judah, now widowed, was traveling in the vicinity where Tamar lived. He did not recognize her, as she sat at the side of the road, veiled. Thinking that she was a harlot, he asked her to sleep with him. She said yes, but only if he would give her his seal, cord, and staff. He agreed.

When Judah is later told that Tamar has become pregnant by harlotry, he becomes incensed and wants her to be burned. She defends herself by showing Judah his own seal, cord, and staff. Realizing at last that he was wrong, he says "She is more right than I, inasmuch as I did not give her to my son Shelah."

Tamar then gave birth to twins, the offspring of Judah. As the first one put out a hand from the birth canal, the midwife took it and tied a scarlet thread onto his hand, saying, "This one came out first." But, as he pulled back his hand, his brother came out! Tamar said: "What a breach you have breached yourself!"

Discussion Question: How does this Genesis chapter about Judah (one of Joseph's brothers) and Tamar relate to the Joseph story or, for that matter, any other Genesis story?

Genesis 38 appears to have nothing whatsoever to do with the Joseph story. Moreover, not only does Genesis 38 interrupt the Joseph story at a crucial moment, but it is chronologically out of place. By that I mean that Genesis 39 returns us to the time when Joseph is seventeen years old. As with the inconsistency previously noted concerning which group sold Joseph to Egypt, questions naturally arise as to this chapter's positioning. Unlike the "inconsistency" question, however, we will learn the answer to the Judah question, but not until Genesis 43.

This chapter also reflects events of the past. Just as it was with the birthing of Jacob and Esau, we witness once again the struggle for dominance between twins. And, just as Isaac could not recognize his son, Jacob (who, at the time, was lamely disguised as Esau), so too could Judah not recognize his daughter-in-law, Tamar. The theme of "recognition" will appear again in Genesis 42 of the Joseph story, and then later in the book of Exodus when the topics of the ninth plague and ninth commandment are introduced. I will address the question, "Why do such hard-to-believe encounters happen so regularly in Torah?" when it next appears in the Joseph story.

Genesis 39 -41: Joseph's Downfall and Rise to Power

Summary: *Potifar, an official of Pharaoh, acquired Joseph from the Yishmaelites. But YHVH was with Joseph, and so he became a man of success. Potifar, seeing that YHVH was with Joseph, appointed him over his house, placing all of his belongings in Joseph's hands.*

Joseph was fair to look at. Potifar's wife fixed her eyes on him and said "Lie with me!" Joseph refused, saying "How could I do this great an ill" to the man who entrusted me. "I would be sinning against God!" One day when none of the house-people were in the house, she grabbed Joseph by his garment and again said, "Lie with me!" Joseph escaped outside, leaving his garment in the clutches of her hand.

She called in her house-people, saying, "See! He (Potifar) brought to us a Hebrew man to laugh at us and lie with me." And, she kept his garment until his lord returned to the house, when she told him what she had told the house-people.

Potifar's anger flared. He put Joseph in the dungeon house, in the place where the king's prisoners are imprisoned. But, once again YHVH was with Joseph, and put his favor in the eyes of the warden, who gave Joseph the responsibility to oversee the other prisoners. And, whatever Joseph did, YHVH made succeed.

Now after these events, the King's cupbearer and baker angered the king, who put them into the dungeon. The two men dreamed a dream, each man his own dream, in the same night. The following morning, Joseph noticed that both were dejected and of ill-humor because there was no one here to interpret their dreams. Joseph said, "Are not interpretations from God? Pray recount them to me."

The cupbearer said, "In my dream, a vine was in front of me and on the vine, three winding – tendrils with blossoms that opened up into clusters of ripened grapes. I picked the grapes and squeezed them into Pharaoh's cup and put the cup into his hands."

Joseph said, "This is my interpretation: The three windings are three days – in another three days, Pharaoh will restore your position and you will put into his hands the cup, according to your practice. But, keep in mind when it goes well for you to keep me in mind to Pharaoh, for I was stolen from the land of the Hebrews, where I did nothing wrong."

When the baker saw that Joseph had interpreted the cupbearer's dream, he said, "I, too, in my dream had three baskets of white bread on my head, the upper basket containing all sorts of baked edibles for the Pharaoh, but birds were eating from that basket." Joseph replied, "The three baskets are three days; in another three days Pharaoh will hang you from a tree and the birds will eat your flesh."

And, on the third day, Pharaoh's birthday, he made a drinking feast for all of his servants, restored the cupbearer to his position and hanged the baker, just as Joseph had interpreted. But, the cupbearer did not keep Joseph in mind.

Now, at the end of two-year's time, Pharaoh dreamt that he was standing by the Nile-stream, and out of the stream came seven healthy- looking cows, who grazed on the reed grass. Soon thereafter, seven gaunt cows came out from the Nile and proceeded to eat the seven healthy cows but remained gaunt. Pharaoh awoke and then dreamt a second dream: Seven ripe ears-of-grain grew from a single stalk, followed by seven thin ears, which proceeded to eat the seven ripe ears, but remained thin.

In the morning, Pharaoh's spirit was agitated for no one could interpret his dream. Then the chief cupbearer spoke up, telling Pharaoh of the Hebrew lad, Joseph. Pharaoh sent for Joseph, who said that it is not he who interprets dreams, but God. Pharaoh tells him his dreams. Joseph listens and then tells Pharaoh that he had but one dream: The seven plump cows and the seven ripe ears of grain represent seven years of abundance in all the land of Egypt. And the seven gaunt cows and the seven thin ears will be seven years of famine, which will destroy the land. Joseph goes on further to say that the reason for the dreams repeating themselves is because the matter is determined by God.

Joseph then tells Pharaoh to select a discerning and wise man to oversee the land, to collect all kinds of food during the good years, and pile them up under Pharaoh's hand as food provisions to be available for the people during the seven years of famine.

Pharaoh says that there is no man as wise and discerning as Joseph to oversee this operation. "To your orders shall all my people submit. Only I will be greater than you." Pharaoh renames Joseph "The God Speaks and He Lives" and he gives him Asenat, daughter of the priest of On as his wife. Now, Joseph was thirty years old as he stood in Pharaoh's presence.

Two sons were born to Joseph and Asenat before the famine came: Menashe, meaning "God has made me forget all my hardships, all my father's house"; and then Efrayim, meaning "God has made me bear fruit in the land of affliction."

Then the famine came and it was over all the surface of the earth. Joseph opened up all the storehouses and gave out food rations. And all the lands came to Egypt to buy rations from Joseph.

Discussion Questions: Why do we see such repetition of the numbers "three," as in three winding tendrils, three baskets, three days; and the number "seven," as in seven cows, seven ears of grain, and seven years each of plenty and of famine? Why was the chief cupbearer saved while the chief baker was killed? Has Joseph "moved forward" from the person he was prior to being brought into Egypt? Who is Joseph's Pharaoh and why do the seven gaunt cows in his dream remain gaunt and the seven ears of corn remain thin?

> **What is the significance of the numbers "three" and "seven"?** We last encountered these two numbers in Genesis 30 ("The Tale of the Two Deceivers"), where "three" signaled the impending arrival of a revelation from YHVH, and "seven" was used to indicate the completion of a cycle of creation. The fact that both numbers are used throughout this chapter, along with repeated reference to dreams (recall that dreams were understood as

prophetic statements from YHVH), suggests that the Joseph story may be taking place more on a spiritual plane than on a physical one.

Why was the cupbearer saved and the baker not? Undoubtedly there is a *midrash* (a collection of Rabbinic literature consisting of commentary on and clarification of biblical texts, first compiled around 500 A.D.) that offers a plausible explanation, but I prefer not to go there. Let's just say that, consistent with the meaning of God's name (YHVH, or "God will be what God will be"), things can happen that defy human explanation.

Has Joseph "moved forward"? In his youth, Joseph seemed to exude a sense of confidence and inner purpose that appeared to his brothers, father - - and to us, as arrogant and offensive. In Egypt, we see none of this. Instead, we witness a very humble Joseph, someone who refused to sin when confronted by Potifar's wife, someone who attributed his ability to interpret dreams entirely to God, someone who accepted without question or complaint the responsibility of providing food to the people of Egypt and surrounding lands. Has Joseph "moved forward" from the person he was during his youth? Has he shown the capacity to go forth without having his past determine his present?

My answer is "no." Joseph was born with the spiritual capacity to begin a new cycle of creation. His name ("God has added') didn't need a transformation, as did the names of Avram and Jacob , because it already contained the name of God in it. (Recall that names in the Torah are intended to reveal an individual's true character.) While his brothers didn't see this in Joseph, *Israel* did. (*"Now Israel loved Joseph more than all of his sons, so he made him an ornamented coat."*)

Again, the name "*Israel*" signifies Jacob's spiritual dimension – the side that recognized in his favored son his own capacity to advance (or "add to") the spiritual well-being of the family through struggle. But, what exactly is Joseph adding to the spiritual journey that his ancestors began? The answer will become clear later in the story when his brothers come to him in Egypt.

Who is Pharaoh? Clearly this is not Moses's Pharaoh from the Exodus story, for rather than having a hardened heart, Joseph's Pharaoh seems to have a very open and sensitive heart.

For example, conscious of the fact that his dream was important and yet at the same time disturbing, he exhibited the humility to turn to an imprisoned Hebrew for council. He sensed in this unlikely person the capacity to hear God.

But, why in his dream is he standing by the river? (Often translated as the "Nile", the Hebrew used in the Torah for this particular river is *ya'or*, or the river of Divine Light.) Consider the imagery: Here he stands by himself, the most powerful person in the region's most powerful and advanced nation. He seems lost in thought, mesmerized by the river that flows before him in a continuous motion from the past to the future, knowing that this river holds the key to his empire's prosperity, for it is the source of all trade, agriculture, culture, and sustenance.

We can only imagine what was going through his mind. Perhaps he was feeling overwhelmed by his responsibility to ensure the well-being of his many subjects, while being fully aware that there are numerous factors - - like the bounty of each year's harvest - - that are beyond his control? Might he have been thinking, "Can I go with the flow, or will I be swept away by its currents? Can I separate myself from the past long enough to deal with a future that is not yet in my present? Are my dreams foretelling that future?"

Why do the cows remain gaunt and the ears of corn remain thin? Why in his dreams do the seven gaunt cows remain gaunt, even after eating the healthy cows, and the seven thin ears remain thin, even after swallowing the seven ripe ears? This imagery may be symbolizing the feeling of being enslaved in Egypt - a time when the people had food and drink, yet no matter how much they consumed, they felt a hollow pit in the stomach, as if something fundamental in their lives was missing.

> Genesis 42: Joseph's Plan for His Brothers' Redemption

Verses 1-5: *When Jacob saw that there were rations in Egypt, he said to his sons, "Why do you keep looking at one another? I heard that there are rations in Egypt – go there and buy us some so that we may live." So, ten brothers went to Egypt, but Jacob did not send Benjamin, "lest harm befall him!"*

Unlike Jacob's father, Isaac, who in his old age favored the senses of taste, smell, and touch (Genesis 27), we are told that Jacob is relying on sight (he "saw") and sound ("I heard"), two senses that are more commonly associated with moments of revelation. For example, Abraham, Sarah, and Hagar were all said to have *heard* YHVH's voice. And, Avram was said, in Genesis 13, to have *seen* long distances in all four directions, as did Moses in Deuteronomy 34. Jacob's reliance on sight and sound seems, therefore, suggest that he remains vibrant and alert; his spiritual light has yet to fade despite the many trials that he has struggled with and prevailed over.

Verse 6: *The sons of Israel came to Joseph and bowed down to him.*

The meaning of Joseph's first dream, the "wheat dream" (*"Here we were binding sheaf-bundles out in the field and my sheaf arose and stood upright, and your sheaves circled around my sheaf and bowed down to it"*) has finally become clear to Joseph. His brothers had presumed that the dream meant that Joseph was predestined to lord over them, yet ironically they are now coming to Joseph and willingly prostrating themselves before him, with the intent of purchasing wheat-rations so that they and their father can live.

Apparently, Joseph's "wheat dream" was foretelling the future and the role that he would be playing in it. As the meaning of his name, "God has added," suggests, Joseph had advanced far enough in the Egyptian power structure to "add" to the physical well-being of his family, including his own descendants and those of his brothers.

Verses 7-12: *Joseph recognized his brothers, but pretended not to, instead speaking harshly to them: "From where do you come?" They did not recognize him. And Joseph was reminded of the dreams that he had dreamt of them and said, "You are spies!"*

Not recognizing family members is a recurring theme throughout the Torah. Lot claimed to have no recollection of sleeping with his two daughters; Isaac mistook Jacob for his brother Esau; Jacob was oblivious to the fact that he was sleeping with Leah rather than her sister Rachel; Judah did not recognize that he was sleeping with Tamar; and none of Joseph's brothers recognized him.

Why do such hard-to-believe encounters happen so regularly in Torah? Surely they are not to be interpreted literally, but instead are presented to warn us against our natural tendency to allow "darkness" into our lives by relying on habitual ways of interacting with our environment and those around us. When we do so, our senses are dulled along with our ability to process reality. Said simply, darkness causes us to go through life half-asleep.

Are Joseph's brothers living in darkness? The text suggests that they are: *"The brothers said each man to his brother: "Truly we are guilty concerning our brother – that we saw his heart's distress when he implored us and we did not listen. Therefore his distress has come upon us"* (verse 21).

The brothers are plagued by guilt - - not only for what they did to their brother, but also because of its effect on their father. We can imagine that guilt preoccupies their daily thoughts and haunts their every moment. It leaves them stuck in the past, unable to inhabit the present and move forward. Their inability to recognize their brother leaves them incapable of taking action despite their desperate situation. Or, as Jacob said to them in the opening lines of this chapter, *"Why do you keep looking at one another?"*

Verse 13-16: *They replied, "No, my lord, we are your servants, honest sons of a single man living in Canaan, who have come to buy food-rations. We are twelve, the youngest is with our father and one is no more." To this, Joseph said, "No, you are spies and shall be tested. You will not depart from this place unless your youngest brother comes here. Send one of you to fetch your brother, while the rest of you remain as prisoners."*

While it might not yet be clear at this point in the story, these verses suggest that Joseph now understands the meaning behind his "celestial dream" (*"Here the sun and the moon and eleven stars were bowing down to me!"*), and -- more importantly -- what he must do about it. In brief, Joseph realizes that he must devise a plan to free his brothers of their guilt, thereby allowing them to shed the darkness that has enveloped them. Only by doing so can he complete his mission of looking after the wholeness of his brothers and "add to" the spiritual well-being of his family - - a mission that began when he said *"hee-ney-nee"* to his father, *Israel*.

Verses 17-20: *Three days later, Joseph told the brothers to return to their father with the wheat that their silver could purchase, but Shimon will remain here, imprisoned as a hostage. "To free him, you will have to return with your youngest brother."*

> Joseph's plan begins with his presenting a dilemma to his brothers: For them to bring food to their father so that the family can live, they will have to put Rachel's second son, Benjamin, at risk. Joseph knows how his father will react to this request and how difficult it will be for his guilt-ridden brothers to tell their father of it. He also knows that his brothers will return to Egypt, not only to save Shimon, but because they will have no choice but to return: The famine will last another six years, meaning that his father and brothers will once again need to purchase more food- rations.

Verses 21 – 24: *The brothers said each man to his brother: "Truly we are guilty concerning our brother – that we saw his heart's distress when he implored us and we did not listen. Therefore his distress has come upon us." To this, Reuben responds: "Did I not say to you, 'Do not sin against the child.' But you did not listen. Now comes the reckoning for his blood!" The brothers did- not know that Joseph was overhearing what they said, for a translator was between them. Joseph turned away (so that they would not see him), and wept and wept.*

> The brothers, particularly Reuben, are beginning to see the connection between the past and their present situation. The verses also bring out the emotional depth of Joseph's character. None of the patriarchs or matriarchs mentioned in Genesis were said to have wept – up to this point, only Hagar wept (Genesis 21:16).

Verses 25 – 28: *On their return trip home, one brother opened his sack to give his donkey fodder and found his silver, saying "My silver has been returned!" The rest trembled, saying, "What is this that God has done to us?" Then they each emptied their sack and each found his original count of silver.*

> At this moment, the brothers realize that they are doomed, but have yet to accept responsibility for their past actions. Instead they place the blame on God (*"What is this that God has done to us?"*).

Verses 29 – 37: *They came home to Jacob and told him all that had befallen them. He replied, "It is I that you bereave, for Joseph is no more, Shimon is no more, and now you would take Benjamin. - My son will not go down with you, for his brother is dead and he alone is left! Should harm befall him on the journey on which you are going, you will bring me down in grief."*

> We can sense Jacob's deep sense of resignation. He knows that he has no choice but to allow the brothers to take Benjamin, but he also understands the risks. Should Rachel's second son meet the same fate as her first son, then he, his family, and his descendants would be left without a worthy heir to the family's birthright. The journey that began with Avram and Sarai would end here.

- ## Genesis 43 and 44: Returning to Egypt

Genesis 43: 1-9: *The famine was heavy in the land and so their father told them, "Return and buy us some food-rations. Judah reminded his father of the man's warning: "You shall not see my face unless your brother is with you." Judah then said to Israel, "Send the lad with me, so that we may all live. And I will act pledge that if I do not bring him back to you, I will be culpable-for-sin against you all the days to come."*

> It was Judah who had convinced his brothers not to physically harm their brother Joseph at the pit. It was also Judah who willingly took responsibility for his improper behavior by making a sincere, though misguided attempt to protect his youngest brother. Why is it that Judah who is willing to play a more active role than are his brothers? The answer might reside in what was stated about him in Genesis 38. There, we learned that Judah had three sons, the first two of whom died soon after marrying Tamar. Perhaps Judah knows what it is like to be a parent and therefore can better empathize and identify with his father, while his brothers still identify themselves as siblings.

Verses 10-14: *Israel replied, "If it must be so, bring the man a little balsam, honey, balm and laudanum, pistachio nuts and almonds, along with silver to purchase the food-rations and the silver that was returned in your packs – perhaps that was an oversight.*

The writers are again drawing our attention to the past for better understanding of the present, but taking it one step further to include the distant future. First, it is important to note that gifts are said to be coming from *Israel* and not from Jacob, suggesting that whatever was given has a more spiritual than an earthly connotation.

The three spices that *Israel* tells his sons to carry (balm, balsam, and laudanum) are the same three that the Ishmaelites were carrying on their trading route down to Egypt when they acquired Joseph. Here we see another past-present linkage: Just as the Ishmaelites used these three spices to cope with the pain of their exile, so *Israel* was offering his sons the wherewithal to ease their feelings of guilt and the "darkness" that it engendered as they, too, journeyed back to Egypt.

Reference to the future may be found in the fact that *Israel* is also giving his sons honey and two types of nuts. We know that honey is used in the expression, "land of milk and honey" to symbolize sweetness and joy in life. We also know that nuts (like milk) are a rich source of sustenance. Perhaps *Israel* was offering his sons a glimpse into what life will be like in the distant future when their descendants leave Egypt and enter into the Promised Land?

> Genesis 43:15 - Genesis 44: 12: *The brothers did as they were told and once again stood in Joseph's presence. When Joseph saw Benjamin, he invited the men into his home. The men were afraid to enter because of the silver that they had found in their pack on the last visit, but Joseph told them not to be afraid: "Your God, the God of your father, placed a treasure in your pack for you to return to me." Joseph brought Shimon out to them and then asked, "Is your father alive?" and his brothers answered, "Yes." Joseph then looked at Benjamin and asked, "Is this your youngest brother?" and the brothers again answered, "Yes." Joseph turned aside and wept. After restraining himself, Joseph ordered that the brothers be served food and drink.*

Joseph commanded his steward: "Fill the men's packs with food along with each man's silver, but put my silver goblet into the mouth of the youngest man's pack." Unaware of this, the brothers started their journey home. They had not gotten far when Joseph said to the steward, "Pursue them and when you catch them, say, 'Why have you paid back ill for good? Is this goblet the one that my lord drinks with?'"

The brothers asked, "Why do you speak such words? We would never do such a thing!" The steward responded, "He, for on whom it is found, shall be my servant, but the rest of you shall be clear." The goblet was found in Benjamin's pack.

Discussion Question: Why does Joseph want to enslave the one brother who shares the same mother? Why does he want to endanger his aging father who still mourns the loss of his first choice for inheriting the family's birthright? And, how will enslaving Benjamin free his brothers of their guilt?

> There are situations in our lives that we wish we could live over and behave differently. For example, knowing what the brothers know at this point in the story – how it affected their father and themselves - would they have put Joseph into the pit and sold him into slavery?

> Joseph's plan is to re-create that defining moment for his brothers. He did so by devising the illusion that they were once again in control over the life of Rachel's son. Will the brothers now abandon Benjamin, the heir apparent to the family's birthright, as they once abandoned Joseph? Will they again allow jealousy and self-interest to over-ride their sense of family *shalem*/wholeness?

> Thanks to Joseph's plan, his brothers have the opportunity to choose differently. The teaching is clear: The road to repentance involves more than seeking forgiveness from those whom we offended; we must also seek forgiveness from ourselves.

Genesis 44:16- 34: *The brothers rent their clothes and returned to the city. Joseph said to them, "What kind of deed is this that you have done!" Judah replied, "What can we say to show ourselves innocent? God has found out your /servants' crime. Here we are servants to my lord, the one in whose hand the goblet was found." But Joseph said, "Heaven forbid that I should do this; only the man in whose hand the goblet was found shall become my servant. The rest of you go in peace to your father!"*

Judah comes closer to Joseph and says, "You once asked us if we have a father and another brother and we replied that we have an old father and a younger brother whose brother and mother are dead. And you said, 'Bring him down to me so that I may set eyes on him.' But we said, 'The lad cannot leave our father, for were he to leave, our father would die' for he had already lost his wife's first son. So, now, pray let your servant stay instead of the lad, for how can I go up to my father, when the lad is not with me – and see the ill-fortune that would come upon my father?"

> Once again, we see that it is Judah who is able to respond in the moment with a passionate plea. And it is Judah, more than his brothers, who shows the willingness to put the family's *shalem*/wholeness ahead of his own interests. Put in Torah terms, Judah has "moved forward." His struggles with things both human and divine (see Genesis 37 and 38) have given him the wisdom to see beyond the "darkness" that has plagued his brothers and - in so doing - to better inhabit the present.

:

Genesis 45- 50: Reconciliation

Joseph could no longer restrain himself. He put forth his voice in weeping, saying to his brothers, "I am Joseph. Is my father still alive?" But his brothers were not able to answer him, for they were confounded in his presence. Joseph said, "Pray come close to me; I am Joseph your brother whom you sold into Egypt. But do not be pained that you sold me here, for it was to save your life from famine that God sent me on before you.

"The famine will last still another five years. Go to my father and say to him, 'Thus says your son, Joseph: God has made me lord of all Egypt. Come down to me and stay in the region of Goshen and I will sustain you there.'" And Joseph flung himself upon Benjamin and both wept. Then he kissed all his brothers and wept upon them.

And Pharaoh heard the news and said to Joseph, "Say to your brothers to fetch their father and all of their belongings and come to me and I will give them the good things of the land of Egypt so that they will eat of the fat of the land." To all of them, Pharaoh gave changes of clothes, but to Benjamin he gave three hundred pieces of silver and five changes of clothes.

> Like Joseph before him, Pharaoh is also re-creating a defining moment for the brothers by lavishing recognition on Benjamin, as Jacob once did upon Joseph by giving him the ornamented coat. In contrast to their earlier behaviors, the brothers are now showing no resentment toward Benjamin. In Torah terms, they have also "moved forward," being less directed by the past and therefore more alert to the moment.

The brothers returned to the land of Canaan and said to their father, "Joseph is still alive and has become the ruler of the land!"

Israel traveled with all that was his and came to Be'er Sheva. And God came to him in a vision in the night, saying, "Jacob, Jacob!," and he said, "Hee-nay-nee (Here I am)." And God said, "I am El, the God of your father. Do not be afraid of going down to Egypt, for a great nation will I make of you there."

> In Torah, stating a person's name twice signifies that the person has advanced. Here, God is recognizing the Jacob of old alongside the new Jacob: - the one still willing to struggle with another life-altering moment, still vibrant enough to say *"hee-nay-nee,"*

And, all of the persons of Jacob's household who came to Egypt were seventy.

> Drawing from the commentary that accompanies Genesis 31, we might think of the number "seventy" as representing seven (which signifies the completion of one cycle of Creation) ten times (where ten represents an amount large enough to command one's attention), Use of the number "seventy" in the text may suggest that Jacob's household had already made significant forward advances. Everett Fox notes that in many ancient

cultures, the number "seventy" symbolized perfection or wholeness ("The Five Books of Moses", p. 357).

Joseph went to meet Israel in Goshen and when their eyes met, they wept continually. Israel said to Joseph, "Now I can die, since I have seen your face." Jacob lived in the land of Egypt for seventeen of his one hundred and forty-seven years. And as he drew near to death, Israel called for his son Joseph, and said to him, "Pray do not bury me in Egypt, but instead at the burial sight of my fathers – at the cave that is in the field of Makhpela, which Abraham had acquired from Efron the Hittite, and where they buried Abraham, Sarah, Isaac and Rifka, and where I buried Leah.

> Why is Jacob/*Israel* asking not to be buried in Egypt/*Mitzrayim*? Is he warning his family that while settling in Egypt is necessary for sustaining life during times of physical scarcity, it is not a place where we can satisfy our spiritual hunger?

> This warning may have already been embedded in Pharaoh's two dreams. Recall the commentary that offered reasons why the seven gaunt cows remained gaunt, even after eating the healthy cows, and the seven thin ears remained thin, even after swallowing the seven ripe ears.

Israel turned to Joseph's two sons and, with eyes heavy with age, placed his right arm on the head of Ephraim, the younger son, and his left arm on the head of the older one, Menasha. He was about to bless his two grandsons, when Joseph intervened, telling his father to place his right arm on his first-born. Israel responded, "I know, my son, I know – the descendants of Menasha will be a great people, but those from Ephraim will be greater."

> This story suggests that *Israel*, even at his advanced age, was able to see into the distant future at least as well as his son, Joseph. This incident speaks volumes as to just how far Jacob had "moved forward" in his personal and spiritual journey, when you think that he began it as a self-serving "heel-sneak."

Now, Jacob called his sons to gather round, "That I may tell you what will befall you in the aftertime of days. Come together and hearken, sons of Jacob, hearken to Israel your father."

And he proceeds to bless each of his twelve sons, likening Judah to a lion, whom his brothers will praise and bow down to, and *Joseph to a wild-ass along a spring.*

Judah is deserving of praise, having transformed himself into a sensitive and generous person, largely on his own.

Israel's blessing to Joseph is harder to decipher. As previously mentioned, the term "wild ass" does not appear to be complimentary. For example, we see this expression in the book of Job 39: 5-8 describing those who live a wandering, lawless life. Yet, Jacob refers to his favorite son and chosen heir, Joseph, using this same term as a compliment. The prophet Jeremiah is also referred to as a "wild ass," as is Ishmael in Genesis 16:12.

Also, we know from Genesis 27 that Isaac loved Esau, in part because Esau reminded him of his brother Ishmael. In light of this, might it be that *Israel*, by likening Joseph to a "wild ass," is seeing qualities in Joseph that he saw in his brother, Esau?

Might *Israel*, in his blessing to Joseph, be trying to unburden himself of his past, when he tricked his father to receive the blessing intended for Esau? His blessing could be intended to reinforce one of the core themes of the Joseph story, which is that until we can make peace with our past, our ability to inhabit the present and move forward into the future is limited.

Jacob's "blessing" to Shimon and Levi appeared more like a reprimand: *"Damned be their anger that is so fierce; I will split htem up in Yaakov, I will scatter them in Israel. To their council may my being never come, in their assemble may my person never unite! For in their anger they kill men, in their self will they maim bulls."* Jacob's anger dated back to the time that Shimon and Levi slaughtered all the men of Shekhem three days after tricking these men into agreeing to be circumcised (Genesis 34: 25, 26). At the time, Jacob said to them, "You have stirred up trouble for me, making me reek among the settled-folk of the land, the Canaanites and the Perizzites, for I have menfolk few in numbers; they will band together against me and destroy me and my household" (Genesis 34: 30).

What makes Jacob's words so interesting is that the descendants of Levi end up holding the esteemed positions in Jacob's family. As we will soon read, Moses was born to Levite parents (Exodus 1); YHVH will request that his brother Aaron (also a Levite), Aaron's four sons, and their descendants assume the priestly roles in perpetuity (Exodus 28:1); and the tribe of Levites oversee the well-being of the Tabernacle (Numbers 1:51).

When Jacob was finished blessing his sons, he expired. And Joseph flung himself at his father's face and wept. He then charged that his physicians embalm his father, which took the required full forty days.

In the "Flood" story, we noted that the number "forty" in Torah represents the birth of a fundamentally new understanding of life - and therefore the death of what we once had held to be true. More specifically, "forty" symbolizes moments of revelation when an individual crosses over into a closer relationship with self, with others, and with YHVH. Here, however, the number's symbolic value does not appear to apply - any more so than it did in Genesis 25, where Esau was said to be forty when he married a Hittite woman. As was the case with Esau's age, it appears that the use of the number "forty" in terms of the embalmment process is simply referring to biological time.

When the days of weeping passed, Joseph and his brothers buried his father, as their father had requested. But, now that their father was dead, the brothers worried that Joseph might hold a grudge against them and repay them for all the ill that they had caused him. They therefore flung themselves at his feet, saying "We are servants to you." But Joseph said, "Be not afraid. You may have planned ill against me, but God planned it over for good in order to keep many people alive."

At the moment that his brothers flung themselves at his feet, Joseph's second dream, the "celestial dream" *("Here the sun and the moon and eleven stars were bowing down to me!")* became a reality. In calming his brother's concerns, he made it clear that the dream was less about him and more about the spiritual well-being and future of the family.

Joseph lived one hundred and ten years, saying to the Sons of Israel that when God takes account of you, he will bring you from this land to that land that he swore to your forefathers. "

When God does so, bring my bones up with you." And he died, and the brothers embalmed him and put him in a coffin in Egypt.

Closing Comments: Joseph's name means "God has added." What did Joseph add? He added compassion and forgiveness to his relationships with his siblings, two qualities that were sorely lacking in the relationships between Cain and Abel; Isaac and Ishmael; and Jacob and Esau. Compassion and forgiveness can serve as the "center of gravity" to counteract a family's many centrifugal forces and keep its members united, even in the face of great adversity. To be compassionate and to forgive is to recognize that the conflict does not begin and end with our bruised ego; compassion and forgiveness dictate that we transcend these blows.

Now that the book of Genesis is completed, with its teachings about how to maintain *familial* peace and its credo that we *are* expected to be our brothers' keepers, regardless of the struggles it might entail, we are ready to "move forward" to the Exodus story, and its teachings about maintaining *communal* peace.

Chapter 6: Israel in Egypt

Introduction: At least three aspects of the Book of Exodus distinguish it from Genesis. First, whereas the Genesis stories involve many key players, linked inter-generationally over a wide expanse of time, all of the Exodus stories take place during the lifetime of one man, Moses. Second, the Genesis stories deal mostly with the challenges of maintaining intra-family peace, concluding that "we all must be our brother's keeper." The Exodus stories extend that teaching into the domain of inter-family dynamics, for Exodus is primarily about nation-building and the challenges of maintaining communal peace. Third, in Exodus YHVH emerges from the background to become the central leadership figure, acting directly in behalf of the people, challenging the Egyptian gods, performing miracles that liberate, guiding those in the wilderness, and setting in stone laws for the people to follow. Whereas YHVH had been known as *El'ohim* or *El-Shaddai* in Genesis, only in Exodus does YHVH make explicit his/her Name.

Interestingly, Moses' life-journey will be almost the opposite of Joseph's. Joseph began his life as a shepherd and ended it as an Egyptian viceroy, while Moses was raised in royalty as an Egyptian prince and ended his days as a shepherd, first of livestock and then of people. Whereas Joseph led the people into Egypt for their physical well-being, Moses led them out of Egypt for their spiritual well-being. And, while Joseph confidently displayed heroic and visionary leadership qualities, Moses acted as a reluctant liberator.

We begin our reading of the Book of Exodus in Chapter 6, at the time leading up to the deliverance from Egypt. Chapter 7 will cover the period from the deliverance up until the time when the Children of Israel receive the Covenant at Sinai. Chapter 8 will conclude the Book of Exodus with an expose on each of the so-called Ten Commandments, as well as description of the Tabernacle and the Priestly Vestments.

In Chapter 6, "Israel in Egypt," we will examine what it means to be a slave in Egypt and, as well, a foreigner (resident alien) in a foreign land: someone who may have been born, lived, and died in the land, but never truly inhabited it. Chapter 6 will also follow Moses' life from infancy to revelation at the sight of the burning bush. And, this chapter concludes by having us delve into the symbolic meaning behind each of the so-called "ten plagues."

➢ The King Who Did Not Know Joseph (Exodus 1, 2)

Summary: *The children of Israel grew so mighty (in number) that the new king said, "Let us use our wits against them" lest they become mightier than we. So, he and his gang-captains afflicted them with crushing labor. He also told their midwives, "When you help the Hebrew woman give birth, if it is to a son, put him to death." But the midwives held God in awe and did not do as the King said. He asked the midwives, "Why have you let the children live?" and they responded: "The Hebrew women are livelier than are the Egyptian women; before we come to them, they have already given birth!" Therefore, Pharaoh commanded that his people throw into the river every Hebrew son that is born, but let every daughter live.*

A man from the house of Levi married a Levite woman, who bore a son. And, when she saw that he was "goodly," she hid him for three months. She then prepared for him a little ark of papyrus, loamed it, and placed it in the reeds by the shore of the Nile. His sister stationed herself far off, to know what would be done to him.

Pharaoh's daughter went down to bathe in the river – and saw the little ark and sent her maid to fetch it. She then opened it and saw a weeping baby boy. She said, "This is a Hebrew child!" Moses' sister said to Pharaoh's daughter: "Shall I go and call a nursing woman from the Hebrews?" The daughter said "Go," and so she called the child's mother, who nursed him. The child grew and became Pharaoh's daughter's son, whom she called Moshe for "out of the water I pulled him out."

Now some years later, Moses went out to his brothers and saw their burdens and an Egyptian man striking one of them. Seeing that no one was there, Moses struck down the Egyptian and buried him in the sand. He went out again the next day and saw two Hebrew men scuffling and asked, "Why do you strike your fellow?" The man replied, "Who made you prince and judge over us? Do you mean to kill me as you killed the Egyptian?" Moses became afraid, saying "Surely the matter is known!" Indeed, Pharaoh heard of this matter and sought to kill Moses, but Moses fled and settled in the land of Midian and sat down by a well.

The priest of Midian had seven daughters who came to draw water for their father's sheep. Shepherds came and drove them away, but Moses rose up and delivered them. When the daughters returned home, their father, Re'uel said, "Why have you come home so quickly?" They replied that an Egyptian man rescued us from the hands of a shepherd and then watered our sheep. Re'uel said, "So where is he? Why have you left him behind? Call him that he might eat bread with us." Moses agreed to settle down with the man and accepted his daughter, Tzippora, who gave birth to their son, Gershom, for Moses said, "A sojourner I have become in a foreign land."

Many years later the king died. The Children of Israel groaned from their servitude, and their cries for help went up to God. God called to mind his covenant with Abraham, Isaac, and Jacob, and God saw the Children of Israel and took notice.

Discussion Questions: Who are the "Children of Israel" and do they differ from those who are referred to as the "Hebrews"? Why was Moses born out of the house of Levi, as opposed to one of the other eleven tribes? What is meant by a "goodly child? What role are women playing in Torah? Did Moses commit murder? Who are the Midianites? What does it mean to be "a sojourner in a foreign land"? Did Moses really exist; did the Exodus actually happen?

- **Who are the "Children of Israel"?** The expression "Children of Israel" is used for the first time in the Torah in Exodus 1:1 and then is used repeatedly thereafter. Moreover, this expression appears to be synonymous with the term "Hebrews," which was used only sparingly in the Genesis stories; it appears for the first time in Genesis 14:13, where Avram is referred to as a Hebrew by a man from Sodom, and is not mentioned again in Genesis until the Joseph story, fifteen chapters later (Genesis 39:14; 39:17; 40:15; 41:12; 43:32.)

  Why the introduction of a new term here? Consistent with what distinguishes Exodus from Genesis, both terms - "Children of Israel" and "Hebrews" - refer to a community of people rather than to specific individuals and their families. That is, the "Children of Israel" refers to those individuals who, while not necessarily biologically linked to Jacob, are descendents of his spiritual side. Thus, whereas in Genesis the question of birthright was limited to the family, in Exodus it is open to anyone who, as the name "*Israel*" suggests, shows the willingness and ability to pursue his or her personal and spiritual journeys by committing to a lifetime of struggle with things both mortal (such as relationships, demands on our time, competing priorities, and our physical well-being) and divine (such as our spiritual well-being, the mysteries of our existence and purpose), while surrendering to that in our lives which we cannot control, own, or understand.

The term "Hebrews" also suggests an open community of spiritual seekers. Recall from our earlier discussion of the Covenant (Genesis 17-20) that the Hebrew word for "Hebrew" is "*Ivri*," which means "crossing-over" when it is used in the context of a "closer relationship with one's self, with others, and with YHVH," for the two words - Hebrew and crossing -share the same three-letter root (*alef-bet- resh*), which is pronounced *ah-ber*. Defined accordingly, Hebrews are "Children of Israel," for they represent anyone who has "crossed over" by advancing on his or her personal and spiritual journeys, as one would who has experienced a revelation -- an insightfully new understanding that helps one "move forward."

We will revisit this core Torah message of inclusiveness when we read about those who left Egypt for the wilderness. Suffice to say here that the message of "inclusiveness" is a fundamental teaching in Torah, first appearing in the Genesis story about Hagar. Recall that she, and not Sarai, was the first female after Eve to whom YHVH speaks (Genesis 16). The Torah is reminding us that you don't have to be biologically related to Abraham and Sarah to hear YHVH. It is not about our status or position in life - - even an Egyptian female slave can hear YHVH, become a "child of Israel" and cross-over into a closer relationship with herself, with others, and with YHVH.

This inclusiveness theme is repeated again in the Book of Ruth, believed to have been written around 1070 B.C.E., or about 130 years after the Hebrews entered the Promised Land from the Sinai. In that Book, it was Na'omi, from the tribe of Ephraim, who heard God speak in the wilderness of Moab. Moreover, her son, Chi'ion, married a Moab woman named Ruth, who would later become the great-great-grandmother of King David. Yet, as we read in Genesis 19, the Moabites, who descended from Lot's illicit encounter with one of his daughters, became great enemies to the decendents of Avram and Sarai. The teaching is clear: "Good" can be found, here in the form of Na'omi and King David, even among one's enemies.

That said, the opening lines of Exodus contain a delicious irony, but one that will only become apparent as we advance in the story. Suffice to say here that while the text refers to the people as a community of spiritual seekers, they are anything but that in the opening chapter of Exodus. Indeed, it will take many of them the full set of ten plagues before they awaken to their inner yearnings. And, it will be that awakening that will ultimately differentiate between those who are Hebrews/ Children of Israel and those who remain Egyptian laborers. Until that awakening, everyone living in Egypt can be considered an Egyptian.

One other point: The text refers to the Children of Israel as being "mighty (in number)." The last time that expression was used was in Genesis 18:18, when YHVH promised Avraham that he will "become a great nation and mighty (in number), and all the nations of the earth will find blessing through him." As of Exodus 1, only the first half of YHVH's prophesy has materialized, for Pharaoh is clearly not viewing the Hebrews as a blessing, but rather as a threat because of their numbers. Might the writers also be telling us that the rest of the Book of Exodus will be about the second half of the prophesy?

- **Why the house of Levi?** This house or, better, *tribe* holds a very special place among the twelve tribes, for from it would come Moses, his brother Aaron, and all future generations of high priests (*Cohen'im*). Based on their past actions, however, this tribe seems undeserving of its esteemed status. After all, it was Levi and his brother Shim'on who reached a peaceful agreement with Hamor and his son, Shekhem, after they had defiled their sister, Dina, and then they proceeded to slaughter Hamor and all the men in his tribe (see Genesis 34). It was this incident, and not the sale of Joseph, that caused their father, Jacob/*Israel*, to curse the two of them on his deathbed, when he said , "These (two) brothers, wronging weapons be their ties-of-kinship. Damned be their anger, that it is so fierce- I will split them up in Jacob and scatter them in Israel" (Gen. 49:5-7).

What is yet to be revealed is how the Levi tribe was able to harness its anger and turn it into something that the rest of the tribes could benefit from, while the Shim'on tribe could not. Indeed, the tribe of Shim'on all but disappeared by the end of the Book of Deuteronomy, consistent with Jacob's condemnation, while the tribe of Levi earned the responsibility for being the guardian of the covenant. We see evidence of Levi's transformation in Moses' positively-worded deathbed blessing of Levi (Deuteronomy 33:8-11).

- **What is a "goodly" child?** Recall from the Creation story in Genesis that "good" refers to that which actualizes the potential to bring forth the life that is embedded within. By referring to the child as "goodly," the Torah is pointing out that the child has life-creating capacity. In the context of the Exodus story, however, "life" is going to refer less to one's physical well-being and more to one's spiritual advancement. Those who follow Moses' lead will learn to be more aware, more able to appreciate life before death, and more able to participate in the ongoing process of creation.

- **What role are women playing in Torah?** Many have criticized the Torah for being male-dominated and overly patriarchal; yet we already have witnessed numerous instances in Genesis where woman play a major role. Without Eve, Adam would not have left the safe confines of home, and the two of them would not have begun their personal and spiritual journey to find out what their lives were about. Without Sarah's prompting, Abraham would not have passed the family birthright on to Isaac. And without Rebecca, Isaac would not have passed the family birthright on to Jacob.

The Book of Exodus continues with this gender-positive view. It was the midwives who bravely chose not to follow Pharaoh's command to put to death all newborn Hebrew males, and then to stand up to Pharaoh when he confronted them. It was Moses' mother who put her life at risk by hiding her newborn son from the Egyptians for three months before setting him adrift on the Nile in a little ark. It was Moses' sister who kept a close eye on the baby as he drifted in the river and then boldly approached Pharaoh's daughter with the plan to bring the child's mother to nurse him. And it was Pharaoh's daughter who chose to raise the child as her own, in clear violation of her all-powerful father's edict. Indeed, men played virtually no role in the first fifteen verses of the Exodus story!

Said simply, without the decisive actions taken by the women in the Genesis stories, the generations of Abraham, Isaac, and Jacob would not have "moved forward." And, without the decisive actions taken by the women in the opening verses of the Book of Exodus, the Torah would not have advanced beyond the Book of Genesis.

- **Was Moses a murderer?** The text states, "*He saw an Egyptian man striking a Hebrew man, one of his brothers – and seeing that there was no man there, he struck down the Egyptian and buried him in the sand.*" The simple answer is "Yes," but with a caveat that goes something like this: Moses murdered the Egyptian because the Egyptian, by virtue of his evil and cruel acts to a Hebrew man, deserved to die. And, in performing this heroic deed, Moses showed YHVH his willingness, ability, and courage to lead his people to freedom. Had Moses not taken the lead at this critical moment in Torah, YHVH would not have been revealed to Moses at the "burning bush."

I find this explanation to be inconsistent with what the Torah (which means "teaching") teaches us, which is, as I noted before to be more human, to value life above death, and to participate in the ongoing process of creation. If we take this telling of Moses' killing literally, as do many commentaries, the teaching would instead be "if you strike my brother, or treat him unjustly, then I have the god-given right to kill you." Clearly, this punishment does not fit the crime. It not only misinterprets the phrase, "an eye for an eye," but goes beyond by implying "two eyes for a bloody nose." As we should know all too well, this kind of misguided cause-and-effect reasoning is the fodder for fundamentalism and terrorism, and not compassion and social justice.

I say "misinterprets the phrase" because as Hillel - one of the most important figures in Jewish history, who lived shortly before the time of Jesus – pointed out, the context in which the "eye for an eye" phrase appears (in Exodus 21, verses 23-27) suggests something very different: Should an individual cause bodily harm to another due to acts of negligence or intent, the perpetrator is obliged to pay the victim the monetary equivalent of what the lost eye – or any other body part -was worth. Taken in this light, the phrase is not about revenge, but rather represents a basis for civil law that is still relevant in today's courts.

Moses' murderous act is also inconsistent with another core Torah teaching: regarding control. In brief, this teaching tells us that we can bring about problems for ourselves and for those around us when we over-reach and try to be more God-like, thinking that we can control that which we cannot control. The sooner we understand this, the sooner we can deal with life's traumas and disappointments, and find inner peace and wholeness.

We learned about the pitfalls of trying to take matters into our own hands in the stories about Adam and Eve, Cain, the builders of the infamous "Babel" tower, and Avram (Abraham) and Sarai (Sarah) in the story about Sarai's Egyptian servant, Hagar. It would seem that, here, Moses also tried to take matters into his own hands and by doing so he over-reached. He attempted to single-handedly resolve a larger societal problem, without any instruction, approval, or assistance from YHVH.

So, back to the question, what Torah-teaching can we draw from the passage, "*He saw an Egyptian man striking a Hebrew man, one of his brothers – he struck down the Egyptian and buried him in the sand*"? In attempting an explanation, I am first reminded of a statement by Moses Maimonides, who said that if our literal reading of the scripture suggests something that is clearly contrary to reason, we must interpret what we read as metaphor, for the Torah often speaks "figuratively and allegorically."

I am also reminded of the lessons from Genesis 21 and 22, about the banishment of Hagar and Ishmael and the binding of Isaac. In brief, the Hagar and Ishmael story, which we read on the first day of Rosh Hashanah, teaches us that we risk our lives and our future if we let our old ways control our present. The teaching of the binding story is that we also risk our lives and our ability to inhabit the present if we try to control our future.

Relating these thoughts to Moses, it is important to note that he was raised in the lap of royalty and likely had aspirations for eventually becoming the next monarch of Egypt. His killing of the Egyptian task-master might have signaled a "*lekh lekha*," or "going forth" moment of profound spiritual importance. With one single action, Moses not only permanently separated himself from his past, which to this point had been controlling his present, but also severed his ties to a future filled with wealth, comfort, and power. (Recall two other *lekh lekha* moments, the first in Genesis 12 when YHVH said to Avram, "*Go forth from your land and from your father's house, to the land that I will let you see.*"; and the second in Genesis 22 when YHVH said to Abraham: "*Take your son, your only one, whom you love, Isaac, and go forth to Mount Mor'iah and offer him up there as an offering-up.*")

This allegorical teaching from the passage is fully consistent with Torah: Moses *had to* "kill" the Egyptian in him that was shepherding his life so that he could give birth to a new and more authentic purpose to his life. Only by this "murder" could he inhabit the present with enough clarity and mindfulness to perceive the "burning bush." Taken in this light, the murder of the Egyptian can be interpreted as a "forty-like" experience in Moses' life; that is, the birth of a fundamentally new understanding about the meaning of life, and therefore the death of what he was once held to be true. For more discussion about the symbolic meaning of the number "40", refer to the commentary to the Exodus 3 question "Was Moses really seventy-nine?" The text provides another clue, this one pointing to the killing as a resolution of an internal struggle, when it states "that there was no man there." No man there? Bear in mind that this is Egypt, a hub of activity and commerce, at a time of day when thousands are employed at various construction tasks – not exactly a setting where anyone could find himself alone. And, while no one was said to have witnessed the killing, the subsequent change in Moses' character was apparent to all who came into his presence, although remarks like "who made you prince and judge over us?" suggests that the others did not yet grasp the meaning of the change. That is to say that while Moses no longer saw himself as an Egyptian prince, the others were still "in the dark" about who he had become. This last remark will take on additional meaning when we discuss the meaning behind the ninth plague.

- **Who are the Midianites?** Recall from Genesis 37 that *"a group of Midianite merchants passed by, hauled Joseph out of the pit, and then sold him for twenty pieces of silver to the Ishmaelites, who then brought Joseph to Egypt."* We observed in that verse the almost interchangeable usage of "Midianites" and "Ishmaelites," suggesting that these two tribes might be close tribes of the same family. This juxtaposition of the two tribes allows us to once again witness how the past, present, and future converge in the story in interesting and sometimes ironic ways. By that I mean that whereas Avram and Sarai banished Ishmael and his mother, Hagar, an Egyptian slave, it was the descendents of Ishmael who not only brought Joseph into bondage in Egypt, but then, four hundred years later, indirectly helped Moses bring the Children of Israel out of that bondage. And, whereas Avram and Sarai tried to protect their blood line from the descendents of Ishmael, the blood lines will once again converge through Moses, by virtue of his close relationship with the Midianite priest Re'uel (Jethro), and his daughter, Tzippora, whom Moses marries. Soon after, she gives birth to their son, Gershom ("sojourner there"), so-named because Moses said, "A sojourner I have become in a foreign land."

- **What does it mean to be "a sojourner in a foreign land"?** Everett Fox points out that, contrary to DeMille's stereotyped portrayal of the horrors of slave labor (in his movie, "The Ten Commandments"), the opening of Exodus limits itself to only a few verses about the Hebrews' physical torment. From the perspective of Torah, of far greater importance to the story is their experience of being strangers in Egypt.

This "stranger" experience is not new. In the story about Hagar, Sarai's Egyptian maidservant (Genesis 16), we learned that her name means "stranger" and Egypt (in Hebrew, *Mitz-rayim*) means a "narrow place" - a place where we give more attention to our material pursuits than we do to the questions of good, evil, and life. "Hagar the Egyptian maidservant" thus becomes "the enslaved stranger who came from a narrow place." Hagar's experience bears close similarity to that now facing the Children of Israel, for in Exodus they too find themselves to be "enslaved strangers in a narrow place." Like Hagar, the Children are being treated as objects in what Martin Buber calls an "I-It" relationship. Their days are spent working solely for the purpose of advancing Pharaoh's own agenda. They are not free to follow their own journey, but rather Pharaoh's journey. They sacrifice their spiritual well-being for material enslavements like job security, shelter, and food.

Sure, working conditions in Egypt were not ideal, but remember that, for its time, thirty-five hundred years ago, a steady job in a prosperous, secure, and orderly empire with an abundance of food and drink was about as good as it got for those not belonging to the ruling class. Indeed, once out in the wilderness, the people talked about how good they had had it in Egypt: "We recall the fish that we used to eat in Egypt for free, the cucumbers, watermelons, green leeks, onions and garlic!"

(Numbers, 11:5). There they had lived, but were not alive. They travelled through their limited time on earth, half asleep, never alert enough to inhabit the moment.

Like Hagar, for them to move their lives "forward" towards a closer relationship with themselves, others, and with YHVH - - and address such fundamental questions as "who am I, why am I, and what is my real purpose" - - they needed to break free from their enslavements and stop allowing others to treat them as victims. Like Avram and Sarai in Genesis 12, they needed to just "go forth" (*lekh Lecha*), for if they do not leave, their lives will remain forever incomplete (i.e., not whole/*shalem*), alienated from their true identify.

- **Did Moses really exist?** As with the Patriarchs and Matriarchs of Genesis, nobody knows, and quite likely will never know. If he lived, it would have been around 1,400 years before the Common Era, that is, about 3,400 years ago. Even the story about the Exodus is suspect. As previously mentioned, the Hebrews were said to have spent four centuries as slaves in Egypt, yet no artifacts have been found in either Israel or in Egypt that reflect an earlier Egyptian influence. Similarly, although it is stated in Exodus 12: 37 that six hundred thousand men left Egypt to wander for forty years in the relatively small region of the Sinai, no evidence whatsoever has been found in Sinai to suggest that such a mass exodus of about 2 million (if we also include women and children) ever took place. Also, the image of Moses as a castaway set adrift on a river bears a resemblance to the lesser known birth of Sargon of Akkad, born in Mesopotamia, who became an Akkadian emperor famous for his conquest of the Sumerian city-states some 4,300 years ago. Again, any lack of historical proof should not diminish the value of these stories, which are all presented in Torah to convey teachings.

➤ The Burning Bush (Exodus 3)

Background: As the story opens, Moses is about seventy-nine years old. By Torah standards, his life until now has been rather uneventful. He was born a slave, raised as a prince, and has lived most of his adult life in exile, tending the flock of his father-in-law, Jethro (Re'uel), the priest of Midian. To date, Moses has never "spoken" with YHVH.

Summary: *He led the flock into the wilderness and came to the mountain of God, to Horev. And YHVH's messenger was seen by him in the flame of a fire out of the midst of a bush. He saw that the bush is burning but is not consumed. Moses said, "Now let me turn aside that I may see this great sight – why the bush does not burn up!" When YHVH saw that he had turned aside to see, God called to him out of the midst of the bush, saying, "Moses, Moses!" And Moses replied, "Here I am." YHVH said to Moses, "Remove your sandals and do not come near for the place on which you stand is holy ground." "I am the God of Avraham Isaac, and Jacob. I have seen the affliction of my people that are in Egypt and heard their cry; I know of their suffering. I have come to rescue them and bring them to the land flowing with milk and honey. I send you to Pharaoh – bring my people, the Children of Israel, out of Egypt." Moses responds, "Who am I that should go to Pharaoh?" YHVH said, "I will be there with you. I will tell the Children of Israel that the God of their fathers has sent me to you and they will say, 'What is his name?'"*

God then replied, "Tell them that my name is EHYEH ASHER EHYEH, the God of your fathers, the God of Abraham, Isaac, and Jacob. Tell them that I will bring them up from the affliction of Egypt to a land flowing with milk and honey. But, I know that the king of Egypt will not give you leave to go, and so I will strike Egypt with all my wonders, and after that he will set you free. And you shall not go empty handed, for each woman shall ask of her neighbor and of the sojourners in her house of objects of silver and gold and clothing."

Discussion Questions: Was Moses really seventy-nine years old at the time of this story? Why does the text say that Moses led his flock into the wilderness when he was already living in the Midian desert, a place that most would agree is very much a wilderness? Why is the mountain of God named "Horev"? What makes Moses' reaction to seeing the burning bush so noteworthy? Why does YHVH call Moses by name twice? Moses may have said "Here I am," but did he mean it? Why does YHVH invoke the names of the Patriarchs? What does God's name mean? Why ask for silver, gold, and clothing? Where do we find ourselves in the story?

- **Was Moses really seventy-nine?** The same question was previously addressed concerning Avraham and Sarah; that is, recent archeological evidence suggests that during biblical times, people viewed two holidays, Rosh Hashanah and Passover, as New Year celebrations. As such, each year as we measure it may have represented two years to them. If so, then Moses was a much more realistic age of about forty when he encountered YHVH at the burning bush and was sixty (not a hundred and twenty) when he died.

    But, we need not try to explain Moses' age literally. Consider for a moment the metaphoric meaning of the number "40" that has been repeatedly used in Genesis, beginning with the flood story. You will recall that a "forty" experience is used to symbolically represent the birth of a fundamentally new understanding about the meaning of life, and therefore the death of what we once held to be true. Put another way, when the text associates an event with the number "forty," it usually means that a revelation has taken place that allows the protagonist to cross-over into a closer relationship with himself/herself, with others, and with YHVH.

    Moses already had one such an experience when he "killed" the Egyptian inside of him; that is, when, with one single action, he not only permanently separated himself from his past, which to this point had been controlling his present, but also severed his ties to a future filled with wealth, comfort, and power.

    Moses, now at the age of seventy-nine, is about to have another "forty" experience in the presence of the Burning Bush. And, as most of us know, he will have one last transformational "forty" experience when, after camping out for forty days and forty nights at the top of Mount Sinai, he experiences his third revelation, the Ten Commandments. Have you done the math? Might this explain why Moses was said to be a hundred twenty years old at the time of his death?

- **Why does Moses lead his flock into the "wilderness"?** As I previously mentioned in the commentary for Genesis 21, the wilderness (*mid-bar*) is where we will hear YHVH speak (*da-ber*). As such, the Torah is making an important distinction between our physical realty (e.g., a desert, or *negba*, which means "parched dry") and a more spiritual reality (wilderness).

In Torah, people do not enter the wilderness unless they are searching for answers. They may know where in their lives they are coming from, but do not yet know where they are going. Moses may be feeling as if there is more to his life than tending to a flock of sheep belonging to someone else.

A final point: While the traditional translation of verse 1 is "into the wilderness," a more literal translation is "after" the wilderness" (the Hebrew word used, *a-khar'ah* literally means "after"). To say "after" changes the meaning of the verse, for we know that in the Torah "after the wilderness" is the Promise Land. The text may therefore be saying that Moses was leading his flock towards the Promised Land. However, between the wilderness and the Promised Land lies the mountain named Horev.

- **Why is God's mountain named Horev?** *Horev* means sword or destruction, suggesting that something in Moses' past is about to be severed. In Torah, this is what revelation is all about: A transformational moment when we realize that what we held to be true in the past is no longer meaningful to us and therefore must be discarded (severed or destroyed). In its place, a new truth will emerge that allows us to more fully inhabit the present and move on, less encumbered, to a more enlightened future. It is that extra-perceptual moment when we are able to glimpse our inner truths (e.g., who we are and what we are about) and find greater clarity, wholeness, and unity (*shalem*).

As an interesting aside, the first time in Torah that the imagery of a sword appears is in the Adam and Eve story (Genesis 3:24) where it is written that Cherubim (or "Winged-sphinxes") with ever-turning swords were placed outside the Garden of

Eden to guard the Tree of Life. The imagery appears again in Exodus 25:18 when these mythical figures were placed outside the Ark (Tabernacle) to "protect" the tablets from Sinai that were housed in the Ark. And, we can find these figures and their swords in most synagogues perched on the outside of the ark *(aron kodesh)* that houses the Torah.

But, why does the Torah use such aggressive imagery, like "sword" and "destruction" to refer to this mountain? The simple answer is that revelation does not happen without a struggle, a commitment to action and often the incurrence of some suffering and pain for letting go of what we had. Said in another way, it is not only about "receiving the word"; it is about "living the word." To move forward and "cross over", something must be left behind; to accept the new, aspects of the past must die.

Interestingly, the need to suffer is paramount in Buddhism, for according to this belief structure, suffering helps to promote the development of our consciousness and teaches us lessons of tolerance and humility. More to the point, in Buddhism, "suffering" refers to the deep sadness that we feel when we discover that nothing in life is permanent – not our possessions, health, friendships, and so on. Even mountains that appear permanent will eventually erode and disappear.

In a similar vein, the need to struggle is central to the teachings of Torah. To advance our understanding of good, evil, and the meaning of life requires that we struggle with the questions posed by each of the two "trees" that are said to lie at the center of the Garden of Eden (Genesis 3). Indeed, struggle is fundamental to being like *Israel*, which is defined in Genesis 35 as the willingness to commit to a lifetime journey of struggling with things both divine and mortal, with the knowledge that we – like all of Creation – exist as uncompleted acts, like verbs conjugated in the future imperfect tense. As such, the writers of the Torah may be saying that our need to struggle and our desire to be more enlightened are woven into the very fabric of Creation.

Did you know that Mount Horev will later in the Exodus story be referred to as Mount Sinai? Perhaps the Torah may be using this literary convention to convey the fact that as we move through time and space, our perspective changes.

- **What makes Moses' reaction to seeing the burning bush so noteworthy?** Rabbi Jamie Korngold notes that "it takes patience to notice that something is on fire which is not burning up because you have to sit with it for a while to observe the changes, or lack thereof" (page 24). While this is true, it also takes an acute awareness to appreciate that what we are seeing transcends (or lies outside of) time, space, and reason. Can we see the extraordinary in the ordinary? Can we experience eternity in the present tense? Can we see with all of our senses those things that we know cannot happen in the physical world, and not try to explain them through scientific investigation or Google search? Moses is experiencing a revelational moment, when he transcends much that he had held to be true.

   It is interesting to observe that Moses first sees YHVH's messenger in the flame of the fire, but when he speaks, he speaks only of the burning bush and not of the messenger. This raises the question, "Who is the messenger?" Might the messenger be Moses' inner voice awakening him to a new calling in his life – the same voice that caused him to lead his flock into (after) the wilderness? Recall that Moses has spent most of his adult life in the Midian desert, a physical reality; perhaps for the first time he is hearing the *da-ber* that can only be heard in the spiritual "wilderness," that place we go to when our spirit is agitated, causing us to search for new, more meaningful answers?

   Moses' response (*hee ney nee*) when God calls him has already been heard in a few other stories in Torah, but only at life-altering moments (for example, in Genesis 22:1 when God asks Abraham to sacrifice his son on Mount *Mor'iah*, the "Mountain of Teaching"). By saying "*here I am,*" Moses was saying that he was totally present, not knowing what was about to be asked of him but nevertheless ready to respond without hesitation. He was saying that his heart was entirely open and that all of his senses were fully awake to fully inhabit the present.

- **Why call Moses' name twice?** This convention of calling a name twice appears in other stories in the Torah. Given the context in which it appears here, we can surmise that it is used to symbolize the old Moses (a herder of sheep and goats) *and* the new, transformed Moses (soon to be the shepherd of the Children of Israel). He is about to do that which he will never retire from.

- **Why does YHVH invoke the names of the Patriarchs?** Moses is being asked to enter into a partnership with YHVH, but he first must understand that he is more than just a shepherd of sheep. He needs to be made aware of his connection to the distant past - - to those individuals who are his spiritual ancestors ("soul community") and the struggles that they went through with things both mortal and divine - - in order to better appreciate the struggles that his community is currently experiencing in Egypt.

- **What does God's name mean?** There are only two verb tenses in Biblical Hebrew, the past/perfect (meaning that the action is completed) and the future/imperfect (meaning that the action is progressing towards an uncertain future). God's name, *EHYEH ASHER EHYEH* (which appears only once in the Torah in its full unabbreviated form) is conjugated as a verb in the imperfect tense, and is translated as "I will be that which I will be" or "I will be present whenever and wherever I will be present."

God's name gives no hint as to who or what God is. Perhaps the writers of the Torah conceptualized God by this abstraction in order to affirm that God is beyond our ability to understand, define, predict, or influence. This conceptualization lies in stark contrast to the image of God that many of us grew up with: the all-wise and all-powerful parent figure who intervenes in our lives when we are at risk, rewards us when we do the right things, and punishes us if we don't.

Perhaps by keeping the concept of God abstract, the writers may also be saying that there are many ways to experience God. Depending on where we are in any given moment of life, we might be experiencing God by looking inward or outward, or in the relationship that we develop with our self, with others, and with nature. The Torah may also be implying that we should be wary of those who hold an anthropomorphic, humanized vision of God, of those who claim to speak or act in God's behalf, and of those who assign meanings that interpret God's actions as if they know what God is.

But is God's name all that abstract? On the one hand, the answer is a resounding "Yes," but at the same time God's name should also be familiar to us. We can say this because, like YHVH, we are all *verbing* through life in the future/ imperfect tense --- we are all uncompleted actions progressing towards an uncertain future. From the perspective of Torah, however, the difference between God's verbing and our verbing is that the uncertainty referred to resides solely with us; it is we who are uncertain about our future. God will be what God will be.

- **Why ask for silver, gold, and clothing?** Some have argued that these three items are symbolic o
- f the provisions that are due to freed slaves. What makes the request so interesting is that the provisions are not coming from the royal family, but from neighbors - - fellow slaves who chose to remain "enslaved strangers in a narrow place." Unlike Avram and Sarai (Genesis 12), these individuals were unwilling to trade the comfort, familiarity, and security of their prosperous surroundings for the uncertainties of a land unknown to them.

Again, the working conditions in Egypt were not ideal, but for its time, a steady job in a prosperous, secure, and orderly empire with an abundance of food and drink was about as good as it was to get for most people. And the fact that these "slaves" had silver, gold, and clothing attests to the fact that they were able to accumulate considerable wealth while working for Pharaoh. This is not to say that prosperity is intrinsically bad. However, it does have an insidious way of causing us to define our lives in terms of its pursuit and making us unwilling to leave.

- **Where do we find ourselves in the story?** Are we still shepherding flocks for someone else? Have we begun to drive them into/after the wilderness? Can we see Mount Horev in front of us? Are we seeing the messenger, or has our attention advanced to seeing the burning bush? Are we ready to say, or have we already said, "Here I am." Has there been a time when we participated in co-creation and did something which was truly "good" (*tov*)?

➢ Returning to Egypt (Exodus 4)

Summary: *Moses expresses concern that the people will not trust him; they will say that "YHVH has not been seen by you!" YHVH transforms Moses' staff into a snake and then back into a staff and says, "So that they may trust that YHVH has been seen by you." Still concerned, Moses says, "Please, my Lord, no man of words am I, for heavy of tongue and mouth am I." YHVH replies, "Who placed a mouth in humans? It is I who will be there with your mouth and instruct you as to what you are to speak." To this, Moses says, "Please, my Lord, find someone else to speak." Then YHVH's anger flared at Moses and said, "Is there not Aaron, your brother, a Levite – I know he can speak, yes, speak well. As you return to Egypt, he will come out to meet you. I will instruct you what to say and you shall put the words in his mouth. He shall be for you a mouth and you shall be for him a god."*

YHVH said to Moses, "I will make Pharaoh's heart strong-willed and he will not send the people free. Then say to him, "Thus says YHVH, my firstborn is Israel; send free my son that he may serve me; but you have refused so I will kill your firstborn!"

Moses went to Jethro, his father-in-law, and said, "Pray let me return to my brothers that are in Egypt, that I may see whether they are alive. Jethro replied, "Go in peace!" So, Moses took his wife and his sons and returned to Egypt. On the way, he encountered Aaron at the mountain of God and told Aaron all of YHVH's words. And the two of them gathered all the elders of the

Children of Israel. Aaron spoke all the words that YHVH spoke to Moses and the people trusted him that YHVH had taken account of them and seen their afflictions.

Discussion Questions: Why is Moses so reluctant to do as YHVH asks? What does Aaron's name mean? Why is YVHV first "making" Pharaoh's heart strong-willed and then punishing him for it by threatening to kill his first born? How are the people to "serve" YHVH? What is the meaning of "alive" in the context of Moses' request to Jethro to return to Egypt? What is the meaning of Jethro's parting words, "Go in peace"?

- **Why is Moses so reluctant to do as YHVH asks?** The Torah considers Moses to be the first prophet. The Hebrew word for prophet is *Navi,* which is constructed on the linguistic root/*shoresh* "la-voh," meaning "to bring." While most define a prophet as someone who predicts the future, the definition is broader than that. The term refers to a person who is told by YHVH to bring YHVH's words to a community at a time when the message is entirely outside the norms of that community. Not surprisingly, a prophet's words are generally not readily received and are likely to be resisted, for the prophet tells others exactly what they don't want to hear. Small wonder, therefore, that many prophets, are very reluctant to deliver the YHVH-given message.[12]

---

[12] Consider the prophet Jonah(whose full name, Jonah ben Amittai, means Dove, Son of My *(God's)* Truth): *YHVH is telling him to go to Ninevah, the capital of Assyria, to those who want to - - and, as we know, soon will-- destroy his nation, the Northern Kingdom of Israel, and ask them, in Jonah's language, which is different from their language, to repent. "Otherwise, in forty days your city will be destroyed!" Feeling as if he would be betraying himself and his nation, he decides instead to go in the opposite direction, away from Ninevah. He goes west (Nineveh is east), down to sea level (Nineveh is at a higher elevation), onto a ship destined for Tarshish (which is located in Spain; that is, further west) and all the way down to the hull of the ship, where he proceeds to fall asleep.*

Let's put it this way: Moses doesn't need YHVH to tell him that Pharaoh will not take kindly to the suggestion that he let his principal source of labor, on which he has built his empire, "go." Would you, if you were Pharaoh? And, fFor that matter, Moses also doesn't need YHVH to tell him that the Hebrews will not willingly give up a steady job (in a prosperous, secure, and orderly empire, with an abundance of food and drink) and march off into the wilderness without food and water, to destinations unknown. Again, would you?

- **What does Aaron's name mean?** We have already learned that names in the Torah reveal core aspects of personality. For example, Isaac's Hebrew name, Yitzhak, is derived from the Hebrew word for "laughter," for he brought laughter to his parents in their old age ; and Jacob's name, Yaakov, means "heel-sneak" or "deceiver," because he tricked his brother and father in his quest to receive the family's birthright; Joseph's name means "God has added," for he added compassion and forgiveness to the relationships with his siblings ; and Moses' name means "pulled from the water." Aaron's name, however, is left undefined, almost as if he has no personality independent of Moses, little more than a mouth for Moses to put words into, as YHVH instructs Moses to do.

- **Why is YVHV making Pharaoh's heart strong-willed and then threatening to punish him for it by killing his first born?** If YHVH is all-powerful, why doesn't YHVH soften Pharaoh's heart? By hardening Pharaoh's heart, which then leads to the death of his first born, isn't YHVH coming across more as an accomplice in crime than a savior. In Exodus 7: 4, YHVH repeats this threat, but adds to it that "I will set my hand against Egypt." And, why must Pharaoh's first born and all Egyptians have to suffer on account of Pharaoh's stubbornness?

We can easily conclude from this passage that YHVH is acting no better than Pharaoh, who, only two chapters before, commanded his people to drown every newborn Hebrew son. The problem with this literal interpretation, as it has been with other literal interpretations, is that it does not lead to a meaningful Torah teaching: Its message of revenge and communal punishment is clearly inconsistent with the earlier teachings that we read in the Book of Genesis.

Moreover, YHVH's comment about making Pharaoh's heart "strong-willed" appears completely out of YHVH's character. Indeed, we have not read in Torah, nor will we ever read, that YHVH removed an individual's freedom to choose between good (*tov*) and evil (*ra*), or about YHVH causing an individual to miss his or her "mark" (the Torah definition of sin, as it is first defined in the Cain and Abel story). As it was with the story about Moses killing an Egyptian, the Torah appears to once again be challenging us to draw meaningful teachings from this passage, by interpreting the passage as a metaphor. Let's try.

To begin with, YHVH didn't have to actively impede Pharaoh's ability to choose, because Pharaoh was already predisposed to harden his own heart. I am referring to the human condition of favoring material comfort, status, power, and leisure over a life of struggling to be more like *Israel* – a life of wrestling with things both human and divine. We witnessed this ego gratification/struggle-avoidance tendency in the choices made by Adam, Eve, and the serpent; the builders of the Babylon Tower; Abraham's nephew, Lot (who, when given the choice of where to settle, chose the resource-rich lands of the east that reminded him of the prosperous homeland that he had left); Jacob and his many deceits; and also, undoubtedly, in choices that we ourselves have made. Moses obviously understood this, by virtue of his great reluctance to deliver this prophecy to Pharaoh and, for that matter, to the Hebrews.

That is to say that there is nothing particularly special about Pharaoh's choice; we can all identify with it, and have at times probably acted on it. And, like Pharaoh, the more that we feel threatened, the more do we tend to dig in our heels and harden our own hearts in an attempt to protect what we have. Our actions do not require the active intervention of YHVH, for the job was already done: Like Pharaoh, we were all "created" this way.

However, while we may all be predisposed to favor gratification over struggle, we are not condemned by our nature to do so. The Exodus story teaches that we still have a choice. Some will choose the path less travelled, a path that leads us out of Egypt, away from *Mitz'ra'yim*, away from the narrow place and into the barren wilderness (*mid'bar*) where we can "hear the speak."

As to the killing of Pharaoh's first-born, to fully comment on this point we will have to decode the first nine plagues, and we are not yet there in the story. Suffice to say here that the tenth plague, "death of the first-born" is best understood in the context of the nine plagues that preceded it; and that in Torah, one's first-born is symbolic of that person's future. To say, therefore, that YHVH will kill Pharaoh's first-born is to say that both he and his offspring will have no meaningful, purposeful future in *Mitz'ra'yim;* they will live, but their spirit will not.

- **How are the people to serve YHVH?** In the Genesis stories of Chapters 17-20, we learned that serving YHVH means living by the Covenant, which means trying to be like *Israel*; that is, showing willingness and ability to struggle on a daily basis with things both human and divine, and, in turn, with questions about good, evil, and the meaning of life. It means trying to fully inhabit the present by giving up control of that which doesn't belong to us, and by living our lives according to the Twenty-third Psalm ("The Lord is my shepherd"). It is about helping future generations to cross-over into a closer relationship with themselves, with others, and with YHVH.

Put another way, serving YHVH means entering into a co-creation partnership with YHVH. This means "working the Garden, watching over it and guarding it" (Genesis 2). This also means showing the willingness to say "Here I am" on a daily basis. It means trying to conform our many actions and decisions to the shape of our soul. Only by doing so will we feel the sense of wholeness that we desire, which comes from being connected to that which is larger and truer than our own egos. To do the reverse, to conform our soul to our actions, is to become like slaves in Egypt.

As these explanations suggest, serving YHVH has nothing to do with faith and acts of faith. Instead, it is about the core teachings of the Torah, which are about learning how to be more human, to appreciate life before death, and to participate in the ongoing process of creation. None of this is possible when we are living and working in a "narrow place."

- **What does "alive" mean?** We are accustomed to think of life and death in physical terms, but we must remind ourselves that the Torah is first and foremost a theological document and, as such, is focused more on conveying ethical and spiritual teachings than on explaining physical realities.

Think back to the "Garden" story (Genesis 2, 3), where YHVH said to Adam and Eve that *"on the day that you eat from that tree, you must die."* As you we know, they did not die on that day, at least not in the physical sense. From the perspective of Torah, the death that they experienced was a spiritual death, caused by having to leave the Garden. In other words, they moved away from their close relationship with YHVH, and towards a place where the "light" from the first day of creation shines less brightly.

So, when Moses said, *"Pray let me return to my brothers that are in Egypt, that I may see whether they are alive,"* he was saying that he wanted to see if the Children of Israel were moving into a closer relationship with YHVH, which, as was suggested in the commentary to the previous question, is the same as "serving" YHVH.

But, how do we serve YHVH? How do we sustain and enhance our "alive-ness"? We addressed this question earlier, but only in a normative way. Expressions like "entering into a co-creation partnership with YHVH," "working the Garden, watching over it and guarding it," and "showing the willingness to say, 'Here I am'" on a daily basis say little about *how* one goes about doing that. However, the teachings of the Creation and Garden stories offer us a plausible three-part answer that has to do with observing Shabbat, attending to our communal soul, and finding a "soul" mate.

(1) **Shabbat**. We learned from the Creation story that Shabbat is the day when God separated the physical world from the spiritual world. The word "Shabbat" comes from the root *shin-beit-tav*, meaning "to stop." The passage, "On the seventh day, God stopped from all labor," implies that "stopping" is woven into the fabric of creation; it is a fundamental part of creation, just like the creation of the land and of all living things. As such, the Torah is telling us that we can actively participate in the creative process and thereby "serve" YHVH, if we learn the importance of stopping.

As mentioned in the Genesis 1 commentary, most of us live in a work-centric world, where we spend much of our waking hours occupying our minds and bodies with those tasks, responsibilities, and ambitions that we hope will increase our family's security, prosperity, and status. Yet, many of us also yearn for something more than "building pyramids seven days a week in Egypt for someone else." Perhaps we sense that our lives are somehow incomplete, we feel alienated from our true identity, and we desire to feel more whole. Within each of us lies a spiritual side with questions that want to be given voice-- questions like "Who am I, who am I not, why am I, and what is my real purpose?"

Shabbat is about taking the time to listen to these questions, and then to discover personally meaningful answers to them. It is a time of introspection and meditation, when we try to quiet our mind of its work-centric dialogues, listening instead to the voice of our heart (what some refer to as our "inner teachings") and being fully present and living in the moment. Shabbat is about stopping what we are doing long enough to build a relationship with ourselves.

In short, Shabbat is a time when we can renew our spirit, nourish our soul, and be transformed by what we learn about ourselves. Only by better knowing who we are can we begin to shape our labor to the contour of our soul, rather than the other way around. By listening more closely to our inner teachings, we can feel more fulfilled, insightful, and joyful - more able to actively participate in the creation process by doing things that are truly *tov* (i.e., good, or life-enhancing). By observing Shabbat, we can feel more alive. To disregard Shabbat is to be disconnected from God and therefore, from the perspective of Torah, to be (spiritually) dead.

(2) **Communal Soul**. We reasoned from the Garden story that we can serve YHVH by attending to our communal soul. From the perspective of Torah, our soul (*neshemah*) comes from YHVH's breath. Just as YHVH is said to have breathed life into Adam (Genesis 2:7), the lives of all of us are said to come from the same source. The teaching here is that our soul doesn't belong only to us, because it comes from YHVH and it is shared among all of us. As such, it is not about us per se, but about community.

From this perspective, the meaning of life and the feeling of being alive are not solely about seeking our own delight but, rather, about taking care of others. This is what we learn in the passage "YHVH took the human and set him in the garden of delight to work and watch it" (Genesis 2:15).

This teaching is reinforced in Isaiah 58, when he said to his community, "This is not the fast that I desire." Isaiah, who lived approximately 600 years before the common era, was telling his community that Yom Kippur is not about performing mindless rituals of self-denial like fasting, which have no bearing on the well-being of others. Rather, Yom Kippur, which is first reference to Yom Kippur in Leviticus 23: 26-32, where no mention is made to the practice of fasting, is about awakening our collective conscience by caring for those in need, whether their needs be physical, material, emotional, or spiritual. It is about serving YHVH and, in the process, becoming more alive ourselves.

This core teaching is consistent with what is stated in Leviticus 19:18 ("Love your fellow as yourself"); and by Hillel in *Sayings from the Fathers* ("What is hateful to you, do not do to your fellow" – and - "If I am not for myself, who will be for me? And if I am only for myself, then what am I? And if not now, when?"); and much more recently, with Parker Palmer (*A Hidden Wholeness),* who defines the "soul" as that which drives our hunger for wholeness and our desire to feel connected to that which is larger and truer than our own egos.

> As a side bar: Daniel Gilbert, a social psychologist known for his research on the nature of human happiness, and the author of a *New York Times* best-seller, "Stumbling on Happiness," has found that the best predictor of happiness is a person's relationships with others and the amount of time that is spent with family and friends. Indeed, these factors are significantly more meaningful than money, material objects, and other such "narrow" pursuits that many of us substitute for social relationships.

It seems that Professor Gilbert has found empirical support for the "Isaiah hypothesis" --- that it is all about people and community and the communal soul. When we walk mindfully with YHVH by responding to our communal soul, we feel a sense of *shalem,* experience a renewal of body and spirit, and feel more alive. But, when we allow ourselves to become overly involved with our personal needs and wants, we disconnect from YHVH, stop serving YHVH, and become, as it were, less alive and more dead.

(3) **Soul Mate.** Finally, we learned from the Garden story that we can better serve YHVH and increase our capacity to "live" through marriage. In that story YHVH says, "It is not good for the human to be alone." Therefore, "a man leaves his father and his mother and clings to his wife and they become one flesh" (Genesis 2: 24). In Ecclesiastes 4: 9-12, Koheleth likens the union of a man and woman to a "threefold cord," such that the whole is stronger than the sum of its parts.

The Hebrew word for marriage is *ki-dushim*, from the word *kadosh*, or " set apart by God." Shabbat is the first time *kadosh* is mentioned in the Torah, when the seventh day is set apart from the other six because of its spiritual nature, which God referred to as "exceedingly good." Similarly, marriage involves a relationship that is to be set apart from all other relationships, because it too entails a spiritual component.

Specifically, marriage involves a lifelong sharing of two souls. It requires continual commitment, effort, and discipline that draws from both the head and the heart. Through marriage, we can feel a sense of wholeness, or completeness, fulfillment, and a sense of being alive. But, to do so, there must be love.

Scott Peck wrote in "A Road Less Travelled" that love, like God, is something too large and deep to be understood and expressed with words. Love is the willingness to extend our self and our soul for the purpose of nurturing the other's spiritual growth. In return we receive something *tov* from that person. Thus, love is both selfless and selfish, altruistic and reciprocal, and like other *tov* acts of creation, self-sustaining.

As a mystical aside, the Hebrew word for man (*ee-sh*) is made up of three letters, *alev, yud,* and *shin,* while the Hebrew word for woman (*ee-shah*) is also made up of three letters, *alev, shin,* and *hay.* These two words share two letters in common (*alev* and *shin*), while two other letters (*yud* and *hay*) appear only once in each word. The latter pair begins the spelling of God's name (*yud, hay, vov, hay*). The story goes that by removing the name of God from the union of these two words (*yud* and *hay*), that is, by taking out that which sets apart a marriage from other relationships, you end up with *ay-sh*, which is the Hebrew word for fire - something which is all consuming rather than self-sustaining.

To recap, when Moses said, "*Pray let me return to my brothers that are in Egypt, that I may see whether they are alive,*" he may have wanted to see if the Hebrews were periodically stopping during the week to renew their spirits, and caring for those in need, and participating in one special loving, soul-sharing relationship.

.

- **What is the meaning of "Go in peace"?** Recall that *Shalom*, which most of us know to mean "peace," shares the same three-letter root as does the word *Shalem*, which means "wholeness" - a deep sense of oneness with who we are (without internal conflicts) and where we are (in the world around us). *Shalem* is similar in meaning to the Hindi word, "yoga," which means "to unite."

➤ Confronting Pharaoh (Exodus 5, 6)

Summary: *Moses and Aaron said to Pharaoh, "Thus says YHVH: Send free my people, that they may hold a festival to me in the wilderness." He replied, "Who is YHVH that I should listen to his voice?" They said, "The God of the Hebrews has met with us; let us go a three day journey into the wilderness to make an offering to YHVH. Pharaoh replied, "For what reason would I let the people loose from their tasks and their burdens?" And he commanded his slave-drivers to stop giving straw to make bricks; " instead, let them gather their own straw and make just as many bricks, for they must be lax to have the time to cry out."*

When the slave-drivers saw that the people had not finished baking their quota of bricks, they beat the officers of the Children of Israel, whom the slave-drivers had set over them. The officers cried to Pharaoh, saying "Why do you do thus to your servants?" He replied, "The fault is your people, for they took time to cry out." The officers then confronted Moses and Aaron, saying "May YHVH judge you, for you have put into Pharaoh's hands a sword to kill us."

Moses returned to YHVH, saying "For what reason did you send me to Pharaoh? You did not rescue your people. Since I mentioned your name, Pharaoh has dealt only ill with them."

YHVH said to Moses, "Now you will see what I will do to Pharaoh, for with a strong hand he will send them free, I am YHVH. Avraham, Isaac, and Jacob, who I established a covenant with, saw me as God Shaddai, for my name was not known to them. Say to the Children of Israel that I am YHVH who has heard their moaning and will bring you out from your burdens of Egypt and to the land that I promised to your ancestors. And, you shall know that I am your God." But, the people, out of shortness of spirit and exhaustion of body, did not hearken to Moses. Moses said to YHVH, "If the people did not listen to me, why will Pharaoh."

Now, these are the sons of Levi: Gershon, Kehat and Merari. Levi lived to be 137 years. Kehat had four sons, Amram, Yitzhar, Hevron, and Uzziel. Kehat lived to be 133 years. Amram married Yokheved, who bore two sons, Aaron and Moses. And Amram lived to be 137 years old.

Discussion Questions: Why ask for a three day journey? Was YHVH not known to the Patriarchs? Who is Yokheved? What does the number 137 mean?

- **Why ask for a three day journey?** Once again we see the number "three" being used to symbolize the coming of revelation - - a quality of time indicating that we know now (in the present) that we are no longer where we were (past), but have yet to receive a vision of where we are to go (future).

- **Was YHVH not known to the Patriarchs?** This statement is not entirely true, for in Genesis 13, verse 3, Avram said to Bera, "I raise my hand in the presence of YHVH, God Most-High" that I will not take anything that is yours, so that you should not say, 'I made Avram rich.' Perhaps YHVH is saying in Exodus 6 that while Avram might have known YHVH's name well enough to utter it, he did not understand YHVH's character to the extent that it was revealed to Moses at the Burning Bush and will soon be revealed to the Egyptians

- **Who is Yokheved?** The mother of Moses, her name means "One who honors or gives weight to God," in contrast to Pharaoh, who gives weight only to his own heart.

- **What does the number 137 mean?** In Exodus *6: 15-20,* we learn of the paternal lineage of Moses and Aaron, all of whom lived more years than Moses' 120 years. Included are Levi, their great-grandfather, who lived 137 years; Kehat; their grandfather, who lived 133 years; and Amram, their father, who lived 137 years. In our studies, we have learned that most numbers have symbolic meaning. But, what is the meaning of "137" and why is the grandfather of Moses and Aaron singled out for living *only* "133" years? Adding to this puzzle, we read in the concluding chapters about Abraham, Sarah, and Hagar that their son, Ishmael, who - like descendents of Levi - settled near Egypt, also lived 137 years. Perhaps the number "137" once had symbolic meaning to ancient Egyptians?

Bear in mind that numbers in the Torah are sometimes used to symbolize the *absence* of a spiritual condition. For example, in an earlier passage (Genesis 26:34) we learned that Esau turned "forty," but without any hint of a revelatory, transformational experience that would have caused him to cross-over into a closer relationship with himself, with others, and with YHVH; a moment when he would have been able to move forward to a more enlightened future by leaving behind the emotional baggage of the past.

Alternatively, could the Torah be saying that it is not the number of years that we live, but whether we use our allotted time to move our self and our community into a closer relationship with YHVH? Consistent with this latter explanation, Moses' age at the time of his death, a hundred and twenty, might in "Torah-speak" represent the three revelational moments in his life, each represented by the number "forty" : the killing of his Egyptian identity, the vision of the Burning Bush, and the receiving of the Ten Commandments on Sinai.

➢ *The First Four Plagues (Exodus 7 and 8)*

Summary: *YHVH said to Moses, "Speak to Pharaoh all that I speak to you," to which Moses replied, "I am of forskinned lips; how will he listen to me?" YHVH said, "I will make you as a god for Pharaoh, and Aaron will be your prophet. But, I will harden his heart and he will not hearken to you and I will set my hand against Egypt. The Egyptians will know that I am YHVH when I bring the Children of Israel out from their midst with great acts of judgment." Now, Moses was eighty years old when he spoke to Pharaoh, and Aaron was eighty-three.*

YHVH said to Moses, "Speak to Pharaoh that he may send the Children of Israel free from this land. And when you speak with him, say to Aaron to take your staff and throw it down before Pharaoh: Let it become a serpent". They did as YHVH commanded. In response to this display, Pharaoh called for his magicians and they did the same with their staffs. But Aaron's staff proceeded to swallow up each of their staffs, yet Pharaoh's heart remained strong-willed.

> *(1) YHVH said to Moses, " Go to Pharaoh in the morning, when he goes to the Nile, and say to him, 'YHVH, the God of the Hebrews, has sent me to you saying: Send free my people so that they may serve me in the wilderness!' By this you shall know that I am YHVH: I will strike -- with the staff that is in my hand -- upon the water that is in the Nile, and it will change into blood. The fish will all die and the river will reek." YHVH said to Moses to say to Aaron, "Before the eyes of Pharaoh, take your staff and stretch your hand over all the waters in Egypt – even in wooden containers - and let them become blood!" But*

the magicians of Egypt did the same, and so Pharaoh's heart remained strong-willed, and he did not hearken to them.

(2) *YHVH said to Moses, "Go to Pharaoh and say, 'Send free My people that they may serve Me And if you refuse, I will smite your entire territory with frogs that will come into your house, bedroom, upon your couch, into your ovens and onto your dough-pans.' Stretch out your hand over the waters of Egypt and make the frogs ascend upon the land."*

The magicians did the same, but this time Pharaoh called Moses and Aaron and said, "Plead with YHVH that he may remove the frogs from me and my people, and I will send the people free." And Moses cried out to YHVH and the frogs died and were piled up heaps upon heaps, and the land reeked. But, Pharaoh made his heart heavy with stubbornness.

(3) *And YHVH said to Moses, "Tell Aaron to stretch out your staff and strike the dust of the land; it will become lice throughout all the land of Egypt and the lice will be on every man and beast." The magicians tried, but could not duplicate this event, and told Pharaoh, "This is the finger of god," but Pharaoh's heart remained strong-willed and he did not listen to them.*

(4) *YHVH said to Moses, "Start early in the morning, and go to where Pharaoh goes for water and say to him that if he does not let my people go so that they can serve me, then I will send flies upon you/him and your/his servants, people, and houses, and you/they will all be covered with them. But, I will keep the region of Goshen distinct, so that there will be no insects there, for it is where my people are situated."*

YHVH did this, and heavy swarms of flies came to Pharaoh's house, into the houses of his servants, and throughout all the land of Egypt. Pharaoh called for Moses and Aaron and said, "Go to your god in the land!" Moses once again asks Pharaoh to let the people go a three day's journey into the wilderness and they shall make an offering to YHVH. Pharaoh replies, "I will send you free, but you are not to go too far! Plead for me!"

Moses pleaded for Pharaoh and YHVH did according to Moses' words and the flies were removed. But, Pharaoh made his heart heavy with stubbornness and did not set the people free.

Discussion Questions: Did the plagues actually happen? Why were there ten plagues? What is the meaning of the first, second, third and fourth plagues?

- **Did the plagues actually happen?** The Hebrew word often translated as "plagues," *ma'kah*, literally means "blows," - - as in the blowing of the shofar - - something that awakens our senses from their slumber and captures our attention. The story tells of how the first few plagues affected everyone, from the royalty down to the cattle in the fields, including Pharaoh's laborers. Only those who were awakened by the blows and grasped their meaning left *Mitz'ra'yim* (a "narrow" place), while those who were not awakened remained enslaved in their narrow place—a place that is materially rich, but spiritually dead

Did the plagues happen? The Torah's stories may contain references to specific historical events, but they were not necessarily written to be historical accuracy. Rather, the Torah, which means "teachings", was written to convey ethical and spiritual wisdoms. Accordingly, "blows" are being used as symbols to make the point that it takes a lot of hardship to get us to change our ways. Will we listen to the "blows?" Will it cause us to leave our narrow places? How many blows will it take?

* **Why "ten" plagues?** Recall from the Book of Genesis the various times that the number ten appears. It appears in Genesis 16, when Sarai says to Avram, *ten* years after being in the Land, that "YHVH has obstructed me from bearing." It appears again in Genesis 23, when the story tells us that Abraham's servant took *ten* camels with him when venturing to find a bride for Yitzhak. And it appears in Genesis 30 when Yaakov says that Lavan "changed my wages ten times over." Think also about the Ten Commandments, the Ten Days of Awe between Rosh Hashanah and Yom

Kippur, the ten generations that separated Adam from Noah and Noah from Abraham, and the custom of "tithing" (see Genesis 14:20 and 28:20). There are said to be Ten Lost Tribes of Israel (those other than Judah and Benjamin). There are Ten Sephirot in the Kabbalistic Tree of Life. And, in Judaism, ten adults (a *minyan*) are the required quorum for prayer services.

In these and other references, "ten" usually signifies a sufficient number to capture one's attention and strike one's spirit. For example, if we cannot find forgiveness during the ten days of awe, we are unlikely to find it on the eleventh day. Ten is the number of times that Lavan will have to change Yaakov's wages before Yaakov finally says, "Enough!" and begins his preparation to leave. Similarly, if ten plagues are not enough to cause the Hebrews to leave Egypt, an eleventh likely won't do it.

- **What is the meaning of the first blow, blood?** The story tells of a time when all the water in this arid land turned to blood; when the "river of life" – which in ancient times was a symbol of fertility, and the source of all life, - became a "river of death," totally undrinkable. Can we taste it? Will the taste of this tainted water awaken us? Is it telling us that we have no future here?

Pharaoh doesn't seem to grasp what has just happened. An Egyptian god – the River – a core in the belief structure of his empire - has just been assassinated, yet he is unmoved. Instead he is comforted by the knowledge that his magicians seem to be able to perform the same effect.

Notice two glaring inconsistencies in the story. First, if YHVH turned all the water in the land into blood, what was left for the magicians to act on? Second, and more telling, while most of the other blows are given an ending date, this first blow is not. Why? Might the Torah be reminding us not to take the story literally, for to do so would lead the story to a very different ending? Namely, if all the water in this narrow place turned, forever, into blood, all living things – Pharaoh, the Hebrews, the Egyptians, all the crops in the fields, all the animals -- would soon die. There would be no exodus into the wilderness and no revelation at Sinai.

- **What is the meaning of the second blow, frogs?** Originating in the waters, these amphibians -- which in ancient Egypt represented rebirth and resurrection -- moved to the land and died. The decaying bodies should be awakening our sense of smell. Their death should be sending the message that narrow places offer no hope of salvation and resurrection. Can we smell it? Will it make us want to leave?

  Evidently Pharaoh can smell it. For the first time in the story, he reluctantly acknowledges YHVH as a force more powerful than that of his magicians. But his awareness is short-lived. The thought of allowing his laborers to leave their jobs even for three days is apparently more obnoxious to him than the stench from the dead frogs. Can we identify with the predicament facing Pharaoh? Do we often find ourselves struggling with our "narrow, *Mitz'ra'yim* side?

- **What is the meaning of the third blow, lice?** Lice afflict our skin and our sense of touch. Notice how the blows have gotten progressively more personal, starting in the water, moving onto the land, and now moving onto us. Also, unlike the first two blows, this blow comes to Pharaoh without warning; even the magicians realize that they are competing with a "finger of god" that is more powerful that anything that they or Pharaoh can duplicate. Pharaoh, however, too stuck in his narrow ways, is unmoved by their plea.

- **What is the meaning of the fourth blow, flies?** If the first three blows weren't enough to awaken Pharaoh and all the other Egyptians from their slumber, how about flies, a constant source of annoyance which can be seen, heard, and felt? If the blood, frogs, and lice weren't enough, might the flies awaken us?

  Apparently it is awakening some, for the text states, *"I will keep the region of Goshen distinct, for it is where my people are situated."* What this means is that for the first time, a distinction is made between those Egyptians who are awakened and those who are not, with those who are awakened being counted among the Hebrews. That said, it will still take six more blows to cause the awakened ones to act on their own behalf and leave their narrow place.

➤ The Next Three Plagues (Exodus 9)

(5) YHVH said to Moses, "Come to Pharaoh and say, 'Thus says YHVH, the God of the Hebrews: Set free my people that they may serve me! If you refuse, then my hand will be on your livestock with an exceedingly heavy pestilence'" And, YHVH again made a distinction, between the livestock of Israel and that of Egypt. And all the livestock of Egypt died.

(6) YHVH said to Moses and Aaron, "Take fistfuls of soot from a furnace and let Moses toss it heavenward before Pharaoh's eyes – it will become fine dust on all the land of Egypt, on every Egyptian man and beast, even upon Pharaoh's magicians, becoming boils that sprout into blisters." But, YHVH made Pharaoh's heart strong-willed, and he did not set the Hebrews free.

(7) YHVH said to Moses, "Start early in the morning, and say to Pharaoh, 'Thus says YHVH: Send free my people so that they may serve me! Otherwise, I will send all of my blows upon your heart and against your servants and people so that you may know that there is none like me throughout all the land.'

'Indeed, by now I could have struck you and your people with pestilence and you would have vanished from the land, but I have not, and instead have let you withstand so that you may see my power and recount my Name.'

'But, still you have not set my people free, so tomorrow I will cause rain to come down as exceedingly heavy hail. Send word to all in the field to seek shelter, for all living things

found in the field – people, cattle, trees and plants - will die!'" And it was so. Only in the region of Goshen was there no hail.

Pharaoh sent for Moses and Aaron and said to them: "This time I have sinned; YHVH is the one in the right, and I and my people are the ones in the wrong! Plead with YHVH; let me send you free." Moses replied: "As soon as I have gone out of the city, I will spread my hands to YHVH and the hail will be no more. But as for you and your servants, I know well that you do not yet stand in fear before the face of YHVH."

When Pharaoh saw that the hail had stopped, he continued to sin, as YHVH had told Moses that he would.

Discussion Questions: What is the meaning of the fifth, sixth and seventh plagues?

- **What is the meaning of the fifth blow, murrain (death to the livestock)?** In ancient times, livestock were not only the main source of wealth, but also of food. Their death symbolized the collapse of the local economy and widespread hunger – things that Pharaoh would feel in his pocketbook and belly.

  Did all the livestock really have to die just to awaken Pharaoh and the Egyptians? If we take the Passover story literally, then the answer is "Yes" ; but, as with other stories in Torah, the writers provide enough hints to discourage us from taking a literal interpretation. For example, if the story about the plagues is true, then all of the animals that died from the first blow would die again with the fifth (murrain) blow, yet be afflicted by the sixth blow (boils), only to die again with the seventh blow, hail.

- **What is the meaning of the sixth blow, boils?** Boils represent a more personal assault than the previous five blows, for they can be thought of as toxic fluids that come from inside of us - what might be thought of as spiritual contamination that comes from living too long in a *Mitz'ra'yim*.

- **What is the meaning of the seventh blow, hail?** It is said to come down from the heavens, striking dead all that are in the fields, including all people and livestock. Hail is frozen water, frozen like the hearts of those who still deny their longing for a more meaningful life. Notice how this blow was introduced with a warning to all *Egyptians* and a chance for them to save themselves. (Something new.)

➢ The Final Three Plagues (Exodus 10, 11)

(8) Moses and Aaron came to Pharaoh and said, "Thus says YHVH: ' How long will you refuse to humble yourself before me? If you refuse to send my people free, I will bring locust into your territory. They will cover the ground, consume what remains for you from the hail, and fill your houses.'"

Pharaoh's servants pleaded with him: "How long shall this one be a snare to us. Send the men free. Do you not yet know that Egypt is lost?"

Pharaoh asked Moses: "Who is it that will go with you to serve your God?" Moses replied, "It will be our elders, our young ones, our sheep and oxen, for it is YHVH's pilgrimage-festival for us." To which Pharaoh said, "Why also the young ones – your faces are set towards ill!"

So, Moses stretched out his staff and YHVH led in an east wind which brought in a horde of locust and the ground became dark. Quickly Pharaoh called for Moses and Aaron, and confessed that he had sinned against YHVH. "Plead that your God remove this death from me."

They did as Pharaoh had asked and YHVH reversed the strong sea wind, which bore the locust away and dashed them into the Sea of Reeds. But, YHVH made Pharaoh's heart strong-willed and he did not send the Children of Israel free.

(9) *YHVH told Moses to stretch out his hand over the heavens and let there be darkness over the land for three days, so dark that "a man could not see his brother." But, for all the Children of Israel, there was light in their settlements.*

Pharaoh called for Moses and said, "Go serve YHVH, even your young ones, but leave your sheep and oxen here." Moses replied "Even our livestock must go with us, for we must give an offering and do not yet know how we are to serve YHVH until we come there." Pharaoh did not consent, but instead said, "Go from me! You shall not see my face again. Be on your watch for should you again see my face, on that day you shall die!"

(10). *YHVH said to Moses: " I will cause one more blow, afterwards Pharaoh will send you free from here. Indeed he will drive you out. But first, ask of your neighbors for objects of silver and gold." YHVH then said, "In the middle of the night, I will go forth throughout the land of Egypt and every first born shall die, even the first born of beasts. Then a cry will be heard throughout the land, the likes of which has never been and which will never be again. But against the Children of Israel no harm will come, in order that you know that YHVH makes a distinction between Egypt and Israel."*

Moses went to Pharaoh in flaming anger, but Pharaoh's heart was too strong-willed to hear.

Discussion questions: What is the meaning of the eighth, ninth, and tenth blows?

- **What is the meaning of the eighth blow, locust?** Like the previous plague, hail, locust seemed to come down from the heavens. They consumed every bit of food left from the hail, leaving nothing for the Egyptians and their livestock to eat. Again, I point out that this event cannot be taken literally, for if it were to have occurred in the manner described, those Egyptians who had not died of thirst (remember that the first plague was never said to end) would soon enough die of starvation. And while the eighth blow did end - in the sense that the locust horde were all blown into the Sea of Reeds - the desolation that they brought would remain at least until the next growing season, months away.

- **What is the meaning of the ninth blow, darkness?** The ninth plague brings us back to Day 1 of Creation, to a time when light was separated from darkness. Recall from the reading of the Creation story that this light was distinguished from that of physical light, for it was said to have been spoken into existence three days before the day that the sun and moon were created. We concluded that the light of Day 1 was intended to represent spiritual light and that darkness represents the absence of that light.

But, what is spiritual light? The writers of Exodus imply that it is the light that enables us "to see the face of our brother." This last point requires some explanation. In ancient cultures, "face" had a special meaning. To say that "I see your face" is to say that I have taken the time to develop a deep understanding of you. It epitomizes what Buber refers to as an "I-Thou" relationship. Recall from earlier comments that to be bonded in such "I-Thou" relationships is to feel grace, love, compassion, insight, and awe. Each such bond offers us the opportunity to glimpse through to the eternal. Accordingly, "spiritual light" can be thought of as the connecting soul-sharing tissue in which a community of relationships is formed and sustained.

In contrast, darkness, at least as the term is defined in the text, connotes relationships that are superficial, disconnected, and rife with conflict. As I previously noted in the commentary on the Joseph story (Genesis 42:7-12), the apparent non-recognition of family members has been a recurring theme throughout the Torah. For example, Lot claimed to have no recollection of sleeping with his two daughters; Isaac mistook

Jacob for his brother Esau; Jacob was oblivious to the fact that he was bedding Leah rather than her sister, Rachel; Judah did not recognize that he was sleeping with Tamar; and none of Joseph's brothers recognized him in Pharaoh's house. It follows that one who cannot "see" another will also have great difficulty "seeing" himself or herself.

The difference between these Genesis examples of darkness and that of the ninth blow in Exodus is that the ninth blow affected everyone and not just relationships within a single family. For those still residing in *Mitz'rayim* (a narrow place), the blow either opened their eyes to what had been missing in their lives, or, as it was with Pharaoh, closed their eyes (and hearts) tighter. Pharaoh, and others like him, was too stuck in the past and the benefits that the past provided to willingly accept change. While he initially appeared enlightened by some of the blows (e.g., *"confessed that he had sinned against YHVH"*), he quickly returned to his habitual ways of interacting with the Hebrews and with himself.

The ninth blow has a different effect on the Hebrews. The light provided these more awakened individuals with a portal to what life might be like in the Promised Land. By doing so, it increased their desire to leave that which had become familiar and to search for a better, more meaningful way.

- **What is the meaning of the tenth blow, death of the first born?** As I have done with other troublesome references in Torah, I will try to draw a meaningful teaching from the tenth blow by avoiding its literal meaning and, instead, delve deeper into its ethical message. In Torah, as in many cultures, children are understood to represent our future. If we raise them in a home imbued with the values of enslavement and narrowness, then they may never learn a better way. They will be living a life that is not their own, a life that is not personally meaningful to them. They will live, but their ability to appreciate life will be dead. As for the "first born", Everett Fox points out that in many ancient cultures, the first born – be they of fruit, animals, or human beings - were viewed as the best that nature has to offer, and therefore often selected for sacrifice to the gods (page 322).

As such, the tenth blow, coupled with the previous nine are signaling all who have the capacity to listen that they need to leave their narrow place because they have no future there. Just as Avram had to *"Go forth from your land and from your father's house, to the land that I will let you see"* (Genesis 12), the purpose of the blows is to prepare the people to participate in a communal *Lekh Lekha*.

Chapter 7: Israel in the Wilderness

Introduction: The tenth blow, the death of the first born, is about to happen, and after it does, Pharaoh will finally agree to set the Children of Israel free. So begins the exodus of the people from *Mitz'rayim*, the narrow place, to the *midbar*, the wilderness where they will "hear YHVH speak." Along the way they will cross the Reed Sea, enter the wilderness of Shur, journey to places with intriguing names like *Sukkot, Maror, Elim, Syn,* and *Refidim*, be attacked by Amalek, and receive their daily portion of *manna*. As Everett Fox points out, those who try to locate the mentioned places or explain the existence of manna miss the point of the biblical writings, which are more concerned with conveying a teaching than with being historically or scientifically correct.

➤ The Initial Preparation (Exodus 12):

Summary: *YHVH said to Moses and Aaron to let this new moon be for you the beginning of new moon of the year. On the tenth day after this moon, each Israel household shall take an unblemished lamb from their respective herd. On the fourteenth day they shall slay their lambs, placing some of the blood on the doorposts of their houses and on their gates.*

They are then to eat the meat, along with matzot and bitter-herbs, while YHVH will proceed through Egypt and strike down every firstborn, from man to beast, but will pass over the entrances of those houses showing the blood sign posts. YHVH said that the people shall celebrate this day as a pilgrimage for YHVH and for seven days eat nothing with ferments until the sun sets on the twenty-first day of the month.

And it will be that when your children say to you: What does this service mean to you, say it is the slaughter meal of Passover to YHVH who passed over the houses of the Children of Israel in Egypt while dealing blows to the Egyptians.

Now it was the middle of the night when YHVH struck down every firstborn in the land of Egypt, even of the beasts. There was a great cry in Egypt, for there was not a house in which there is not a dead man.

Pharaoh arose and called for Moses and Aaron, saying "Go out from amidst my people, you and the Children of Israel, even your herd, serve YHVH according to your words and bring a blessing even on to me!"

Now the Children of Israel did as Moses said, which was to ask the Egyptians for silver, gold, and clothing. YHVH had given favor in the eyes of the Egyptians and they let themselves be asked of.

The Children of Israel and a mixed multitude of others, including about 600,000 men, moved from Ra'amses to Sukkot, along with their many livestock.

Discussion questions: When is the New Year celebrated? Why take an unblemished lamb and why do so "ten" days after the year's first new moon? Where is Egypt? Why did the Egyptians hold a favorable view of the Children of Israel? Who were included in the "mixed multitude" that left Egypt? Where is Sukkot? Did the Exodus from Egypt really happen? And, to quote one of the Four Questions asked at the Passover Seder, "Why on other nights do we eat leavened or unleavened bread, but on this night only unleavened bread?"

- **When is the Hebrew "New Year"?** The tradition is to celebrate the New Year on the first two days of the year's seventh new moon, which occurs at the beginning of the month of *Tishrei*. This is the holiday of *Rosh Hashanah,* which means "the head of the year." It is during this holiday - also known as the Day of Remembrance, and the birthday of the world - when New Year wishes are extended and the numeric year of the Hebrew calendar advances.

Exodus 12, however, hints at Passover as a second New Year. It begins on the 14th day of the year's first new moon (the month of *Nisan*), which falls on the second Shabbat of the new calendar year. This day coincides with the year's first full moon (given the moon's 28 day cycle) and continues for seven days, or up to the time when YHVH dealt the tenth blow (plague) on the Egyptians. Whereas Rosh Hashanah is associated with the birth of the world, Passover, a springtime holiday, is symbolizes the re-birth of nature and the birth of the Israelite nation.

Two New Year holidays in the same calendar year? Some believe that during biblical times each year as we now measure it may have represented two years. This would mean that Avram left home when he was at a much more realistic age of 37.5, Sarai gave birth to Isaac when she was 45, and Moses died at the age of 60.

Notice that the number "seven" plays a prominent role in the dating of Rosh Hashanah and Passover. As a quick review, the Hebrew calendar is organized around the notion of spiritual time and therefore uses the number seven as the base to represent the completion of a cycle of creation. Further discussion on the significance of this number can be found in Chapter 2's commentary on Genesis 1.

- **Why "ten days"?** The number "ten" in Torah represents an amount sufficiently large to capture our attention and affect our behavior. For example, ten days should be adequate time to prepare our household for departure from Egypt if we are fully committed to leaving. For more examples of the use of the number "ten" in Torah, refer to the commentary on the question, "Why ten plagues?" in Chapter 6.

- **Where is Egypt?** In the story about Hagar, Sarai's Egyptian maidservant (Genesis 16), we learned that the Torah refers to Egypt as *Mitz'rayim,* meaning a "narrow place" - narrow not only in a physical sense - it's population was and is centered around the Nile for obvious reasons of physical and commercial necessity - but also spiritually. That is to say that *Mitz'rayim* is any place where we give more attention to our material pursuits than we do to the questions of good, evil, and life.

Contrast the spiritual meaning of *Mitz'rayim* with that of wilderness. The Hebrew word for "wilderness" is *mid-bar*, which is built on the same three letter root as the word *da-ber*, meaning "speak." From the perspective of Torah, *Mitz'rayim* are are narrow places where we cannot hear YHVH speak (or if you prefer, "our teacher from within"), while the *mid-bar* are those places where we can. In the *mid-bar*, we come to terms with who we were, while getting a glimpse at who we have the capacity to become. It is both a place of struggle and a source of inspiration. David Ben-Gurion said, "The true appeal of the wilderness is that it brings one closer to the divine. Here a person sees primeval nature in all its strengths, unchanged and undisturbed by human hands."

- **Why an unblemished lamb?** The Hebrew word for unblemished is "*tam*." It is used to refer to a sacrificial animal or person (only three individuals are described as being *tam*: Noah, Job, and the simple son at the Passover Seder) that is uncorrupted, pure, and beyond reproach. In Exodus 12, YHVH appears to be testing the sincerity of the people: Will they voluntarily give up control of something valuable which they had no hand in creating? Are they ready to make the kind of sacrifices that are required to leave their narrow place? Are we?

- **Why did the Egyptians hold a favorable view of the Children of Israel?** The Torah mentions that the Egyptians freely gave the Children of Israel silver, gold and clothing. What makes their act of generosity appear so astounding is that it came on the heels of the tenth blow, a time when every Egyptian household experienced the deaths of all first-born humans and animals. This final plague came soon after the first nine, each said to have brought great suffering to every Egyptian household. So, why a favorable view?

Like many stories in the Torah, the tale of the ten blows clearly should not be taken literally. Had it been based on historical fact, the tenth blow could not have happened for the simple reason that there would be no Egyptians alive, first- born or otherwise, to suffer that blow. The first blow (all water turned to blood) would have wiped out the entire population due to thirst, as would the eight blow(locust) due to hunger. As for the livestock, they would also have perished from the first blow, only to die again with the fifth (murrain), sixth (boils), seventh (hail), and eighth plagues.

What then did the blows/plagues represent? In the previous chapter we likened them to the sounding of the *shofar* (ram's horn), each blow representing a different assault on our senses: each intended to awaken us from our slumber, capture our attention, and make us more aware of our need to leave our narrow place.

To this explanation I would add that at the time of the blows, most everyone living in *Mitz'rayim*, including the descendants of Jacob were Egyptians, living a narrow existence, distracted by material pursuits and thus unable to hear YHVH speak. Bear in mind that four hundred years have passed since Jacob and his family settled in this land, more than enough time for the Children of Israel to be fully assimilated and absorbed into the culture of the larger population, whether through friendships, intermarriage, or coercion.

Thus, the Egyptians weren't gifting their enemies, but rather their friends, neighbors, and in some cases even some family members. The Egyptians – now defined as those who chose not to leave in their narrow place - might have admired the courage of those who were leaving, wishing that they could summon the resolve to do so. Again, it is not easy to change our ways, particularly when we live in a prosperous society and are reaping the benefits of that prosperity.

- **Who were included in the "mixed multitude"?** The simple answer is anyone – be they Jew or Egyptian or whoever – who was awakened by the "blows" to the realization that there is more to life than building pyramids for someone else in *Mitz'rayim* seven days a week. Put another way, the mixed multitude included those individuals who, while not necessarily biologically linked to Abraham and Sarah, were like them in spirit: willing to trade the comfort, familiarity, and security of their prosperous homeland for the uncertainties of a land unknown to them.

- **Where is Sukkot?** In the context of Exodus 12, "*Sukkot*" is not referring to temporary dwellings that those who left *Mitz'rayim* inhabited during their forty-years in the wilderness, nor necessarily to a specific location. Instead, the term relates to the seven-day harvest festival that begins on the first full moon of the seventh month, on the fifth day after Yom Kippur in the early autumn. It is a holiday of thanksgiving for nature's bounty. Perhaps the text is telling us that the Children of Israel, having planted the seeds of freedom in the year's first new moon (Passover), are now experiencing the sweetness of their first harvest (Sukkot) and a glimpse into what their lives could be like in the future when they enter the Promised Land.

- **Did the Exodus really happen?** Like many Biblical stories, the Exodus tale appears to be recounting a historical event, and yet presents details that are inconsistent with reason. Consider the claim that about 600,000 men left *Mitz'rayim*. We can assume that roughly another 600,000 women left with them and with the women at least another 600,000 children. (And in Exodus 17: 3 we learn that those who left brought their livestock: *"For what reason did you bring us up from Egypt, only to bring death to me, to my children, and my livestock?"*) All in all, the test is therefore suggesting that approximately two million people wandered for 40 years in a relatively small region of the Sinai desert- - and yet curiously not a single artifact has been found in that region to suggest that a mass exodus ever happened!

If the Exodus story did not happen as depicted, then why do we celebrate Passover every spring to commemorate such an event? What Torah teaching can we derive from this folklore? Why do we say at the Passover Seder that we were once slaves in *Mitz'rayim*, when in fact we weren't slaves – at least not slaves as we think of them from the stories of the pre-Civil War days in America? And, why does Moses' name not appear even once in the *Haggadah* - the book about the Exodus story which was written about one thousand years ago and read aloud each year at the Seder – when Moses is clearly the lead character in the Torah's telling of the story?

In the attempt to address these questions, let's examine what some of the key symbols in the narrative represent, beginning with *matzot*.

(1) Why *matzot* and not ferments? Or, as phrased as the second of the four questions in the *Haggadah* : "Why on other nights do we eat leavened or unleavened bread, but on this night only unleavened bread?"

The traditional explanation is that the Children of Israel had to eat unleavened bread on the night of the tenth plague because they knew that they would soon be chased by the Egyptians, and therefore they did not have the time to let the dough rise. "*And thus you are to eat, your hips girded, your sandals on your feet, your sticks in your hand*" (Exodus 12:11). This is why *matzot* is often called the "bread of haste and affliction."

With all due respect to the tradition, I find this literal explanation lacking because it offers no teaching. Remember, the word, "Torah" means teaching. What lessons does this explanation hold that would enable us become more human, appreciate life before death, and participate in the ongoing process of creation? What guidance does it provide to help us to transform our consciousness to more life-enhancing levels of awareness, even during mundane or trying times? How can this explanation help us move forward on our personal and spiritual journeys?

To begin to answer these questions, it is important to first note that the word *matzot* means "to drain out." That is to say that unlike ordinary leavened bread, which is made from yeast, flour, water, sugar, eggs, butter, and salt, *matzot* is made only from flour and water. Put in symbolic terms, *matzot* represents something pure, unblemished, consisting of only the basics and drained of any extras – of any *chu-matze*.

What does *matzot* have to do with being freed from slavery? We can think of it as symbolizing our true essence – our inner voice that we have difficulty hearing until we can drain out all of the extras that "enslave" us by hiding our authentic selves from ourselves and from others. Were there "extras" in Egypt 3,400 years ago? Remember, at this time in history, long before there was a "middle class", Egypt was the place to be. It was a center of culture, trade, and military might; a place where its so-called "slaves" were provided with shelter, food, water, and steady work, protection from neighboring nations, material comfort, and even some silver, gold, and livestock.

So, what teaching does this second explanation hold? Why on this night do we only eat unleavened bread? Might the Torah be telling us to eat *matzot* on this night to remind ourselves that prosperity often exacts a cost: It can enslaves us, cause us to not hear the "blows"; cause us to focus more attention on accumulating *chu-matze* (unessential extras) than on building closer relationships with ourselves, our family, and our community. We eat *matzot* on this night to remind us of whom we really are and why it is important to leave narrow places.

(2) **Why do we eat "bitter herbs"?** The literal explanation is that the bitter herbs (*maror*) are eaten at the Seder to remind us of the bitterness of Egyptian bondage. The less literal explanation is that the bitter herbs symbolizes the sadness that we feel once we realize how much time we've wasted chasing after the "extras" while ignoring what truly matters.

(3) **Why does the "*charoset*" that we also to eat at the Seder taste sweet?**
Charoset represents the mud bricks that the workers formed as they toiled to build Pharaoh's pyramids. Therefore, we would expect it to taste at least as bitter as the herbs, yet it tastes sweet. Some have explained that its sweetness symbolizes the seductive, almost narcotic quality of *chu-matze,* specifically how it can draw us in and enslave us with promises of pleasure, comfort and status, all the while taking control of our thoughts and actions.

(4) What is the Exodus story really about? It is about the journey that many of us face as we struggle with the big questions like: Who am I? Am I living a meaningful life and what is my relationship with the eternal? As with Avram and Sarai in Genesis 12, the Exodus story is also about leaving (*lekh lekha*) the security and comforts of home for a journey into the unknown (the "Wilderness"), with the hope of discovering a more meaningful life (our "Land of Promise"). And, as implied by the *Haggadah* – we don't need Moses to show us the way, for the teachings from the Torah can serve as our moral compass.

(5) Who are the four sons? The *Haggadah*, tells of four sons, three of whom asks a question pertaining to the Passover Holiday. The "wise" son asks "What are the meaning of the precepts, laws and regulations the YVHV commanded you to do?" The "wicked" son asks "What does this service mean to you?" The "simple" son asks "What does all this mean?" The fourth son, meanwhile, does not yet know how to ask.

These questions come directly from the Torah. The wise son's question, which reflects a greater level of informed inquiry than do those from his brothers, can be found in the Book of Deuteronomy 6:20. The wicked son's question comes directly from Exodus 12:26. The careful reader will note that there is nothing particularly wicked about this son's question. Rather, it is the kind of question expected from a boy in his teens as he tries to establish his own identity by separating himself from that of the adults around him. The "simple" son also suffers from an unfortunate label, for there is nothing "simple" about his question, which is found Exodus 13:14. In Hebrew, this son is referred to as "*tam*", which we previously defined as meaning unblemished and pure, holding no preconceptions – the kind of naiveté that we might associate with a young child. Recall that aside from the simple son, only Noah and Job are referred to as "*tam*". Finally, the son who doesn't ask is referenced in Exodus 13:8.

Why four sons? Recall from Chapter 3's commentary on Genesis 13, where we asked, "What was Avram really seeing?" that the number "four" appears numerous times in Torah, usually to signify the components of spiritual wholeness. In the case of the four sons, we witness the fullness of a family's past, present and future, as our children pass through their natural and normal stages of development, beginning with the son too young to ask ("primal emptiness"), to the son still unblemished by life's trials ("naivetés"), to the rebellious teenager ("individuation") and finally, to the son that is approaching adulthood.

(6) Why do we read four questions? The Haggadah presents four questions, which are customarily read by the family's youngest member: (1) Why is this night different from all other nights? (2) Why on other nights do we eat leavened or unleavened bread, but on this night only unleavened bread? (3) Why on other nights we do not dip (immerse) even once, and on this night twice? (4) Why on all other nights do we eat and drink either sitting or reclining, but on this night we all recline?

The answer to the first question is obvious: This night commemorates the night that we left the safe confines of our narrow places and began in earnest our personal and spiritual journeys. We already addressed the second question under the recent heading "Why *matzot* and not ferments?" We partially addressed the third question: Dipping symbolizes spiritual purification. We dip once in the Reed Sea to wash away the enslavements that we accumulated while living in a narrow place. We dip a second time to prepare ourselves to enter the Promised Land, a place of enlightenment, when we cross the Jordan River in order to cleanse ourselves of the questions, fears and doubts that we faced in the wilderness.

As for the fourth question, "reclining" represents the freedom to periodically stop, rest, reflect, and appreciate where we came from, where we are, and where we are going. To recline is to observe the Sabbath and say *dai'yay-noo*; that is, to truly feel and know that where we are on our journey at any given moment is sufficient.

➤ The Journey Begins (Exodus 13, 14)

Summary: *YHVH went before the people by day in a pillar of cloud to lead them the way, and by night in a pillar of fire to light their way. Going by day and by night, the people moved from Sukkot to Etam, lying at the edge of the wilderness, by way of the Sea of Reeds.*

YHVH told Moses to speak to the Children of Israel, saying that they may turn back and encamp before Pi ha-Hirot, between Migdol and the sea, before Baal-Tzefon.

Seeing this, Pharaoh will say, "They are confused in the land. The wilderness has closed them in!" And with a strong-willed heart, he will also say, "What is it that we have done, that we have sent free Israel from serving us?" He had his chariot harnessed along with all of Egypt's other chariots and the army and pursued the people, overtaking them by their encampment by the sea.

The people lifted up their eyes, saw Egypt marching towards them, and cried out to YHVH. To Moses, they said, "Is it because there are no graves in Egypt that you have taken us out to die in the wilderness? Didn't we say to you to let us alone that we may serve Egypt? Indeed, it is better for us serving Egypt than our dying in the wilderness!"

Moses replied, "Do not be afraid; stand back and watch YHVH's deliverance which he will work for you today."

YHVH said to Moses, "Hold your staff high, stretch it out over the sea and split it." I will cause the sea to go back with a fierce east wind all night so that the Children of Israel can move through the sea upon dry land. The Egyptians will follow. When they do "stretch out your hand over the sea and the waters shall return." It will cover the chariots and all of the riders. None will remain. The Egyptians will know that I am YHVH.

And when Israel saw Egypt dead by the shore and the great hand that YHVH had wrought against Egypt, they held YHVH in awe and trusted YHVH's servant, Moses.

Discussion Questions: Why is YHVH represented by pillars of clouds and fire? Where is the Sea of Reeds? Why did so many Egyptian soldiers have to drown? Where are Pi ha-Hirot and Baal-Tzefon? Are the "Children" the true "Children of Israel"?

- **Why depict YHVH as pillars of clouds and fire?** YHVH was described in Genesis 1 as a wind-spirit (*ru'akh elohim*) or "God's breath" that hovers (as, in being fluid or always moving) over the dark face of the waters of pre-creation. The Torah was likening YHVH to something that lacks form and substance yet can be observed in the things that it touches - like a bush or a field of wheat. In other words, we can experience YHVH, but never know YHVH's true essence because *Ehyeh asher ehyeh;* "YHVH will be whatever YHVH will be."

  This characterization of YHVH as an unknowable abstraction is seen again in Exodus 13. We know that clouds and fire are light and airy; therefore they cannot be imagined to take on discrete geometric forms like pillars. As with "wind-spirit", the juxtaposing of pillars with cloud and fire suggests a counter-intuitive opposite intended to transcend our understandings of reality.

- **Where is the Sea of Reeds?** Many of us are familiar the movie, "The Ten Commandments". We recall the scene where Moses - played by Charlton Heston - first separates the Red Sea to allow the Children of Israel safe passage, then closes it to bring the total demise of the Egyptian war machine. But, is this scene fact or folklore?

  I strongly suspect "folklore". To begin with, the name "Red Sea" never appears in the Torah, which instead refers to the sea as the "Reed Sea." There is a quantum difference between those two bodies of water. The Red Sea is a large and wide body of water, deep enough to easily handle large, ocean-bound cargo ships. In contrast, a

Sea of Reeds points to a shallow, marshy body. It may not be perplexing why so many continue to refer to the Reed Sea as the Red Sea, for the parting of the Red Sea would represents the "mother of all miracles."

A word about large-scale miracles: They play a relatively minor role in Torah. As we read in 1 Kings 19, the presence of YHVH is not to be found in grand interventions like the forty-day flood or the parting of the Sea - - but rather in "soft murmuring sounds" and "still, small voices."

Not surprisingly, the location of the Sea of Reeds has never been identified. This may well be because like many places mentioned in the Torah, this sea was never intended to represent a physical reality. Rather, it is mentioned for its symbolic value: The Reed Sea represents the Israelites final contact with the Egyptians. It is also where the Israelites took their first ritual bath (*mikvah*) to purify themselves of their past shortcoming and enslavements; that is, the first of the two "dips" referred to in the third question at the Passover Seder (*Why on other nights we do not dip even once, and on this night we dip twice?*). Some have likened the Reed Sea to a birth canal, for it was from the Sea that an Israelite nation was born.

- **What about the vast number of Egyptian said to have drowned?** Did the Israel nation have to be born on the backs of so many deaths? And, what kind of God is YHVH to have acted with so little compassion?

If taken literally, the story about the parting of the Reed Sea poses some troubling moral and spiritual questions; but again, many scenes from the Torah including this one are not meant to be taken at face value. Instead we can think of this story as we did the previous ten blows (plagues); that is, assaults on the people's senses to get them to change their ways, leave the comforts of their narrow place, and begin their personal and spiritual journeys.

We can also think about the drowning of the Egyptian military as an "eleventh" blow – a final assault, meant to assure the Israelis that they are doing the correct thing by separating themselves from *Mitz'rayim* and putting their trust in YHVH, and to remind those who chose not to leave that they are jeopardizing their future.

We can also view this story as we did in Exodus 2 where Moses killed the Egyptian taskmaster. Just as Moses had to "kill" the Egyptian in him, so too did the Children of Israel have to put their Egyptian way of life behind them. In the case of Moses the killing represents one person's internal struggle, while the Reed Sea incident symbolizes the internal struggle of a whole community. With the closing of the Sea on the Egyptian military, the Israelites now understand that returning to Egypt is no longer an option.

- **Where are Pi ha-Hirot and Baal-Tzefon?** YHVH is telling Moses to set up camp in the proximity of *Pi ha-Hirot* and *Baal-Tzefon*. Why? Might it be that YHVH is testing the Children of Israel? I say this because neither of these two locations can be located on a map for the simple reason that neither place existed. Perhaps both are introduced to symbolize the dilemma facing the Children of Israel as they arrive at the first critical crossroad in their journey. They can either go towards *Pi ha-Hirot*, which translates as "the mouth of freedom," or towards *Baal-Tzefon*, which means "the hidden (false) god of the north."

The Torah is implying that there is more to leaving *Mitz'rayim* than simply heading north in the wilderness, for even in the north the Israelites will find false gods like *Baal-Tzefon* - religious sects which claim to offer comfort and certainty without the need to struggle.

This raises the question, "Is *Mitz'rayim* marching after them, or are they marching to *Mitz'rayim*?" They seem to be doing the latter. Recall their cry to YHVH: *"Is it because there are no graves in Egypt that you have taken us out to die in the wilderness? Didn't we say to you to let us alone that we may serve Egypt? Indeed, it is better for us serving Egypt than our dying in the wilderness!"* - - this seems to reflect a fear not of returning to their narrow way of living, but rather of the uncertainties that lie ahead for them should they continue on their journey into the unknown.

Said simply, they are viewing *Mitz'rayim* not as the problem, but rather as the solution. They may understand that they can never return to *Mitz'rayim*, yet they still miss the comfort they experienced there.

- **Who are really are the Children of Israel?** The Torah makes repeated reference to those who left *Mitz'rayim* as "Children of Israel," meaning those individuals who, while not necessarily biologically linked to Jacob, are descendants of his spiritual side. They are anyone who, as the name *Israel* suggests, shows the willingness and ability to pursue his or her personal and spiritual journeys by committing to a lifetime of struggle with things both mortal (such as relationships, demands on our time, competing priorities, and our physical well-being) and divine (such as our spiritual well-being, the mysteries and purpose of our existence), while surrendering to that in our lives which we cannot control, own, or understand.

Given this definition, it therefore seems inappropriate to refer to the generation who left *Mitz'rayim* as "Children of Israel," for they seem to be giving every indication that they would willingly give up the struggle if they could return to the safe confines of *Mitz'rayim*. They will be tested other times during their desert journey and each time fall short of truly deserving the label "Children of Israel." Perhaps a more fitting designation for this generation would be "Children of Jacob," for they seem to be more aligned with Jacob's materialistic side then with his spirituality.

➢ Journey in the Wilderness (Exodus 15:1 to 15:26)

Summary: *Moses had Israel move from the Sea of Reeds to the wilderness of Shur, where they travelled for three days but found no water. They came to Maror, but its water was too bitter to* *drink. The people grumbled against Moses, saying: What are we to drink? Moses cried out to YHVH, who directed Moses to wood which he was to throw on the water to make it sweet. There YHVH imposed law and judgment for them, and there YHVH tested them, saying, "If you hearken to My voice and do what is right in My eyes, follow the commandments and keep all of my laws, then I will not impose the sicknesses on you that I did on the Egyptians.*

Discussion Questions: Where or what is the wilderness of Shur? Where or what is Maror? How could "wood" make the water of Maror sweet?

- **Where or what is the wilderness of Shur?** *Shur* shares the same *shoresh* (3-letter root) with the word, *ya'shar,* which means "straight", and wilderness (*mid-bar*) shares the same *shoresh* with *da'ber*, which means "speak or talk." To walk in the "wilderness of straight talk" is to walk in a land free of enslavements, where the people are free to struggle with concepts of good, evil, and the meaning of life. That said, straight talk requires honesty, trust, and truthfulness with oneself and with others – attitudes and behaviors largely foreign to the current generation of Israelites, given their upbringing in a narrow place.

- **Where or what is Maror?** *Maror* means "bitter" as in the bitter herbs that are placed on the Passover Seder plate. The people named the place "bitter" because that is how the water tasted to them. Maror is also a place where they will soon receive a revelation. We know this because the text states that it took them three days to get there. Recall that the number "three" usually represents the coming of revelation - - meaning an awakening to a new direction in life, and recognition of what was previously held true is no longer meaningful. The revelation at Maror will take the form of the law and judgment imposed by YHVH on the people.

- **How could "wood" make the water of *Maror* sweet?** Few verses in Torah are as difficult to decipher as is verse 25 in Exodus 12: "*Moses cried out to YHVH, who directed Moses to wood which he was to throw on the water to make it sweet. There*

YHVH imposed law and judgment for them, and there YHVH tested them, saying, "If you hearken to My voice and do what is right in My eyes, follow the commandments and keep all of my laws, then I will not impose the sicknesses on you that I did on the Egyptians."

Let's try to decode this verse, first by addressing the question: Why did the water of *Maror* taste bitter? Perhaps it tasted bitter because those who drank from it had, only three days before, sacrificed their past for a present that is totally foreign to them, and for a future that holds no certainties. True, these people were now free -- but like Hagar, also "an enslaved stranger from a narrow place" who was sent out into the wilderness of "seven wells" (Genesis 16) - - the Israelites are unsure how to inhabit their newly gained freedom. Rather than feeling joy at their liberation, the Isrealites are experiencing unease, fear, a longing for *Mitz'rayim* and regret at having left. Thus, the bitterness refers not so much to the water as to the people who are drinking it, yet unable to appreciate the sweetness of their newly found freedom. They need instructions on how to be free, which came in the form of the revelation that they received when Moses threw the wood into the water.

But, how can water be sweetened by throwing wood into it? To answer this question, we need to know the symbolic meaning of "throw" and "wood." The Hebrew word for "throw" is *yor'eh,* constructed from the same 3-letter root (*shoresh*) as *mor'eh* (teacher). This indicates that the two words share a common conceptual base. *Yor'eh* suggests the tossing of an object towards a target, while *mor'eh* refers to someone who helps others to better hit their mark. By instructing Moses to "toss the wood directly at the desired mark," YHVH was thus having Moses teach the people about wood.

But, what can the people learn from "wood"? What does wood symbolize? I suspect that wood is being used in this passage as a metaphor for the two trees that lie at the center of the Garden of Eden: the Tree of Life and to the Tree of Knowledge of Good and Evil. From the Tree of Life comes the law that YHVH imposed on the people and from the Tree of Knowledge of Good and Evil comes the judgment – both teachings are necessary to help the Israelites fully appreciate their newly gained freedom.

As these people will soon reveal by their actions, however, what they have yet to learn wisdom – the ability to put their knowledge into practice. That said, it can be argued that there was nothing revealed at Sinai that wasn't already revealed by the thrown wood at *Maror*, given the deep philosophical and spiritual meaning represented by these two trees (for more about the two trees, refer to the commentary about them in Chapter 2 under the heading "The Garden of Eden").

One other point worth mentioning from verse 25 concerns the bitterness of the water at *Maror* and the first blow (plague). Recall from the story about the plagues that all but the first had an ending date. Before Moses threw the wood into the water, the river of life remained a river of death, unable to sustain or enhance life. The wood (that is, the teachings from the two trees) transformed the water back into something "*tov*" (acts that serve to realize the potential to bring forth life that is embedded in the creation by YHVH), and by so doing, ended the first blow.

➢ The Journey Continues (Exodus 15:27- 16)

Summary: *From Maror, they went to Elim, where there were twelve springs of water and seventy palms – and from there to the Wilderness of Syn.*

On the fifteenth day after the second New Moon after their leaving of Egypt, they again grumbled to Moses, saying "Better had we died by the hand of YHVH in the land of Egypt, where we ate bread till we were satisfied, than to bring us to the wilderness and die of starvation."

YHVH said to Moses: Tell the people that at sunset I will give them flesh to eat. And at daybreak, I will make it rain bread from the heavens, and the people shall go out in the mornings and glean each day's amount, each person according to that he could eat. On the morning of the sixth day, each shall glean a double portion, saving the surplus for the Sabbath, for YHVH has given you the Sabbath, a day of ceasing when you will see the glory of YHVH. And it was so; at sunset a horde of quail covered the same, and at daybreak a layer of dew covered the surface of the wilderness, which dried into what the people called "mahn-hu." They ate the manna for the forty years, until they came to settled land.

Discussion Questions: *Where or what are Elim and Syn? Why twelve springs and seventy palms? Why do the people continue to grumble? What is Manh-hu?*

- **Where or what are *Elim* and *Syn*?** The word "*Elim*" is made up of two words, "El" which is one of YHVH's names, and "*im*" which is the Hebrew word for "with." In other words, having been introduced to the "tree" lessons, they were able to walk "with YHVH" – at least until they came to the Wilderness of *Syn*, where they once again displayed a lack of trust in their divine leader.

As for the meaning of "*Syn*", it is tempting to define the word by its association with its English homonym, but this association is pure coincidence, for the Hebrew word for "sin" is *chet,* and not *syn*. Perhaps by saying that the people entered the Wilderness of *Syn*, the text was implying that they had moved away from the Wilderness of *Shur*, where for a brief time they demonstrated the ability to engage in "straight talk."

- **Why twelve springs and seventy palms?** In the commentary on the Garden of Eden story (Genesis 2 and 3), the Promised Land was defined as a state of mind where we find both milk (symbolic of sustenance) and honey (symbolic of sweetness and joy), even during mundane or troubled times. Of course, it doesn't have to be milk and honey – other metaphors also work. For example, in Genesis 43, sustenance was represented by nuts – another high source of protein. And, when journeying in the arid wilderness, as the Israelites are doing, water becomes an obvious means of sustenance, while dates from desert palm trees are a readily- available source of sweetness. So, when verse 27 states that *"They came to Elim, where there were twelve springs and seventy palms"*, keeping in mind that the meaning of *Elim* (with YHVH), the message being conveyed is that even in the wilderness, when we are "with YHVH," we can glimpse into what our lives could be like in the future if and when we enter the Promised Land.

Now, why "twelve" springs and "seventy" palms? The numbers may be referring back to Genesis 46: 8-27, which lists the names of the twelve sons of Israel and then states: *"Thus, all the persons of Jacob's household who came to Mitz'rayim were seventy."* By coming upon the twelve springs and seventy palms in *Elim*, the people are not only glimpsing into the future, but also seeing their connection to the deep past. Put in modern terms, by linking the past with the future, the Torah is teaching us that to better know where we are going, it is important to know from where we came.

- **Why do the people continue to grumble?** Only one month has passed since the tenth blow (death to the first born). During that time, the Israelites left their narrow place, drained themselves of their "extras", experienced the sweetness of their first harvest (*Sukkot*), safely crossed the Reed Sea, journeyed in the wilderness of straight talk, were taught the lessons of wood (law and judgment), and walked with YHVH. Yet, when put to the test, they continue to show a preference for enslavements over freedom and physical comforts over spiritual struggle. They may be journeying in the wilderness, but for them it has yet to become a *mid'bar* - a place where they can hear YHVH speak. Rather, they continue to experience it as a *negba* – a parched dry, desolate wasteland that does not support life; a place where all that they can hear is the beckoning call of their past enslavements and where they thirst and hunger for the extras, the *chu-matze*.

- **What is *mahn-hu*?** *Man-hu*, or what has been Anglicized as "manna", translates into English as "what is this?" What is it? Over the years some have tried to explain this "bread from the heavens," but as Everett Fox points out in his commentary to Exodus 15, they miss the point of the biblical writings, which is more concerned with conveying a teaching than with being historically or scientifically correct. (That said, later in the Torah, specifically in Chapter 11, versus 7 and 8 of the Book of Numbers, manna is likened to that of a coriander seed which can be ground in a millstone, crushed in a crusher, or boiled in a pot to make cakes that taste like something rich in oil.)

Perhaps the Torah introduces manna into the story to complete a test: What will it take? Now that our physical needs for water and food are satisfied, will we finally be able to separate ourselves from our past, so that it is no longer determining our present? Will we be able to move forward (*lekh Lekha*) to a sense of spiritual awareness, as Avram and Sarai did as they journeyed away from their homes to a land that YHVH had yet to reveal to them?

And, if water and food aren't enough, how about receiving the gift of the Sabbath? Will we then stop our grumbling and realize that it was our thirsting and hunger for wholeness (*shalem*) that brought us out of *Mitz'rayim*? In *Refidim*, we learn that the answer is "no." Not only do the Israelites not stop their grumbling, but it is they who are now proposing a test to YHVH when they ask "Is YHVH among us, or not?"

➤ That Last Stops Before Sinai (Exodus 17 and 18)

Summary: *The community moved from the Wilderness of Syn to Refidim, where once again there was no water to drink. They quarreled with Moses, saying "For what reason did you bring us up from Egypt, only to bring death to me, to my children, and my livestock?" And they tested YHVH: "Is YHVH among us, or not?"*

Moses cried out to YHVH, saying "What shall I do with these people?" YHVH replied, "Take your staff and with some elders looking on, strike the rock at Horev; water will come out of it, and the people will drink."

Amalek came and made war upon Israel in Refidim. Moses said to Joshua: Choose us men and make war upon Amalek! I will station myself on top of the hill with the YHVH's staff in my hand. And it was that whenever Moses raised his hand, Israel prevailed and whenever he lowered his hand, Amalek prevailed. Aaron and Hur helped to support Moses's hand, and in the end, Joshua and his men weakened Amalek. YHVH said to Moses: "I will wipe out Amalek and the memory of Amalek under the heavens. To that, Moses replied, "War for YHVH against Amalek, generation after generation!"

Now Jethro, the priest of Midyan and Moses' father-in-law, heard all that YHVH had done for Moses and his people. He took Tzippora, Moses' wife, and her two sons, Gershom, and Eliezer, and came to Moses where he was encamped. Moses greeted Jethro with a bow and kiss, and together they went into Moses' tent where he told Jethro all that YHVH had done.

Now it was on the morrow that Moses to judge the people, settle their legal matters, and make known to them YHVH's laws and instructions. Jethro said, "Why do you sit alone, while the entire people are stationed around you? You will become worn out. Be there, yourself, for the people in relation to YHVH. But select honest men of caliber to be chiefs of thousands, chiefs of hundreds, chiefs of fifties and chiefs of ten. They will bring every great matter to you, but every small matter they shall judge by themselves."

Discussion Questions: Where or what is Refidim? Who are the Amalekites and why is YHVH calling for their extermination? What role is Jethro playing in this story?

- **Where or what is *Refidim*?** The word is rooted in two other words, the first pertaining to "healing" and the second to "hand." In other words, the community - once again thirsting for water - moved to the "healing hand." Ironically, this name appears as a misnomer for no healing seems to take place there. Not only do the people continue to grumble, but Moses has apparently joined the chorus.

That said, the passage also suggests that *Refidim* is situated close to *Horev*, which is where Moses encountered the "burning bush." In Chapter 6 we learned that *"Horev"* means sword or destruction. Its name is meant to suggest a place where we realize that what we held to be true in the past is no longer meaningful to us and therefore must be discarded (severed or destroyed). It is a place where new truths can emerge that allows us to more fully inhabit the present and move on, less encumbered, to a more enlightened future.

In short, Horev is a place where revelation is possible. In Exodus 3, *Horev* was referred to as the "Mountain of God," which soon will become known as Mount Sinai. From the perspective of Torah, therefore, it may not be surprising that the "healing hand" is in close proximity to the "mountain of God."

- **Who are the Amalekites and why is YHVH calling for their extermination?** Few verses in Torah can make us cringe more than Exodus 17: 14, where YHVH offers Moses to "wipe out the memory of Amalek from under the heavens!" (According to biblical lore, the Amalekites are a tribe who descended from Amalek, who was one of Esau's grandsons and, therefore, one of Isaac's great-grandsons {Genesis 36:12}). Apparently Moses fails, because years later YHVH similarly commands Saul, Israel's first king, to wipe out the Amalekites (I Samuel 15:1-34). Saul fails as well, for in the Book of Esther 13:1 we learn that Haman, the evil Persian councilor, is an Amalekite king. The Amalekites are mentioned numerous other times in the bible, including Numbers 14:39-45; Judges 3:12-13; and 1 Samuel 27-30.

This is not to say that the Amalekites were Israel's only enemy, for there were also the Canaanites, Assyrians, Babylonians, and Philistines, to name a few. But four things make the Amalekites unique: First, rather than being limited to one location, they seemed to appear across wide expanses of time and space, showing up one year at *Refidim* in the Sinai Desert, thirty-nine years later at the threshold of Canaan, and almost a millennium later in the capital of Persia during the Babylonian exile. Second, there is no mention of Amalekites in any text other than the Bible, which raises the question of their actual existence. Third, in contrast to those living in the great city of Nineveh (mentioned in the Book of Jonah) - Israel's powerful enemy to the north - YHVH never offered the Amalekites the opportunity to repent. And, fourth, of all of Israel's enemies, only the Amalekites were marked for extermination.

Taken in total, this evidence suggests that Amalekites were never an external threat to Israel, unlike Israel's other enemies. Rather, they represent that which impedes Israel's ability to move forward, particularly at critical moments in its development. For example, the Amalekites mysteriously appear at Refidim, Israel's last stopping point before encamping opposite Mount Sinai, and again as the Israelites are about to enter the Promised Land.

So, who or what is Amalek? We can think of the Amalekites as internal threats – our behavioral tendencies which, if left unguarded, can cause us to taste sweet water as bitter, prefer complacency over struggle, and choose evil (*rah*) over good (*tov*). Said differently, Amalek represents our willingness to abandon our journey of becoming more "like *Israel*" and instead direct us towards more "narrow" paths. It should therefore not be surprising to read that YHVH is calling for Amalek's extinction. The Torah is not advocating genocide, at least not in a literal sense. Rather, it is using stories about the Amalekites to teach us the importance of struggling with, and ultimately conquering, our non-covenantal urges.

- **Who is Jethro?** From the perspective of Torah, biological linkage plays a lessor role in one's moral development than spiritual linkage. This is why YHVH refers to Abraham - but not Isaac - as Jacob's father, while Isaac was Jacob's biological father (Genesis 28). Torah further suggests that one's spiritual link is capable of originating outside the family lineage, as in the case of David who refers to Saul as his father and Saul calls him "my son."

The same can be said for the relationship between Jethro, the priest of Midyan, and Moses, even though the two men never address one another a "father' or "son." Still, Jethro's fatherly influence on Moses is undeniable. It was Jethro who offered shelter to Moses while the latter was fleeing from Pharaoh's wrath. It was Jethro who welcomed Moses into his family by allowing his daughter *Tzippora* to marry Moses without any preconditions. (Jethro's openness on this matter lies in stark contrast to the way that Lavan treated his nephew Jacob when Jacob requested permission to marry Lavan's daughter, Rachel.) It was Jethro who understandingly replied *"Go in peace"* when Moses asked *"Pray let me return to my brothers that are in Egypt, that I may see whether they are alive."* And, it was Jethro who in Exodus 18 advises Moses on how to manage the large number of people who have become increasingly difficult to lead.

Some may find it ironic that Moses had such a close relationship with Jethro. Recall from Chapter 6 that the tribe of Midyan and that of Ishmael may be one and the same. This means that Moses, the leader of the Children of Israel, is being nurtured and advised by a descendent of Jacob's uncle, Ishmael. Recall also that Avram and Sarai had banished Ishmael and his mother, Hagar, in the attempt to protect their blood line from the descendants of Ishmael and Hagar. With the birth of Moses' two children with Jethro's daughter, *Tzippora*, however, their blood lines have once again merged. Adding to the apparent irony, had Ishmael and Hagar not been banished, there would have been no Jethro to help Moses lead the Children of Israel from *Mitz'rayim* to the Promised Land. Yet, the Torah treats this notable turn of events not as ironic, but fully consistent with its message of inclusiveness and that there is no divinely chosen people. Everyone is given the opportunity to struggle with things both human and divine, regardless of where they are born or who they are born to.

This theme is also evident in the stories about Lot and Ruth. It was Lot who dimwittedly allowed his two daughters to get him drunk on consecutive nights – so drunk that each daughter could "lay with him" and become pregnant by him – so drunk that he "claims" to have known nothing about the illicit encounters (Genesis 19). As it turned out, the two sons born to Lot's daughters became the tribal leaders of the two great enemies of the Israelites, the Moabites and the Ammonites. Yet, we later learn in the "Book of Ruth" that the great-great grandmother of King David was Ruth, a Moabite. And, Moab became the site of Moses' final resting place (Deuteronomy 34:1-9).

Chapter 8: Revelation at Sinai

➢ Encamping Opposite the Mountain (Exodus 19)

Summary: *On the third new moon after leaving Mitz'rayim, they moved on from Refidim and came to the wilderness, where Israel encamped, opposite the mountain. Meanwhile, Moses went up to YHVH, as YHVH called out to him from the mountain, saying, "You have seen what I did to Mitz'rayim, how I bore you on eagles' wings and brought you to me. So say to the House of Jacob, tell the Children of Israel: If you hearken to my voice and keep my covenant, you shall be a special treasure from among all people, a kingdom of priests, a holy nation."*

And the people answered, "All that YHVH has spoken, we will do."

YHVH said to Moses, Tell the people to make them holy, and scrub their clothes, so that they will be ready for the third day, the day when I will come down upon Mount Sinai. Have no one touch the mountain, for whoever touches the mountain shall be put-to-death.

Now it was that on the third day at day-break, there were thunder sounds and lightning and the mountain trembled and shook; a heavy cloud lay on the mountain, and an exceedingly strong shofar (ram's horn) sound was heard. Moses brought the people from the camp and stationed them beneath the mountain.

YHVH had come down upon the mountain in fire and, from behind the heavy cloud and dense smoke, told Moses to come up the mountain with Aaron.

Discussion Questions: Why has it taken three months to reach the wilderness of Sinai (when it should have taken only one day)? Who exactly are encamped opposite the mountain? Are we the "chosen people?" Why put to death those who touch the Mountain? What does the mountain represent?

- **Why three months?** A map of the area shows that the Sinai desert lies adjacent to Egypt proper, meaning that on the day that one leaves Egypt, one arrives in the Sinai. However, it is one thing to enter a desert (*negba*) and quite another to enter a wilderness (*midbar*) - those places where we can hear YHVH speak. By stating that the journey took three months, the Torah is again reminding us that the people's journey is at least as much metaphysical as it is physical.

And, once again the Torah is using the number three ("*on the third new moon*") to symbolize the impending arrival of revelation which they can "see" from where they are standing. Since leaving *Mitz'rayim*, the people were first purified of their past enslavements (by dipping in the Reed Sea), then received physical sustenance (water and manna) and, finally, spiritual sustenance (the Sabbath). In other words, it has taken the Israelites "three" months to sufficiently abandon former habits – i.e., their misguided ways of thinking - to be able to hear that which will soon be revealed to them. In the meantime, separated from their past, they anxiously await an uncertain future in a state of heightened alertness.

The number "three" appears a second time when YHVH says, "*for the third day, the day when I will come down upon Mount Sinai.*" As this will be the third day of the third month after leaving *Mitz'rayim*, the Torah may be signaling that the people will soon be given the "Revelation of all revelations."

- **"Who" are encamped next to the mountain?** Notice how the text presents the people as a progression from the most general ("they *moved on from Refidim*") - to the more specific *("where Israel encamped")* - to the very specific (*"Moses went up to YHVH"*). Similarly, YHVH commands Moses: "*So say to the House of Jacob, tell the Children of Israel.*" The Torah is reminding us that it was a "mixed multitude" who left *Miz'rayim*, and it is that same mixed multitude who are now encamped next to the mountain.

We are like those people. We "come to the Mountain" with differing abilities to "hear"; some clinging largely to our past ways of thinking while an enlightened few, like Moses, enter with a nearly "blank slate." Some of us come seeking answers to our spiritual, "*Israel*-like" questions, while others are more concerned with our more earthly "Jacob" concerns. Some seek answers on both, while others ask neither. Each of us will have our own unique relationship with the Mountain; each will experience revelation differently.

* **Are we the Chosen People?** Exodus 19:5 states: *"If you hearken to my voice and keep my covenant, you shall be a special treasure from among all people, a kingdom of priests, a holy nation."* Many misinterpret this verse as suggesting that only the Children of Israel are the "chosen people." However, the verse does not imply that YHVH chose this mixed multitude of people at the exclusion of all others. Rather, the if/then structure of the verse suggests that it is *we* who must do the choosing. That is, anyone – Jew or otherwise – who actively and willingly keeps YHVH's covenant will become one of the "chosen." This message of inclusiveness is reinforced throughout the Torah. For instance, the name "Hebrew" refers to all those who cross over into a closer relationship with themselves, their neighbors, and the Divine; while "Israel" denotes those engaged in human and Divine struggle.

* **Why put to death those who touch the Mountain?** *"Have no one touch the mountain, for whoever touches the mountain shall be put-to-death"* (Exodus 19:12). Once again we are confronted with the kind of reference in the Book of Exodus that can make us "moderns" cringe. Other such references include the suffering inflicted on the Egyptian people during each of the ten blows (plagues); the drowning of the Egyptian military in the Reed Sea; and the calling for the extermination of the Amalekites. It is therefore not surprising that many biblical scholars have argued that the God depicted in Exodus is more demanding, more powerful, less approachable, and less compassionate than the God of the Genesis stories. But, from the perspective of Torah, is this characterization of YHVH fair? I will argue that it is not fair, based on the position I have put forth throughout this book: that the Torah should not – and indeed, cannot – be interpreted literally.

> I say "should not" because the text's primary function is to provide ethical and spiritual insights that help us to become more humane, to appreciate life before death, and to participate in the ongoing process of creation. A literal reading of the "death to those who touch the mountain" example, however, offers little such developmental wisdom. What we get instead is what Rabbi Harold Kushner describes as a parental god who demands respect, faith, and dependency - - the kind of god that can engender in us feelings of arrogance, guilt, intolerance and fanaticism; the kind of god that many of us grew up with: the all-wise and all-powerful parent figure who intervenes in our lives when we are

at risk, rewards us when we do the right things, and punishes us when we don't. Freud described this parental view of God as "immature," while Einstein labeled it "childlike."

I also say "cannot be" because the text contains many inconsistencies which, when taken literally, defy reason. The first blow/plague (transformation of all the water in Egypt into blood) is one of many such examples. Recall that while most of the plagues were associated with starting and ending dates, the first plague has only a starting date. If taken literally, this would mean that every person in this arid land would have died within a few days; from Pharaoh and his royal magicians to each slave, including Moses. No one would be alive to endure the other nine plagues or drown in the Reed Sea! There would be no Exodus from Egypt, no Revelation at Sinai, and no Torah. I therefore join others before me in arguing that this inconsistency - and the many others found in the Torah - should not be viewed as evidence of sloppy writing or poor editing, but rather as periodic reminders not to literalize that which is intended as allegory.

So, what might be a non-literal interpretation of *"Have no one touch the mountain, for whoever touches the mountain shall be put-to-death"*, and what developmental wisdom can be drawn from it? The answer, I believe, resides in the teaching from the Adam and Eve Story in Genesis 3. Recall that YHVH said to them, *"On the day that you eat from that tree, you must die."* Remember what happened? They disobeyed YHVH, ate from the tree, and yet did not die, at least not until many years later when their biological clocks ran out.

What did we learn from this early Genesis story that could assist us in better understanding YHVH's "death threat" in Exodus 19:12? We learned that while we are accustomed to think of death in physical terms, the Torah tends to define death spiritually. Accordingly, while Adam and Eve did not biologically expire upon eating from the tree, they suffered spiritual death by being driven out of the Garden. From the perspective of Torah, this means that they moved away from their close relationship with YHVH and spiritual perfection, to a place where the "light" from the first day of Creation shines less brightly.

The same can be said of those who were to touch the Mountain. Like Adam and Eve, the Israelites were being tested: *If you hearken to my voice and keep my covenant, you shall be a special treasure from among all people, a kingdom of priests, a holy nation.* Some among their mixed multitude would undoubtedly choose not to listen or to listen halfheartedly. And, if choosing to hearken to God's voice – the "voice that creates" (Genesis 1) - allows the possibility of moving forward towards the "light," then not doing so means the opposite. It means returning to the dark times of the ninth blow when we "cannot see the face of our brother" and are thus unable to engage in a community of deeply grounded "I-Thou" relationships with our neighbors.

It follows that whereas death for Adam and Eve meant being driven from the Garden, death for those who would choose to touch the Mountain is defined by separation from *"a kingdom of priests, a holy nation."* In other words, they were to be cut off from the ones who agree to live their lives in service to God.

And, what does service to God entail? As we read in earlier chapters, it involves keeping the Sabbath (Genesis 1); working and guarding the Garden (Genesis 2); being willing and able to struggle with things both human and Divine (Genesis 32); being our brother's keeper (Genesis 45-50); putting into practice the laws and judgments learned from the two Garden trees (Exodus 16); and, as we will soon read in Exodus 20, using the Ten Commandments as our moral compass.

Said succinctly, living in service to God is about living in service to ourselves, our community, and the Garden in which we live. Those who would choose this service understand that YHVH's message is not a "death threat" but instead a "life-gift."

- **What does the mountain represent? And, why is YHVH so adamant that it not be touched?** Answers to these two questions again reside in the teaching from the Adam and Eve Story. Recall that Adam and Eve were tempted by the prospects of becoming more "God-like" - they wished to possess the knowledge of good and evil and to see the light of Creation as it appeared on Day 1.

Of course, there is nothing inherently wrong with their desire to be enlightened. What was wrong, from the perspective of Torah, was the way that they sought such knowledge. Specifically, they tried to take direct control over their own destiny, symbolically illustrated by their eating the forbidden fruit from the Tree of Knowing Good and Evil. They imagined that they could attain gratification instantly and without struggle. Said simply, they tried to control the uncontrollable. This story reminds us that there is much about our lives that we cannot control, and the sooner we understand this, the sooner we can deal with life's traumas and disappointments and find inner peace and wholeness. Other stories in the Torah offer much the same lesson, including the sagas of Cain (Genesis 4); the builders of the infamous "Tower of Babel" (Genesis 11); and Avram and Sarai (a.k.a. Abraham and Sarah) in the story of Sarai's Egyptian servant, Hagar (Genesis 16).

Think of touching the mountain as tantamount to eating from the Tree of Knowledge. Bear in mind that the Israelites are only three months into their journey as free people. With one critical exception, the Israelites are like an assembly of naïve children, with mixed multitudes of unbridled desires and undeveloped consciences. There are many life-lessons with which they must yet struggle before they are ready to enter into the Promised Land ("Land of Promise", or an awakened state of awareness) where they will discover their true purpose – first as individuals and then, finally, as a nation. As such, the story of the Israelites in Exodus 19 is like Adam and Eve's "coming-of-age," but on a grander scale (it now pertains to a community rather than two individuals).

Moses, of course, is the exception. Having already experienced two revelations (life - altering moments) - first when he "killed" the Egyptian in him that had been shepherding his life so that he could give birth to a new and more authentic purpose in his life (Exodus 2); and second when he saw the burning bush, which awakened him to a new calling to his life (Exodus 3) - he was not only allowed to touch the Mountain, but was asked by

YHVH to ascend it. Said metaphorically, Moses climbed the ladder that Jacob (in Genesis 28) only dreamed of climbing.

➤ Receiving the Ten Sayings/Commandments (Exodus 20)

Background: The messages contained in the first fourteen verses of Exodus 20 are among the most important in Western religious thought; yet they are often misunderstood. To begin, the Torah uses the word *d'va-reem*, which translates as "sayings" or "things" but is often misinterpreted as "commandments." It is only in the last four hundred years that these sayings have come to be known as commandments. Indeed, the first Saying - *I am YHVH your God, who brought you out from the land of Mitz'rayim, and from the house of serfs* - cannot be construed as a commandment. Second, some of the Ten Sayings – most notably the tenth – contain multiple messages. Moreover, the numbering of the ten items differs in the Jewish and Christian traditions. The Jewish tradition lists the First Saying as *I am YHVH your God*. This is omitted from the New Testament, which instead divides the second saying in the Jewish tradition into two separate expressions; first "You are not to have any other gods before my presence"; and second *"You are not to make yourself a carved-image or any other figure that is in the heavens above, earth below, or the waters beneath the earth."* Third, it is also not clear how the Fourth and Ninth Sayings are worded, for when they are repeated in Deuteronomy 5:12-15, their wording changes. Fourth, given the symbolic meaning of the number ten in the Torah,[13] (specifically, it represents an amount sufficiently large to capture our attention and affect our behavior), it is no small coincidence that we think of the sayings as numbering ten even though there are as many as 613, at least according to Jewish mystical thinkers. Finally, many biblical scholars once assumed that Ten Sayings were minor extensions to the Code of Hammurabi, an earlier assembly of seven law coming from Mesopotamia - and there are in fact some broad similarities between the two. However, the current thinking is that the two compilations differ significantly in their intent: Hammurabi's Code is now understood to have been used

---

[13] Think also about the Ten Blows (plagues), the Ten Days of Awe between Rosh Hashanah and Yom Kippur, the Ten Generations that separated Adam from Noah and Noah from Abraham , and the custom of "tithing" (see Genesis 14:20 and 28:20). There are said to be Ten Lost Tribes of Israel (those other than Judah and Benjamin). There are Ten Sephirot in the Kabbalistic Tree of Life. And, in Judaism, ten adults (a *minyan*) are the required quorum for prayer services.

by Hammurabi to show gods and people alike that he is a just king, while the Ten Sayings are presented as decreed directly by God.

So, what are the "Ten Commandments/Sayings?" As we will read, they are more than simply a list of do's and don'ts. Taken as a whole, they are like the "wood" at Maror - able to transform that which tastes bitter into something sweet (Exodus 15). Collectively, they are designed to help us along our personal and spiritual journeys as we struggle with questions about good, evil, and the meaning of life. They serve as a pathway for attaining a closer relationship with ourselves, our community, and the metaphysical, while acting as a blueprint for truly "loving our neighbors as ourselves" (Leviticus 19:18). If being *Israel* entails "struggling with things both Divine and human and proving able" (Genesis 32), the Ten Sayings teach us how to be "able."

Indeed, it can be said that all of the Torah's teachings are summarized in these fourteen verses of Exodus 20. Hard to imagine? We'll begin by stating each of the Ten Sayings as they appear in the Jewish tradition.

God spoke all these words, saying:

> *I am YHVH your God, who brought you out from the land of Mitz'rayim, and from the house of serfs.*

> *You are not to have any other gods before my presence. You are not to make yourself a carved-image or any other figure that is in the heavens above, earth below, or the waters beneath the earth. You are not to bow down to them nor serve them, for I, YHVH am a zealous God, calling to account the iniquity of the fathers upon the sons, to the third and fourth generations of those who hate me, but showing loyalty to the thousandth of those who love me and keep my commandments.*

> *You are not to take up the name of YHVH for emptiness, for YHVH will not clear him that takes up his name for emptiness.*

> *Remember the Sabbath and make it holy; no one in your household is to do any kind of work for in the first six days YHVH made the heavens and earth and all that is in it, but rested on the seventh day and blessed it.*

> *Honor your father and your mother in order that your days may be prolonged on the soil that YHVH is giving you.*

> *You are not murder.*

> *You are not to commit adultery.*

> *You are not to steal.*

> *You are not to bear false witness against your neighbor.*

> > *You are not to desire the house of your neighbor, the wife of your neighbor, nor his servant, ox, or donkey, nor anything that is your neighbor's.*

Notice that the first four Sayings pertain to our relationship with God, while the next six concern our interactions with other people. This ordering is consistent with the view during Biblical times that everything originates with God. A more contemporary view and the one that I endorse begins with the individual. Accordingly, I will comment on the Sayings in reverse order, starting with the Tenth. What should become apparent, however, is that the Ten Sayings are interdependent, such that any one Saying cannot be fully understood without accounting for its effect on others. It should be equally obvious that the Ten Sayings, when taken as a whole, are about discovering who we are and who we are not. The purpose is to help us to build intimate relationships, first with ourselves and then with others. Consequently, the Ten Sayings represent the continuation of the journeys towards personal and spiritual awareness that began with the Ten Blows.

* What is meant by the Tenth Saying, "*You are not to desire the house of your neighbor, the wife of your neighbor, or his servant, ox, or donkey, or anything that is your neighbor's*"? Or, put in positive terms, as is done in the "Zohar" (the foundational work for Jewish mystical thought known as Kabbalah) "we are to desire our own life" – who we are, what we have, and who we were meant to be – and be able to say with an appreciative heart, "it is sufficient" (*di-ya'noo*).

(Why make specific reference to an ox and donkey? In Biblical times, these two animals were essential for one's livelihood and therefore were easy to desire: the ox pulled the plow and the donkey helped to transport the final products to the market place.)

And, while it is normal to aspire to that which may belong to others, we should avoid the temptation of desiring their belongings, for doing so distracts us from our own journey; makes us feel disgruntled and diminished; preoccupies our mind with thoughts that deaden our senses; and removes us from fully living in the moment. Put another way, envious thoughts prevent us from ascertaining reality; impair our judgments; diminish our ability to engage with others; and promote relationships that are superficial, disconnected, and rife with conflict. For example, it was the desire to become more "God-like" that drove Eve to eat from the "forbidden fruit" (Genesis 3) and the "tower builders" to reach for the heavens (Genesis 11). It was jealousy that caused Cain to murder his brother Abel (Genesis 4) and Joseph's brothers to hate him.

In contrast, when we desire our own lives, we are more open to experience that which life has to offer; hear our "teacher from within"; and act with compassion and love. We are more accepting of the fact that there is much about our lives that we cannot control. The sooner we accept this fact, the better we are able to cope with life's traumas and find inner peace and *shalem* /wholeness. When we are satisfied with what we have, we are able to say *Hee-nay-nee*, or "here I am," as did Abraham in the *Akedah* Story (Genesis 22) and Moses in the presence of the burning bush (Exodus 3). These are life-altering moments when we are totally present, our hearts entirely open and all of our senses fully awake. In summary, when we desire our own life, ourselves, we are more able to bear true witness on others (the Ninth Saying).

*What is meant by the Ninth Saying, *"You are not to testify falsely against your fellow witness."*? That is, we are to bear true witness for our fellows. The essence of this message is that we are to understand others deeply enough to support them in attaining what they need, that we can give them what they need in real time with what we have at hand; or, put in Martin Buber's terms, bearing true witness is about engaging in " I-Thou" relationships.

However, we cannot bear true witness on others until we can bear witness on ourselves, and we cannot bear true witness on ourselves until we learn to desire our won life. As such, the ninth and tenth sayings are interconnected and self-reinforcing: the more that we are satisfied with what we have, the more freely we can offer ourselves to others and, in turn, the better we feel about ourselves. By engaging in this virtuous cycle, we create a community based on a self-sustaining climate of reciprocity and wholeness - one in which we feel connected to that which is larger and truer than our own egos. This is what the Promised Land is all about.

Hillel understood this 2,000 years ago when he said, "If I am not for myself, who will be for me? And being for my own self, what am I? (see *"Sayings from the Fathers"*). The prophet Isaiah also understood this 2,600 years ago, when he criticized the way that Yom Kippur was being observed, saying "This is not the fast that I desire!" (Isaiah 58). His point is that this "Day of Judgment" is not about denying ourselves food for one day. Rather, the day is to remind us of our year-round responsibility to take care of those who are in need, whether those needs be physical (e.g., food, clothing, and shelter) or psycho-social (e.g., companionship). In addition, Yom Kippur serves to draw attention to our own needs. In making his case, Isaiah was staying true to the first reference to the Holy Day that appears in Leviticus 23: 26-32. Those passages make no mention of the practice of fasting or any other act of self-denial. Instead, they state that we are to "afflict our souls" - in Hebrew, *v'ee-nee-tem nafsho- ta'chem* - which, in the context of Leviticus 23, means "attend to our soul and those of our community."

The Torah contains numerous instances of bearing false witness. For example, we read about Isaac's inability to distinguish between his two sons at the time that he blessed them (Genesis 25-27) and Judah's mistaken claim that his daughter-in-law, Tamar, was a harlot (Genesis 25-27). Another example of bearing false witness comes from the Ninth Blow , a time when it became too dark to "see the face of our brother." Another example is from the Book of Job, which tells that three friends came to visit Job soon after he had suffered unimaginable hardships. They may have come with the good intention of comforting him, but their visit produced the opposite effect. What Job needed to hear was that not everything happens for a higher purpose; doing all the correct things doesn't guarantee a good outcome; he had every right to feel grief and anger; and being angry at God would not cause further misfortune to come his way. Had his friends borne true witness to his character, they would have understood his grief deeply enough to tell him that. Instead, they told Job that in God's eyes, he and his family must have deserved their fate; for a just and all-knowing God doesn't act capriciously. In so doing, Job's friends caused him to suffer twice: once for the tragedy that befell him, and a second time for the guilt that he felt for believing that he was somehow responsible.

(For further interpretation of the Book of Job and the importance of bearing true witness, I recommend Rabbi Harold Kushner's book, "When Bad Things Happen to Good People." Some may know that, like Job, the Kushner household suffered a great tragedy when their son, Aaron, died in his early teens of a rare, incurable condition that causes premature aging.) Other examples in Torah of bearing true witness include the stories about: the mysterious man who wrestled with Jacob and acknowledged Jacob's spiritual advances by renaming him *Israel* (which we read in Genesis 32); the time when *Israel*, while on his death bed, blessed each of his twelve sons (Genesis 25-27); and how Joseph interpreted Pharaoh's two dreams (Genesis 39).

* What is meant by the Eighth Saying, *"You are not to steal?"* The Torah recognizes many forms of stealing aside from the obvious. For example, we read about how Sarai tried to steal Hagar's humanness by treating her like an "it," an object whose sole purpose was to advance

Sarai's own agenda. We also read about Jacob's stealing of Esau's birthright (Genesis 25) and about how Jacob's uncle, Lavan, stole seven years of Jacob's life and labor by denying his wishes to marry Rachel until he first agreed to marry Leah (Genesis 29). The teaching from these and other such examples is straightforward: We cannot build an intimate relationship with ourselves and with others if we act on our desires by taking things that do not belong to us.

Like the previous two sayings, the Eighth Saying also has a positive take: We are to give with a generous heart rather than steal with a selfish one. One example comes from Genesis 43, which tells of how Joseph created the means for his brothers to relive that moment in their lives when they had allowed jealousy and self-interest to over-ride their sense of family wholeness. By so doing, Joseph gave his brothers the opportunity to seek forgiveness not only from those whom they offended, but also from themselves.

Another "giving" example is found in Leviticus 23:22: *"Now when you harvest the harvest of your land, you are not to finish-off the edge of your field, but leave it for the afflicted and the sojourner."* Other examples include *hee ney nee* (here I am*)* moments; that is, times when a person is ready to give without hesitation before knowing what YHVH is about to ask of him/her. Abraham said *hee ney nee* just before being asked to sacrifice his son (Genesis 22). Moses also said *hee ney nee* at the sight of the burning bush, moments before YHVH asked him to return to Egypt and bring the Children of Israel out (Exodus 3). .

Before commenting on the Seventh Saying, let's stop for a moment and compare the ordering of the Sayings with that of the plagues. In Chapter 6, I pointed out that the ordering of the plagues had meaning, in that each blow got progressively more personal and therefore harder to ignore. The First Blow (blood) took place in the water, the Second (frogs) moved up to the land, and the Third, lice, moved on to our bodies. This progression continues to the tenth and most threatening blow, death to the first born. We can infer a similar "personal" pattern in the reverse ordering of the second half of the Ten Sayings, which begins with desire (ten), and then progresses to false witness (nine), stealing (eight), adultery (seven) - which we will address next - and finally murder (six).

*What is meant by the Seventh Saying, *"You are not to commit adultery?"* Most interpret the Seventh Saying in the context of marriage, and rightfully so. Indeed, the Torah, like religious texts from all denominations, views marriage as something Divine. As I mentioned in the Chapter 6 commentary on Exodus 4, the Hebrew word for marriage is *ki-*

dushim, derived from the word *kadosh*, meaning "set apart by God." Shabbat is the first time *kadosh* is mentioned in the Torah, a day that is set apart from the other six because of its spiritual nature, which God referred to as "exceedingly good" (Genesis 1). Marriage is the second *kadosh*; the very construction of the word (*ki-dushim*) is intended to signal that it is different from other relationships. Thus, from the perspective of Torah, to be unfaithful to one's spouse is not only a sin (missing our mark) against another, but a sin against the "unknowable force of what was, is and will be."

The Seventh Saying, however, is not limited in Torah to extra-marital sexual relations, but extends beyond that to any act of deceit or breach of trust that "adulterates" or contaminates the relationship between two or more individuals. Consider the deception committed by Lot's two daughters, who got their father so drunk that each could lay with him (Genesis 19). Consider also the lies that Joseph's brothers told their father when, after dipping Joseph's coat in the blood of a goat, they said, *"This is what we found and we know not if it is your son's coat or not"* (Genesis 37). And, consider the false accusations that Potifar's wife made against Joseph that caused Potifar to place Joseph in a dungeon (Genesis 39). In these and other such cases, the consequences to the perpetrator, the victim, and the community can be exceedingly bad. Whereas acts of integrity bring people together by creating a climate of reciprocity that is self-sustaining and life-enhancing, acts that adulterate relationships cause the opposite. Put simply, one good deed invites another, while one bad deed incites another.

Finally, the Seventh Saying can also apply to a kind of self-deception that affects our relationship with our self, with others, and with our ability to bear true witness. Consider *Jonah ben Amitai* (or "Jonah" as he is more commonly referred to) who deluded himself into following the "truth" that he desired rather than the teaching of his namesake, which means "Dove, Son of My God's Truth." (Like most Biblical names, Jonah's name is intended to reveal core aspects of the bearer's personality.) Jonah acted untrue to his name by believing that he could deny God's request that he go to the people of Ninevah, who were at that time the powerful enemy of Israel's Northern Kingdom, and ask those people to repent. As mentioned in Chapter 6, rather than go to Ninevah, Jonah went west (Nineveh is east), down to sea level (Nineveh is at a higher elevation), onto a cargo ship destined for Tarshish (a destination in Spain, further away from Nineveh), and all the way down to the ship's hull. There he fell into a deep sleep even as a mighty tempest threatened the seaworthiness of the ship and the lives of all aboard it.

The Jonah story reminds us that when we are untrue to ourselves, we run the risk of harming others as well. Said more broadly, when we commit adultery, whether by deceiving our spouse, our neighbors, or ourselves, we are more prone to steal, bear false witness, and desire that which doesn't belong to us.

We must now ask ourselves: Who among us has not committed adultery in one form or another at some point in our lives? The Hebrew Bible identifies only three such unblemished (*tam*) individuals: Noah, Job, and the "simple son" at the Passover Seder.

*What is meant by the Sixth Saying, "*You are not to commit murder?*" As it did with desire, witness, stealing, and adultery, the Torah recognizes at least six forms of "murder" and its synonym "kill." The six can be broken into two groups of three, one group representing "good" (*tov*) murders, that is, murders that you should commit because they help to actualize the potential to create life that is embedded in the creation by YHVH; and a second group of murders which you should not commit because they are "evil" (not good, or *rah*) in that they negate, destroy, or kill the actualization of good. (The terms good and evil were defined in the first three chapters of Genesis.)

Let's address the "evil" murders first, as they are easier to understand. The most potent example appears in Genesis 34. We are told of how two of Joseph's brothers, Levi and Shim'on, slaughtered Hamor and all the men in his tribe for defiling their sister, Dina (Genesis 34). It was this case of cold-blooded murder that caused their father, Jacob/*Israel*, to curse the two of them on his deathbed, when he said, "*These (two) brothers, wronging weapons be their ties-of-kinship. Damned be their anger, that it is so fierce- I will split them up in Jacob and scatter them in Israel*" (Gen. 49:5-7).

Did their punishment fit the crime? It did from the perspective of Torah, for the curse that they received was coming from YHVH through *Israel,* meaning that they were being sentenced to a death of spirit.

A second kind of an evil (*rah*, or life- destroying) murder was committed by King David as it is told in II Samuel Chapters 11 and 12). While at the height of his power, he sees a woman, Bathsheba, bathing on a roof top, desires her (Tenth Saying), and acts on his desires (Seventh Saying). Then, with the intent of stealing her from her husband (Eighth Saying), he sends the latter off to the front line of a battle and to certain death (Seventh Saying).

What makes the murder that David committed different from that by Levi and Shim'on is that the two brothers actively participated in the killings, while David used his position of power and influence to avoid any direct involvement? In so doing, he bore false witness (Ninth Saying) by deluding himself into believing that it wasn't he who killed Bathsheba's husband, but rather the war-time circumstance.

Later in life, David - older, wiser, and less egotistical - admits to his transgressions (2 Samuel 12:13: "*I stand guilty before the Lord!*") and accepts his punishment: While it was his life's mission to build the Temple - a "*resting place for the /Ark of the Covenant*" and the spiritual center for the twelve tribes of the nation that David was instrumental in forming – that honor went to his son, Solomon, for God said to David: "*You will not build a house for my Name, for you are a man of battles and have shed blood*" (1 Chronicles 28: 2-3). Solomon is the second child from his union with Bathsheba, the first having died seven days after his birth as predicted by the prophet Nathan as further punishment.

The third form of evil/*rah* murder does not concern death of body, but rather of spirit. I am referring to the story of Cain and Abel from Genesis 4. As you may recall from the Chapter 2 commentary, Cain was said to have killed his brother, but the fact that Abel's name (*Hevel*) means something ephemeral or momentary suggests that what Cain killed was not a human, but rather something *Hevel*-like, or metaphysical. Recall also from Chapter 2 that at the time of the murder, Cain was likely preoccupied with unresolved issues from the recent past (*"exceedingly upset that YHVH had no regard for Cain's gift"*) and anxious about how this setback would affect his future status in the family. Cain's preoccupations with the past and his anxieties about the future distracted his attention and deadened his senses, preventing him from being cognizant of the present. The Torah teaches us that without being fully awake and mindful to what the world is offering in the moment, one exists without truly living. Consequently when Cain murdered Abel, given the symbolism in the story, I argued that what he really killed was a moment in his own life when he might otherwise have actualized the potential to create life that is embedded in the Creation (Genesis 1); perceived a bush burning, but not consumed (Exodus 3); or heard YHVH in the "smallest of still voices" (I Kings 19:11-12). A message that we can draw from the story of Cain is that we are more able to follow the precepts of the previous four Sayings when we are fully present and engaged with life.

Having examined three forms of life-destroying murders, let's now consider three forms of life-creating murders mentioned in Torah - that is, murders that help to actualize the potential to create life. The first of these three good/*tov* murders was committed by Moses at the time when "h*e saw an Egyptian man striking a Hebrew man, one of his brothers – he struck down the Egyptian and buried him in the sand*" (Exodus 2). I argued in Chapter 6 that Moses wasn't a murderer; for his struggle was entirely internal. He had to "kill" the Egyptian in him that was shepherding his life in order to create a new and more authentic purpose to his life. Only by this "murder" could he inhabit the present with enough clarity and mindfulness to perceive the "burning bush", which in turn enabled him to choose to live "good."

The second of the three *tov* murders involved the extermination of the Amalekites. Specifically, YHVH orders Moses to "wipe out the memory of Amalek" (Exodus 18) and then tells Saul to do the same (I Samuel 15:1-34). However, as discussed in the Chapter 6 commentary, YHVH was not calling for *ethnic cleansing*, but rather *ethics cleansing*. The

Amalekites represent our tendency to prefer complacency over struggle and choose evil (*rah*) over good *(tov)*. Killing those tendencies better equips us to advance forward into a closer relationship with ourselves, our community, and the Divine.

The third and final example of a *tov* murder appears in the story of David and Goliath, which is found in 1 Samuel 17:1-40. Most remember the basic story line: The Philistine army was advancing on the Israelite army when a young boy named David challenged and killed Goliath, the giant Philistine warrior, and in so doing saved the nation.

That in a nutshell is the literal take on the story. Let's now briefly examine its allegorical meaning. The narrative likely takes place around 1000 BC, at a time when Israel's first king, Saul, was struggling to unite the nation's twelve tribes. At the same time, the Philistines (who probably were Greek) were posing a huge challenge to Israel, not only because of their military might (their armor and weapons were far more advanced due to their superior metallurgical technologies), but because of their prosperity (they profited from being at the center of trade and culture). To top it off their leader, Goliath, was said to be six cubits high (about ten feet tall).

Who was Goliath? His larger-than-life imagery suggests that he was not a real person. Instead, he appears in the story as a symbol, representing the extent of the Philistine challenge; for it was he alone who challenged any Israelite to a one-on-one, winner-take-all battle. Specifically, he said *"Choose one of your men and let him come down against me. If he beats me in combat and kills me, we will become your slaves"* (I Samuel 17:8-9).

Bear in mind that in military terms, Goliath's challenge (risking the well-being of an entire military regiment on a single soldier) is totally unorthodox and without precedent. But again, this is Torah - where stories are intended less for historical accuracy than to convey personally meaningful teachings.

So, what was Goliath's challenge and what lesson can we derive from it? First, the challenge: The Philistines, like the Egyptians before them, offered the Israelites all the trappings of advanced civilization, but with it a way of life that tends to become narrow – one in which people willingly sacrifice their spiritual well-being for material enslavements such as job security, shelter, and food. Said differently, Goliath's battle with David can be viewed as a battle between polytheism and monotheism. Will the Children of Israel, only a few generations removed from *Mitz'rayim,* abandon the Promised Land that they are still trying to settle, in favor of their polytheistic ways? Will they continue to move forward into closer relationships with themselves, their community, and the Divine, or will they spend the rest of their days chasing after false gods?

Now, the teaching: By killing Goliath - - or more accurately killing what Goliath stands for - - David reminded the people of what they should have learned from the Ten Blows/plagues, their exodus, and forty years of wandering. Specifically, our potential to create is better actualized when we control the extras (*chu'metz*) than when they control us. . Thus, from the perspective of Torah, the killing of Goliath was a "good" murder, as were those of the Egyptian task master and Amalek.

* What is meant by the Fifth Saying, "*Honor your father and your mother in order that your days may be prolonged on the soil that YHVH is giving you*"? Perhaps no Saying is more quoted and less understood than this one, particularly by parents who interpret the Hebrew word "Honor" (*ca'vode*) to mean "love" or "obey." It doesn't. *Ca'vode* shares the same linguistic root (*sho-resh*) with the word for "heavy", *ca'ved*. Thus, the word "honor" in the expression, "Honor your father and your mother" literally translates as "give weight, or close attention to" your parents. This is another way of saying, "bear true witness on your parents" (the Ninth Saying).

By stating this Saying separately from the Ninth, the Torah is recognizing the obvious: There is something undeniably powerful about the relationship between parents and their children. Witness the relationship between Eve and her first son, Cain, the first of many stories in Genesis pertaining to parent-child relations and their effect on a child's ability to "move forward" on his or her personal and spiritual journeys. Other Genesis stories also bear noting, in particular those about Avram, Sarai, and Hagar and their son, Ishmael; Abraham, Sarah and their son, Isaac; Isaac, Rebecca, and their twin sons, Esau and Jacob; and Jacob, Leah, Rachel and each of their twelve sons. If the point of the Ten Sayings is about building an intimate relationship with ourselves so that we can do the same with others, then these stories suggest that there is no better place to start than by bearing true witness with our parents. In them we see ourselves close-up: the good and the not-so good, our past and our possible future.

Moreover, there is nothing in the Biblical stories to suggest an obligation to obey or love our parents. Consider Avram and Sarai, who went forth from their parents' home, never to return or see their parents again (Genesis 12). They were neither vilified nor reprimanded for their actions, but rather esteemed as the forebears of *Israel*. Indeed, the Torah encourages us to choose which of our parents' footsteps to follow and which of their wells to dig (see the Isaac story shortly after his binding on Mount Mor'iah in Genesis 22), because like YHVH's name, we too "will be what we will be." Or, as expressed more recently in a Kahlil Gibran poem about children in which he wrote that our children may come through us, but they do not belong to us.

The Saying "Honor your father and your mother" also begs the question, "Who are our parents?" The Torah emphasizes the distinction between physical and spiritual reality. For example, YHVH refers to Abraham as Jacob's father, even though Isaac is Jacob's biological father. This is because Isaac's spiritual identity started to fade at an early age, in contrast to that of his father, Abraham, and ultimately of Jacob himself.

From the perspective of Torah, our spiritual parentage can also originate outside the family lineage. For instance, David refers to Saul as his father and Saul calls him "my son," even though the two are not biologically linked.

One additional note about David's relationship with Saul: We are told in I Samuel 17: 38 that Saul tried to prepare David for battle with Goliath by "clothing David in his own garment." Saul's garments included a bronze helmet, breastplate, and sword. These garments had worked for the previous generation; yet David quickly rejected them, saying, "I cannot walk in these, for I am not used to them." Clearly, David's decision was not motivated by obligation or love, but instead the recognition that what had worked for his father was not going to work for him. That is to say that David gave weight, or close attention, to his father, while at the same time bearing true witness to himself.

Finally, often overlooked in the Fifth Saying is its ending clause: *"in order that your days may be prolonged on the soil that YHVH is giving you."* Of course, the soil refers to the Promised Land, which we earlier defined as a state of mind of awakened awareness, where we find both milk (symbolic of nourishment) and honey (representing sweetness and joy), even during mundane or troubled times.

* What is the meaning of the Fourth Saying, *"Remember the Sabbath and make it holy; no one in your household is to do any kind of work for in the first six days YHVH made the heavens and earth and all that is in it, but rested on the seventh day and blessed it"?* The Creation Story (Genesis 1) tells of how YHVH created the physical world during the first six days through a process of separation, or "setting apart." On the seventh day, YHVH created the Sabbath by separating the physical world from the spiritual world.

The Hebrew word for the Sabbath, *Shabbat*, derives from the root *shin-beit-tav*, which actually means "to stop" although it is commonly mistranslated as "to rest." As such, Shabbat is intended to be a time of introspection and meditation, when we try to quiet our mind of its labor-centric dialogues and listen instead to the voices of our heart (sometimes referred to as our "inner teachings") and be fully present in the moment. This is our opportunity to renew our spirit, nourish our soul, and be transformed by what we learn from the experience. In other words, Shabbat is about stopping what we are doing long enough to build a relationship with ourselves. By remembering Shabbat, we are better able to comprehend the teachings from each of the previously discussed six Sayings. By observing the Shabbat, we can better advance forward on our personal and spiritual journey to *"the soil that YHVH is giving you."*

*What is the meaning of the Third Saying, *"You are not to take up the name of YHVH for emptiness, for YHVH will not clear him that takes up his name for emptiness"?* This Saying is telling us to not trivialize YHVH's name by using it for self-serving purposes, as some politicians and religious leaders often do. Moreover, don't claim to understand YHVH, know what YHVH wants, or speak on YHVH's behalf; but instead bear true witness on YHVH by accepting YHVH's abstract name, *Ehyeh asher ehyeh* ("I will be whatever I will be") as it was revealed to Moses at the Burning Bush. Accept also the fact that YHVH's name gives no hint as to who or what God is. Therefore be wary of those who hold an anthropomorphic, humanized vision of God, claim to speak or act on God's behalf, or assign meaning to God's actions as if they know God's true essence. . Be wary also of our own temptation to misuse God's name. Finally, accept that YHVH isn't so much a name - in the sense that names are nouns - but instead is a verb, conjugated in the first person, imperfect tense to signify an ongoing movement into an unbounded future.

Why the Third Saying? It teaches us that like YHVH's name, we too "will be whatever we will be." Implied in the Third Saying, therefore, is the message that the sooner we can bear true witness to YHVH by not "taking up YHVH's name in emptiness," the sooner we can bear it to ourselves and others (Ninth Saying), for we are created in the image of YHVH. Once we are able to do this, we will become "spiritually clean" (in Hebrew, *na'kee*): Forgiven for our movements backward and made again *tam,* or unblemished; that is, restored to our original state of purity in which we were born *"in order that your days may be prolonged on the soil that YHVH is giving you"* (Fifth Saying).

On the other hand, not taking *"up the name of YHVH for emptiness"* can leave us with a totally unrealistic understanding of ourselves and others. For example, Rabbi Harold Kushner argues in his book "When Bad Things Happen to Good People" that most of us grew up with a "non-empty" image of God as being an all-wise parent figure who treats each of us with infinite fairness, rewarding us when we do right and punishing us when we don't. As he notes, this image can engender feelings of guilt (e.g., "We must have brought this tragedy on to ourselves"), anger (when our prayers are not answered), and jealousy (when our neighbors' prayers appear to be answered). These are the kinds of emotions that can preoccupy our thoughts and distract us from remembering the Sabbath and honoring our parents. This empty image of God can also engender feelings of self-righteousness, impatience, and intolerance (e.g., "If they worked harder, they wouldn't be poor") – emotions which can encourage actions like martyrdom that can "murder" the potential to create life and adulterate relationships (Sixth Saying). These emotions can also promote stealing, bearing false witness, and desiring that which doesn't belong to us (Sayings Seven to Ten).

* What is the meaning of the Second Saying, "*You are not to have any other gods before my presence. You are not to make yourself a carved-image or any other figure that is in the heavens above, earth below, or the waters beneath the earth. You are not to bow down to them nor serve them, for I, YHVH am a zealous God, calling to account the iniquity of the fathers upon the sons, to the third and fourth generations of those who hate me, but showing loyalty to the thousandth of those who love me and keep my commandments"?* Though this is the longest of the Ten Sayings, its message is straightforward and captures the monotheistic essence of the Torah. To us moderns, however, it appears passé; for few among us think of ourselves as polytheists. This is probably because we hold an outdated image of polytheists as deeply superstitious individuals, usually from primitive, agrarian-based societies, who pray in front of clay or golden calves that symbolize fertility and other such basic human desires.

Torah hints at a more modern view of polytheists as those who choose to live their lives in *mitz'rayim*" – narrow places where we focus more on *material* than *spiritual* pursuits (Recall from earlier commentary that spiritual pursuits include seeking knowledge of good (*tov*), evil (*rah*), and life; as well as answers to personal questions such as "Who am I?", "Who am I not?", "Why am I?", and "What is my real purpose?") Said differently, polytheists are those who define their lives in terms of pursuits other than the seeking of *shalem* (wholeness) and trying to be like *Israel* (both willing and able to struggle with personal and spiritual matters). Polytheists are also those who engage in *melachah* on Shabbat, or activities intended to grant us control over our physical environment for our own material gain (Genesis 1).

Polytheists are also those who "*take up the name of YHVH for emptiness*" by holding a humanized view of God - for such a view tends to be idol-like, carved in *our* own image (Third Saying). For example, consider parents like Abraham and Sarah. In their attempt to control the future they treated their son Isaac for 37 years like an idealized possession, "a god before YHVH's presence." This prevented Isaac from leaving his home to embark upon his personal and spiritual journey, while keeping Abraham and Sarah from fully perceiving YHVH's presence. (For more about the relationship between Isaac and his parents, refer to the Chapter 3 commentary about the Sacrifice of Isaac.)

The point of the above examples is that we are all polytheists, placing "other gods before YHVH's presence" and allowing worldly possessions and aspirations to distract our attention, preventing us from being fully present and engaged in life. In so doing, we "murder" a moment in our lives in which we might have otherwise actualized the potential to create life that is embedded in the Creation (Sixth Saying). The question, therefore, is not whether we are polytheists, but to what extent. Put in terms of the Exodus story (Chapter 7), are we in control of our *chu-matze* (extras, or non-essentials that can enslave us) or does our *chu-matze* control our relationship with ourselves, others, and the Divine?

The consequences of "placing other gods before YHVH's presence," according to the Second Saying, do not stop with us. Indeed, they extend to future generations. Implicit in that prediction is that we have the capacity to bring upon ourselves the Tenth blow, "Death of the first born." Recall the Chapter 6 commentary on Exodus 11: If we raise our children in a home imbued with the polytheistic values of enslavement and narrowness, they may never learn a better way. They will be living a life that is not their own - a life that is not personally meaningful to them. They will live, but their ability to appreciate life will be dead, as in turn will the ability of their offspring, *"for I, YHVH am a zealous God."*

Often translated as "jealous," "zealous" suggests that half-hearted attempts to reach the soil that YHVH promised us will not get us there. If we *"take up the name of YHVH for emptiness"* and if we *"place other gods before YHVH's presence,"* we will never experience *shalem*/wholeness - - never experience a deep sense of oneness and peace with who we are (with no internal conflicts) and where we are (in the world around us);

never reach a state of mind where we are fully aware of receiving nourishment (milk) and sweetness (honey) from life, even during mundane or troubled times.

***What is the meaning of the First Saying, "*I am YHVH your God, who brought you out from the land of Mitz'rayim, and from the house of serfs*"?** The First Saying refers to an event in the past. This is done to convey the meaning that in order to hear the Ten Sayings, we must first be sufficiently awakened by the Ten Blows, for it was these Blows that caused us to leave our narrow places and our enslavements. This is not to imply that only three months since leaving *Mitz'rayim,* we are now free. Rather, the First Saying is reminding us of our monotheistic relationship with *Ehyeh asher ehyeh* ("I will be whatever I will be").

Now, who is YHVH, aside from "being whatever YHVH will be"? The Third and Second Sayings tell us who YHVH is not (i.e., not empty and not one of many), but offer no clues as to who YHVH is. Inferred from the First Saying, however, is the message that we need not concern ourselves with things that we cannot understand, for those concerns serve to distract our attention from ourselves, our parents, and our community. Rather, the First Saying is telling us to be content simply in knowing that YHVH exists, by virtue of YHVH's actions (e.g., "I brought you out from the land of Mitz'rayim"); is "one" (the monotheistic essence of the Torah); and offers Ten Sayings to help us move closer to "the soil that YHVH is giving us." The ultimate message is that the unfathomable life force that we call YHVH is, was, and forever more will be without limits (*ein sof*) and without other (*ein od*). Our challenge is to bear true witness on YHVH by accepting comfort in the fact that we will never understand YHVH.

Closing Comments: We observed how the Ten Sayings are interdependent: The meaning of each is augmented by its interactions with the other nine. As such, the Ten Sayings taken as a whole offer a more enriched lesson than do the sum of its Ten individual parts. For example, it is not possible to fully grasp the meaning of the three Sayings about YHVH (i.e., the first three) without first struggling to understand who we are and who we are not (Sayings 4-10). It is also not possible to fully understand ourselves without trying to understand YHVH. The Ten Sayings are thus presented to represent a limitless array of personal, communal and spiritual challenges, far more than can be learned and put into practice in a lifetime. But take heart; for this is what leaving Mitz'rayim for the Promised Land is all about. It is about willingly committing our lives to something that is forever beyond our human ability to reach and master. This is not to say that we were not born with the capacity to move closer to the Tree of Life and its promise of enlightenment. However, like Adam and Eve, we can never get so close as to eat from it.

Chapter 9: Receiving the Covenant

Exodus 20:15 through Exodus 23: A System of Justice

Summary: *The people were seeing the thunder sounds, the flashing-torches, the shofar sound, the mountain smoking, and stood far off, saying to Moses, You speak with us, and we will listen, but let not YHVH speak with us, lest we die! Moses replied: Do not be afraid, for it is to test you that YHVH has come, to have awe of YHVH so that you do not sin.*

YHVH then said to Moses to tell the Children of Israel that they are not to make beside Me gods of silver and gold. Instead, make for Me slaughter sites of soil and un-hewn stones where the people can make sacrifices of shalom of your sheep and oxen.

And, YHVH said to Moses: These are the regulations to set before the people to deal with:

- *The rights of the slaves (e.g., Exodus 21:2: "On the seventh year the slave is to go free") as well as regulations to protect widows, orphans, the poor (e.g., Exodus 23:10, 11: "For six years you are to sow your land and gather in its produce, but in the seventh you are to let it go that the needy may eat and what they allow to remain, the wildlife of the field may eat.")*
- *Actions that cause personal injuries (e.g., Exodus 21:24-25: "- eye for an eye, tooth in place of tooth, hand in place of hand, foot in place of foot, burnt scar in place of burnt scar, wound in place of wound, bruise in place of bruise")*
- *Instances of damage done to another's property due to negligence or intent (e.g., Exodus 21:33: "When a man digs a pit, and does not cover it up, and an ox or a donkey falls into it")*
- *Capital crimes of violence like murder, striking one's parents, kidnapping, and denigrating one's parent; as well as non-capital crimes such as theft, rape, bribery, and bearing false witness*
- *Protecting the rights of strangers (Exodus 23:9: " for once we were strangers"); and livestock (Exodus 23:12: "on the seventh day, you are to cease your labor so that your ox and donkey may rest"; and Exodus 23:19: "You are not to boil a kid in the milk of its mother.")*

> *Avoiding disrespect on religious matters, such as idolatry or blasphemy, as well as guidance on observing the three Pilgrimage Festivals (Passover, Shavu'ot, and Sukkot).*

These regulations conclude with the promise that if the people do all that YHVH speaks, then YHVH will be an enemy to their enemies ("cause them to perish"); remove hunger and sickness from among their midst; and make their territory from the Sea of Reeds to the Sea of the Philistines (the Mediterranean), from the Wilderness (the Negev) to the River in the north (Euphrates).

Discussion Questions: What is the test that Moses refers to at the beginning of this passage? Why is Moses told to make a slaughter site of soil and unhewn stones? What is the relationship between the "regulations" that Moses is to set before the people and the Ten Sayings?

* What is the test that Moses mentions at the beginning of this passage? The stories of Genesis and Exodus that we have read up to this point contain many instances where the lead characters are tested to see what they learned, what lessons remained in store for them, and whether they were truly ready to apply that which has just been revealed to them. As was previously discussed, revelations can be thought of as epiphanies; that is, those sudden intuitive leaps of understanding when we realize a better and more personally meaningful way to live with ourselves, others, and the Divine.

However, Moses's remark (*Do not be afraid, for it is to test you that YHVH has come, to have awe of YHVH so that you do not sin*) is only the second instance in Torah where the reader is being explicitly told that what is about to transpire in the story is a test. Testing was first mentioned in the context of the Akedah story (Genesis 22), which opened with the line, "*God tested Abraham.*" In that instance I interpreted this to mean that what was about to happen in the story was "not the real thing"; that is, Isaac's life was not really going to be sacrificed.

We can apply a similar interpretation to Moses's statement in Genesis 20. The Israelites are being given the opportunity to demonstrate what they have learned from their experiences to date, without yet running the risk of being denied entry into the Promised Land. Their experiences began with the first of the Ten Blows in *Mitz'rayim* and continued as they glimpsed the Promised Land at Sukkot, safely crossed the Sea of Reeds, drank sweetened water at Maror, ate *man-hu* and quail at Elim, received the gift of Shabbat in the Wilderness of Syn and, most recently, received the Ten Sayings at Sinai.

How did they do on their latest test? The answer is, not well. Despite these many reassurances to body, mind and spirit, they are still unable to live in awe of YHVH and accept the First Saying (*"I am YHVH your God, who brought you out from the land of Mitz'rayim, and from the house of serfs"*). To the contrary, they continue to fear for their lives should YHVH speak directly to them.

It is interesting to note that their performance on the test lies in stark contrast to that of Abraham, who - moments before being asked to take his son Isaac and offer him up - responded *hee-nay-nee* ("here I am"), an expression used in Torah to indicate a complete readiness to obey without hesitation despite not knowing what was about to be asked (Genesis 22). Moses said the same in Exodus 3 just as YHVH was about to tell him to return to Pharaoh and bring the Children of Israel out of Mitz'rayim.

➤ **Why is Moses told to make a slaughter site of soil and unhewn stones?** YHVH goes on to say that "*you are not to build it smooth-hewn, for if you hold high your iron-tool over it, you will have profaned it*" (Exodus 20: 22). As we know, it was and still is customary to demonstrate one's faith by building elaborately decorated houses of worship. YHVH is saying that these adornments are not what a relationship with YHVH is about. In making this statement, YHVH is reiterating the Second Saying: "*You are not to have any other gods before my presence. You are not to make yourself a carved-image or any other figure that is in the heavens above, earth below, or the waters beneath the* *earth."* Said simply, what has been created in the heavens, on earth and in the waters are sufficient (*di'yay-noo*) and good (*tov*) and therefore not in need of human attempts to improve them. Finally, YHVH is saying that because soil and unhewn stones are found everywhere, so too can be our relationship with YHVH. We don't have to climb to the top of high mountains to get in touch with our spirituality.

What will soon transpire in the Exodus story, however, will appear to contradict these spiritual calls for simplicity; for as some of us already know, YHVH's instructions for building the Tabernacle and Ark are detailed and ornate. Moses also ends up climbing the mountain twice. I will try to reconcile these two seeming contradictions as they show up in the text.

➢ **What is the relationship between the "regulations" that Moses is to set before the people and the Ten Sayings?** The Ten Sayings conveyed a set of visions and values for creating a community of spiritual seekers, deserving of entry into the Promised Land. The regulations, appearing in the Book of Exodus between Chapters 21:2 and 23:33 lay the groundwork for translating those visions and values into a body of civil law. This groundwork is later extended, in the Torah's third and fourth books, Leviticus and Numbers.

As brief as they are, three features distinguish the regulations as a body of civil law. First, they are fair, providing guidance for doling out punishments that fit the offense. Second, they are also flexible, recognizing that extenuating circumstances are often involved. Third and finally, the regulations are compassionate in that they offer protection for the powerless. [14]

---

[14] As a brief aside, consider the regulation, *"You are not to boil a kid in the milk of its mother,"* which appears in Exodus 23:19. Taken at face value, this regulation suggests that it is acceptable to eat milk and chicken together because chickens are obviously not milk producers. Therefore, why do the dietary laws of *kashrut*, which developed during post-biblical times, call for separation of meat and dairy/milk? I suspect that the answer may lie in the Jewish mystical tradition of the Middle Ages,

> Exodus 24: Beginning the Ascent

Summary: *Moses recounted to the people all of YHVH's words and regulations, and then wrote them down. He built a slaughter site beneath the mountain with twelve stones, one for each of the twelve tribes, and then read the covenant to the people, who responded in one voice, "We will do and we will hearken!" Moses offered up slaughter offering, took half of the blood and tossed it on the people, saying "Here is the blood of the covenant that YHVH has cut with you by means of all these words."*

YHVH told Moses to go the mountain with Aaron and Aaron's two sons, Nadav and Avihu, and seventy elders. As they went up, they saw sapphire bricks beneath their feet.

YHVH then said to Moses: Go up to me on the mountain, only you, and remain there, that I may give you tablets of stone: the Instruction and the Command that I have written down. A cloud covered the mountain for six days. On the seventh day YHVH called to Moses from amidst the cloud. And the sight of the Glory of YHVH to the Children of Israel was like a consuming fire. Moses went up into the midst of the cloud and was on the mountain for forty days and forty nights.

Discussion Questions: Why twelve stones and seventy elders? What is the "blood of the covenant"? What are the "sapphire bricks"? Why did Moses stay on top of the mountain for "forty days and forty nights"? How is revelation experienced?

> ***Why twelve stones and seventy elders?** We have come across these numbers before. For example, Genesis 46: 8-27 lists the names of the twelve sons of Israel and then states: *"Thus, all the persons of Jacob's household who came to Mitz'rayim were seventy."* Reference to the number 70 appears again in the opening lines of the book of Exodus:

---

which viewed milk as a "life giving" source of sustenance (as in "the land of milk and honey") that should be kept apart from all types of flesh, which is viewed as representing death.

"Now these are the names of the Children of Israel coming to Egypt - - so all the persons were seventy persons" (Exodus 1:1-5). Then, in Exodus 15:27 we read of the journey out of Mitz'rayim: *"From Maror, they went to Elim, where there were twelve springs of water and seventy palms – and from there to the Wilderness of Syn."*

Regarding the Exodus 15 verse, I wrote that by coming upon the twelve springs and seventy palms in *Elim*, the people are not only glimpsing into the future, but also seeing their connection to the deep past at the time of their first arrival in Egypt. This connection is symbolically revisited in Exodus 24, when YHVH tells Moses to go to the mountain with seventy elders.

What is the significance of the number "seventy"? Perhaps it was chosen because it represents the product of seven (which signifies the completion of one cycle of Creation) times ten (considered an amount large enough to command one's attention). It may also derive from the Flood Story and the number of Noah's descendants, listed in Genesis 10, who repopulated the world. The Torah may be implying that the seventy elders represent those esteemed individuals who will populate the Promised Land.

➤ **What is the "blood of the covenant"?** During biblical times, a covenant (in Hebrew, *brit*) referred to a formal agreement or contract with God, which was generally sealed by an exchange of blood. Why blood? It represents one's life-source; therefore to exchange it represents the offering of an intimate part of one's own being. As such, an exchange of blood was viewed as more enduring than a simple verbal commitment or handshake, akin to a signature on a legal document today.

Of course, the ritual of blood-exchange mentioned in this passage and elsewhere in Torah involved the blood of sacrificial animals rather than humans. And, while most today view animal sacrifice as a barbaric custom, we can agree that it was a major advance over the practice of human sacrifice which was common in the surrounding cultures at that time. Moreover, the sacrificial animal had to be unblemished (*tam* in Hebrew*)*, and therefore dear to the owner. Referring back to the story of Cain and Abel (Genesis 4), we will recall that Abel gave the choicest of the first-born from his flock, suggesting a generous offering from the heart. Cain's gift, in contrast, was described as half-hearted.

As an aside, the earliest recording of a blood exchange is found in the ancient Sumerian story of Gilgamesh, thought to have been written more than 4,500 years ago. In that story, Gilgamesh and his friend Enkidu become blood brothers, thus acting as a single being until death. The "blood covenant" took on new meaning in the Christian Bible. For example, we read in Matthew 26:28 that *"This is the blood of the covenant, which is poured out for many for the forgiveness of sins."*

➢ **What are the "sapphire bricks"?** Bricks have appeared twice before in the Torah. In the Tower of Babel story (Genesis 11) bricks were used by the people in an attempt to reach the heavens and make a name for themselves. Later, in Exodus 5, the enslaved people living in *Mitz'rayim* (a narrow place) used bricks to build Pharaoh's cities. Here in Exodus 24, sapphire bricks line the pathway up the Mountain of God.

These three stories raise the question: "Whom are we serving?" Are we making bricks to serve ourselves (as in the Tower story) or another (like Pharaoh)? Or, are the bricks meant to help us move closer to YHVH? By the time that Exodus 24 is read, the answer should be obvious, even without having to rely on the sapphire metaphor

Why sapphires? These semi-precious stones are intensely blue, so much so that legend has it that they offer a vision of the heavens. In fact, sapphires are mentioned in numerous other biblical stories, including Exodus 39, Job 28:6, Isaiah 54:11, Ezekiel 1:26, and Ezekiel 28:13.

➢ **Why did Moses stay on top of the mountain for "forty days and forty nights"?** The number 40, which appears forty times in the Torah beginning with the Flood story (Genesis 5), is used to symbolize the birth of a fundamentally new understanding about the meaning of life, and therefore the death of what we once had held to be true. "Forty" also represents a moment of revelation when an individual has developed a deeper understanding of the meaning of the Ten Sayings. (The number 40 has a similar meaning in the Christian Bible. For example, Jesus went by himself into the wilderness for forty days and forty nights, and returned with a New Testament.)

➤ **How is revelation experienced?** The Exodus stories hint at a progression. At the lowest level are the Israelites who, while looking up from the base of the Mountain, saw a consuming fire, which they feared was going to destroy them. Their response to the Mountain suggested that they have not moved forward from where they were four chapters ago in the Exodus story when Moses said to them *"Do not be afraid! For it is to test you that YHVH has come, to have awe of him be upon you"* (Exodus 20:17). Once again they were tested and one again they underperformed.

At the next level is Moses, who in Exodus 3 felt awe rather than fear upon seeing the bush burning but not being consumed; for he realized that he was experiencing the extraordinary in the ordinary. At the third and highest level is a more mature version of Moses, who in later years willingly surrendered to the "unknowable." By allowing himself to be totally enveloped by the cloud, he gave up all control of who he was and who he may have wanted to be. At this level, Moses attained freedom from all ego-induced enslavements, understood better than any the meaning of the phrase: "I will be whatever I will be," and experienced the future in the present tense.

Those who study Kabala and its mystical view of the Torah refer to these moments as *ein sof* experiences. This translates as "without limits" - an experience that is so vast, so deeply penetrating, so filled with clarity and awe - that it seemed to reside less inside of Moses than did he inside of it. Other *ein sof* experiences include those felt by Avram in Genesis 13 and Moses in Deuteronomy 34: 1-4, when each was allowed to see the Promised Land in all directions.

> **Exodus 25-31: Instructions for Building the Tabernacle.**

Background: These seven chapters contain detailed instructions for the building and décor of the sanctuary and its sacred center, where the ark or tabernacle is to be held. This ark is to contain the two tablets engraved with YHVH's words, referred to as the "Testimony." Also mentioned in these chapters is a description of the garments that the priests are to wear and the many steps that they are to follow when sacrificing an animal.

Summary: *And YHVH spoke to Moses, saying: Speak to the Children of Israel. Let them make Me a Holy-Shrine, according to all that I grant you to see, the building pattern of the Dwelling and the building pattern of all its implements that I may dwell amidst them. They are to make the Tent of Appointment and the /Ark of Testimony; and the purgation-cover that is over it; and all the implements of the Tent and the Table; the pure lampstand and all of its implements; and the site for smoke-offering-up and all of its implements; and the basin and its pedestal and the officiating garments; and the garments of holiness for Aaron the priest and the garments of his sons for being priests; and oil for anointing and fragrant smoke for the holy offerings according to all that I have commanded you, they are to make. However, my Sabbaths you are to keep, for it is a sign between Me and you, a covenant throughout all generations, to know that I, YHVH, hallow you. And when YHVH finished speaking to Moses on Mount Sinai, he gave to him the two tablets of the Testimony, tablets of stone, written by the finger of YHVH.*

Discussion Question: Why are the instructions for the Tabernacle and the priestly garments so detailed and ornate, as opposed to unhewn? Why were the Ten Sayings written on two tablets rather than some other number?

> *** Why build it so ornate?** There have been several attempts to reconstruct various objects in Torah, like Noah's Ark, the Ark of Testimony, and the Temple, only to discover that the descriptions fall short of providing complete blueprints. Moreover, there are aspects of the instructions that do not hold up to reason. As Everett Fox (pp. 395-396) points out, the Israelites are only three months removed from slavery and currently residing in the wilderness; how could they have acquired the precious materials mentioned in the text that are required to build the Tabernacle or, for that matter, learn the building and artistic skills necessary to complete the task?

Fox's answer is that those who reject the story because of its practical and logical inconsistencies miss the point of its non-literal teaching: By positioning the Ark of Testimony in the sacred center of the Sanctuary, and the Ten Sayings in the center of the Ark, the text is telling us how we can develop a closer relationship with YHVH and consequently move closer to the "soil that YHVH is giving us." In brief, we can do this by focusing our attention on the moral code that lies at the "center of the center" and not on its sacred source; for, as the Second and Third Saying tell us, YHVH is unknowable. The layout of the sanctuary is thus envisioned as the physical manifestation of a spiritual philosophy.

That said, why have the sanctuary so ornate? Wasn't it only a few chapters ago that YHVH said to Moses: *"You are not to build it smooth-hewn, for if you hold high your iron-tool over it, you will have profaned it"*? (Exodus 20: 22). Wasn't YHVH saying that these adornments are not what a relationship with YHVH is about?

The answer depends on YHVH's audience. When it is Moses, unhewn stones are enough. After all, who in Torah has moved closer to an enlightened relationship with YHVH, having just experienced his third revelation? His first revelation came when Moses killed the Egyptian (representing a force from within that was shepherding his life) in order to create a new and more authentic purpose to his life (Exodus 2). Only by this "murder" could he inhabit the present with enough clarity and mindfulness to perceive his second revelation, the "burning bush" (Exodus 3). It was through this experience that he understood a new direction for his life, one in which he would partner with YHVH to lead the mixed multitude of the enslaved people living in Egypt from their narrow places. The third revelation is the receiving of the Ten Sayings directly from YHVH. If the number "40" in Torah is used to symbolize the birth of a fundamentally new understanding about the meaning of life, as we have already observed numerous times in the biblical stories, then Moses by the time of receiving the Ten Sayings has reached the symbolic age of 120 years, or 40 times 3, the age that he will remain until the time of his death.

For the rest of the Israelites, however, unhewn stones are not enough. Remember that when they looked up from the base of the Mountain, they saw a consuming fire which they feared would destroy them. They have also been tested repeatedly, and underperformed each time. While Moses was transformed during his forty days and forty nights on top of the Mountain, those who remained below became more anxious and doubtful.

By providing detailed and ornate instructions for building the Tabernacle and Ark, YHVH is offering the Israelites a kind of tangible bridge linking their physical reality to the Divine in a way that the average person could understand. The need for such precise direction from YHVH is necessary since the people have yet to show an understanding of the first three Sayings. This will soon be evident in the upcoming Golden Calf Story, when they regress to the rituals and practices that were familiar to them in Egypt.

➢ **Why "Two" Tablets?** Might the Sayings be written on two tablets to separate those five behaviors that we are told to engage in (for example, remember the Sabbath and honor our parents) from the five which we are told to avoid (murder. adultery, stealing, bearing false witness, and coveting)? Alternatively, might two tablets have been chosen to symbolically represent the two trees lying at the center of the Garden of Eden/Delight (Genesis 2, 3)? The Tree of Life and its associated questions - "Who are we?" and "What is our purpose in life?"- refer to the positive behaviors expressed in the first five Sayings, while the Tree of Knowledge of Good and Evil relates to the five negative behaviors mentioned in the second five Sayings.

> Exodus 32: The Golden Calf

Summary: *When the people saw that Moses was shamefully late in coming down the mountain, they assembled against Aaron and said to him to make us a god who will go before us, for we do not know what has become of Moses. Aaron replied, "Bring to me all of your gold," which he then took and fashioned into a molten calf, and said, "This is your God, O Israel, who brought you up from the land of Egypt." He then called out that "Tomorrow is a festival to YHVH." Starting early on the morrow, the people offered shalom-offering, and then sat down to eat, drink and revel.*

YHVH said to Moses: Go down, for your people are a stiff-necked people, having quickly turned away from that which I commanded them. My anger may flare against them, and I may destroy them, but you I will make a great nation.

Moses soothed the face of YHVH, saying, For what reason should your anger flare against your people? Should the Egyptians say that I brought them out with the evil intent of killing them in the mountains?

And YHVH felt sorry for the evil that YHVH had spoken of doing to his people.

Now, Moses began to descend the mountain with the two tablets of the Testimony in hand. And it was that when he saw the calf and the dancing, his anger flared and he threw the tablets, smashing them beneath the mountain. He then took the calf and burned it, ground it up until it was thin-powder, stewed it in water, and then made the Children of Israel drink it.

Moses then said to Aaron, "What did this people do to you that you have brought upon it such a great sin!" Aaron replied, "Let not my lord's anger flare up, for you yourself know this people and how set-on-evil it is."

Moses positioned himself at the camp's gate and said, "Whoever is for YHVH – to me." And there gathered all the sons of Levi. He then said, "Thus says YHVH, take your swords and kill every man who is not for YHVH." And the sons of Levi did according to Moses's words and on that day some three thousand men fell.

The next day Moses said to his people, "You have sinned a great sin. So now I will go up to YHVH, and perhaps I may be able to purge away your sin."

Moses went up to YHVH and said, "So now, if you would only bear their sin – but if not, pray blot me out of the record that you have written." YHVH replied, "Whoever sins against me will be blotted out of my record. Now, go, lead the people to where I have spoken to you, but on the day of my calling to account, I will call them to account for their sins." And, YHVH plagued the people because they made the calf that Aaron made.

Discussion Questions: Who is Aaron? Why did Moses have the people drink a solution of powdered gold? Did YHVH order the killing of every man who is not for YHVH? How does the Golden Calf story compare with the stories of the Flood and of Sodom?

> **Who is Aaron** (aside from being the patriarch of the priestly tribe)? As I noted in Chapter 6's commentary on Exodus 4, most names in the Torah reveal core aspects of personality (e.g., Moses's name means "pulled from the water"). Aaron's name, however, is left undefined. It is as if he has no personality independent of Moses. Indeed, he has been little more than a mouth for Moses to put words into. This is how YHVH viewed Aaron, when he said to Moses: *"Is there not Aaron, your brother, a Levite – I know he can speak, yes, speak well. As you return to Egypt, he will come out to meet you. I will instruct you what to say and you shall put the words in his mouth. He shall be for you a mouth and you shall be for him a god."*

With the exodus, however, Aaron's situation changed. For the first time in the story, he does not have his brother around to put words into his mouth, for Moses is presumably alone at the top of the Mountain, enveloped in the clouds that looked like fire to those below him, and has not been seen or heard from for at least 40 days. Aaron can finally speak for himself.

But, does he? I think not. Despite all that he experienced as Moses's second-in-command in dealing with Pharaoh and in personally witnessing each of the Ten Blows; despite seeing sapphire bricks as he and his two sons accompanied Moses and the seventy elders part-way up the Mountain of God; despite this and so much more, Aaron continues to act as someone else's mouthpiece. Rather than speak the words of Moses, we find him in Exodus 32 speaking the words that the mixed multitude wants to hear. Of course, I am referring to the passage when he tells the people to bring to him their gold so that he could fashion out of it a calf (an Egyptian symbol of fertility). He calls this calf YHVH, the god "that brought you from the land of Egypt" – and not a single person objected. It was as if no one - including Aaron himself - was influenced in the slightest way by the first three Sayings that YHVH had spoken to them just a few days before!

What I find particularly telling about Aaron's behavior is that rather than take responsibility for his actions when confronted by Moses, he shifts the blame to the others when he tells Moses, *"You yourself know this people and how set-on-evil it is."*

Curiously, Moses does not appear disturbed by Aaron's behavior. Instead he shows him compassion, saying: *"What did this people do to you that you have brought upon it such a great sin!"* Why? Perhaps Moses understood the pressures that "this people" could place on their leader, having felt it many times himself. Alternatively, perhaps Moses realized that by treating his brother as little more than a mouthpiece, he had stunted Aaron's personal and spiritual development. This explanation bears similarity to what Abraham and Sarah inadvertently did to their son Isaac by keeping him under their parental control well into his thirty-seventh year. Recall the observation in the commentary to Genesis 22 that Isaac, due to having been homebound for so many years, had difficulty establishing his own identify and consequently never advanced as far on his journey as did his parents or his son, Jacob.

➢ **Why did Moses force the people to drink a solution of powdered gold?** The drink is serving as a wake-up call, a refresher "blow" to remind the people of why they left Mitz'rayim and undertook the journey to the Promised Land. They left because the prosperity that they enjoyed while living in that narrow place was not fulfilling their spiritual needs. They left because they hungered for a life filled with sustenance (milk) and joy (honey). The left because living in Mitz'rayim was like drinking a powdered gold solution that offered them neither.

➢ **Did YHVH order the killing of every man who is not for YHVH?** By telling Moses to order the Levites to kill with their swords every man who is not for YHVH, YHVH seems to be instructing Moses to do something that is not only inconsistent with the Sixth Saying ("not to commit murder"), but also with the system of civil justice that we read about in Exodus 20-23. We described that system as being fair (providing guidance for doling out settlements that fit the offense); flexible (recognizing extenuating circumstances); and compassionate (offering protection for the powerless). As it was with the Exodus 19 statement *"Have no one touch the mountain, for whoever touches the mountain shall be put-to-death,"* we are once again confronted with a God that appears demanding, jealous, passionate, and capricious – a God that evokes fear, not awe.

Before jumping to that conclusion, however, it is important to remind ourselves that the Torah is first and foremost a theological document, concerned primarily with conveying spiritual and ethical teachings rather than historical or physical happenings. Accordingly, the Torah tends to define death in spiritual terms. For example, Adam and Eve did not biologically expire upon eating the forbidden fruit. Instead they suffered spiritual death, being driven out of the Garden and away from their close relationship with YHVH, to a place where the Light from the first day of Creation shines less brightly.

Secondly, the teachings from the Torah assume a degree of free will: We can choose to move either closer to the Light or as far away from it as imaginable, as depicted in the book "Night" - Elie Wiesel's first-hand account of a Holocaust experience. When we opt for the first path, we become one of the "Chosen" – but note that it is we who do the choosing. As we read in Exodus 19:5, *"If you hearken to my voice and keep my covenant, you shall be a special treasure from among all people, a kingdom of priests, a holy nation."*

Torah's treatment of death and free will offers us clues for decoding YHVH's killing order. Specifically, those who chose not to be for YHVH were exercising their Divine right of free will to not be among the "Chosen People." In so choosing, however, they denied themselves and their offspring the opportunity to enter into the Promised Land. Put differently, we all have the freedom to invoke the tenth blow/plague (death of the first born) on ourselves by choosing a life imbued with the polytheistic values of enslavement and narrowness. However, when we make such choices, we limit the life journeys of our children and their children, making it more difficult for them to discover their life's true purpose, even after the ten blows/plagues. Said bluntly, we all have the freedom to choose a life that is spiritually dead.

As for the Levites' swords, it is tempting to view them as lethal weapons, but I prefer a less literal interpretation based on how the term "sword" is used in Torah. The first usage of "sword" (in Hebrew, *horev,* which also means "destruction") appears in the Garden of Eden story when *"YHVH then placed Cherubim and flashing, ever-turning swords to watch over the Tree of Life" (Genesis 3:24).* The next instance, in Exodus 3:1, refers to the mountain, Mount Horev, where Moses encounters the "burning bush." The third mention of swords pertains to those held by the Levites.

What do these three references have in common? In each case, the word is used to signify purification; that is, the destruction of what we once held to be true so that *new* truths can emerge. Taken in this light, the Levites swords represent a form of communal cleansing, that which cuts off the non-spiritual seekers from having any further contact with those who yearned for a closer relationship with YHVH, so as to allow the communal "light" to shine more brightly.

How many were cut off? The text states "some three thousand men" (Exodus 32:28). What makes this number interesting is that it is the first time in Torah that a number is presented as an approximation, an amount representing a very small percentage of those 600,000 men (about half of one percent) who were said to have left Egypt (Exodus 12:37). Perhaps the text is suggesting that the possibility remains open for a life of sustenance (milk) and joy (honey) for the vast majority -- if not for themselves, then for their children.

- **How is the Golden Calf story similar to the one about the Flood?** When YHVH expressed anger against the people and threatened to destroy all but Moses, YHVH's statement was strikingly similar to the "new beginning" message after the Flood, when YHVH instructed Noah to *"Bear fruit and be many and fill the earth"* (Genesis 9:1). Recall also that YHVH's covenant with Noah promised to never again bring all flesh to ruin (Genesis 8:15). YHVH holds to this promise in his narrative with Moses, where only the third clause of Exodus 32:10 is stated definitively. Specifically, YHVH said, "my anger *may* flare up against them, and I *may* destroy them, but you I *will* make a great nation."

Thus, just as the Flood Story establishes Noah as a kind of second Adam, the Golden Calf tale presents Moses as a kind of second Noah, with one important difference: Noah's story suggests that he will be biologically linked to all who fill the earth after him. Moses, with only two sons, will not hold this distinction but is being promised an even greater one: that he will become the spiritual father to all who eventually enter the Promised Land. (Additional discussion about spiritual lineage is found in the Chapter 8 commentary on the Fifth Saying: *"Honor your father and your mother in order that your days may be prolonged on the soil that YHVH is giving you."*)

➤ **How does the Golden Calf story compare to the tale of Sodom ?** In Sodom (Genesis 18:1-22), Abraham pleaded with God on behalf of the Sodomites. Once he obtained assurance that the city would not be destroyed if fifty righteous people were found, he bid the number down to forty-five and then to forty, thirty, twenty and finally ten. Moses similarly tried to shield his people from YHVH's wrath, saying, *"For what reason should your anger flare against your people?"* (Exodus 32:11).

Of course it would be presumptuous to advise YHVH as to what to do, but that may not be the intent of these two stories. Instead, they allow us further insight into who Abraham and Moses were and how they viewed their relationships with YHVH. Of the two, Abraham showed himself to be the crafty negotiator. Rather than immediately reveal his end-game number, he approached it incrementally, perhaps fearing YHVH's reaction had he pursued the desired number too aggressively. Moses, in contrast, stated exactly what was on his mind.

Moreover, Abraham seemed genuinely concerned with the well-being of the Sodomites despite their evil, life-destroying ways, while Moses's compassion showed signs of wearing thin. Indeed, his question "Should the Egyptians say that I (i.e., YHVH) brought them out with evil intent of killing them in the mountains?" (Exodus 32:12) seemed to be suggesting less concern for his flock and more concern with what the Egyptians might think of him. If this were the case, then Moses's sudden concern for "self" may not be surprising. He would have every reason to be frustrated, given all that he has sacrificed to bring the people to the Mountain. Perhaps now he began to doubt the mission that he had willingly accepted at the sight of the Burning Bush, and he began to wonder if the people would ever shed their narrow ways?

On the other hand, this is Moses – the man who is later described in the Torah as "the most humble of all humans" (Numbers 13:3). From the perspective of Torah, humbleness is the capacity to extend one's self non-judgmentally so as to nurture and support the spiritual growth of others. There are undoubtedly those who would be surprised were he to show sudden concern with his own ego.

So, who is Moses? He is like all of us. He is on his own personal and spiritual journey alongside the people whom he is leading. Enlightened as he may be at this point, some lessons he has yet to learn. For example, he is about to discover that ascending the mountain is relatively easy, with the potential for revelation everywhere. The real challenge lies in the descent, as he must take care not to break the tablets. Once we experience revelation large or small, our challenge lies in integrating that lesson into reality. Can we transform knowledge into wisdom? Can we use the lesson to improve our relationships with ourselves and with others? Can we accept that our journey, like Creation itself, will never be completed? Moses, like all of us, is struggling with these questions.

> Exodus 33, 34: The New Covenant

Summary: *YHVH said to Moses: Go you and those who you brought up from the land of Egypt, to the land which I swore to Abraham, Isaac, and Jacob. I will send a messenger before you and will drive out the Canaanite, Amorite, Hittite, Perizzite, Hivvite and the*

Yevusite. Say to the people that I will not go up in your midst, lest I destroy you, for you are a hard-necked people.

Moses pitched a tent far from the camp, which he called the Tent of Appointment. Whenever Moses went into the Tent, a column of cloud would descend and position itself at the tent's entrance. And YHVH would speak to Moses, face to face, as a man speaks to his neighbor. When Moses would return to camp, his attendant, the lad Joshua, would not depart from within the Tent.

Moses said to YHVH, "If I have found favor in your eyes, pray let me know your ways that I may truly know you. Please, let me see your glory."

YHVH responded, I will cause all of my goodness to pass in front of your face. I will call out the name YHVH before your face. However, you cannot see My face, for no human can and live! Station yourself in the cleft of the stone on top of the Mountain and I will screen you with my hand until I have passed by. I will then remove my hand so that you can see my back, but my face shall not be seen.

Then YHVH said to Moses: Carve two tablets like the ones that you smashed and I will write on them the words that were on the first tablets. Moses did as YHVH said. And YHVH passed before his face and called out "YHVH, YHVH" and then shouted: "showing mercy, favor, grace, loyalty, truthfulness, faithfulness, and loving kindness to thousandth generation; slow to anger; forgiving of immorality, transgressions, and sin; and clearing of guilt."

YHVH then said, Here I cut a covenant" before all of you I will do wonders such as have not been created in all the earth. And, all of your people will see the work of YHVH. Take care, do not cut a covenant with those already settled in the land which I have promised to you; do not marry their whoring women nor bow down to their gods. Keep the festival of Matzo. Every first born of your sons you are to redeem with an offering of the first fruits of the soil. Observe the Sabbath and the Pilgrimage Festival of Weeks and the Pilgrimage Festival of Ingathering. You are not to boil a kid in the milk of its mother.

And Moses was beside YHVH for forty days and forty nights, without eating bread and without drinking water while writing down on the tablets the Ten Sayings of the covenant He then came down from Mount Sinai with the two tablets of Testimony, not knowing that the skin of his face was radiating because of his having spoken with YHVH.

Aaron and the Israelites saw Moses's radiating face and were afraid to approach him. Moses called to them and they came. He then commanded them all that YHVH had spoken to him on the Mountain. When he finished peaking, he put a veil upon his face.

Whenever Moses would come before the presence of YHVH, he would remove the veil, as he would whenever he was about to speak to the people, so that they could see his radiating face. But he would then put the veil back on, removing it only when speaking with YHVH.

Discussion Questions: Why is Moses' tent referred to as the Tent of Appointments? Did Moses see YHVH's face? What did Moses "see" while standing in the cleft? What is meant by the "cleft of the stone"? Is there a relationship between the Thirteen Attributes and the Ten Sayings/Commandments? Why a "radiating face"? Who is Joshua?

> ➤ **What is the "Tent of Appointment"?** The Hebrew word, "*ma'ode*", generally translated as "appointment" or "meeting", was used in day four of the Genesis 1 Creation Story to mean "set times." In the Hebrew calendar, the set times include Shabbat and the three festival holidays, Passover, Sukkot, and Shavuot. Thus, by entering the "Tent of Set-Times", Moses was entering that place in time which bridges the physical world (days 4, 5 and 6) with the spiritual world (days 1-3).

> ➤ **Did Moses see YHVH's face?** The text appears to contradict itself. First it states "And YHVH would speak to Moses, face to face, as a man speaks to his neighbor" (Exodus 33:11). However, soon after, in Chapter 33, YHVH tells Moses, "I will screen you with my hand until I have passed by. I will then remove my hand so that you can see my back, but my face shall not be seen" (Exodus 33:22, 23).

Both verses can be true. Recall from the discussion of the Ninth Blow/Plague, when for three days it was so dark that *"a man could not see the face of his brother,"* that in ancient cultures, "face" referred to more than physical appearance. To say that "I see your face" meant that I have taken the time to develop a deep understanding of who you are and can see glimpses of your "inner light." To say that "Moses saw YHVH's face" is to say that he momentarily attained a level of consciousness so awakened that he could be fully present and at perfect peace with the universe's eternal life-giving force.

The question, therefore, is not *whether* YHVH and Moses have developed a neighborly sense of intimacy (which should be apparent from our readings of the first thirty-three chapters of the Book of Exodus); but *how* intimate is their relationship? Are there aspects of YHVH that remain a mystery to Moses?

The answer, from the perspective of Torah, could only be "yes." We have already been told by the first Three Sayings/Commandments that YHVH is without limits - existing outside the constraints of space and linear time - and therefore transcends our human ability to understand. Thus Moses, while having a close relationship with YHVH, can never fully "see" YHVH's face; for to do the impossible would destroy Moses's humanness. It would be tantamount to seeing the Light of the first day of Creation, unobstructed by any darkness. To do this, one would have to return to the time that preceded the Sixth Day and the introduction of humans, and then *"take from the Tree of Life and eat and live forever"* (Genesis 3:22). Said simply, for Moses to do this he must cease being mortal, for *"no human can see YHVH's face and live"* (Exodus 33: 20).

> **What did Moses "see" while standing in the cleft?** Moses pleaded with YHVH to be allowed to "truly know You and see Your glory." What YHVH revealed to Moses has become known as the "Thirteen Attributes" (see Exodus 34:6-7). As Everett Fox notes on page 450, "It is almost as if the text is saying that this is all that can be known, intimately, of this God, and this is all one needs to know. There is no shape, no natural manifestation; only words, which describe God's relationship to human beings."

It is nevertheless interesting to note that two of God's Thirteen Attributes are God's name. That is, the list of thirteen begins with YHVH YHVH. The convention of calling a name twice appears throughout the Torah. For example, we read in Exodus 3 that YHVH calls out Moses's name twice. Given the context in which this occurred, we surmised that it was done to symbolize the old Moses (a herder of sheep and goats) *and* the new, transformed Moses (soon to be the shepherd of the Children of Israel).

We can apply a similar reasoning to YHVH although, unlike Moses, *Ehyeh asher ehyeh,* ("I will be whatever I will be") is eternal and therefore unchangeable. What changes with the revealing of the Thirteen Attributes is YHVH's relationship with humans. This becomes more apparent a few verses later when, in Exodus 34:10, YHVH offers the people a new covenant, the terms of which are spelled out in verses 10 through 28 in Chapter 34. In brief, the covenant promises the people continued wonders, but in return they are warned against mixing with the Canaanites.

For example, YHVH says, *Take care, do not cut a covenant with those already settled in the land which I have promised to you; do not marry their whoring women.* "Whoring women?" In the context of biblical Hebrew, this term refers not to prostitutes but to any individual who is not true to self, to neighbors and to the Divine. Torah defines a whore as anyone who chooses to behave in a manner inconsistent with the teachings of the Ten Sayings.

- **What is meant by the "cleft of the stone"?** On Moses's first descent of Mount Sinai, he carried the two tablets with YHVH's Ten Sayings, but he was unable to deliver their meaning to the Israelites. Angry at their behavior, he failed to act on the revelation that he had just received. In his frustration, he instead threw the tablets to the ground and broke them.

YHVH is about to give Moses a second chance, but with an important difference: He is being told to first stand in a crevice that separates two pieces of stone at the mountain top. It is fair to ask what is being suggested by this imagery. Might it be that the two pieces of stone that YHVH referred to in verse 33:22 are the two new stone tablets, with Moses holding one in each hand? Might YHVH be telling Moses to stand in that cleft so that he can feel as one with the tablets, meaning that his survival will now depend on the tablets remaining whole (*shalem*) and their wholeness, in turn, depending on him?

In this case, we can assume that this event was staged to teach Moses a lesson. Specifically, should he once again throw down the tablets, he would be destroying not only himself but also the promise of YHVH's relationship with the people. This experience should have demonstrated to Moses that there is still work to be done; Put differently, the event reminded Moses that his mission as a servant to God - which he agreed to on that day he said "here I am" in front of the Burning Bush (Exodus 3) -is not yet complete. True, he helped to lead the Children of Israel out of Egypt, but he has yet to lead them to the land flowing with milk and honey.

- **Is there a relationship between the Thirteen Attributes the Ten Sayings?** Consider the staging: Moses is standing alone at the top of the mountain, holding on to the two recently carved tablets, when YHVH passes before him calling out the Thirteen Attributes. Written onto the tablets are ten Saying, proclaiming with unqualified certainty which acts are acceptable and which are not. In contrast to the Sayings, each of the Attributes conveys messages of compassion and understanding. Why juxtapose these two monumental lists?

In Kabbalistic terms, the Ten Sayings – as well as all the laws and regulations that will soon follow from them- represent examples of *Gevurah,* which is translated as strength, judgment, severity and discipline. Gevurah is the foundation of stringency: absolute adherence to the letter of the law, with justice meted out strictly. Like the Ten Sayings, Gevurah is "etched in stone." By itself, it results in a legal system that is rigid and narrow – more a contract than a covenant.

Complimenting Gevurah's stringency is *Hesed,* translated as loving kindness, boundless and ever-flowing mercy, and forgiveness. Hesed serves to soften the harsh judgments of Gevurah, thus acting as the antidote to the narrow legalism and religious dogma. Defined accordingly, we can think of the Thirteen Attributes (*"YHVH, YHVH; showing mercy, favor, grace, loyalty, truthfulness, faithfulness, and loving kindness to thousandth generation; slow to anger; forgiving of immorality, transgressions, and sin; and clearing of guilt."*) as representing examples of Hesed. The downside of a legal system consisting of Hesed alone is that it would be incapable of distinguishing the boundaries between good and evil. .

Thus, the reason for juxtaposing the two lists should be clear: The Torah is recognizing a fair and just legal system requires both Gevurah and Hesed. We will return to this teaching when we consider the merits of the many laws and regulations that follow in the Torah's next three books: Leviticus, Numbers, and Deuteronomy.

- **Is there a relationship between the Thirteen Attributes the Ten Sayings?** Consider the staging: Moses is standing alone at the top of the mountain, holding on to the two recently carved tablets, when YHVH passes before him calling out the Thirteen Attributes. Written onto the tablets are ten Saying, proclaiming with unqualified certainty which acts are acceptable and which are not. In contrast to the Sayings, each of the Attributes conveys messages of compassion and understanding. Why juxtapose these two monumental lists?

In Kabbalistic terms, the Ten Sayings – as well as all the laws and regulations that will soon follow from them- represent the essence of *Gevurah,* which is translated as strength, judgment, severity and discipline. Gevurah is the foundation of stringency: absolute adherence to the letter of the law, with justice meted out strictly. Like the Ten Sayings, Gevurah is "etched in stone." By itself, it results in a legal system that is rigid and narrow – more a contract than a covenant.

Complimenting Gevurah's stringency is *Hesed,* translated as loving kindness, boundless and ever-flowing mercy, and forgiveness. Hesed serves to soften the harsh judgments of Gevurah, thus acting as the antidote to the narrow legalism and religious dogma. Defined accordingly, we can think of the Thirteen Attributes (*"YHVH, YHVH; showing mercy, favor, grace, loyalty, truthfulness, faithfulness, and loving kindness to thousandth *generation; slow to anger; forgiving of immorality, transgressions, and sin; and clearing of guilt."*) as representing examples of Hesed. However, the downside of a legal system consisting of Hesed alone is that it would be incapable of distinguishing the boundaries between good and evil behaviors.

Thus, the reason for juxtaposing the two lists should be clear: The Torah is recognizing a fair and just legal system requires both Gevurah and Hesed. We will return to this teaching when we consider the merits of the many laws and regulations that follow in the Torah's next three books: Leviticus, Numbers, and Deuteronomy.

- **Why a "radiating face"?** The answer is simple: Moses got closer to YHVH than any person in Torah ever had or ever will - - so close that he could almost "glimpse" into YHVH's truth and feel the welcoming warmth of the first day of Creation when light was separated from darkness. Moses in fact got close enough to hear the Ten Sayings, Regulations, and Thirteen Attributes spoken directly to him by YHVH - - close enough to experience a sense of enlightenment.

What is enlightenment? In his book "*After the Ecstasy, the Laundry,*" Jack Kornfield defines enlightenment as moments of heightened consciousness when one is fully awake and able to perceive the mysteries of the universe and the realities of the world. The Torah describes it as a momentary sense of wholeness (in Hebrew, *shalem*) - a feeling of oneness and peace with ourselves and the world around us. When one is experiencing enlightenment, it is as if our inner light is radiating outward.

Let's bring the "radiating face" imagery more down to earth. Most of us have felt the presence of an enlightened person – perhaps a spiritual leader, a yoga instructor, an artist, or a special teacher. This person appears to know who we are and who we are not, and is comfortable with that knowledge. This person accepts us without judging and makes us feel at ease. This is a person we would like to emulate. While his or her face may not radiate as brightly as Moses's did, it nevertheless shines brightly enough to be seen, even by those who "*could not see the face of their brother.*"

➤ **Who is Joshua?** We first encountered Joshua in Exodus 17, during the war against Amalek in Refidim. Recall Moses saying to Joshua: *"Choose us men and make war upon Amalek- - and in the end, Joshua and his men weakened Amalek."*

Joshua's Hebrew name is *Yehoshua,* which means "salvation." (Jesus's name comes from the Latin form of Joshua's Greek name, Ἰησοῦς (*Iēsous*).) With a name meaning Salvation, it is safe to say that he will eventually play a key role as the Exodus story progresses! Suffice to say now, however, that by virtue of assigning responsibilities of military leadership to Joshua, as well as sharing the Tent of Appointment with him, Moses appears to be grooming this young lad to be his successor.

> Exodus 35-40: The Building of the *Mishkan*/Dwelling, Part 2

Summary: Chapters 35-40 of Exodus contain YHVH's detailed instructions, as dictated to the people by Moses, for building the Tabernacle (in Hebrew, the *Mishkan.*) This is the second time that the building instructions have been given; the first time was in Chapters 25-31. The difference is that the earlier set focused primarily on the *Mishkan's* interior, like the designs of its tapestries and various ritual objects, while the current set of instructions focuses more on the dwelling's overall design, including its outer courtyard, where the slaughter-site and basin are to be placed, and its inner courtyard, which is to contain a menorah and the two Tablets of Testimony.

As these latter six chapters point out, the structure's defining feature is its portability: Accordingly, its roof is to be made of cloth and animal skins, while its walls are to be built so that they can be readily dismantled and transported by carrying poles. It will serve as YHVH's dwelling place during the Israelites 'desert wanderings.

Most of what is written in these six chapters of the Book of Exodus represents details that offer little in the way of discussion or teachings. That said, a few points are worth mentioning.

- First, before dictating any of YHVH's instructions for building the *Mishkan*, Moses reminded the people that *"for six days is work to be made, but on the seventh, there is to be holiness for you"* (Exodus 35:2). With this reminder, Moses was reinforcing a central tenet of the Torah, which was first mentioned in Genesis 1 and most recently stated as the fourth commandment: *Remember the Sabbath and make it holy; no one in your household is to do any kind of work for in the first six days YHVH made the heavens and earth and all that is in it, but rested on the seventh day and blessed it.* Moses understood that the people required one day a week to quiet their minds of their labor-centric dialogues and listen to the voices of their hearts; otherwise they would gravitate back to an Egyptian-mindset, rather than move forward to *"the soil that YHVH is giving them."*

- Second, the text in Exodus 35 and 36 makes it abundantly clear that all of the requisite materials for building the Mishkan are being supplied on a voluntary basis, as are all of the construction tasks. Exodus 35:29, for example, states: *"Every man and woman whose mind made-them-willing to bring (anything) for all the workmanship that YHVH had commanded (them) to make, through Moses, the Children of Israel brought a freewill-offering for YHVH."* This is also evident in verses 5, 10, 21, and 24 of Chapter 35, as well as in verses 2 and 3 of Chapter 36. Indeed, the people's willingness to contribute exceeded YHVH's expectations, to the point that YHVH finally said to Moses: *"The people are bringing in much more than enough"* (Exodus 36: 5) and Moses, in turn, announced to the people: *"Man and woman – let them not make ready any further work materials for the contribution of the Holy-Shrine"* (Exodus 36:6).

These verses suggest a marked change in the way that the Israelites viewed their relationship with work. When they lived in Egypt (*Mitz'rayim* - " a -narrow place"), the Israelites were working at tasks like the "building pyramids in Egypt, seven days a week for somebody else" - - work that did not nourish their spirit. Now, for the first time in their lives, they are working at tasks that they find to be personally meaningful, as is evidenced by the whole-hearted enthusiasm that they brought to their work.

- Third, in dictating YHVH's instructions for building the *Mishkan*, Moses asks the people to voluntarily contribute gold, silver and bronze (Exodus 35:5); oil for lighting, spices for fragrant incense, and onyx stones (Exodus 35:8 and 9); large tapestries and tanned leather skins (Exodus 36:8 and19); as well as tools for the skilled craftsman to measure, cut, shape, weave, sew and assemble the various materials.

The fact that the people were able to respond to Moses's request with "more than enough" to complete the work begs the question: "Where did all of these supplies come from?" How were these people - - who had been slaves in Egypt for four hundred years; who had left Egypt in haste; who lacked even food and water; and who had only recently contributed their gold to build the Calf - - how were they able to come up with the kind of bounty mentioned in the text?

These questions do not have reasonable answers. As we have already observed in numerous other stories, the Torah may contain references to specific historical events, but it was not written with the intent of historical accuracy. As Everett Fox said, those who reject these stories because of their practical and logical inconsistencies miss the stories' non-literal teachings.

So, what might we have learned from this story? We learned that not only was Moses able to descend the Mountain the second time without throwing down the Tablets, but that some of his "radiating face" may have rubbed off on the people. Whereas in the past, the people had mistrusted YHVH's words and feared YHVH's presence, they are now expressing appreciation, commitment, and love.

The question, however, remains: Will this state of communal enlightenment last? Have the lessons from the past year, beginning with the First Blow/Plague and culminating with the Golden Calf, finally sunk in, or will the people return to their polytheistic ways? Have the Children of Israel finally accepted revelation and been transformed; that is, acknowledged a fundamentally new understanding about the meaning of life, while discarding that which they had once held to be true? And if so, why does the Torah not recognize this transformation by interjecting the number "40" into the text, as it had in all of its other stories that tell of this kind of personal transformation?

We also learned that the people responded with more enthusiasm and commitment when the order of instructions began with the Sabbath, followed by the layout of the *Mishkan's* structure, and lastly the details of the interior adornments (Exodus 35-40), than they did when the order was reversed(Chapters 25-31). What we don't know is whether the ordering of the instructions affected the people's attitude toward their work; or was it the intervening material/events - specifically the lessons learned from the Golden Calf fiasco (Exodus 32) and the receiving of the new Covenant (Exodus 33 and 34)that account for their change?

- Fourth, we are told in Exodus 39:17 that the construction of the *Mishkan*, with all of its adornments, was completed on the first day of the first new moon in the second year. Put into perspective, this date is two weeks shy of one year since Israel left Egypt (they left on the fifteenth day, that is, the first full moon of the New Year), and ten months after the people had first camped opposite Mount Sinai.

Why two weeks? We learned in Genesis 1 that the number " 7" represents the completion of a cycle of creation. As such, the text is suggesting that while the Children of Israel have been wandering for fifty weeks, they still have a long way (two weeks, or two times seven) to go on their spiritual journey.

Why ten months? Recall that the number "10" in Torah usually signifies a sufficient number to capture one's attention and strike one's spirit. Think the Ten Days of Awe between Rosh Hashanah and Yom Kippur; the Ten Sayings/Commandments; the Ten Blows/Plagues: If Ten Plagues were not enough to cause the Hebrews to leave Egypt, an eleventh likely won't do it. Recall also from Exodus 19 ("Encamping Opposite the Mountain") that the people came to the mountain with differing abilities to "hear"; some clinging largely to their past ways of thinking, while an enlightened few, like Moses, enter with a nearly "blank slate." Some came seeking answers to their spiritual, "*Israel-*

like" questions, while others were more concerned with their more earthly "*Jacob*" concerns. Some sought answers on both, while others asked neither. It follows that if camping against YHVH's mountain for ten months wasn't enough for an individual to experience revelation, regardless of the reasons for coming, then it isn't likely to happen by staying an eleventh month.

Chapter 10: The Book of Leviticus

Introduction: Leviticus is the third of Torah's five Books. The name, meaning "Priestly Instructions," is derived from the descendants of Levi, the third son of Jacob. As the stories in the Torah clearly illustrate, the "Levites" were designated by YHVH to be the priestly tribe, given the responsibility for caring for the Tabernacle and attending to the needs of high priests (see Book of Numbers 1:51 and 2:6, 7). In turn, the high priests, or *Co'ha-nim,* were selected from this tribe to be "priests for YHVH from amidst the Children of Israel" (Exodus 28:1). Originating with Aaron, the *Co'ha-nim* included his four sons (Nadav, Avihu, Elazar, and Itamar) and their descendants.

Many find Leviticus to be the least interesting of the Torah's five books. Rather than offer the kind of rich literary narratives that characterize the other four, Leviticus consists primarily of lists of stringent ritualistic details that promote little in the way of memorable stories and meaningful ethical discussion. Moreover, some of the details, like the protocols for ritual animal sacrifice, appear to us today as offensive, cruel, and grossly outdated.

As with most difficult portions in the Torah, however, there is more to Leviticus than what meets the literal eye. Suffice here to say that it is probably no coincidence that Leviticus is the only book whose stories take place entirely at Mount Sinai, the logical place in the wilderness to receive priestly instructions. Even the book's positioning in the Torah is noteworthy. Sandwiched between the other four books, Leviticus appears to serve as a bridge, linking all that led up to the Revelation at Sinai - which began with the departure from the Garden -with all that will follow (culminating at the end of the book of Deuteronomy with the entry into the Promised Land).

Not only does Leviticus lie at the center of the five books, but the verse "You shall love your neighbor as yourself", which appears in Leviticus 19:18, lies at the precise geographic center of the Torah! Sometimes referred to as the "Golden Rule", this single sentence is said to capture the ethical cornerstone of Torah. As Hillel put it when asked to summarize all of Torah in one sentence, "Everything else is commentary" (see Saying from the Fathers: 1:14).

As an aside, Hillel, who is considered to be one of the leading rabbis of the Talmudic era, is often compared to Jesus. The two men lived around the same time, though Hillel is thought to be about twenty years older. Both drew from Leviticus 19:18 when citing their version of the d neighbors") appears in the negative, as are many of the Ten Commandments, while Jesus' formulation ("Love your neighbor as you would yourself") is stated in the positive.

Many have debated which formulation represented the higher ethic. On one hand, Jesus' expression is clearly more upbeat and closer to the original wording of Leviticus 19: 18. On the other hand, Hillel's expression is easier to apply in our everyday interactions, for he is not telling us to love our neighbors, many of whom we may not even like. All he is saying is that regardless of our feelings, we should treat our neighbors in the same ways that we would want to be treated.

Fox (1997; pp. 499) offers additional insights about the Book of Leviticus. He views the book as one of separations, in that it sets up a strict set of rules to distinguish the Levite priests from the common folk; the holy from the profane; life from death; order from disorder; social justice from social injustice; and permitted sexual acts and foods from forbidden ones. These and other such separations can be thought of as continuing the creative process that began in the Genesis 1 story of the Creation. Just as we were told in that story that YHVH created the universe through a series of separations (e.g., light from darkness; the heavens from the earth; the oceans from dry land; and the Sabbath from the other days of the week), the Israelites are now being invited to participate in the process through a set of instructions to help them create a society set-apart from others by its ethical values.

➢ Rules of Sacrifice (Leviticus 1-7)

Background: The first seven chapters of Leviticus lay out stringent priestly rules for sacrifice, including the four types of offerings: the *minha* sacrifice, or the gift offering of grain; the *shalom* sacrifice, an expression of sincere gratitude; the *hattat* sacrifice, done to decontaminate or purify (that is, to rid oneself of sins committed unintentionally); and the *asham* sacrifice, or the guilt or reparation offering. For each type of offering, instructions are given as to the kinds of grains and/or domestic animals suitable to be offered; the preparations, presentation, and disposal of the offerings; the tasks of the priests; and the level of involvement by the worshipper.

Because these seven chapters contain mostly lists of ritualistic details that do not readily lend to commentary, I will comment only on the first six verses from Chapter 6, which I feel adequately captures these chapter's overall tone and message.

Summary: *YHVH spoke to Moses, saying command Aaron and his sons, saying "This is the instructions for the offering-up that is what goes up on the blazing hearth on the slaughter-site (alter) all night until daybreak, while the fire of the slaughter-site is kept blazing on it. The priest is to clothe himself in his wide-raiment of linen, with breeches (knee length pants) over his flesh. He is to set-aside the ashes which the fire has consumed on the slaughter site. He is then to strip off his garment and clothe himself in other garments, after which he brings the ashes outside the camp to a ritually pure place. The fire at the slaughter is to be kept blazing – it must not go out! And the priest is to stoke on it in the morning, every morning. He is also to arrange on it the offering-up and turn into smoke on it the fat parts of the shalom offerings. A regular fire is to be kept blazing upon the slaughter site, not to go out!*

Discussion Questions: Why must the fire not go out? What is special about linen clothing? Why change garments midway through the ceremony? Where is the ritually pure place lying outside the Tabernacle? What is special about the "fat parts"? Why sacrifice an animal to convey a *shalom* gift of gratitude? What purpose is served by the inclusion of so many ritualistic details?

- **Why must the fire "not go out"?** Three references are made in the first six versus of Chapter Six to the importance of not allowing the fire to go out at the slaughter-site, which is the alter built in the outer courtyard of the Tabernacle. Why this insistence? Perhaps the fire's light is intended to represent the spiritual light from the first day of Creation, a light that offsets the darkness of the ninth blow (plague): *YHVH told Moses to stretch out his hand over the heavens and let there be darkness over the land for three days, so dark that "a man could not see his brother." But, for all the Children of Israel, there was light in their settlements"* (Exodus 10: 21-23).

    Or, perhaps the fire's importance is attributed to the belief that it has the capacity to purify that which is *tamie* (unclean, blemished or polluted). After all, the act of purifying or setting-apart that which is *tam* (pure, unblemished, beyond reproach) from that which is *tamie* is a core theme of Leviticus.

- **Why linen?** Linen is a fiber derived from the stem of a flax plant. This plant also yields oil from its seeds. Like fire, the oil is used for creating light as well as to purify. It follows that the people may have viewed the fiber from a flax plant as inherently enlightened and pure.

- **Why change garments midway through the ceremony?** The act of changing clothes symbolizes the difficulty in separating the pure from the impure and keeping them apart, primarily because purity was understood in Torah to be easily blemished.

- **Where is the ritually pure place that is said to lie outside the Tabernacle?** The text may be referring to the Promised Land -- a place (*ma'kome*) lying outside space and time. This place was in close proximity to where the people were camped and had received revelation at Mount Sinai, which yet remained a generation away.

- **What is special about the "fat parts"?** Dieticians tell us to avoid fatty foods, but for most of us, our taste buds tend to prefer them. So do our eyes: Watching fat burn over an open flame has a hypnotic-quality. Unlike lean cuts, fat burns with a lot of fanfare, exciting our senses of sight, sound and smell with its snaps and crackles that seem to dance across the dark sky with the rhythms of their own. It is thus easy to imagine that the fat parts represented to these people the "first and the choicest" part of the animal offerings or sacrifice.

You might remember that this phrase originated in the Genesis 4 saga of Cain and Abel and refers to an expression of deep gratitude; a recognition of impermanence and an understanding that that which is dearest to us doesn't really belong to us, though we may be fortunate enough to share precious moments with it. Abel made such an offering when he willingly sacrificed the "first and the choicest" from his flock, while Cain's offering was half-hearted - nothing extraordinary, just some fruit collected from the soil for which he played a minor role in harvesting.

The notion of offering "our first and choicest" was then extended in later stories to father-son relationships. One such example appears in Genesis 22:2 where we read that YHVH asked Abraham to "*take your son, your only one, whom you love ... and offer him up.*" A second example is found in the Joseph story, when *Israel* (the spiritually enlightened side of Jacob) placed his son Joseph, whom he loved "*more than his other sons*" (Genesis 37:3) at great risk when he told Joseph to "*look into the well-being of your brothers,*" whom we soon learned wished him dead (Genesis 37:8).

- **Why sacrifice an animal to convey a *shalom* gift of greeting - -or for that matter, to convey *hattat* and *asham* sacrifices?** The Torah specifies that only domestically raised livestock that are set apart from the herd by virtue of being unblemished (*tam*) are acceptable to be offered up. However, given that only a minority of the worshipper's herd meets this criterion, we can surmise that these animals must have represented prized possessions. We can also assume that the worshipper formed tight bonds with these prized animals since they raised them from birth. To willingly offer them up, therefore, must have represented a deeply personal expression of sacrifice and introspection, akin to Abel's offering of his "first and his choicest."

While not coming to the defense of animal sacrifice, Fox (pp. 508) makes an interesting point by contrasting the ritual of animal sacrifice with the mechanized, mass-processed, and emotionally disconnected way that animals are slaughtered today – done entirely for our own well-being and with virtually no direct involvement on the part of the farmer and consumer.

- **Why so much ritualistic details?** The first seven chapters of Leviticus contain little other than a set of detailed formal instructions pertaining to animal sacrifice. Why?

Perhaps the instructions were intended to build a common culture across the twelve tribes, helping to transform the twelve into a single, unified community with a shared set of values and customs, set apart from other communities. Another possible interpretation is that these instructions, like those for building the Tabernacle and Ark which we read about in the later chapters of Exodus, serve as a needed bridge between the physical world and the metaphysical, particularly in the minds of the common (non-priestly) folk who held only a surface understanding of the first three Sayings (Commandments). One can imagine the deep sense of awe that must have been felt by these folks as the priests, shrouded in a veil of mystery, preceded with the utmost care and intent, through the formal ceremony.

➤ Death to Aaron's Elder Two Sons (Leviticus 8-10)

Background: Chapters 8 and 9 describe the many steps taken by Moses, under the guise of YHVH, to purify and clothe Aaron and his four sons as they prepare for the public ceremonies that will become the bulk of their priestly responsibilities. The ceremonies were done in silence; neither the priest nor the public engaged in chanting or song, perhaps to convey the sanctity and solemnness of the preparations.

With these two chapters having set the ceremonial context, we come upon Chapter 10, which tells of the flash-fire from YHVH that instantly killed Nadav and Avihu, leaving us to wonder exactly what great offense against YHVH did these two sons of Aaron commit so as to warrant their sudden demise.

Summary: *Now Aaron's sons, Nadav and Avihu, each lit his own pan, put incense on the alien fire, and brought it before the face of YHVH, such as YHVH had not commanded them to do. The fire went out from the presence of YHVH and consumed them, so that they died.*

Moses said to Aaron, It is what YHVH spoke, saying, 'Through those permitted near to me, I will be proven holy and accorded honor.'" Aaron was silent.

Moses then called the two sons of Aaron Uzziel, Aaron's uncle, and said, "Carry your brothers from in front of the holy Shrine to beyond the camp." Moses further said to Aaron and his two remaining sons, Elazar and Itamar, "Your heads do not bare and your garments do not tear, so that you do not die. The entire House of Israel can grieve over the burning that YHVH caused to burn (but not over the deaths of Nadav and Avihu). Do not go out from the entrance of the Tent of Appointment, for the oil of anointing of YHVH is upon you."

Now, about the hairy-goat of hattat, Moses inquired, yes inquired, and found that it had already been burned! He became furious at Aaron's remaining two sons, asking them "Why did you not eat of the hattat offering in the place of the holy Shrine, for it is the holiest holy portion, given to you to bear the guilt of the community to effect purgation for them? You should have eaten it in the Holy-Shrine, as I commanded!

But, Aaron said to Moses, "Here today they brought their hattat offering before YHVH and such things as these have happened to me! Had I eaten the hattat offering today, would it have been good in the eyes of YHVH?" Moses hearkened, and it was good in his eyes.

Discussion Questions: Who are Nadav and Avihu? What did they do that so offended YHVH? Did the two really die? Why weren't Aaron's remaining two sons consumed by fire when they did not eat of the *hattat* offering? Who is Aaron?

- **Who are Nadav and Avihu?** The name of Aaron's eldest son, Nadav, means "gift" while the name of Aaron's second son, Avihu, means "he is my father." Their names bear resemblance to that of Cain and his brother Abel. Recall from Genesis 4 that Eve named her first-born Cain - "a gift from God!" – while referring to her second son, Abel, as "Cain's brother," as if he had not personality of his own.

As we concluded earlier, coincidences in Torah almost always serve some purpose, and names are intended to reveal core aspects of the character's personality. What then might the writer(s) have wanted to convey by likening Nadav's name with that of Cain, and Avihu's name with that of Abel? Perhaps the similarities between the names of the two sets of brothers meant to suggest likenesses in their personalities as well. Specifically, while Cain embodied the "Jacob-side" of a person - that which is self-serving, controlling, and conniving, - so too did Nadav. Avihu, by contrast, perhaps represented a person's "*Israel*-side" – temporal, sincere, and spiritual, as had Abel before him.

Of course, no one's personality mirrors that of either Jacob or *Israel*, nor does anybody encompass all characteristics of either Cain or Abel. Combine Nadav and Avihu's personalities, however, and we get a more holistic and realistic portrayal of a single, everyday person -- someone with short-comings and long-comings, imperfections and perfections, insecurities and securities. Perhaps the writer(s) were suggesting that while the high priests may have been given the responsibility for the spiritual well-being of the community, there is nothing innately special about them. Like it was with Abraham, Isaac, and Jacob – and like it will be for Moses, David, and Solomon, in Torah we are all to be judged by our actions and not by our position.

- **What offence did Nadav and Avihu commit?** They might have meant well by bringing their own pan of incense, but by putting the incense on alien fire (*aysh ze'rah*) -- meaning fire that is not "set-apart" -- they demonstrated a lack of understanding of the third Commandment (Saying): "*You are not to take up the name of YHVH for emptiness, for YHVH will not clear him that takes up his name for emptiness*". This saying asserts that we are not to claim to understand YHVH, know what YHVH wants, speak on YHVH's behalf, nor try to improve upon that which YHVH tells us to do. From the perspective of Torah, YHVH dictated a set of detailed priestly guidelines for a reason. It is not for us to claim that we know the reason, but only to know that individual initiatives like the one committed by Nadav and Avihu will be neither appreciated nor tolerated.

- **Did YHVH really kill the two brothers?** Verse 2 appears to leave no doubt when it states that "*Fire went out from the presence of YHVH and consumed them, so that they died.*" In other words, unlike the bush in Exodus 3 that burned, but was not consumed, Nadav and Avihu burned and were consumed. If this is so, however, then we are again confronted with questions like, "Did the punishment fit the crime?" and,

"What is Torah teaching us from this episode?" (Recall that we struggled with these two questions in Exodus 2, where Moses was said to have killed the Egyptian taskmaster.) True, the brothers' sin could not go unnoticed (recall again that "sin" is first defined in the Cain and Abel story as simply "missing our mark; that is, failing to realize our potential). Apparently, the Torah's writer(s) felt the need to be unambiguous: YHVH's priestly guidelines are not open to debate or modification.

Nevertheless, what kind of message is conveyed to the people from the brothers' fiery death? How can YHVH expect us to be compassionate while acting in such a seemingly uncompassionate manner? After all, Nadav and Avihu had never before performed the priestly duties - nor for that matter had anyone else. Inexperienced and lacking any role model, it is only natural to imagine that they were nervous, unsure, and anxious to impress. Surely the case can be made that extenuating circumstances were at play; that the sin that they committed was one of *avon* (committed unknowingly) rather than of *pesha* (premeditated with purpose and intent).

Then again, we might be interpreting Verse 2 too literally. We must remind ourselves that the Torah is first and foremost a theological document, concerned more with conveying spiritual and ethical teachings than with explaining physical realities. Consequently, the Torah repeatedly makes the distinction between physical death - which usually happens to those characters of advanced age - and spiritual death, defined as a loss of intimacy with self, others, and YHVH. For example, we read that Adam and Eve did not die physically when they ate the forbidden fruit, but instead incurred the death of spirit. Thinking of death in this spiritual way also changed the way that we interpreted the tenth blow (Death to the First Born).

The same reasoning can apply to the deaths of Nadav and Avihu. Perhaps they did not physically die, but instead became forevermore separated from their priestly responsibilities. The text provides some indirect support for this assertion: We are told in verses 4 and 5 that Moses asks the two sons of his uncle Uzziel, namely Mishael and Eltzafan, to "carry your brothers from in the front of the Holy Shrine to beyond the camp." The two sons did so by the tunic worn by Aaron's older sons. Had the fire truly consumed the brothers, there would be little left of them and their clothing but a pile of ashes, surely not enough to require two adults to carry. Moreover, had the fire consumed the two brothers, it would have been heartless for Moses to tell Aaron and his two remaining sons to avoid mourning at all costs (Verse 6: "do not bare your heads nor tear your garments, lest you die").

- **Why were the lives of Aaron's remaining two sons spared when they did not eat the *hattat* offering?** A *hattat* offering, also referred to as a "de-sin" offering, was used by the priests to purify or decontaminate – be it an individual or the sanctuary. In verses 12-19 we read about the time, shortly after the death of Nadav and Avihu, when Moses instructs Aaron's two remaining sons to make a *hattat* offering, following the ritualistic procedures commanded by YHVH. It appears that Elazar (meaning "God helps") and Itamar (a name derived from the word "*tamar*" meaning a "date-palm") did not follow procedures. Specifically, Moses was furious that the two brothers had not eaten the *hattat* offering as instructed in the place of the Holy-Shrine. Bear in mind the consequences: Should the brothers face the same fate as did their two older brothers, the family of high priests would have no descendants - - and, no one to tend to the future spiritual needs of the community.

Fortunately, Aaron's response calmed Moses' anger, for in defending his son's actions, he convinced Moses that what they did was the correct thing to do. Specifically, he argued that his sons were not ready to eat the "de-sin" offering because they still felt soiled from the sins committed by their two older brothers. Aaron's point is that some forms of sin are not easily removed, for forgiveness (*tchew'va)* entails a process, preceded by atonement and repentance. (This process is core to the observance of the Rosh Hashanah - Yom Kippur High Holidays.)

This episode is loosely similar to that of the time when Joseph devised a plan for his brothers' redemption (Genesis 42). Recall that ever since selling Joseph into slavery, his brothers have been plagued with the kind of guilt which leaves them stuck in the past, unable to inhabit the present and move forward. Joseph's plan was to re-create that defining moment for his brothers so that they have the opportunity to act differently and in so doing, unburden themselves. Perhaps a similar plan was devised for Aaron and his two remaining sons. By affording them a second opportunity to get it right soon after their older brothers failed, the family of high priests proved ready to tend to the spiritual needs of their community.

- **Who is Aaron?** In the commentary to Exodus 4, I wrote that Aaron's name was left undefined, almost as if he has no personality independent of Moses - little more than a mouth for Moses to put words into. In Leviticus 10, however, we witness a change: Not only did Aaron demonstrate an understanding of the rituals surrounding the *hattat* offering that is equal to, or even surpasses that of his more respected brother, but for the first time he showed the confidence to express his point of view.

What might have precipitated this change? Perhaps it started when he and his descendants were selected to be "to be priests for YHVH from amidst the Children of Israel" (Exodus 28:1)? Another possible turning point might have been come when YHVH spoke directly to Aaron for the first (and only) time (Leviticus 10:8)?

➢ Rules of Pollution and Purification (Leviticus 11-18)

Background: Up to this point, Leviticus has focused primarily upon priestly rules for sacrifice. Starting with Chapter 11, the book turns to issues of separation that affect various aspects of everyday life. We read in this chapter that only domestically-raised mammals that have a cleft in their hooves, bring up their cud, and are not found dead are permitted; as are fish that have fins and scales and fowl that are not birds of prey. All other living things are *tamei* (profane); and therefore we are forbidden to eat them. We then read in Chapter 16 of the mindful respect that is to be given to an animal as it is about to be slaughtered for food.

Chapter 12 defines the border between life and death, as expressed through the sexual functions and discharges. Chapters 13 through 17 discuss boundaries with other surfaces. On the *tamie* side, there is *tzaraat*. This term is commonly translated as "leprosy", but in the Torah it refers not only to skin diseases, but to other visible evidence of death and decay like fungus, mildew, dry rot and mold on clothing and walls. While not mentioned in these five chapters, *tzaraat* is also used in Torah to refer of death and decay of inner surfaces, like one's spiritual well-being.

Included also in these chapters are the rituals to decontaminate the pollutants, including the role played by the priests. Their responsibilities are straightforward: Examine the patient, make a diagnosis, and then recommend the proper ritual to treat the problem. There is no indication whatsoever in the Book of Leviticus that the priests behaved as witch-doctors or exorcists.

Finally, Chapter 18 addresses the boundaries between acceptable and unacceptable sexual behavior and unions. "*What is done in the land of Egypt, wherein you were settled, you are not to do; nor are you to do that which is done in the land of Canaan, to which I am bringing you*" (Verse 3). Among these prohibitions are sexual relations /unions with one's family members, those who marry into the family, and those of the same sex (more on the subject of homosexuality will soon follow).

Let's re-emphasize the point served by the long list of ritualistic borders portrayed in these chapters because it is easy to lose sight of their purpose in all the pages of detail. First and contrary to the popular understanding, none of the rituals concern hygiene (e.g., there is nothing inherently profane and unhygienic about non-Kosher foods). Rather, to repeat an earlier cite by Fox (1997; pp. 499), the rituals pertain to separations. Second, the rituals aim to build a community with a shared desire to live a tightly ordered life, directed towards mindfulness (i.e., the capacity to sense the extraordinary in the ordinary) and perfection. Third and finally, the rituals attempt to create a society set-apart from others by its ethical values and worthy of entering the Promised Land.

➢ Torah's Spiritual Center: Leviticus 19

Background: Unravel the Torah scroll, as is done on the holiday of *Sim-khat Torah*, and you will find that Chapter 19 lies at the center of the book with verse 18 at the exact center point. This verse, often referred to as the Golden Rule, states in part, to be "loving to your neighbor (as one) like yourself." A coincidence? Not likely; for every lesson in the Torah is embedded in this chapter, either explicitly or implicitly. The chapter also extends the concept of separation to virtually all aspects of life – family, calendar, business, civil and criminal law, social relations and sexuality. In so doing, Leviticus 19 serves to review the commandments, sayings, regulations and rituals that went before it, providing additional clarity for some of them.

Summary: *The Lord spoke to Moses saying: Speak to the entire community of the Children of Israel, and say to them: You shall be holy, for holy am I, YHVH your God! Each-man – his mother and his father you are to hold in awe and my Sabbaths you are to keep: I am YHVH your God! Do not turn your faces to other gods nor to make molten gods, for I am YHVH your God!*

When you slaughter an offering of shalom to YHVH, sacrifice it so that it may be accepted on your behalf. It shall be eaten on the day you sacrifice it, or on the following day; but what is left by the third day must be consumed in fire. If it should be eaten on the third day, it is an offensive thing, not acceptable. He who eats of it shall bear his guilt, for he has profaned what is sacred to the Lord, that person shall be cut off from his kin.

When you reap the harvest of your land, you shall not reap all the way to the edges of your field, or gather the gleanings of your harvest. You shall not pick your vineyard bare, or gather the fallen fruit of your vineyard; you shall leave them for the poor and the stranger: I am YHVH, your God!

You shall not steal, lie, or bear falsely, each man with his fellow! You are not to swear by my name falsely thus profane the name of your God, I am YHVH!

You shall not withhold property from your neighbor, nor commit robbery, nor keep overnight the working wages of a hired hand, nor insult the deaf, nor place a stumbling block before the blind. Rather, you are to hold your God in awe, I am YHVH.

You are not to render an unfair decision, do not show favor to the face of the poor, not overly honor the face of the rich. With equity you are to judge your fellow! You are not to traffic in slander among your kins-people, nor profit by the blood of your neighbor, I am YHVH!

You are not to hate your kinsfolk in your heart; nor take vengeance or bear grudge against them. Love your fellow as yourself: I am YHVH.

Now when there sojourns a sojourner in your land, you are not to maltreat him, but like a native born among you shall he be to you. Be loving to him like yourself, for once you were strangers in the land of Egypt. I am YHVH your God!

You are to not allow the mating of two animal kinds, mixing crops on a single field, and wearing garments made of two kinds of fabric. You are not to eat anything with blood, nor practice soothsaying, nor make a skin etching. You are not to round off the edge-growth of your head nor diminish the edge-growth of your beard. Honor the face of the elderly, thus holding your God in Awe. I am YHVH.

You are not to commit corruption in justice, for I am YHVH your God who brought you out of the land of Egypt! You are to keep all my laws and all My regulations and guard them. I am YHVH!

Discussion Questions: Why was Moses told to speak to the entire community? What does it mean to say that we are holy? What distinguishes this chapter's listing of behavioral expectations from the lists of commandments, regulations and rituals mentioned in previous chapters? How are we to "keep all my laws and all my regulations and guard them"?

- **Why was Moses told to speak to the entire community?** The key word is "entire"; for it distinguishes verse 19:2 from the other instances when Moses is asked to speak publicly. It implies that the community has moved far enough from their serfdom ways to truly hear YHVH's message without the need for thunderous sounds, flashing-torches, smoking mountains, or other such attention-getting fanfare.

* **Are we holy?** The word "holy" is first used in Torah to describe the Sabbath (Genesis 1). It means that which is "set-apart" or "separated" by YHVH. To say that we are holy, therefore, is to say that we prove ourselves able to inhabit the "day of stopping" which YHVH separated in time and space from the other six days. Being holy is also about discovering those aspects of ourselves which sets us apart from others in ways that bring us together in community. Holiness thus involves a process of purification by which we drain out our impurities (*chu'matze*) in order to approach our essential or authentic selves, symbolically referred to here as the *matzot* within us (for more on the symbolism of the Passover Seder, see Chapter 7: "Israel in the Wilderness."). As such, becoming

holy entails a continuously unfolding process of awakening. True holiness, therefore, cannot be achieved, but some can come closer than others. Thus, the question to ask is not "Am I holy?", but rather "Am I doing holy?"

- **What distinguishes this chapter's lists of behavioral expectations from previous lists?** At first glance, Leviticus 19 appears largely to serve as a review, - a restatement of the commandments, sayings, regulations and rituals set forth in previous chapters. However, these expectations are now presented in no discernible order. For example, the Fifth Commandment about honoring one's parents is mentioned in verse 3 before the Fourth Commandment to keep the Sabbath. Verse 4 then restates the Second Commandment, which is turn is followed by four verses describing the rituals to which priests must adhere when making a shalom-offering. Verses 9 and 10 concern/address the protection of the rights of the poor and strangers, regulations first mentioned in Exodus 23:11 (see "A System of Justice" in Chapter 9). Verse 11 restates commandments 7-9, followed by a repetition of the Third Commandment, and so on.

What might have been the point of randomizing the items from previously introduced lists of commandments, regulations and rituals - within each list and across different ones? I suspect it was to convey the message that each rule is important in its own right, such that none is to be consistently placed above or listed before any other.

A second distinguishing feature of the rules discussed in Leviticus 19 is that the "System of Justice" is extended to include the rights of hired workers (Verse 13: "*You are not to keep overnight the working wages of a hired-hand with you until morning*"); the deaf and blind (Verse 14: *You are not to insult the deaf; before the blind you are not to place a stumbling block*); the poor and the rich (Verse 15: "*You are not to lift up in favor of the poor, nor overly honor the face of the great, but with equity you are to judge your fellow*"); and the elderly *(*Verse 32: "*Honor the face of the elderly*").

Finally, Leviticus 19 introduces new expectations concerning blending (verse 19: "You are to prevent the mating of two animal kinds, avoid the mixing of different crops on a single field, and not wear garments made of two kinds of fabrics"; soothsaying (verse 26); facial hair (verse 27: *"You are not to round off the edge-growth of your head, you are not to diminish the edge-growth of your beard")*; and skin etchings (verse 28).

The prohibitions against mixing are consistent with the theme of Leviticus; namely, separation represents the means to approach divine-like purity. (Recall the earlier commentary in this Chapter explaining why the Priests wore linen.) Also consistent with this theme is the prohibition against skin-etchings or self-inflicted blemishes, which were seen as making the body impure.

Soothsaying plays into the Torah's concern about cultic practices such as the summoning of the dead (again, Leviticus emphasizes the importance separation, including that of life from death), or the telling of the future. Regarding the latter, many define a prophet as someone who predicts the future. However, prophets in the Jewish liturgy are not portrayed as "soothsayers," but instead are a chosen few who are told by YHVH to bring YHVH's words to a community, usually at a time when that community least wants to hear them.

Finally, regarding facial hair, the early adopters of the particular hair style described in verse 27 were known as the Nazarites (the best known of whom was Sampson), that is, those individuals who dedicated their lives to God (see Book of Judges, chapters 13-16).

- **How are we to keep and guard "all my laws and my regulations"?** "Keeping" all the laws and regulations requires "disciplined passion"; in other words, both cognitive awareness (discipline, or order and boundaries) and psychological attachment (passion, or kindness and compassion) are required. To be disciplined but psychologically detached is to relegate the "keeping" task to a seemingly endless series of mind-numbing responsibilities, done mostly by habit. To be passionate but not mindful is to lack the requisite rudder to channel our energy. (In Kabbalism, the attributes of discipline are referred to as *"gevurah"* and those of passion as *"hesed."*)

In turn, "guarding" the laws and regulations means to look after and protect the well-being of others (family, neighbors, and strangers); sacred time (the subject of Leviticus 23); and the land (the subject of Leviticus 25). The word "guard" (*shomer*), also translated as "observe," first appeared in Genesis 2, when Adam and Eve were told to work and guard the Garden. Use of the same word in Leviticus 19 suggests that we can return to the Garden, and thereby enter the Promised Land, if we prove ourselves able to guard the laws and regulations.

➢ Serious Offenses and Resulting Punishments (Leviticus 20)

Background: Leviticus 20 puts forth a litany of offenses like insulting parents, bestiality, incest, adultery, homosexuality, and the worshipping of Moloch[15]. For most of these misdeeds, the offender "is to be put to death, yes death ... their bloodguilt is upon them." And, unlike previous references to death in the Torah, the text here appears to be referring to physical death and not, death as it is characterized in many of the earlier stories; that is, the death of one's spirit or a movement away from an intimate relationship with self, other, and YHVH. The punishment for those who worship Moloch is even more severe: not only is the violator to be put to death, but it is to be done by "the people of the Land who are to pelt the offender with stones" (verse 2).

The books of Numbers and Deuteronomy mention other offenses punishable by public stoning until death. For examples, in Numbers 15:32-36 we will read that should a man be found picking wood on the Sabbath day…the entire community is commanded by YHVH to pelt him with stones until he died. A similar fate is to befall the rebellious, stubborn son "who does not hearken to our voice" (Deuteronomy 21:18- 21). Also to be stoned to death is the young bride who falsely

---

[15] Moloch is the name of an ancient an Ammonite god. Moloch worship was practiced by the Canaanites and Phoenicians. What made Moloch worship particularly offensive to Israel was that it included child sacrifice by parents.

claims to be a virgin (Deuteronomy 22: 13-21) and a man who has an affair with a married woman (Deuteronomy 22:22).

Citations like these leave many of us in a quandary about the Torah in general and specifically YHVH, for as moderns we tend to prefer a more compassionate, forgiving, and loving God over one that evokes fear. Moreover, in that the word "Torah" means "the teaching", the question must be asked, "What can we learn from these citations?" Is it to "love your neighbor as yourself" (Leviticus 19:18), or to behave with the same self-righteous intolerance and barbaric cruelty as do today's Taliban? Can YHVH really claim to embody the Thirteen Attributes mentioned in Exodus 33 ("*YHVH, YHVH; showing mercy, favor, grace, loyalty, truthfulness, faithfulness, and loving kindness to thousandth generation; slow to anger; forgiving of immorality, transgressions, and sin; and clearing of guilt"),* and then command us to meter out justice in such an abhorrent way? Furthermore, can we be expected to emulate YHVH's attributes when YHVH seems to be telling us to behave otherwise? And, isn't the way that YHVH is defining justice in these three Books inconsistent with how justice was defined in Exodus 20-23; that is, being fair (providing guidance for doling out settlements that fit the offense); flexible (recognizing extenuating circumstances); and compassionate (offering protection for the powerless)?

These kinds of questions have troubled readers of the Torah for thousands of years. Some try to defend what was written by arguing that the understanding of justice that is expressed in this ancient document should not be held up to today's standards. Others note that the apparent inconsistency in YHVH's nature is due to the fact that the Torah was likely written by different writers at different times and with different points of view.

However, if we interpret the above mentioned passages in the context of another teaching in Torah - the one that encourages us to actively question YHVH's words when these words pose rulings that challenge our sensibilities – then we will not find these passages troubling, nor conclude that YHVH is capricious and inconsistent. I am referring to the Genesis 18 story about Abraham who, upon hearing YHVH's intentions to destroy the cities of Sodom and Gamora, convinced YHVH to do otherwise. Abraham argument was that regardless of how corrupt are these two cities, there are innocent people residing within them.

I am also referring to Numbers 14, which tells of the rebellion against Moses, incited by the scouts' report that the Promised Land cannot be successfully entered. This report and the rebellion that it triggered caused YHVH to lose all patience with the people and tell Moses, "Let me strike them down and make you a great nation!" Moses, however, talks YHVH out of this decision, arguing that this will look badly to the Egyptians, who will say "It was from a want of YHVH's ability to bring this people into the land of promise."

Some might say that Abraham and Moses were testing YHVH judgment; however, I prefer the explanation that YHVH was testing them, assessing their ability to lead - not by faith, but by their level of compassion and moral character. Just as YHVH tested these two men's ability to lead, might it be now that YHVH was testing the Children of Israel's ability to follow? Will they administer the capital punishments that YHVH commands them to do, even though it violates the ethical code that YHVH had been teaching them during the past forty years, the core to which had appeared only one chapter before in Leviticus 19:18; that is, "we shall love our neighbor as ourselves"? Will they rationalize their brutal actions by claiming that they were "only following orders"? Or will they, like Abraham and Moses before them, object when they sense that the punishment does not fit the crime? And who is more ready to inhabit the Promised Land; that is, who has advanced further on their personal and spiritual journey, those who are willing to follow orders or those who question the ethical nature of those orders?

While the Torah doesn't directly address these questions, we can infer an answer from the fact that there is scant evidence, written or otherwise, to suggest that public stonings were a common practice. [16] Indeed, the Mishnah (also known as the "Oral Torah") points out that leading rabbinic scholars from around the second century CE imposed so many restrictions on the implementation of capital punishment in general and specifically stoning as to effectively ban

---

[16] Only a few are mentioned in the Tanakh: Leviticus 24: 23, which deals with blasphemy, a violation of the 3rd Commandment; Numbers 15: 36, which deals with gathering wood on the Sabbath, a violation of the 4th Commandment; Joshua 7: 25, which deals with stealing, a violation of the 8th Commandment; and I Kings 12: 18, which deals with an abuse of power. The last of these four examples occurred around the time of King Solomon, or about three thousand years ago,

it. [17] What makes this point particularly salient is these rabbis were some of the most ardent of believers – those who regard the Torah as flowing directly from the mouth of YHVH. Apparently even they are willing to question YHVH's words when questioning is called for - and by doing so, passed YHVH's test.

We can also infer an answer from Deuteronomy 30. Contrary to the previous three chapters, which list a multitude of possible offences and the dire consequences associated with each, Deuteronomy 30 ends the Torah on an optimistic note. It is as if YHVH expects us to stray, but also leaves the door open for us to return. When we do, "YHVH will restore your fortunes… have compassion on us… and collect us from all the peoples to which we have been scattered and bring us back to the land that our fathers possessed" (Deuteronomy 30:3-5). The content in these Deuteronomy chapters lead me to believe that the "us" in the abovementioned cite includes those who were sentenced to death, like the person who insults his parents, the rebellious son, the Sabbath wood picker, the philandering man, and so on.

Of course, if the death sentence was never intended to be carried out, why was it so graphically described? Perhaps the answer is that the writer(s) understood that the very threat of a public stoning would be enough to maintain social order by deterring those who are inclined to stray.

---

[17] The Makkot, a book of the Mishnah states: A Sanhedrin (Israel's High Court) that puts a man to death once in seven years is called destructive. Rabbi Eliezer ben Azariah says that this extends to a Sanhedrin that puts a man to death even once in seventy years. Rabbi Akiba and Rabbi Tarfon say: Had we been in the Sanhedrin none would ever have been put to death. The restrictions were to prevent execution of the innocent, and included many conditions for a testimony to be admissible that were difficult to fulfill. To that, Moses Maimonides wrote in his book *The Commandments, Neg. Comm. 290,* that "It is better and more satisfactory to acquit a thousand guilty persons than to put a single innocent one to death." He viewed of commission as more threatening to the integrity of law than errors of omission.

➤ Guarding Sacred Time (Leviticus 23)

Background: Leviticus's central theme is that because YHVH is perfect, we should strive for perfection as the means by which we can move closer to YHVH. Previous chapters have addressed this challenge in such areas as priestly rituals, worship, sacrifice, social relations, family life and ethics. Chapters 21 and 22 continue this theme with a list of laws and regulations to which the priests must adhere in order to be worthy of serving in the sanctuary. Like much of Leviticus, the lists in these two chapters are presented in a matter-of-fact manner that offers little opportunity for commentary or discussion. We will therefore skip ahead to the more provocative material contained in Chapter 23, which discusses how time is marked in the Torah.

In brief, Chapter 23 details the underlying structure of the Hebrew calendar. While most other calendars are based solely upon either lunar or solar cycles, the Hebrew calendar derives from both and is therefore known as "luni-solar." Specifically, it relies on a fixed year comprised of twelve lunar months, each containing twenty-nine or thirty days, with a leap month added seven times every nineteen years to synchronize it with the slightly longer solar year. Moreover, each day in this calendar begins at sunset and runs to the next sunset, consistent with the order of the wording used in the Creation Story (Genesis 1): "...there was evening and there was morning..."

What truly sets-apart this calendar from others, however, is that it is organized around the number seven -- be it seven days, weeks, months, or years. What is the significance of this number? As previously mentioned, "seven" refers to the completion of one cycle of Creation and the start of a Sabbath (*Shabbat*). The word "Shabbat" derives from the root *shin-beit-tav*, meaning "to stop" (although it is commonly mistranslated as "to rest"). The passage, "*On the seventh day, God stopped from all labor*" thus implies that stopping is woven into the fabric of Creation, as are the land, wildlife, and humans. Given the central theme of Leviticus, it is not surprising that the number seven is central to the structure of the Hebrew calendar. The thought is that if we practice the art of stopping on a regular basis, as the calendar prescribes, we can move closer to YHVH, and in so doing begin to see the extraordinary in the ordinary, just as Moses did when he saw the bush burning without being consumed.

Summary: The first holiday mentioned in Chapter 23 is the Sabbath, which begins on the seventh day after the year's first new moon in the month of *Nisan*. (Verses 1-4: *"YHVH spoke to Moses, saying, Speak to the Children of Israel and say to them: 'The appointed times of YHVH, you are to proclaim to them as proclamations of holiness. For six days may work be done, but on the seventh day is Sabbath, Sabbath-ceasing... a day that you are not to do any kind of work.'"*)

Passover then begins on the second *Shabbat* of the month of *Nisan,* which coincides with the year's first full moon. (Verse 5-12: *"On the first full moon, on the fourteenth after the new moon is the Passover to YHVH. On the fifteenth day after this new moon, is the pilgrimage festival of matzot to YHVH, for seven days matzot you shall eat."*) Passover lasts for seven days and marks the time when we were freed from our enslavements.

- **Why on the fifteenth day,** and not on the day when the holiday begins? Passover begins on the fourteenth day, which is the calendar's second Sabbath. Like the first Sabbath, it is a day of stopping -- not a day for leaving Egypt, nor a day to participate in the other activities associated with this pilgrimage festival.

- **What is a "pilgrimage festival"?** We can suppose that these were ancient attempts to graft the agricultural cycles with the sacred times of the year; i.e., those organized around the number seven. The way that it works is that three times a year, once each in the spring (Passover/*Pesach*), summer (*Shavuot*) and fall (*Sukko*t), every Israelite was expected to journey to Jerusalem and give thanks for their seasonal harvest. For Passover, this meant the harvest of wheat; for Shavuot, the summer fruits; and for Sukkot, it meant giving thanks for the final harvests and praying for a bountiful harvest in the coming year.

Shavuot, which translates as the "Festival of the Weeks," occurs on the seventh Sabbath after Passover and marks the time when Torah was received at Sinai. (Verses 13-22: *"From that day, count seven Sabbaths. Then you are to bring near a grain fit of new crops to YHVH... When you harvest the land, do not finish off the edge of it, for that is for the afflicted and sojourners that you are to leave them."*) Shavuot falls in the month of *Sivan*, the third month in the Hebrew calendar.

- **Why is this pilgrimage holiday celebrated by only a few?** While Easter occurs at the time of year close to Passover and Thanksgiving close to Sukkot, *Shavuot* has no parallel holiday in the non-Hebrew world. Maybe this is because *Shavuot* is a summertime holiday, when many families are on the go. Or, as Harold Kushner postulates in his book "To Life", while the other two pilgrimage holidays are family-oriented and fun to celebrate, *Shavuot* is not. Rather, it is about committing one's self to living a holy life set-apart from others by the laws, regulations and expectations received at Sinai.

As we will later read in Leviticus 25, the Shavuot that comes every seventh year is called the "sabbatical year" and the Shavuot that comes after seven cycles of seven years is called in Leviticus 25:23 the "Jubilee Year." The Jubilee Year Shavuot serves to remind us that the Land does not belong to us – we are only sojourners and resident settlers.

Rosh Hashanah, the "Head of the Year," begins on the year's seventh new moon in the month of Tishri; and ten days later comes *Yom Kippur*, the "Day of Atonement." (Verses 23- 32: *"On the seventh New Moon, you are to have a Sabbath-ceasing, a reminder by horn-blasting, a proclamation of holiness. Mark on the tenth day after this seventh New Moon it is the Day of Atonement. You are to afflict your selves and bring near a fire offering to YHVH."*)

Lastly comes the seven- day harvest pilgrimage holiday known as *Sukkot,* which translates as "little huts." This holiday begins on the first full moon of the seventh month, *Tishri*. (Verses 33-44: "On the fifteenth day after this seventh New Moon, is the seven-day pilgrimage-festival of Huts. *You are to take the fruit of beautiful trees, branches of palms, boughs of thick tree-foliage, and willows of the brook."*)

Interestingly, in ancient times, *Sukkot* rather than *Yom Kippur* was considered to be the High Holy Day. Also interesting is that the holiday is celebrated with four species from nature: the Lulav (a ripe, green, closed frond from a date palm tree); Hadass (boughs with leaves from the myrtle tree); Aravah (branches with leaves from the willow tree) and the Etrog (the fruit of a citron tree). Why four species? From Genesis 2 and 13, we learned that the number "4" symbolically represents a spiritual path back to the Garden.

- **What about those holidays not mentioned in Leviticus 23?** There is *Simchat Torah*, which falls on the seventh day of Sukkot (consistent with the organization of the calendar around the number seven) on the seventh day of Sukkot. This holiday celebrates the annual cycle of Torah reading. On that day, the last line of Deuteronomy is read followed by the first line of the opening chapter of Genesis.

Then there are two holidays that celebrate historical events: Hanukkah, which happens during *Kislev*, the ninth month of the year, and Purim, coming during Adar, the year's twelfth month. What these and other less observed holidays like *Tish B'av* and *Lag B'omer* have in common are that they are neither connected to sacred time by the use of the number "seven"), nor directly associated with the cycles of agriculture.

➤ Unfinished Business (Leviticus 24- 27):

Summary: Most of what appears in Leviticus 24 involves rules, regulations and behavioral expectations that either review or further clarify that which was presented in earlier chapters, leaving me and others to question the placement of this chapter's material in the Book of Leviticus, or even its purpose. For example, the opening verses of Chapter 24 detail the ritual objects to be used in the Tabernacle, a topic which had already been discussed in Exodus 25-31 and 35-40. The closing verses of this chapter meanwhile provide examples of capital crimes, a topic previously addressed in Leviticus 20. Furthermore, neither of these two topics appears to logically follow Chapter 23's discussion of sacred time, nor precede that which will be presented in Chapter 25. What might explain this apparent lack of fit? Perhaps Chapter 24 was a late addition to the Book of Leviticus? Or, perhaps the purpose of this chapter was to serve as a repository for details that didn't readily fit elsewhere?

In contrast, Leviticus 25 addresses two ethical concerns not previously mentioned: the proper treatment of the land and those who are impoverished. Specifically, the chapter introduces the notion of the sabbatical year ("*In the seventh year, there shall be a Sabbath of ceasing for the land, a Sabbath to YHVH. The after growth of your harvest you are not to harvest. The Sabbath yield of the land is for you, your servants, strangers who journey through, domestic animals and wild beasts to eat*") and the Jubilee year (verses 8-10: "*On the seven Sabbath cycles of years, on the seventh New Moon, on the tenth after the New Moon, on the Day of Atonement, you are to blast the shofar throughout all of the land. You are to hallow this fiftieth year, proclaiming freedom throughout the land and to all of its inhabitants; it shall be a homecoming for you. Each is to return to his holding, to his clan.*")

The message from these verses should be clear: Just as humans deserve the Sabbath, so too does the land; for Torah views the land as a living entity, having the capacity to give birth to other forms of life if it is properly cared for. Caring for it means that every seventh year it should be left fallow; whatever grows that year, even if self-propagated, should be neither harvested nor eaten by anyone other than the poor. These verses serve to remind us of the importance of regarding the land with respect, rather than as an object whose sole purpose is to advance our own agenda.

A second message from these verses is that the land does not belong to us. It is not ours to own in perpetuity, for every fifty years it returns to its rightful owner. In Torah, its rightful owner is YHVH. (The Jubilee Year, also known as the Home-bringing Year, falls on the fiftieth year rather than the forty-ninth, when it is to lay fallow as it does at the last of every seven-year cycle.) However, this second message begs three prickly questions:

- **Do the rules of the Jubilee Year apply to the "Land" that the Israelites will soon enter?** That is, will the ownership of "Promised Land" revert back to YHVH every fifty years? Or, did YHVH relinquish ownership of the "Promised Land" upon saying to Abraham in Genesis 13: "*I give to you and your descendants for the ages*", or to Moses in Leviticus 25:38: with the words "*I am YHVH your God who brought you* *out of the land of Egypt to give you the land of Canaan to be for you a God"*?

Verse 23 of Leviticus 25 suggests the answer: *"The land is not to be permanently owned, for the land is Mine, for you are sojourners and resident settlers with me, throughout all the land of your holdings, you are to allow for its redemption."* Said more simply, the Land may have been promised to us, not to own, or permanently inhabit, but instead to pass-through.

- **Do the rules of the Jubilee Year apply to *"the cave that is in the field of Makhpela, which Abraham had acquired from Efron the Hittite?"*** (Genesis 45). Will the ownership of this site return to Efron or his descendants in fifty years? (It is at this cave where Abraham, Sarah, Isaac, Rifka, and Leah are buried). The text implies that the answer is "yes" to both questions, but with the following caveat: Leviticus 25 tells us that the caves no more belong to the descendants of Efron than they do to Abraham's descendants, *"for the land is Mine (YHVH's)."*

- **Is the Jubilee Year for land practical?** Can a society exist without clear property rights? The simple answer is that nobody knows, for the concept has never been tested. That said, I suspect that the Jubilee Year, particularly as it applies to the ownership of land, is too idealistic a concept to be practical. This is because most places are "narrow" like *mitz'rayim* in the sense that they are inhabited by people who are more concerned with their material wants than their spiritual needs (consider Lot in Genesis 13; Lavan in Genesis 30; Jacob in his youth, and the Pharaoh in the book of Exodus). In narrow places, basic civil law (such as that governing property rights) is essential to prevent their inhabitants from engaging in behavior that is morally hazardous – that is, taking advantage of others because of an inadequate set of formal enforcement mechanisms. Put more simply, people are prone to act in self-serving, opportunistic ways when they know that they are not likely to be caught.)

That said, I suspect that the Jubilee year was never envisioned for narrow people in narrow places, but only for those communities that have crossed-over into the Promised Land in the sense that all of their inhabitants are "sojourners and resident settlers" there. Like the Jubilee Year, the "Promised Land" is defined in idealistic terms. It is not so much a physical entity as it is state of mind where we find both milk (symbolic of nourishment) and honey (symbolic of sweetness and joy), even during mundane or troubled times. As such, the Promised Land implies a place devoid of any moral hazards or the accompanying need for formal enforcement mechanisms (laws). It is the only place where the Jubilee Year for land could be honored.

A third message from these verses (and verses 25, 35, and 39) is that just as perpetual ownership of the land is forbidden, so too is that of people, even those who have *"sunk down into poverty."* Similarly, we are not permitted to assign them to *"crushing labor"* (verse 46), for *"it is to Me that the Children of Israel are servants"* (verse 55). The text offers various ways that a serf can be redeemed prior to the Jubilee Year. However, if his debt is too great, then, *"He shall be beside you as a resident-settler and serve you only until the Home-bringing year, after which he and his family can go free and return to his clan"* (verses 40, 41). This Leviticus chapter also recognizes that not every serf will want to be redeemed. This is particularly true of the non-Hebrew serfs; for by returning to their clan they would likely have to give up the opportunity to stop all work activities once a week – a privilege/luxury they were afforded during their servitude to the Israelites.

Compared with the Jubilee Year dictum regarding land ownership, the one concerning people is less vulnerable to moral hazard because it is influences by one's innate sense of justice. As such, it is readily transferable into practical civil law in terms of meeting the following three criteria: Fairness, in by providing guidance for doling out punishments that fit the offense; Flexibility in recognizing that extenuating circumstances are often involved; and Compassionate, in offering protection for the powerless.

Leviticus 26 provides a logical conclusion to Leviticus by presenting a list of rewards for adhering to the rules, regulations and behavioral expectations discussed throughout the chapter as well as a list of punishments for not following them. The rewards, detailed in verses 6 through 12, include an abundance of food, protection from enemies, inner peace, wholeness, and closeness with YHVH: *"I will walk about in your midst; I will be for you a God and you will be for me as a people"* (Verse 12).

Meanwhile the punishments, listed between verses 16 and 39, occur in three waves and are dire. The first wave begins with *"If you do not hearken to me by not observing My commandments and regulations and violate my covenant… you will experience consumption and fever, and be hit by plague (Egypt). Your land will not give forth its yield."*

The second wave is more severe: *"If you walk in opposition to me, I will continue against you blows … I will set loose wild-beasts against you and your animals, so that they will make you few. You will eat but not be satisfied."*

The third and most drastic wave is as follows: "After *all this if you will not hearken to me, but still walk in opposition to me. . . I will discipline you. You will also eat the flesh of your sons and daughters. I will place your corpses atop the corpses of your idol-clods, make your cities a wasteland, and scatter you among the nations. Those of you that remain I will bring faintness to your hearts and cause you to flee from the sword, though there is no pursuer. You will perish among the nations. Those that remain will rot in the land of your enemies."*

The chapter concludes with verses 41 through 46, which I summarize: *"But, that if your heart should humble itself and find acceptance, I will bear-in-mind my Yaakov covenant and my Abraham covenant and not finish you off, for I am YHVH, your God. These are the laws, regulations, and instructions that YHVH gave to the Children of Israel at Mount Sinai by the hand of Moses."*

- **Why such gruesome punishments?** In addressing this question we need once again to remind ourselves not to interpret the passages literally, but instead view them as a collection of symbols, all intended to convey a deeper ethical understanding.

Our search for deeper meaning begins with the observation that the list of punishments contains multiple references to the time when the Israelites were still living enslaved lives in *Mitz'rayim* (a "narrow place). The most obvious connections to this time period are the expressions "hit by plague" (verse 17) and "I will continue against you blows" (verse 21). Recall that the Hebrew word often translated as "plagues" (*ma'kah*) actually means "blows" - - something that awakens our senses from their slumber and captures our attention. Finally, just as the Ten Blows (Plagues) were ordered from the least to the most personally threatening, so too are the three waves of punishment ordered from mildest to most severe.

A less obvious connection is "*You will eat the flesh of your sons and daughters*" (verse 29), which is reminiscent of the Tenth Blow (plague): "*In the middle of the night, I will go forth throughout the land of Egypt and every first born shall die, even the first born of beasts.*" Bear in mind that in Torah, as in many cultures, children are understood to represent our future. Just as "death to the first born" implies that our decision to remain in *Mitz'rayim* will cost us our future, it follows that "*not observing all these commandments*" (verse 14) and "*walk in opposition with me*" (verse 27) will produce the same result. Also bear in mind that just as the plagues never actually happened (for the many reasons explained in Chapter 6 of my book), the same can be said of the punishments, such as eating of one's children. They are presented not with the intent of being historically accurate, but instead to convey ethical and spiritual lessons. Said simply, the stories were never about the wholesale killing of one's children, but rather symbolic underlying meaning (in this case, the future).

- **Why draw our attention back to the time of the Plagues?** What types of ethical and spiritual wisdom can we draw from the story of the blows (plagues) that apply to Leviticus 26? These stories intend to convey the significant degree of hardship and struggle that are required for us to change our narrow ways. Will the promise of rewards and the threat of punishments in this chapter awaken our senses and capture our attention as the blows did? Will we voluntarily move forward as a community and cross-over into the Promised Land, as we once crossed over into the wilderness; or will we give into our weaker side and again seek out the comforts of Mitz'rayim?

Leviticus 26 contains other symbolic associations that communicate similar questions. For example, verse 26 threatens famine by stating that "You *will eat but not be satisfied*," a throwback to Pharaoh's dream about the seven gaunt cows in Genesis 41 that ate the seven healthy cows, but remained gaunt. A second example appears in verse 33, with the threat to "*scatter you among nations*". This is a reference to the Tower of Babel discussed Genesis 11, and the builders' fear of being at the mercy of others and facing the ever-present threat of leaving without a trace.

- **What can we learn from this chapter?** First, the list of punishments, coupled with the list of rewards, is based on the notion that humans have the capacity to influence their own fate; they can choose to move either forward backwards and face the resulting consequences. Second, the final six verses of Leviticus 26 suggest that our choice need not be permanent. No matter how far we have regressed back to Mitz'rayim, we still have the opportunity to reverse course and be redeemed.

➢ Closing Comments (Leviticus 27)

Summary: Throughout the entire Book of Leviticus, the people were camped beside Mount Sinai being schooled in how to prepare themselves for leaving the wilderness and entering the Promised Land. The lessons, coming in the form of commandments, sayings, regulations, and expectations, all had to do with raising their spiritual and ethical consciousness. Their last lesson appeared to come with the closing verse of Leviticus 26, which states, *"These are the laws, regulations, and instructions that YHVH gave between Himself and the Children of Israel at Mount Sinai, by the hand of Moses."* In theory, therefore, the people are ready to put their teaching into practice, except for one worldly detail: How are they going to pay for the upkeep of the sanctuary?

This question is addressed in Leviticus 27. Unlike the other chapters in Leviticus, there is nothing spiritually uplifting about the content of this chapter. It focuses entirely on what practical realities to expect in the Promised Land, where life would certainly not be free of struggle. It may be a place where we find nourishment, sweetness, and joy, even during mundane or troubled times -- but that of course implies that there will be mundane and troubled times. Specifically, Leviticus 27 details a tax schedule that differentiates based upon each person's gender, age, and financial well-being. Noteworthy in this chapter is the introduction of the ten percent tax known as a "tithe" (described further in Deuteronomy 14:22).

This chapter and Book end abruptly with verse 34 ("*These are the commandments that YHVH commanded Moses for the Children of Israel at Mount Sinai*"), a verse that largely restates the closing verse of the previous chapter, perhaps implying that the last chapter in Leviticus did not offer a whole lot of forward movement. Whatever the reason for repeating this closing verse, we are now ready to advance to Torah's fourth book, the Book of Numbers.

Chapter 11: The Final Preparations

Introduction: The Torah's fourth book, "Numbers" (*Be'mid-bar* in Hebrew) appears to be mistitled. *Be'mid-bar* means "in the wilderness" suggesting that the book will tell of the Israelites wandering for many more years before they are allowed entry into the Promised Land. To be sure, the book does contain stories about their continued wandering, but the majority of the book's content involves other subjects including census-taking, taxation, and the camp layout; the responsibilities of the Levites; laws regarding adultery and the removal of ritual pollution; stories about several mutinous rebellions; and the early battles in land of Canaan. Moreover, some of these subjects seem misplaced, pertaining more to the stories previously told in the Books of Exodus and Leviticus than to the challenges of wandering in the wilderness. Even the writing style in Numbers is inconsistent, sometimes resembling that of Leviticus with its long lists of ritualistic details, while at other times containing the kind of rich literary narratives that characterized Genesis and Exodus.

Why does Numbers appear so disorderly? There are various explanations for this. My take is that the book was written in its oddly structured manner to convey the message that reaching the Promised Land entails more than simply meeting challenges of surviving in the wilderness. It requires that the people all be like Israel; that is, show the willingness as a community to struggle with things both divine and mortal, and prove able (recall how Jacob came to be renamed "Israel" in Genesis 32). Therefore the non-wandering subjects in Numbers - when taken in concert with the rules, regulations, and expectations that were detailed in the previous two books - concern the completion of the people's preparation for meeting those struggles.

But, which people? Numbers makes clear that the slave generation - - those of us who were born and raised in *Mitz'rayim* and left this "narrow place" for the uncertainties of the wilderness – will never be prepared to enter the Promised Land. However, the book suggests that our children -- the new generation-- will be. Our own upbringing conditioned us to focus on our material pursuits while ignoring questions of good, evil, and life. But it is the new generation – those who are born free in the wilderness (*mid-bar*) – who will have the ability to "hear YHVH speak" (recall that the Hebrew word for "wilderness" shares the same linguistic root with the word *da'ber*, which means "speak"). They will be more receptive to the Covenant and its many rules, regulations and expectations that "set apart" their generation from our generation, and their nation from other nations. Compared with our generation, they will have the capacity to be more like Israel and in so doing, find both milk (symbolic of nourishment) and honey (representing sweetness and joy) in their lives, even during mundane or troubled times. And it is they who are more likely to "love our neighbors as ourselves" (Leviticus 19:18) in ways that we never could.

Numbers will be presented in three parts. Chapter 11, titled "Final Preparations," covers the Book's first ten chapters, which discuss the remaining details that must be addressed before the people are ready to leave the Wilderness of Sinai and start their journey to the Promised Land. Chapter 12, "Tales of Rebellion," describes the thirty-eight years of wandering until the arrival at Moab, and the six mutinous attempts by the people (mentioned in Numbers 11 – 25) to abandon their journey. Finally, Chapter 13, "Preparations for Battle," describes the steps taken by the people in Numbers 26 through 36 as they prepare to conquer the land of Canaan.

➢ Census Taking (Numbers 1-4)

Summary: *Numbers 1 opens with YHVH speaking to Moses in the Wilderness of Sinai on the first day after the second new moon in the second year after the exodus from Egypt. YHVH tells Moses that he, Aaron, and the heads of each of the twelve tribes (Reuven, Shimon, Judah, Yissakhar, Zevulun, Efrayim, Menashe, Benjamin, Dan, Asher, Gad, Naftali) are to take a census of every man in the community "from the age twenty and upward, everyone is going out to the armed-forces with Israel" except those from the tribe of Levi (Jacob's third son, mothered by Leah), who are not to be counted for battle for they are to be accountable for the Tabernacle (the portable sanctuary used in the wilderness).*

The total, excluding the Levites, came to 603,550. This figure included 46,500 men from the Tribe of Reuven (Jacob's firstborn; mothered by Leah); 59,300 thousand from the Tribe of Shimone (Jacob's second son, mothered by Leah); 45,650 from the Tribe of Gad (Jacob's seventh son, mothered by Leah's maid, Zilpa); 74,600 from the Tribe of Judah (Jacob's fourth son, mothered by Leah); 54,400 from the Tribe of Yissakhar (Jacob's ninth son, mothered by Leah); 57,400 from the Tribe of Zevulun (Jacob's tenth son, mothered by Leah); 40,500 from the Tribe of Ephraim (Jacob and Rachel's grandson and son of Joseph); 32,200 from the Tribe of

Menashe (Jacob and Rachel's grandson and son of Joseph); 35,400 from the Tribe of Benjamin (Jacob's twelfth son, son of Rachel); 62,700 from the Tribe of Dan (Jacob's fifth son, mothered by Rachel's maid, Bilha); 41,500 from the Tribe of Asher (Jacob's eighth son, mothered by Zilpa); and 53,400 from the Tribe of Naftali (Jacob's sixth son, and mothered by Bilha).

YHVH then commanded Moses to count the Levite men between the ages of thirty and fifty years; for these men were to do the specific tasks assigned to their clan including guarding, dismantling, and transporting the Tabernacle and its holy objects. Their numbers totaled 8,580. YHVH also told Moses to count this tribe a second time, every male from the age of one month and upward. Moses did so and found 22,000 males among them, including the sons (and grandsons) of Levi: Gershon (Livni and Shim'i); Kehat (Amram, Yishar, Hevron and Uzziel); and Merari (Mahli and Mushi).

Discussion Questions: Why is Numbers 1 taking place on the second new moon of the second year? What is meant by "going out to the armed-forces with Israel? What might the size of each tribe mean?

- **Why the "second" new moon in the "second" year?** The symbolic meaning of the number two is explained in detail in Genesis 41:32, where Joseph tells Pharaoh that the repetition of his dream (about the seven years of abundance followed seven lean years) "means that the matter is determined by YHVH, who will soon carry it out." In the context of Numbers 1:1, the second new moon in the second year means that thirteen months have passed since exodus from Egypt. What "is determined and will soon be carried out" in this case are thirty-nine more years of wandering.

- **What is meant by "going out to the armed-forces with Israel"?** Decoding of this statement begins with the recognition that "Israel," as defined in Genesis 32, refers not so much to a person, as to the willingness and ability to pursue a path of spiritual yearning. Armed with the Covenant and all that it entails, the Israelites are about to be tested again regarding their readiness to face the personal, communal, and spiritual challenges of the unknown.

To understand the reference to the "armed forces," we must note that the book of Numbers contains numerous militaristic references, beginning with verse 1:3. This would seem to contradict the ethical cornerstone of Torah: the instruction to "love your neighbor as yourself" which appears in Leviticus 19:18. We once again face the challenge of understanding what the writer(s) might have had in mind by inserting this particular inconsistency.

I will offer my thoughts later in this chapter when the ensuing battles are described in all their brutal detail, beginning in Numbers 21. Suffice to say here that like many other narratives in the Torah, those concerning the military conquests by the Israelites are presented as folklore, suggesting that they should not be interpreted literally nor seen as actual historical happenings. Joshua might never have fought a Battle of Jericho and there is no archeological evidence that any of its walls came tumbling down!

- **What about the sizes of the twelve tribes?** The head-count of 603,550 men of fighting age, in addition to the thousands of Levite men, is nonsensically large for all the reasons previously mentioned in Chapter 7 of this book. (You will recall from that chapter that Exodus 12:37 stated that "about six hundred thousand men" left Egypt, implying a total population of about two million people when women and children are included.) Let's put this number into a historical perspective: Best estimates put the numbers living in Jerusalem shortly after entering the Promised Land during the time of King David at only about three thousand people.

While the total count is clearly an exaggeration, the relative sizes of the tribes may symbolize their stature in the community. I say this because in the patriarchs and matriarchs introduced in the Book of Genesis held "size" in high esteem, viewing it as both a reward for keeping YHVH's covenant and a sign of greatness. For example, in Genesis 15:5, YHVH says to Avram, "Look towards the heavens and count the stars… so shall your seed be." Refer also to Genesis 18:18 where the three messengers tell Abraham and Sarah that they will "become a great nation and mighty in numbers" and to Genesis 26:4 where YHVH makes a similar promise to Isaac: "I will make your seeds many, like the stars in the heavens."

Viewed accordingly, it may not be surprising that the tribe of Judah (descended from Leah) is said to be the largest with 74,600 men of fighting age. In Torah terms, Judah's large size can be seen as a partial fulfillment of Jacob/Israel's blessing, which likened "Judah to a lion, the king of beasts; who dares rouse him up? Your brothers will praise you and bow down to you" (Genesis 48:8-9).

In Chapter five, I commented that Judah was deserving of this praise, having transformed himself into a sensitive and generous person-- largely on his own. After all, it was it was Judah who had convinced his brothers not to physically harm their brother Joseph at the pit (Genesis 43). It was also Judah, more than his brothers, who showed the willingness to put the family's well-being ahead of his own interests (Genesis 44). In short, Judah, like Joseph, acted as his "brother's keeper" while the other sons of Jacob/Israel did not.

(Recall that the question "Am I my brother's keeper?" was first asked by Cain in Genesis 4 and remained unanswered until Genesis 37. The many chapters in between communicated the message that every sibling has the responsibility to attend to the *shalem* of his or her family; for the cost of sibling rivalry is painfully high. It resulted in the murder of Abel, the exile of Ishmael, and a death threat to Jacob as well as putting Joseph's life at risk.

Interestingly, three of the four smallest tribes are Ephraim (40,500), Benyamin (35,400), and Menashe (32,200) – all descendants of Rachel, the woman that Jacob loved. She was the mother of Joseph, the son whom Jacob/Israel "loved more than all of his sons…the son that Israel made him an ornamented coat" (Genesis 37: 3); the mother of Benjamin, Joseph's younger brother; and the grandmother of Joseph's two sons, Ephraim and Menashe. Given the elevated positions that Rachel and Joseph played in the family, coupled with the symbolic importance played by size in the Torah, we might have expected that the three tribes would be among the largest.

Why the discrepancy? Perhaps the Torah wants us to think of these three tribes not as separate entities, but as part of a unified familial whole, consisting of 108,100 men --

far outnumbering the Tribe of Judah? After all, it was Joseph - and when Joseph was presumed dead, Benjamin - who was chosen by Jacob/Israel as the rightful heir to receive the family birthright that Jacob/Israel received from his father Isaac, who in turn received it from his father, Abraham.

Again, the birthright in Torah has nothing to do with the family's material possessions or net worth. The rightful heir is the one deemed most able to accept the responsibility of living one's life in accordance with the Covenant so that the current and future generations can "move forward" into a closer relationship with ourselves and each other (our personal challenges) and with YHVH (our spiritual challenge).

➢ Water of Bitterness (Numbers 5)

Summary: As with the Book of Leviticus, Numbers 5 contains priestly instructions for dealing with a wide assortment of scenarios. For example, this chapter provides detailed instructions for priests concerning the treatment of those who suffer from skin impurities (tzaraat) or have had recent contact with the dead (tamie), with the objective of preventing these two types of pollution from infecting the others. Numbers 5 also offers directions for those who seek forgiveness after intentionally committing sins: These individuals are to confess their sin and then make restitution to those people whom they offended by paying a guilt-payment worth twenty-percent above the value of their wrong-doing.

Beginning with verse 11, Numbers 5 becomes somewhat provocative, instructing priests on how to address instances where a husband accuses his wife of having an affair. Unlike in Leviticus 20, there are no witnesses to the alleged affairs mentioned in Numbers 5 to either confirm or refute the husband's accusation.

Lacking witnesses, the priests put the wife through a ceremonial ordeal to assert her innocence. She is told to drink some unspecified liquid formula called "the water of bitterness." She is then informed that if she is innocent, the formula will pass through her system without causing any physical discomfort. However, if she is guilty, it will cause "her thighs to fall and her belly to flood." She would then have to "swear the oath curse," after which the priests would say to her "may YHVH make you a curse and cause-for-oath in the midst of your kinsfolk."

- **Is the "water of bitterness" a just ritual?** On the surface, the answer appears to be "no." Indeed, the process seems grounded on supernatural intervention, superstition, and dark magic – the kind of false justice metered out during the times of the Spanish Inquisition and Salem Witch Trials. Moreover, this kind of trial was completely inconsistent with the definition of justice outlined in Exodus 20-23 in being neither fair (providing guidance for doling out settlements proportional to the offense); flexible (recognizing extenuating circumstances); nor compassionate (offering protection for the powerless). Of course, previous commentary has already established that very little about the Torah resides on the surface. With that in mind, we must ask ourselves what the "water of bitterness" might represent.

We are afforded a defining clue in Exodus 15, where bitter-tasting water is defined. Recall that soon after crossing the Sea of Reeds, the Israelites came to *Ma'ror*, so named because the water there was too bitter to drink. . (*Ma'ror* literally means "bitter" as in the "bitter herbs" that are placed on the Passover plate to remind us of what life was like in Mitz'rayim.) We concluded that the water's bitterness in *Ma'ror* had more to do with the people who were drinking it than with a physical reality. Having just left *Mitz'rayim*, their enslaved, narrow-minded view of reality prevented them from appreciating the sweetness of their newly found freedom.

We can make similar observations about the "water of bitterness" in Numbers 5. Like the waters of *Ma'ror*, it is not some putrid concoction that can cause real physical harm. Rather, it represents a state of mind triggered by one's conscience. Having the accused drink the liquid, while "standing in the presence of YHVH" (verse 18) and under the close scrutiny of the priests, the ordeal bears resemblance to a modern day polygraph (lie-detector) test: Those who know of their guilt will have a difficult time suppressing a physical reaction to the water; while those who are innocent will likely elicit no apparent reaction -- for to them the water will not taste bitter.

Also like a polygraph, the "water of bitterness" test is understood in Torah to not be fool-proof. There will always be a few who can mask their guilt, while others who committed no real sexual impropriety may nonetheless harbor some guilty thoughts and feelings. In the spirit of fairness and justice, therefore, those found guilty in Numbers 5 received a milder punishment ("swear the oath curse" while being cursed by the priests), than did the guilty in Leviticus 20 where, with witnesses present to confirm the affair. In these cases, the priests were instructed to put the offending adults to death (though – for the reasons given in the commentary to that Leviticus chapter under the heading "Serious Offenses and Resulting Punishments" --the death sentence was never applied).

Interestingly, the "water of bitterness" test serves another function aside from assisting justice: It helps to heal wounded marriages. It does so by allowing the accused a formal means to convince the husband of his wife's innocence – something which might not be possible without the test. That is to say that without the test, the emotions of jealousy and suspicion -- which initially led to the husband's accusations -- would likely deepen over time, causing the sweet water of matrimonial bond to taste bitter and poison whatever may be left in their relationship.

In sum, the "water of bitterness" test reflects a fair, flexible, and compassionate understanding of human nature that seems years ahead of its time. It must be noted, however, that it also reflect the first overt example of gender bias in the Torah. Were the Torah being consistent, it would also apply this test to husbands who are accused of going astray.

I find this gender bias perplexing, considering that we read in Leviticus 20 that the punishment for extra-marital affairs was doled out to equally to both offending partners. I also find this bias troubling because it makes light of the positive role that women have played up to this point. As a refresher, recall that without Eve, Adam would not have begun their personal and spiritual journey. Without Sarah's prompting, Abraham would not have passed the family birthright on to Isaac. Without Rebecca, Isaac would not have passed the family birthright on to Jacob. What about the midwives in Exodus 1 who bravely chose not to follow Pharaoh's command to put to death all newborn Hebrew males, and then to stand up to Pharaoh when he confronted them? What about Moses' mother who put her life at risk by hiding her newborn son from the Egyptians for three months before setting him adrift on the Nile in a little ark? It was Moses' sister who kept a close eye on the baby as he drifted in the river and then boldly approached Pharaoh's daughter with the plan to bring the child's mother to nurse him. And it was Pharaoh's daughter who chose to raise the child as her own, in clear violation of her all-powerful father's edict.

In short, up to Numbers 5, the Torah has treated woman as key and trusted players, deserving of equal treatment by the priests. I cannot explain this sudden and troubling shift towards gender inequality, at least when it entails accusations of sexual misconduct and there are no witnesses to either confirm or refute those accusation.

➤ The Priestly Benediction (Numbers 6)

The sixth chapter in the Book of Numbers is similar to the fifth in that it contains mostly priestly instructions for dealing with a mixed assortment of situations. For example, it instructs ascetics like Sampson (for more about Sampson, see Book of Judges, chapters 13-16) who wish to dedicate their lives to God and feel that the normal demands of religious life are not enough. First mentioned in Leviticus 19, these individuals, called Nazarites (meaning those who are consecrated or separated), vow to abstain from alcohol, never shave their hair, and never come into contact with the dead.

Perhaps the most topical portion of Numbers 6, however, lies in its final four verses (24-27). Known as the "Priestly Benediction," these four verses are read to this day at most Sabbath services. They are commonly translated as: "May YHVH bless you and guard you! May YHVH shine his face upon you and favor you! May YHVH lift up his face towards you and grant you shalom! So are they to put my name upon the Children of Israel that I myself may bless them."

While short in length, these verses are deep in message. However, to understand that message, we must first decipher some of its key words. Let us begin with the word "may," which appears in most English translations but is not found in the original Hebrew. A more precise translation of the Hebrew is, "YHVH *will* bless you; *will* guard you; *will* shine his face upon you; YHVH *will* lift up his face towards you." Notice how this affirmative tone lies in stark contrast not only to the common translation, but also to the conditional wording previously used by YHVH in the Book of Leviticus. There, in the 26th chapter of that book, YHVH promises rewards for acting in accordance with YHVH's wishes, but also threatens severe punishments for failing to do so (e.g., "If you do not hearken to me by not observing my commandments and regulations and violate my covenant… you will experience consumption and fever, and be hit by plague. Your land will not give forth its yield."). Might the positive tone in the Numbers 6 passage be suggesting that the people have advanced beyond where they were in Leviticus 26, when the primary motivation to choose YHVH's ways seemed to be fear of reprisal rather than the benefits for doing so?

Discussion Questions: What is the meaning of each of the four versus?

> - **What does "*will bless you*" mean?** The word "bless" (*ba'rokh*) shares the same three letter root (*sho'resh*) with the word *ber'ech*, which means "knee." To be blessed, therefore, is to kneel down and receive – but receive what? The answer resides in the story about Jacob's wrestling with the mysterious man (Genesis 32). As you will recall, at the end of their struggle Jacob was blessed by having his name changed to *Israel,* marking a fundamental transformation in his identity. He was no longer Jacob, the "heel-sneak and deceiver," but rather a person who he was always meant to be – someone willing and able to commit to a life defined by the precepts of the Covenant.
>
>   And, what does it mean "to live by the Covenant"? As explained previously, it involves more than adhering to YHVH's commandments, regulations and expectations. It is about helping future generations realize their potential in terms of their human and spiritual relationships. Said simply, living by the Covenant is about learning how to be more human, to appreciate life before death, and to participate in the ongoing process of creation.

The teaching from the Jacob story is clear: Even a heal-sneak and deceiver is born with the potential to be more Israel-like and live by the Covenant. To be blessed is not only to recognize that potential which lies within all of us, but to act upon it as well. According to Torah, a blessed person is someone who is ready to cross over into the Promised Land.

> **What does *"will guard you"* (also translated as "will keep you") mean?** The word "guard" first appears in the Garden Story (Genesis 2), where it referred not to protection from physical harm but rather to the care of one's spirit. This is to say that those who are blessed and guarded will not waver in their state of mind even in the most troublesome or threatening times. While others see darkness and despair, they will see light. It is they who will find milk (sustenance) and honey (joy and happiness), even during times of hunger, drought, and duress.

It is also the "guarded" who will successfully rid themselves of the fallacy of control. Recall the Genesis stories about Abraham and Sarah, which teach us that believing we can control that which we cannot can bring suffering to ourselves and others. In this and many other tales in the Torah, we are reminded that the sooner we accept those things we cannot control, the better equipped we are to cope with life's traumas and disappointments and therefore find inner peace and wholeness. In sum, those who are blessed and guarded have already crossed over into the Promised Land – without the aid of armed-forces - and they know it.

* **What does *"YHVH will shine His/Her face upon you"* mean?** In Torah, "face" symbolizes one's inner truth or authentic self. To say "I see your face" is to say that I have a deep enough understanding of you to bear true witness (think 9th plague and 9th Commandment). To say that "YHVH will shine His/Her face upon you" therefore means that YHVH is offering the blessed and guarded a face-to-face relationship. In other words, nothing is blurring either party's vision of the other and no other gods hinder the relationship (see the 2nd Commandment).

* What does "*YHVH will lift up Her/His face toward you*" mean? The expression "lift up" symbolizes a moment of clarity of thought and purpose. We witnessed this in Genesis 14 when YHVH told Avram to lift up his eyes and everything that you see in; and in the Akidah story (Genesis 22) when Abraham "lifted his eyes and saw the place from afar"; and in Genesis 33 when "Jacob lifted up his eyes and saw Esau coming." The difference is that in the Promised Land, YHVH joins in the lifting.

*What does *"to put my name upon the Children of Israel"* mean? As previously mentioned, names in Torah are intended to reveal core aspects of the character's personality. YHVH's name, however, isn't so much a name, in the sense that names are nouns. Instead it is a verb, conjugated in the first-person imperfect tense to signify a yet-to-be completed action. The construction of YHVH's name suggests an ongoing two-way movement between the distant past and an unbounded, ever-unfolding future - - an unknowable force of infinite oneness, residing without the limits of time, form and space (*ein sof*), and for which there is no other (*ein ode*).

Therefore, to say that YHVH will put his/her name upon those who are blessed and guarded is to imply that the characters of these individuals have been fundamentally transformed to a more spiritual state. We witnessed this kind of transformation when the letter '*hey*' from YHVH's name was added to the names of Avram and Sarai (to become Abraham and Sarah), and when Jacob was renamed Israel.

*Are the people ready to enter the Promised Land? The people have already received four essential necessities for entering: Revelation at Sinai (Exodus 20); the building of the Tabernacle (Exodus 25-31, 35-40 and Leviticus 24); the formation of the Priesthood (Leviticus 8 and 9); and the guarding of Sacred Time (Leviticus 23). The priestly benediction, which acknowledges the people's readiness, is the fifth and final requirement. The question is, will the people will be able to act on that readiness? An affirmative answer to this question begs a "Catch-22," for it implies that we are ready to enter into the Promised Land only if we are we are already in it. As we will soon read, the Children of Israel are clearly not in it, nor do they show the readiness to enter.

➢ Last Days in the Wilderness. (Numbers 7-10)

The Torah will have us believe that the Tabernacle (also called the *Mishkan,* Dwelling, or Sanctuary) was completed in four stages. Exodus 25-31 describes the set of instructions for the first stage. These deal primarily with the construction of the Tabernacle's interior: the building and décor of the sanctuary, like the designs of its tapestries and various ritual objects; and its sacred center, where the ark or tabernacle is to be held. Exodus 35-40 defines the second-stage, which focuses more on the dwelling's overall design. This includes its outer courtyard where the slaughter-site and basin are to be placed, and its inner courtyard which is to contain a menorah and the two Tablets of Testimony. Leviticus 24 tells of the third stage, identifying the ritual objects to be used in the Tabernacle.

The seventh chapter of the Book of Numbers details the final stage. It happens to be the longest chapter in Torah in terms of number of verses (1-89), dedicated in part to recording the inventory of "near-offerings" brought by each Tribe's leader for the initiation of the slaughter-site. The offerings included silver, gold, grains, goats, and cattle. The leader from the Tribe of Judah made his offering on the first day, followed on consecutive days by the leaders from the Tribes of Yissakhar; Zevulun; Reuven; Shimon; and Gad. The leaders from the Tribes of Ephraim, Menashe, Benjamin, Dan, Asher and Naphtali made their offerings on Days 7 – 12, again one per day, respectively.

What makes the ordering curious is that all of the offerings made during the first week were from descendants of Leah or her maid, Bilha; while the offerings made during the second week were all descendants of Rachel or her maid, Zilpa. The lone exception was the Tribe of Gad, who descended from Bilha. I suspect that there was a meaning to this break in the pattern, but that it was lost in the annals of time.

In Numbers 8, YHVH tells Moses to take the Levites from the midst of the Children of Israel, separate them from the others, and then elevate them as an offering before the presence of YHVH. Moses was then to purify them by sprinkling them with the *Water of Hattat* (i.e., the Water of Decontamination), "for Mine are the Levites to be!"

Moses is then told that not only will the Levites be responsible for the Tent of Appointment and for assisting the priests, but they will also serve as ransom for everyone's firstborn, for while "Mine is every firstborn among the Children of Israel… I now take the Levites in place of these firstborn." In addition, YHVH instructs Moses that the Levites between the ages of twenty-five and fifty are to perform their assigned tasks, after which they are to retire and no longer engage in heavy serving tasks. However, they can still attend meetings in the Tent of Appointment with their fellow brothers.

Discussion Questions: Why substitute a Levite for every firstborn? Why are the Levites told that they are to enter the work force at the age of twenty-five and retire at the age of fifty? What is the Torah teaching us by placing this chapter out of chronological order? What does the movement of cloud and fire tell us about the people? Why is the tribe of Judah leading the way? Who is Hovav and why is Moses pleading with him to stay?

> ➢ **Why substitute a Levite for every firstborn?** We learned in the Book of Genesis that "firstborn" are not necessarily the firstborn, but rather the ones deemed best suited to receive and pass on the family birthright (think of Isaac born after Ishmael; Jacob born after Esau; and Joseph, born after ten of his brothers). In general, the firstborn shows the greatest capacity to lead the current and next generation forward into closer relationships with the community (our personal challenge) and with YHVH (our spiritual challenge). They also bear the greatest responsibility to live their lives as an offering to YHVH, in the sense that Abel offered "first and the choicest" of his flock to YHVH.
>
> To advance on their mission, however, firstborn sons may not belong to anyone other than YHVH. Abraham learned this first-hand in the Akidah story in Genesis 22, which told of the "binding of Isaac" that took place on Mount Mariah (the Mountain of Teaching). It was there where he willingly sacrificed his relationship with his son so that Isaac could live his life as an offering to YHVH. Put in more modern terms, it was on the mountain where Abraham came to understand that his son needed to be freed from the shackles of parental control and expectations, which were stunting his growth and development.

In the Book of Numbers, we read of YHVH extending the designation of firstborn from a few select individuals to that of a whole tribe. The Levites' mission as the "tribe of firstborns" will be to represent "every firstborn among the Children of Israel" by dedicating their lives to the personal and spiritual well-being of each household.

This new designation has organizational implications. On one hand, it reaffirms the Levites' elevated position among the other tribes. The Levites are to act as intermediaries between the firstborn of each tribe and YHVH. Further, as elevated firstborn children, the Levites may belong to no one other than YHVH, living out their lives beyond the control of the other tribes and special interest groups.

On the other hand, the centralizing of authority and responsibilities may have unintended consequences. While it may simplify the challenge of maintaining overall order, it might also engender resentment. Said simply, the elevation of one tribe's position must effectively lower those of the other tribes. What had once been a direct relationship with YHVH for these tribes is now downgraded into an indirect relationship, through no apparent fault of their own.

* Why are the Levites told that they are to enter the work force at the age of twenty-five and retire at the age of fifty? As we have many times witnessed, numbers in Torah generally have symbolic meaning. For example, the number "fifty" represents the Jubilee year, a time of emancipation when that which is owned is returned to its rightful owner, YHVH (Leviticus 25:23). This designation has a different meaning for Levites; for as a tribe of firstborn children they never left their rightful owner. For them, turning fifty simply meant that they were freed from heavy labor. As elders, they were still welcomed guests at Tribal meetings.

The number twenty-five, however, appears nowhere else in Torah. I cannot discern if it has symbolic meaning or what might that meaning might be.

The ninth chapter of Numbers tells of the second Passover: YHVH spoke to Moses in the Wilderness of Sinai in the second year of their going out of Egypt at the first New

Moon, saying: "The Children of Israel are to sacrifice the Passover offering on the fourteenth day after this New-Moon according to all of its laws and regulations." However, some men in the community could not make the sacrifice offering because they were *tamei* (impure), meaning they had come in contact with a dead person. They complained to Moses, "Why should we have our privilege taken away?"

Moses replied, "Stand by and let me hear what YHVH shall command regarding you." And YHVH said, "Any man who is *tamei* by reason of a dead person or is on a long journey is to sacrifice a Passover-offering on the fourteenth day of the second New-Moon."

* What is the Torah teaching us by placing this chapter out of chronological order? Chapter 9 begins with instructions for observing the first day after the first new moon in the second year after leaving Egypt, while the book of Numbers opens 28 days later with YHVH speaking to Moses on the first day after the second new moon of that year. Some might argue that this inconsistency is the result of an editorial oversight, but I prefer a different explanation; that is, the Torah is less concerned with linear time than with sacred time. As we have read in previous passages, the past doesn't necessarily proceed the present in sacred time, nor must the present precede the future. Look no farther than Genesis 1 and its depiction of the first three days of Creation, which existed before the sun and moon were introduced on the fourth day to mark time. Another example can be seen in Genesis 16 when YHVH tells Avram of his future, saying that his descendants' will journey to a land not theirs where they will be enslaved for four hundred years.

In the later portions of Chapter 9, the subject shifts from the second Passover to that of cloud and fire: "Now at the time that the Dwelling was set up, the cloud covered the Dwelling over the Tent of Testimony, and after sunset it remained over the Dwelling, as the appearance of fire, until daybreak." When the cloud lifted, the Children of Israel would march on; in the place that the cloud took up the dwelling, there the Children would encamp. "Whether by day or by night, when the cloud lifted, they would march on . . . and when it lingered over the dwelling, the Children would remain."

*What does the movement of cloud and fire tell us about the people? Recall that cloud and fire were both used in Exodus 24 to represent the presence of YHVH. For example, we read in the Exodus chapter that while the people were stationed beneath the Mountain, a cloud covered the mountain for six days. On the seventh day YHVH called to Moses from amidst the cloud. "And the sight of the Glory of YHVH to the Children of Israel was like a consuming fire." This Exodus passage helps us to interpret Numbers 9 by highlighting how far the people have advanced in the past few months.

First, by moving only when the cloud moved, the people demonstrated their willingness to trade their illusion of control for the uncertainty of the future (i.e., the ever-unfolding movement into the unknown). No one questioned why the cloud would sometimes stop and sometimes go; they all seemed to accept YHVH's promise to "guard" them.

Second, by building the Dwelling according to YHVH's specifications, the people displayed the capacity to bring the cloud down from the mountain top, and in so doing brought themselves closer to YHVH. . At the same time, they observed that the fire that burns all night above the Dwelling is not a consuming fire. As Moses did in front of the burning bush, the people are now able to see the extraordinary in the ordinary.

Finally, in Numbers 10 we read that the Israelites are ready to begin their journey from Sinai to Canaan: "Now it was, in the second year, in the second New-Moon, on the twentieth after the New-Moon, the cloud went up from the Dwelling of Testimony, and the children of Israel marched forth from the Wilderness of Sinai to the Wilderness of Paran, led by the tribe of Judah. Moses said to Hovav, his brother-in-law, the son of Re'ul the Midyanite and the brother of Moses' wife, Tzippora: 'Go with us and we will do good for you, for YHVH has promised good things for Israel.' But Hovav replied, 'I will not go, but rather go to my land and to my kindred.' Moses pleaded, 'Pray do not leave us, for after all you know the best places to encamp in the wilderness; you shall be our eyes…If you go with us, the goodness with which

YHVH will do-good for us, we will do good for you!' The people then marched from the mountain of YHVH for three days. When the cloud of YHVH was over them as they marched and when it would rest, they would rest.

* Why is the tribe of Judah leading the way? This should not be surprising, for the tribe of Judah was said to be the largest with 74,600 men of fighting age. Recall also that when near death, Jacob/Israel likened "Judah like the lion, like the king of beasts, who dares rouse him up? Your brothers will praise you and bow down to you." (Genesis 48:8-9).

*Who is Hovav and why is Moses pleading with him to stay? Hovav is the son of Re'uel (also known as Jethro, Moses' father-in-law) and the brother of Moses' wife, Tzippora. Coming from the surrounding area, Hovav knows the terrain well enough to lead the Israelites, but feels it time for him to return to his people. The text is ambiguous as to whether or not Hovav is swayed by Moses' plea. What is clear, however, is that Moses is panicking: Burdened with the responsibility for leading hundreds of thousands of people, he doesn't know where he is or where he is to go. Rather than trust YHVH for guidance and support, he instead turns to Hovav. For the moment, Moses has forgotten the cloud that has accompanied the Israelites' journey since the time that they left *Mitz'rayim*. For the moment, he is not trusting YHVH's promise to guard the people (verse 25 of Numbers 6: the Priestly Benediction).

Chapter 12: The Tales of Rebellion

Much of the material in the Books of Exodus and Leviticus covers the people's preparations for seeing the "mountain," not as *Horev* (defined in Exodus 3 as the mountain of sword and destruction), but as *Sinai* (the mountain of God where revelation takes place). The preparation to journey beyond Sinai begins with the first ten chapters of the Book of Numbers, as the people try to put into practice all that has been revealed to them. It becomes clear with the opening verses of Numbers 11, however, that this will not be easy, for every step toward to the Promised Land is met by a rebellion. Some are against Moses and others initiated by him, but common to all is a general lack of trust in YHVH.

The first rebellion is sparked by hunger and described in Numbers 11. The second rebellion, which appears in Numbers 12, is initiated by Moses' siblings. Numbers 13 and 14 present the scout's rebellion; Numbers 16 describes the Korah Rebellion; Numbers 17 details the fifth rebellion, which involves the entire community; and finally, Moses' rebellion against YHVH appears in the first 21 versus of Numbers 20.

> The First Rebellion: Hunger (Numbers 11)

Summary: *This chapter tells of the time during their second year of wandering in the Wilderness when the people began to grieve over a lack of meat: "We recall the fish that we used to eat in Egypt for free, the cucumbers, watermelons, green leeks, onions and garlic. But now our throats are dry; there is nothing at all except for the manna."*

Moses heard the people weeping and called to YHVH: "For what reason have I not found favor in your eyes, that you have placed the burden of this entire people on me . . . Where should I get meat to give to this entire people? I am not able, myself alone, to carry this entire people, for it is too heavy on me. Pray kill me, so that I do not have to see my ill-fortune!"

YHVH responds: "Gather seventy men of the elders of Israel and take them to the Tent of Appointment. I will then extend to those elder the rushing-spirit that is upon you, so that they will carry along with you the burden of the people. They are to say, 'Hallow yourselves for the morrow, for YHVH will give you meat, not only for one day, but for a month-full of days, until it comes out of your nostrils and become for you something disgusting,' for you have spurned YHVH by saying 'For what reason did we leave Egypt?'"

Moses turns to YHVH and asks, "Where will all this meat and fish come from?" YHVH replies "Is the arm of YHVH too short?" YHVH then comes down in a cloud and extends some of the rushing-spirit on the seventy elders and it was as if they acted like prophets.

Now, it happened that two of the elders, Eldad and Meidad, did not go to the tent, but instead remained in the camp and acted like prophets. Joshua told Moses of this, saying, "Contain them!" But, Moses replied, "Are you jealous for me? If only all of the people were prophets!"

A rush of wind from YHVH then swept in quails from the sea and spread over the land, two cubits high and a day's journey in each direction. And the people who had rebelled ate all day and night and all the next day. The meat was still between their teeth, yet the supply was not exhausted, when the anger of YHVH flared and struck them down with a great striking. So they called the place Kivrot Ha-Taave (Place of Great Craving), for there were buried those who had the craving.

Discussion Questions: How does this rebellion compare to the hunger rebellion that took place one year earlier? How do the roles of the seventy elders differ from those played by the tribal leaders? What is meant by acting like a prophet? Who are Eldad and Meidad, and why is Joshua threatened by their behavior?

> ***Compare the first rebellion to that which occurred soon after the Israelites left Egypt.** In the earlier rebellion – the one described in Exodus 16 that took place in the second month after the tenth plague/blow (death to the first born) - the people grumbled to Moses, saying, "Better had we died by the hand of YHVH in the land of Egypt, where we ate bread till we were satisfied, than to bring us to the Wilderness and die of starvation."
>
> Much has changed in the year since the first hunger rebellion. Specifically, the people have now received six necessities for entering the Promised Land: the gift of the Sabbath, the Revelation at Sinai, the building of the Tabernacle, the formation of the Priesthood,

the guarding of Sacred Time, and the priestly benediction. However, as we read in Numbers 11, some still continue to hunger for the abundance they left behind in Mitz'rayim, although they now do so with a greater longing and more vivid memories of the many delicacies that Mitz'rayim had to offer (e.g., fish, cucumbers, watermelons, green leeks, onions and garlic).

Moses has also changed. In Exodus 15, he trusted YHVH's ability to address the people's thirst and hunger. By Numbers 11, however, he appears more cynical. Seemingly exhausted by his leadership responsibilities and frustrated by the inability of the people to advance beyond their narrow, non-spiritual ways, he became angry at YHVH, questioning YHVH's powers (as we see in the question, "Where will all this meat and fish come from?"), fairness ("For what reason have I not found favor in your eyes?"), and wisdom (Why have you placed the burden of this entire people on me?").

* What is the significance of the seventy elders? As in many cultures, elders in the Torah are held in high regard for the wisdom they might have accumulated over the years. Therefore, it may not be surprising that when Moses asks YHVH for help, YHVH tells him to gather seventy elders "to carry along with you the burden of the people."

We might ask, "Why not the tribal leaders?" After all, these leaders served an important administrative function for Moses. As Moses' father-in-law, Jethro, explained in Exodus 18: 21, the tribal leaders are "the chiefs of thousands, chiefs of hundreds, chiefs of fifties and chiefs of ten…responsible to bring every great matter to you, Moses, but every small matter they shall judge by themselves." These chiefs allowed Moses to "be there for the people in relation to YHVH" (that is, focus on the spiritual well-being of all the people) without being distracted by the mundane details and petty disputes that inevitably crop up at the tribal level. However, even with their assistance, Moses realized that the task of "being there for the people" was proving too much for him. He needed others like himself who had the "rushing spirit."

Why seventy? As noted in earlier commentary, this number symbolizes completeness or perfection. It first appears in the Genesis 10 story of the Flood to represent the number of Noah's descendants who repopulated the world. It shows up again in Genesis 46: 8-27 ("Thus, all the persons of Jacob's household who came to Mitz'rayim were seventy"); in Exodus 1:1-5 ("Now these are the names of the Children of Israel coming to Egypt - - so all the persons were seventy persons"); in Exodus 15:27 ("From Maror, they went to Elim, where there were twelve springs of water and seventy palms"); and in Exodus 24 (when YHVH told Moses "to go the mountain with Aaron and Aaron's two sons, Nadav and Avihu, and seventy elders").

*What does "acting like prophets" mean? While most regard a prophet as someone who predicts the future, the definition is broader than that. The term refers to a person who is told by YHVH to bring YHVH's words to a community, usually at a time when the message is entirely outside of that community's norms. Not surprisingly, a prophet's words are generally not readily received and are likely to be resisted, for the prophet tells others what they don't want to hear. Small wonder, therefore, that many prophets like Jonah are reluctant to deliver YHVH's messages.

- **Who are Eldad and Meidad and why is Joshua finding their actions threatening?** The names of these two elders loosely translate as "coming from the family of God." The episode about them covers only four verses (26-29) in Numbers 11 and does not mention what these two elders said that so upset Joshua. Perhaps Joshua, not being an elder and not yet having the "rushing spirit upon him," is lacking in the wisdom and experience needed to distinguish a true prophet from a false one? Perhaps he fears that these two elders will supplant him as Moses' closest advisor? Or perhaps Eldad and Meidad, as true prophets, are telling things that Joshua doesn't want to hear? Whatever Eldad and Meidad might have said, it is clear from the story that it was appreciated by Moses who, himself an elder and a prophet, wished others in the camp would be as close to YHVH's words as were these two.

> The Second Rebellion: Family (Numbers 12)

Summary: *This chapter describes the jealousy that Moses' closest family members, Miriam and Aaron, unleashed against him. The story begins with this chapter's first two verses: "Now Miriam spoke, and Aaron, against Moses on account of his Cushite wife that he had taken in marriage, saying 'Is it only through Moses that YHVH speaks? Is it not also through us that YHVH speaks?' And, YHVH heard." Now, Moses was exceedingly humble, more than any other human.*

YHVH told the three of them to go to the Tent of Appointment, where YHVH descended in a column of cloud and called out, saying, "Pray hear my words; if there should be a prophet among you, I will make myself known to you in a dream. Not so, however, with Moses, for he is trusted more so than anyone in my house. I speak to him, 'mouth to mouth.' So, why are you not awestruck and instead speak against him?" YHVH then left, leaving behind Miriam with tzaraat.

Aaron said to Moses, "Please, do not impose on us guilt for sin, for we were foolish and sinned." Moses cried out to YHVH for his sister to be healed. YHVH replied, "Let her be shut up for seven days outside the camp, afterwards she can return." And when she returned, the people marched to the Wilderness of Paran where they camped.

Discussion Questions: What about Moses suggests him to be so humble? Why was Miriam punished with *tzaraat* while Aaron was left unblemished?

- **What about Moses suggests humility?** No person in Torah has had a closer relationship with YHVH, having spoken with YHVH "face to face, as a man speaks to his neighbor" and having seen YHVH's "glory" (that is, the thirteen attributes named in Exodus 33 and 34). No person has been given greater responsibility than Moses, who was charged with leading the people out of Mitz'rayim, through the Wilderness, and into the Promised Land. By virtue of his elevated position, no person has been granted more authority.

    Through it all, however, Moses remained the reluctant, unpretentious leader who never desired power nor allowed himself to become corrupted by it. Perhaps this point is made most evident in Numbers 14: 11-12, when YHVH threatens to strike all the people down and start again with Moses, saying, "I will make of you a nation greater and mightier than it!" Moses declines the honor for himself and his descendants. Instead, he pleads to have the people spared.

Moses did the same in Exodus 32:10 shortly after the incident with the golden calf, when YHVH made him the same grandiose offer; and again in Numbers 16:21-22 at the time of the "Korah rebellion." During that rebellion, soon to be described, YHVH tells Moses and Aaron to "Separate your selves from the midst of this community, that YHVH may finish the people off in an instant." To this, Moses argues, "When one man sins, at the entire community will you be furious?"

- **Why was only Miriam punished with tzaraat?** In that Aaron received no such affliction, it is tempting to conclude that Miriam's punishment -- like the "water of bitterness" test described in Numbers 5 -- is another example of gender bias in the Torah. However, the chapter's opening verse ("Now Miriam spoke, and Aaron, against Moses") suggests otherwise; for it implies that it was Miriam who took the lead in this rebellion.

This may not be surprising. After all, all accounts of Aaron up to this point depict someone who rarely spoke his own mind, preferring instead to speak the words of others. On the other hand, the few stories about Miriam show her to be outspoken and bold. It was she who risked her life watching over Moses as he floated on the Nile in an ark (Exodus 2:4). And it was Miriam who approached Pharaoh's daughter and presumptuously asked the princess if she, Miriam, should call a Hebrew woman to nurse the child (Exodus 2:7).

We are given no clues as to why Miriam, who previously had looked after the well-being of her brother, Moses, would suddenly turn against him -- for she all but disappeared from the text after Exodus 2. Perhaps she became jealous of the family position assumed by her Cushite sister-in-law, Moses' wife Tzippora. Perhaps Miriam felt slighted because her brother, Moses, was the only family member who had a close face-to-face relationship with YHVH. Whatever the case, her skin ailment, *tzaraat* -thought to be leprosy – is symbolic of her insensitive behavior. (Leprosy is a progressive degenerative skin disease which stops the flow of blood to one's extremities, thus causing desensitization.)

> The Third Rebellion - The Ten Scouts (Numbers 13, 14)

Summary: *These chapters in the Torah, titled Sho'lekh Lekha ("Send for Yourself" or "Send for Your Own Sake"), opens with YHVH telling Moses to "send" the twelve tribal leaders to scout out the land of Canaan. The tribe of Judah is led by Calev, and the tribe of Ephraim by Hoshea, whom Moses called Yehoshua (or Joshua).*

Moses instructs the twelve to go through the Negev until they reach the hill-country, and see what the land is like: good or ill, fat or lean, fortified or not - - and also see what the people are like: Are they strong or weak, few or many?

So the scouts went into the Wilderness of Tzyn as far as Hebron, where they came to the Wadi of Eshkol. There, they cut a cluster of grapes, and along with some pomegranates and figs, returned to where the Israelites were encamped, having been away a total of forty days.

Coming before Moses, Aaron, and the entire community in the Wilderness of Paran at Kadesh, the scouts (other than Calev and Joshua) shared their report and let the people see the fruit, saying, "Yes, the land is flowing with milk and honey ... but the towns are large and fortified and the people are fierce. We saw Amalek settled in the Negev; the Hittite, Yevusite, and Amorite settled in the hill-country; and the Canaanite settled by the Sea."

Calev reported differently: "Let us go up and possess it, for we can prevail against it!" He was quickly shouted down by the other scouts, who went on to say that the land devours its inhabitants. "All the men who we saw were giants – Children of Anak; we were just like grasshoppers to them."

Upon hearing the scouts' report, the entire community wept that night, grumbling against Moses and Aaron, saying, "Would that we had died in the land of Egypt? Why is YHVH bringing us to this land, to fall by the sword . . . would it not be better for us to return to Egypt? Let us head back!"

Moses and Aaron flung themselves on their faces before the entire community, while two of the scouts, Joshua and Calev, rented their garments, saying, "The land that we scouted is exceedingly good... if YHVH is pleased with us, YHVH will bring us to this land." The community listened and thought of pelting them with stones.

The cloud descended onto the Tent of Appointment, where YHVH said to Moses, "How long will this people scorn me and not trust me, despite all the signs that I have done among them... Let me strike them down and make you a great nation!"

But Moses replied: "The Egyptians will hear of this. Do you want them to say 'It was from want of your ability to bring the people to the land about which you swore to them, and so you slew them in the Wilderness?' [18] *Pray, let the power of my Lord be as you had spoken: Long suffering and of much loyalty, bearing iniquity and transgression, yet clearing, not clearing (the guilty), calling into account the iniquity of the fathers upon the sons to the third and fourth generation. Pray grant pardon for the iniquity of this people, for your loyalty is great, just as you have done for this people from Egypt until now!"*

YHVH agreed, saying that these people have tested me ten times by not hearkening to my voice. All who have grumbled against me will not see the Land. You and your children shall graze in the Wilderness for forty years, according to the number of days that you scouted out the land – in this Wilderness shall your corpses fall. Only Calev and Joshua shall I allow to enter the land that I promised you because they followed me fully - only those two and your little-ones, those less than twenty years.

---

18 Moses' argument is markedly similar to that which he used to dissuade YHVH from destroying the people after the incident with the Golden Calf. Specifically, he said, "For what reason should the Egyptians say that with evil intent YHVH brought them out, to kill them in the mountains and destroy them from the face of the soil?" (Exodus 32: 11,12).

The people mourned their fate; starting early in the morning, they went up to the top of the hill-country, saying, "Let us go to attack the place that YHVH promised!" But, Moses warned them, "Do not go, for YHVH is not among you ... the Amalekite and Canaanite are there to face you... you will fall by the sword." But they did not listen, and so were crushed.

Discussion Questions: What do the names Calev and Hoshea mean? Why did Moses change Hosea's name to Yehoshua (in English, Joshua)? What is the relationship between Canaan and the Promised Land? Did Moses send out twelve tribal leaders to scout the Promised Land? Where exactly is the Promised Land? How long did the scouts stay away? How many times did the people beg to return to Egypt? How many times did the people test YHVH? Did Moses really sway YHVH's opinion? Is Moses going to be allowed entry into the Promised Land?

- **What is the meaning of the names Calev and and Hoshea, and why did Moses refer to Hosea as Yehoshua?** "Calev" means "like the heart," and Hoshea means "He will help." Moses renamed Hoshea "Yehoshua" by prefixing to it the letter "*yud*", which is the first letter in YHVH's name. In so doing, he altered the meaning of Hoshea's name to "Salvation" (meaning redemption: the actualization of the promise to save someone from harm). As with the addition of the letter "hey" from YHVH's name to the names of Avram and Sarai in Genesis 17, the altering of Hoshea's name signaled a fundamental change in his personality, indicating progress in his spiritual journey.

- **What is the relationship between Canaan and the Promised Land?** It is easy to conclude from the story of the scout's rebellion that the lands of Canaan and Promise are one and the same. They are not. The two lands encompass very different world views - one human and physical; the other Divine and spiritual. We should note that this two-level view of reality is not unique to the Book of Numbers; it permeates much of the writings of Torah. (Consider the meaning of *Israel* that was revealed in Genesis 35: "those who show the willingness and ability to struggle with things both human and divine.").

This means that depending on where an individual is on their personal and spiritual journey, some will experience Egypt as a place rich in material comforts and food, while for others it is *mitz'rayim*, as a spiritually narrow place where more attention is given to our physical needs than to questions of good, evil, and life. Similarly, for some the Wilderness is the about parched dryness and desolation, while for others it is the *mid'bar*, a place to go to hear YHVH speak.

We can thus say that Canaan is to the Promised Land, as Egypt is to Mitz'rayim, and the Wilderness is to the Mid'bar. As such, Canaan refers to a specific geopolitical local, while the Promised Land denotes an awakened state of consciousness that is rife with both nourishment (symbolized by milk) and pleasure (honey). We will find this distinction useful when addressing the next question.

- **Did Moses send the twelve tribal leaders to scout the Promised Land?** Based on the 17th verse of Numbers 13, the answer appears to be "no," for it clearly states that Moses sent out these twelve tribal leaders "to scout out the land of Canaan." The story, however, suggests a different answer, depending on where each leader is on her/his journey to the spiritual and Divine.

    Specifically, the report that the leaders gave to the community of their expedition suggests that ten of them reside primarily in the human and physical world. What they scouted was Canaan; what they returned with was a cluster of grapes, along with some pomegranates and figs –all seed-bearing fruits suggesting Canaan's potential to bring forth the life that is embedded within them by creation. Put in terms of Genesis 1 (the Creation Story), the ten scouts viewed the land of Canaan as being primarily "so"; that is, rich in unactualized potential.

    In contrast, Calev and Joshua had advanced far enough on their journey to perceive the "promised" aspect of what they scouted. It was they who said, "The land that we scouted is exceedingly good." Genesis 1 defines "good" (*tov*) as that which is life-enhancing; meaning that which actualizes the potential to bring forth the life that is embedded in the Creation. The expression "exceedingly good" was said by YHVH at the end of the sixth day of Creation, when YHVH saw all that was made.

- **Where exactly is the Promised Land?** Perhaps the Torah is intentionally vague on the question of which locations lie within the Promised Land to remind us that the stories about it are presented as allegories. That is, we should think its location as having fluid borders rather than those defined by a set of specific geographic coordinates. We can enter the Promised Land whenever our consciousness is awakened, wherever we might be -- whether wandering in the Wilderness or walking the streets of Manhattan.

- **Why did Moses send the twelve tribal leaders to scout out the Land?** YHVH has already told the people that the Promised Land is not only good, being filled with milk (sustenance) and honey (sweetness and joy); it is also promised to them. Why, then, did Moses send the leaders out to scout the land? Was he asking for a second opinion? Did he doubt YHVH's words? Or, was he testing the people's readiness to enter into the Promised Land by putting into practice the revelation that they received at Sinai?

- **Were the scouts away for forty days?** Recall that the number "forty" in Torah often refers to spiritual time – that which existed before the fourth day of Creation. It signals the birth of a fundamentally new understanding about the meaning of life, and therefore the death of what was once had held to be true. Based on the scouts' reports, the forty days that they spent exploring the Promised Land had spiritual connotations for only Calev and Joshua.

- **How many other times have the people pleaded with Moses to return to Egypt?** They first did so in Exodus 13 as they stood by the Reed Sea while the Egyptian soldiers advancing to them, and frequently repeated this plea during their months of wandering in the Wilderness. Despite the physical distance they traveled since leaving Mitz'rayim and the many the reassurances they received from YHVH, the people remained stuck in the past, showing little progress on their personal and spiritual journeys. They were once slaves in Egypt and it seems they will always be so --all too willing to give up the struggle and return to the comforts and certainty that they enjoyed in Mitz'rayim.

- **How many times did the people test YHVH?** The text states, "these people have tested me ten times by not hearkening to my voice," but this amount of times should not necessarily be interpreted literally. Recall from earlier commentary on the Books of Genesis and Exodus that the number "ten" is used to signify a sufficient number to capture one's attention. For example, ten is the number of times that Lavan will have to change Yaakov's wages before Yaakov finally says, "Enough!" and begins his preparation to leave. Similarly, if ten plagues are not enough to cause the Hebrews to leave Egypt, an eleventh likely won't do it. The fact that YHVH is now referring to "ten" as the number of times that YHVH has been tested by the people, suggests that YHVH has run out of patience with them.

As readers of this story, it is tempting for us to be critical of these people. How could they not see the light after all that YHVH has done for them? How could they be so set in their ways? Before trying to answer these questions, let's first ask ourselves this: Would we have acted any differently in their place? Would we be less resistant to change? Sadly, the answer - based on years of research in the field of social psychology - is probably no. The general consensus among these researchers is that change – whether in values, politics, strategy, etc. --is hard to accomplish because attitudes and opinions are formed below the surface. Our worldview is based on mental maps of embedded assumptions, narratives and terms of reality that organize our thinking. As the Torah intuited many millennia ago, people rarely change their underlying narratives or unconscious frameworks. Said simply, if given the choice, most of us would have acted as did all but Calev and Joshua; that is, reject the future that is promised to us and instead elect to return to Egypt.

- **Was Moses able to sway YHVH's opinion?** YHVH appears to have lost all patience with the Children of Israel and now desire to strike down everyone except Moses. The question is: Would YHVH have done so had Moses not mentioned YHVH's glory (i.e., the Thirteen Attributes that YHVH revealed to Moses on Sinai in Exodus

33 and 34)? Or, is Moses being tested again? Perhaps this narrative is meant to show us that Moses, in spite of his frustration with the people, still adhered to the attributes that brought him face-to-face and mouth-to-mouth with YHVH, according to YHVH's likeness.

- **Is Moses going to be allowed entry into the Promised Land?** Verse 30 makes it abundantly clear that only Calev and Joshua from the generation who left Egypt will be allowed to enter, because only those two "followed YHVH fully." What is striking about this verse is that it not only implies Moses will not be allowed entry, but also that he did not follow YHVH fully.

Without knowing the whole story (and we won't until the end of the Book of Deuteronomy), it is easy to jump to the conclusion that YHVH is not a just and fair God. Can it be that YHVH is so uncompassionate as to rebuff his humblest of servants: a person who willingly sacrificed his life in service to YHVH; a prophet like no other; a man whom – as it is written in Deuteronomy 34: 11 -- "YHVH knew face-to-face"? Not follow YHVH fully? What acts of insubordination did Moses commit to deserve dying in the Wilderness along with all the others from his generation? We will have to wait to Numbers 20 for an answer to this last question.

As an aside, verse 30 is not the first suggestion that Moses will be denied entry. It could have inferred it from Exodus 3, verses 6 through 13. There, YHVH tells him that he will lead the people out of Egypt, but does not mention Moses' name when speaking of entry into the Promised Land.

Interestingly, the remaining fifteen verses of Numbers 14 convey the sense that Moses is unmoved by what he has just heard. Rather than bemoan his personal fate, he appears more concerned about the hundreds of thousands of his flock who also learned that they will be denied entry.

> First Intermission (Numbers 15)

The fifteenth chapter in the Book of Numbers offers a three-part pause from the rebellion theme. The first part covers verses 1 through 31 and addresses the sacrificial procedures that the people are to follow once they "enter the land of your settlements that I am giving you." Included in the instructions is the reminder that sojourners (resident aliens) are to be treated with the same respect and held to the same laws and privileges as the permanent residents. One is left to wonder why the instructions in these 31 verses are placed about midway through the stories about rebellion, as they have nothing to do with the topic at hand. Rather, they seem to be a continuation of that which was introduced in the first seven chapters of Leviticus.

The topic covered in the next five verses, beginning with verse 32, is also unrelated to rebellion. It deals with a person who knowingly violates the Sabbath by collecting wood on that day. Not knowing what to do, Moses turns to YHVH, who tells him that the entire community shall put the man to death by pelting him with stones. As with the chapter's first 31 versus, these five verses fit better in Leviticus -- specifically Chapter 20, which addresses serious offenses and resulting punishments. (Recall that in the commentary to that Leviticus chapter, I argued that the references to stoning were never intended to be taken literally, nor is there any evidence that such punishments were ever administered.)

The topic addressed in this chapter's third pause part is also disconnected from that which went before it. Specifically, verses 39-41 contain YHVH's message that the Children of Israel are to put tassels (*tzitzit*) on the four corners of their garments. These tassels are to serve as reminders to keep the commandments. Why four corners of the garment? As I mention in the commentary to Genesis 13, the number "four" is number appears numerous times in the Torah, each time suggesting spiritual wholeness, a portal into the infinite, and a pathway back to the Garden and forward to the Promised Land.

> The Fourth Rebellion – Korah (Numbers 16)

Summary: *Chapter 16 tells of Korah, a Levite and first cousin of Moses and Aaron. Along with Datan and Aviram (from the tribe of Reuven) and two-hundred and fifty community leaders, he* *rose up against Moses and Aaron, exclaiming, "Too much is yours! Indeed, the entire community is holy... why then do you exalt yourselves over the assembly?"*

Moses replied, "Is it too little for you (as a Levite) that YHVH has separated you from the community... would you seek the Priesthood as well? What is wrong with Aaron that you should grumble against him?"

Moses then called for Datan and Aviram, but they said "We will not go up! Is it too little that you brought us from the land flowing with milk and honey to cause us to die in the Wilderness that you should also play prince over us?

Upon hearing this, YHVH said to Moses and Aaron, "Separate yourselves from the midst of this community, that I may finish them off in an instant." To this they pleaded, "When one man sins, must you be furious at the entire community?"

To Korah, Datan, Aviram, and the others, Moses said, "YHVH will make known who among us is holy... and this you shall know – it was YHVH, not me, who sent me to do all these deeds."

Just as Moses finished his words, the earth opened its mouth and swallowed up them and their households, and they all went down alive, into Sheol. The earth covered them and they perished from the midst of the assembly.

Discussion Questions: Why was this rebellion championed by members of the Levite and Reuven tribes? What was the basis of their challenge and why was it flawed? Where (or what) is Sheol?

- **Why was this rebellion championed by members of the Levite and Reuven tribes?** Both tribes felt reasons to be jealous of Moses and his immediate family. Regarding Korah and his fellow Levites, on one hand they held an honored position in the community. Designated by YHVH as the "priestly tribe," their responsibilities included caring for the Tabernacle; acting as intermediaries between the first born of each tribe and YHVH; and attending to the needs of high priests. However, Korah was displeased because none from his tribe were allowed to hold the esteemed position of high priest (*Co'han-nim*) other than Aaron and his direct descendants.

Datan and Aviram had other motives for challenging Moses' leadership. These two individuals were descendants of Reuven, the first born of Jacob's twelve sons, who naturally expected to inherit the family birthright. It went instead to his younger brother, Joseph, a person who Reuven resented. It was Reuven who, when seeing Joseph approaching him from afar, suggested to his brothers that they "strip him of his ornamented coat and drop him into a dry pit" (Genesis 37: 22-24). And it was Reuven who further eroded his relationship with his father by having sex with Bilha, his father's concubine. For this act his father cursed him and --by inference -- his descendants (see Genesis 35:22 and Genesis 49: 3). It follows that by the time the census was taken in Numbers 1-4, the tribe of Reuven would be one of the smallest (in Torah, a tribe's relative size symbolized its stature in the community).

- **What was the basis of their rebellion and why was it flawed?** Korah accused his cousins, Moses and Aaron, of unfairly concentrating power into the hands of too few. He argued that the entire community is holy and therefore deserving of a more equitable distribution of roles and responsibilities. From the perspective of Torah, Korah's argument falls short on three accords. First, by accusing his cousins of nepotism, he missed the point that the priestly positions assigned to the Levites and the especially prestigious roles given to Aaron's lineage were ordained by YHVH. Second, if the entire community was as holy as Korah claimed, then they would have already crossed over into the Promised Land. That is, they would all be living by the precepts of the Covenant. They would therefore be blessed and guarded – and all would know it (see the Priestly Benediction in Numbers 6).

Third, Datan and Aviram accused Moses of acting like royalty. Just as the Hebrew slave challenged Moses in Egypt by demanding, "Who made you prince and judge over us?" (Exodus 2: 14), Datan and Aviram similarly griped, "Should you play prince over us?" (Numbers 16: 13). The problem with their accusation is that their jealousy of Moses caused them to lose perspective. They may have journeyed with Moses out of Egypt, but their spirit still resided back in Mitz'rayim, which they liken to the Promised Land ("Is it too little that you brought us up from the land flowing with milk and honey to cause us to die in the Wilderness?") It is as if Datan and

Aviram are hopelessly stuck in the past, having made little progress on their personal and spiritual journeys.

- **Where (or what) is Sheol?** While generally regarded as the biblical underworld, it is nevertheless a word of uncertain origin and meaning. Preceding concepts of heaven and hell, it is commonly thought of as a dwelling place for the dead. Numbers 16: 33 suggests something different, however, in stating that those who rebelled against Moses "went down alive into Sheol." Other equally vague references to Sheol can be found in Genesis 37:35 and 42:38; 1 Samuel 2:6; 2 Samuel 22:6; 1 Kings 2:6 and 2, 9; Job 7:9 and 17:13; , Psalms 30:3; Isaiah 38:10; 57:9; Ezekiel 31:15-17; Hosea 13:14; Amos 9:2; and Jonah 2:2.

> The Fifth Rebellion – Community (Numbers 17)

Summary: *This chapter tells of the people grumbling on the day after the earth swallowed up Korah and the other rebels, accusing Moses and Aaron of causing the death of YHVH's people. YHVH said to Moses, "Move aside from this community that I may finish them off in an instant!" The plague began. Moses said to Aaron, "Go quickly to the community and effect forgiveness for the people so as to stop the plague. He did this, but not before 14,700 members of the community died, not counting the rebels who perished in Sheol.*

(The plague referred to in Numbers 17 is not the same as the ten plagues that afflicted the Egyptians. The word used for plague in the Egyptian story, ma'kah, translates as "blows." It pertains to the ten means used to awaken the people to the need for leaving their narrow place. In contrast, Numbers 17 uses the word na'gaf, which means to strike or smite.)

YHVH then spoke to Moses, telling him to take a staff from the leaders of each of the twelve tribes, plus Aaron's staff, and put them into the Tent of Appointment. The staff of the man whom I choose will sprout. Moses entered the tent on the next day and saw that it was Aaron's staff that sprouted flowers.

YHVH said to Aaron, "You, your sons, and your father's house for the ages are to be in charge of all matters having to do with the priesthood… no portion of land shall be yours, for I am your portion… and to the sons of Levi, I give over all tithes in Israel in exchange for their servicing the tasks of the Tent of Appointment… Only the Levites are to serve the tasks of the Tent throughout the generations. They are not to inherit Land but instead will inherit the tithing from the people in exchange for servicing the Tent."

> Second Intermission: The Red Heifer (Numbers 18, 19)

These chapters offer a second reprieve before the fifth and sixth rebellion. In Numbers 18, the Levite's tasks and responsibilities are clarified so that incidents like the Korah rebellion will not be repeated. Numbers 19 addresses the aftermath of the Korah and Communal rebellions that brought death to the rebels, their households, and 14,700 members of the community via the subsequent plague; and how the Priests and the Levites would remove the widespread contamination wrought by these many deaths through a ritual known as the "Red Cow" or "Red Heifer."

According to the chapter, the ritual requires a cow in perfect health that never performed any work and has no hairs of any other color but red. The heifer is then ritually slaughtered and burned outside of the camp, with the ashes placed in a vessel containing pure water. In order to purify a person, the water from the vessel is sprinkled on him, using a bunch of hyssop, on the third and seventh day of the purification process.

> The Sixth Rebellion - - Moses Against YHVH (Numbers 20: 1-13)

Introduction: The first thirteen verses of Numbers 20 cover one of the most widely misunderstood episodes in the Torah. We learn that not only will Moses and Aaron be denied entry into the Promised Land, but it will be for what appears to most readers as a minute infraction: a momentary indiscretion reflecting an understandable display of pent-up emotions.

Summary: *The Israelites came, the entire community, to the Wilderness of Tzyn and stayed in Kadesh at the time of the first New Moon, where Miriam died and was buried. Now, there was no water and so the people assembled against Moses and Aaron, saying, "Why did you bring the assembly of YHVH into the Wilderness, to have us and our cattle to die? Why did you make us go up from Egypt to bring us to this evil place, where there are no seeds, figs, vines, or pomegranates to eat and no water to drink?*

Moses and Aaron heard their moaning and flung themselves to their faces. YHVH spoke to Moses, saying, "Take the staff and with Aaron, assemble the community, and then speak to the boulder before your eyes so that it gives forth its water." And Moses assembled the community, said to them, "Hearken, you rebels!" He then raised his hand and struck the boulder with his staff twice. YHVH said to Moses and Aaron, "Because you did not have trust in me, you two shall not bring this assemble into the land that I am giving them!"

Discussion Questions: Where is Kadesh? Has the Israelite's hunger changed in the past 39 years? Why is Moses, along with Aaron, being denied entry into the Promised Land?

- **Where is Kadesh?** In Numbers 13:26, we are told that the Israelites came upon Kadesh during their first year of wandering when Moses sent twelve tribal leaders on a scouting expedition. At that time Kadesh was said to be located in the Wilderness of Paran. Thirty-nine years later, the offspring of those who left Egypt came upon it a second time, only now Kadesh is said to be in the Wilderness of Tzyn (Numbers 20:1).

    Why is the text ambiguous regarding Kadesh's location? The answer may lie in its name, for it shares the same three-letter root (*sho'resh*) with the word *kadosh*, meaning "set-apart by YHVH" as we saw in Genesis 1. The Torah is implying here that Kadesh does not necessarily have a specific geographic position. Rather, it represents a spiritual place -- a line of demarcation that "sets-apart" either the Promised Land from the Wilderness, or the Land of Canaan from the Wilderness. (See the commentary to Numbers 13 and 14, where Canaan and the Promised Land are said to represent different levels of reality.) The question left open in Numbers 20 is whether the people will "cross-over" the Promised Land boundary this time, unlike the first time that they encountered Kadesh, when only Caleb and Joshua crossed-over.

As an interesting aside, Kadesh first appears in the Torah in Genesis 16: 14. It is where Hagar, the first woman in the Wilderness to hear YHVH's voice, finds a well which she names the "Well of the Living-One Who Sees Me."

- **Has the community's hunger changed over the past 39 years?** We read in Numbers 11:5 that at the time of the first rebellion, the people were longing for fish, cucumbers, watermelons, green leeks, onions and garlic – all foods that were familiar to this generation of ex-slaves from their days in Egypt. However, by the time of the sixth rebellion, only Moses, Aaron, Miriam, Calev and Joshua remained from that generation. It is now the younger generation – those born in the Wilderness – who are expressing a different craving -- for seeds, figs, vines, and pomegranates -- foods which the twelve scouts had brought back from the Promised Land thirty-nine years earlier (Numbers 13: 23). These are foods that the youthful generation had never encountered, so why would they be expressing a desire for them?

Might their new cravings be symbolic for a shift in the orientation of the two generations? While the parents' generation focused on the past and grieved over that which they once had, their children (those who began referring to themselves in Numbers 20:4 as "the assembly of YHVH," a term their parents never used) looked to the future, eager to cross over into the Promise Land. For the children, the Wilderness (*mid-bar*, or where they could hear YHVH speak) had become an "evil" place in the sense described in Genesis 2 as being the opposite of "*tov*" (that which serves to bring forth life that is embedded in Creation by YHVH) - evil in the sense that what it was mostly engendering were rebellions that were blocking the future.

Interestingly, Moses and Aaron appeared to have missed this shift altogether. The new cravings did not suggest to them that the Israelites have moved forward as a community. Instead, when hearing the people's latest longings, Moses and Aaron "flung themselves upon their faces" (Numbers 20: 6) and accused the people of being "rebels" (Numbers 20: 10).

- **Why is Moses, along with Aaron, being denied entry into the Promised Land?** And, why "talk" to the rock (rather than hit it)? A Torah story that most of us remember from childhood tells of when YHVH instructs Moses to speak to the rock, but instead Moses strikes it twice. For this, YHVH tells him that he will be denied entry into the "the land that I am giving you" because, "You did not have trust in me" (Numbers 20:12).

What is this story trying to teach us? Is the message that we are to always trust in YHVH no matter what we are asked to do; for any single moment of doubt can undue a lifetime of trusting? Haven't we already encountered many instances in the Torah where YHVH welcomed and even encouraged the questioning of YHVH's pronouncements, rather than demand that they be taken on blind faith? (For some examples, see commentary to Leviticus 20.) What might have caused Moses to ignore YHVH's instructions? And, is getting water from the rock by striking it any less of a miracle than doing so by speaking?

Let's begin by recalling that this is not the first time that the people complained about a lack of water. We first encountered such a scenario in the seventeenth chapter of the Book of Exodus, while the Israelites were camped at Refidim during their first year in the Wilderness. There, YHVH instructed Moses to take his staff, stand before the rock at Horev and strike it. "Water shall come out of it and the people shall drink" (Exodus 17: 6).

Much has changed during the thirty-nine years that separate Exodus 17 from Numbers 20. For example, the people received the six requirements required to enter the Promised Land; all but Moses, Aaron, Caleb and Joshua from the older generation has passed away; and the younger generation is expressing hunger for the Promised Land. However, Moses seems oblivious to these changes; he is treating the rock as if everyone was still back in Refidim.

Is Moses too worn down by his leadership responsibilities and the numerous rebellions that had been waged against him to recognize the people's advances? Perhaps his striking of the rock twice represents his frustration with the people and with the life that YHVH asked him to live? Might his action represent an act of defiance against YHVH? Bear in mind that for the past 39 years, Moses may have been harboring remorse and resentment over what YHVH had told him in Numbers 14 during the tale of the scouts' rebellion. It was then that YHVH said that only Calev and Joshua shall enter the Promised Land because they followed me fully – "only those two and your little-ones, those less than twenty years."

Perhaps by striking of the rock twice rather than following YHVH's instructions by "speaking to the boulder", Moses was acting in an egotistic (non-humble) way. Maybe he wanted to prove to himself and all who witnesses him that he had the power to draw water without YHVH's help.

Moreover, Moses doesn't seem to grasp YHVH's message in telling him to "speak to the rock." YHVH was not asking Moses to engage in sorcery, but rather to use the spoken word as YHVH did in the Creation Story (Genesis 1) to generate something *tov* -- for this is the language of the Promised Land. That is to say, YHVH was inviting "this man of no words…heavy of mouth and heavy of tongue" (Exodus 4:10) to "create as he speaks" (the meaning of the phrase *abra-ka-dabra)* so that Moses could then teach it to the others.

Unfortunately for Moses, he did not appear up to the challenge. After spending most of his life speaking the language of the Wilderness, he finds himself unable to cross-over into a more enlightened way of speaking. In YHVH he had the best of all teachers, yet he still "did not have the trust" to carry out the task. Like the others from his generation, he was looking backwards, while the "assembly of YHVH" is looking forward.

Finally, why did Moses strike the rock twice in Numbers 20 but only once in Exodus 17? We recall some insight from the Joseph story into the significance of repetition. Specifically Genesis 41: 32 told us that a repetition means that "the matter is not only determined by YHVH, but YHVH is also hastening to do it." What is YHVH hastening to do? Is it to relieve Moses of his leadership responsibilities and deny his entry into the Promise Land?

Chapter 13: Preparations for Battle

Introduction: The first thirteen verses of Numbers 20 deal mostly with internal struggles faced by the Children of Israel that were largely of their own making. However, from verse fourteen onward, the struggles become more external as the Israelites encounter other tribal nations. Many of these encounters deteriorate into military confrontations, for which the people have been prepared since the first chapter of Numbers. It was then that YHVH instructed Moses to count every male from the age of twenty upward to be "going out in armed-forces in Israel." As you will recall, that count was made only thirteen months after the exodus from Egypt, approximately thirty-nine years prior. From that count, only Keleb, Joshua, Moses and Aaron remain alive, with Aaron to die soon thereafter. Not until Numbers 26 will a new count be taken.

> ➢ **The Edomites and the Death of Aaron (Numbers 20: 14-29)**

Summary: Moses sent messengers from Kadesh to the king of Edom: "Thus says your brother Israel, you know about all the hardships that have found us: that our fathers went down into Egypt and were mistreated by them. We cried out to YHVH and he heard our voice, sent us a messenger, and brought us to the edge of your territory. Please let us cross through your land – we will not cross through your fields or through your orchards, nor drink water from your wells."

But Edom said, "You shall not cross through me, lest with the sword I come out to meet you!" Refused, the Israelites turned away from him and instead marched to the Mount Hill by the border of the land of Edom. There, YHVH said to Moses and Aaron, "Let Aaron be gathered by his kins-people, for he is not to enter the land that I am giving to the Children of Israel, since you both rebelled against my orders. Take Aaron and his son El'azar and bring them up to Mount Hill, strip Aaron of his garments and place them on El'azar, for Aaron will die there.

After Aaron died, Moses and El'azar came down from the Mountain. When the community saw that Aaron had expired, they wept for him thirty days.

Discussion Questions: Who are the Edomites and why did their king deny the Israelites' request? Where is Edom? What is Mount Hill? Why was Aaron's death mourned while Miriam's was not? When did Aaron die?

> *** Who are the Edomites?** They are the descendants Esau, Jacob/Israel's twin brother. We know this from what Moses' messengers said to the king of Edom in verse 14: "Thus says your brother Israel…" We also know this from Genesis 36:43, where Esau is identified as "the tribal father of Edom."

> *** Why did the king of Edom deny the Israelites' request?** The messengers tell the king of Edom of all the hardships that befell this long-separated side of the family during their enslavement in Egypt. Their story, however, did not seem to arouse any sympathy; for when the messengers asked the king for permission to cross through his land, he responded: "You shall not cross through me, lest with the sword I come out to meet you!"

The king's response is in marked contrast to that made hundreds of years earlier by his tribal-father, Esau, when Jacob made a similar request of him. At that time, Esau responded with kindness and forgiveness, saying "I have plenty, my brother, let what is yours remain yours" (Genesis 33: 9). It would seem from Esau's earlier remarks that his anger towards Jacob for stealing the family birthright had since dissipated.

Why, therefore, did the king act so unwelcoming? What might have rekindled the Edomites' anger towards their tribal brothers? Had so much time elapsed since their last meeting that spiritual light that had once bonded them grew so faint that the king, in the words of the ninth plague, could no longer recognize the "face" of his brother? Did the two tribal nations grow so far apart over time, geography, and experience that they could no longer relate to one another?

Might the Edomites' anger result largely from the doings of Jacob and his descendants? Recall that Jacob never atoned for the offences he committed against his brother – he never sought nor received forgiveness. Consider also that the Israelites in Numbers 20 show no more sensitivity than did their forefather. They do not acknowledge the pain that Jacob caused, much less express remorse over it. Moreover, they show no interest whatsoever in how the Edomites fared over the past four hundred years, speaking only of the hardships that they had to endure --and apparently for no other purpose than to gain passage through Edom. We can see that while the people may consider themselves as descendants of Israel, they in fact appear more like Israel's non-spiritual alter ego, their conniving forefather, Jacob.

The grandson of the Baal Shem Tov referred to the mistreatment of Esau by saying, "Messiah will come when the tears of Esau have dried." There is nothing written or implied in Numbers 20 to suggest that they have.

* **Where is Edom?** The Israelites find themselves once again in Kadesh, thirty-nine years after the twelve scouts had tried to enter the Promised Land from the same location (though only Calev and Joshua succeeded). As you will recall from my commentary to Numbers 13, Kadesh refers either to a specific physical locale which borders the land of Canaan, or to a metaphysical boundary that sets apart the Promised Land from t the *mid'bar* (wilderness). Since Edom lies in close proximity to Kadesh, it follows that Edom is close to one of these lands.

Which one? I presume that it is Canaan, based on the way that the king greeted the Israelites. Had Edom been close to the Promised Land, the king would have been more welcoming. He would have acted more in the manner of verse 34 of Leviticus 19 (the chapter that lies at the physical and ethical center of the Torah). That verse states: "Now when there sojourns a sojourner in your land, you are not to maltreat him, but like a native born among you shall he be to you..."

The "Jacob-like" way that the Israelites tried to manipulate the Edomites in order to gain passage through their land also suggests a closer proximity to Canaan than to the Promised Land. In short, neither the King nor the Israelites seemed to have advanced much on their personal and spiritual journey; nor behaved in the kind of enlightened ways that would suggest that they were nearing the Promised Land.

***What is Mount Hill?** Only a few mountains are mentioned in Torah: Mor'iah, Horev, and Sinai. Mor'iah, or the "Mountain of Teaching," is the setting for the *Akidah* ("Binding of Isaac"), which appears in Genesis 22. It is where Abraham learned to stop trying to control his future through his son. Horev ("Mountain of Sword and Destruction") is where Moses encounters the Burning Bush in Exodus 3. This is where he discovers the need to abandon the beliefs of his Egyptian past that were no longer serving him well so that new, more meaningful truths could emerge. Sinai ("Mountain of Revelation") is where the Israelites were introduced to the Ten Sayings, which contained an almost limitless array of personal, communal and spiritual wisdoms. If being "Israel" entails "struggling with things both Divine and human and proving able" (Genesis 32), the Ten Sayings are about how to be "able."

The common thread that binds these three "mountain" stories is the learning of a particularly difficult life-altering lesson. Like the physical sacrifices that are required to train for, and then ascend a mountain, each lesson involves giving up something of value. In the case of Abraham, it was about sacrificing his close relationship with his son to allow his son the freedom to begin his own journey. For Moses, it was about surrendering the beliefs formed during his princely upbringing that narrowed his view of the world. And, for the Children of Israel, the lesson involved giving up the material comforts of Mitz'rayim for a lifetime of struggle.

Similar to the views revealed at a mountain's summit, each lesson enables us to experience a moment of enlightenment when we can see clearly into the distant future in all directions. And, similar to descending a mountain's slippery slopes, putting our newly acquired knowledge into practice often proves to be the most difficult aspect. Can we descend the mountain without breaking the tablets, as Moses did in Exodus 32? Can we use our newly gained insights to improve our relationships with ourselves and others? We won't know if the lessons have truly transformed us until we leave the lofty heights and return to people, routines, and enslavements that had once defined our life.

Mount Hill fits this mountain metaphor. Prior to Numbers 20, the people have been primarily engaged in summiting a mountain of revelations, without ever being tested by reality. The Edomites represented the first such test. When confronted by them, the Israelites turned away without so much as a whimper. Not so, however, after "the

Children of Israel, the entire community" came to Mount Hill (Numbers 20: 22). While we are not told what transpired at this mountain (other than that Aaron died there), the people nevertheless seemed transformed by the experience. No more will they turn away when challenged. From this point forward in Torah, the people show the willingness to risk their lives, descend the slippery slopes, join the "armed forces for Israel," fight for what they believe – and prove able.

*When do the Torah characters mourn a loss of life? There appears to be no discernible pattern. On the one hand, the text barely acknowledges Miriam's death, stating only that she "died and was buried in Kadesh," saying nothing about how her two brothers, Moses and Aaron, reacted to her passing. Similarly, Aaron showed no emotion when his two older sons, Nadav and Avihu, were vaporized in Leviticus 10 for introducing alien fire into a ceremony. In kind, Moses expressed no remorse upon first learning that he would be denied entry into the Promised Land, nor did Abraham when he was told to sacrifice his son.

On the other hand, Hagar was said to have wept when thinking that both she and her child, Ishmael, would soon die in the Wilderness (Genesis 21: 16). Hers was the first display of deep emotion in Genesis. The next one came when Jacob was told that his son, Joseph, had died at the hands of a beast (Genesis 37: 4). Joseph later wept when his father died (Genesis 50: 1). It is not until Numbers 20: 29 that an outpouring of emotion appears again in the Torah, this time by the entire community who mourned for Aaron for thirty days after his death (Moses' death was the only other instance in Torah when people were said to mourn for thirty days).

Why the inconsistency? Perhaps the writers are reminding us that the Torah is not about any particular person, not even Moses -- rather, it is an account of the inter-generational movement of a community on their personal and spiritual journey towards that more enlightened state known as the Promised Land. This might explain why so little is revealed about the emotions of the lead characters. The same can be said of their appearance; no (or little) attention is paid to their facial expressions, distinguishing features, clothing or other physical attributes. By omitting these details, the writers of the

Torah may have been inviting each of us in our own way to "fill in the blanks." This allows the characters to I become more real to us, almost as if we knew them - - or are them.

***When did Aaron die?** Only in verse 38 of Numbers 33 are we told that he died on Mount Hill "in the fortieth year after going-out…from the land of Egypt."

➢ First Victory and Seventh Rebellion: Food and Water (Numbers 21)

Summary: The king of Arad, a Canaanite ruler of the Negev, heard that Israel was approaching and so waged war against them. Israel made a vow to YHVH: "If you will give this people into my hand, I will devote their towns to you." YHVH heard their voice and gave them the towns at a place that they called Horma (meaning "Destruction"), for it was there where they destroyed the Canaanite cites.

The people then marched from Mount Hill by the Reed Sea Road to go around Edom, and again became short-tempered, complaining to YHVH and to Moses: "Why did you bring us up from Egypt to die in the wilderness? There is no water here and the food is despicable!"

So, YHVH sent to the people vipers that bit them and many died. The people came to Moses and said, "We have sinned by speaking against YHVH and you. Ask YHVH to remove from us the vipers." And YHVH did so.

The Children of Israel marched on, stopping at Ovot, Iyyei Ha-Avarim, Wadi Sered, Be'er (The Well), and then at Mattana, Nahliel, and Barmot, where they sent messengers to Sihon the King of Amorites, saying, "Let us cross your land and we will stay will not drink your water nor spread out in your vineyards. But Sihon would not give permission and gathered all of his fighting people and went to meet Israel in the wilderness. Israel struck back, took possession of his land, and settled in all of the Amorite towns – in the king's town, Heshbon, and all of its daughter towns – dispossessing those who had lived there.

Israel then faced Og, King of Bashan, and all of his fighting people at Edre'i. YHVH said to Moses, "Don't be afraid of him, for into your hand I give him and all of his people and land." So, Israel struck until not a survivor was left to him – and they took all of his land.

Discussion Questions: Is Israel's vow to YHVH a conditional vow? Have the people advanced far enough to enter the Promised Land? Why are the Israelites acting with so much brutality in battle and so little compassion?

> *** Is Israel's vow to YHVH a conditional vow?** The answer certainly seems affirmative: Israel promised to dedicate the Canaanite towns to YHVH *if* YHVH gives the Canaanite people into the Israelites' hands. Not only does this vow not represent the kind of unrequited trust in YHVH that we would expect from a people who are nearing the Promised Land; it is actually reminiscent of the vow made by Jacob when he was running away from home to escape Esau's wrath: "If God will be with me and will watch over me on this way that I go and will give me food to eat and a garment to wear, and if I come back in peace to my father's house, YHVH shall be God to me" (Genesis 28: 20). The plea of Israel (through his descendants) is akin to the one issued by his spiritually unenlightened alter-ego, Jacob: It is all about what YHVH can do for Israel.

Why present Israel's vow in this conditional manner? Is the Torah telling us that after forty years of wandering and despite all that transpired during that time, this people who now call themselves Israel and an "assembly of YHVH" are no further along on their spiritual journey than was their forefather near the beginning his journey?

Or, is this story intended to remind us of our humanness: Our journey, like that of our spiritual ancestors will not always follow a one-way path. , As we advance forward, we can expect a few steps backward. Just as Jacob becomes Israel, Israel repeatedly returns to the struggles with his day-to-day "Jacob-like" shortcomings.

This is what the seventh rebellion was all about. Just as the people are nearing the entry point to the Promised Land, they regress to where they were during the first and sixth rebellions – back even to where they were while living in Mitz'rayim. Becoming once again preoccupied with issues of physical sustenance, they give scant attention to their spiritual needs. We need not become disheartened or impatient, however; for we will see that this setback – like all others they experienced – will soon pass.

*Why so much brutality? The Book of Numbers contains numerous militaristic references, beginning with verse 1:3 which states that "every male of the age of twenty years and upward are going out to the armed forces for Israel." The Israelite military not only goes on to conquer its opponents, but shows no mercy in the process. For example, "Israel struck until not a survivor was left…" (Numbers 21:35).

All of this may seem to contradict the ethical cornerstone of Torah, the command to "love your neighbor as yourself" which appears in Leviticus 19:18. Once again we are faced with the challenge of understanding what the writer(s) might have had in mind when inserting this particular inconsistency. And once again, we find ourselves asking why the nation of Israel had to be born out of so much suffering and violence. What kind of God would act with so little compassion? What are we to learn from the brutal, take-no-prisoners detail that is described in some of the conquests?

In addressing these questions, it is useful to remind ourselves that like previous references to mass killings in the name of YHVH –e.g., the Ten Plagues, the drowning of the Egyptian military in the Reed Sea, and the extermination of Amalek – the battles described in the Book of Numbers are presented as folklore, and as such they should not be interpreted literally as actual historical happenings.[19] Joshua might never have fought a battle at Jericho and there is no archeological evidence that any of its walls came tumbling down. Therefore, we should be asking not, "Why did YHVH instruct his

---

19 I say "folklore" because the head-count of 603,550 men of fighting age is unrealistically large for all the reasons previously mentioned in Chapter 7 of this book. You will recall from that chapter that in Exodus 12:37, it was stated that "about six hundred thousand men" left Egypt, implying a total population of about two million people. However, the best historical estimate put the number living in Jerusalem during the time of King David at only about three thousand people. As I have stressed throughout this book, the Torah was never intended to read as a historical account but rather a collection of philosophical and practical lessons for living a meaningful and socially conscious life. After all, the word "Torah" means "teachings."

people to use so much brutality?", but "What lesson can we learn from these battle stories?" In the case of the Ten Plagues, the lesson concerns the imperative of leaving the materially rich but spiritually dead place known as *Mitz'rayim* for the uncertainties of the *mid'bar*, a place where we can "hear YHVH speak." The drowning of the Egyptian military is about assuring those of us who left Mitz'rayim that they are doing the correct thing by putting their trust in YHVH. The Amalek story is directed at those who did so, teaching us the importance of struggling with and ultimately conquering their urges to return to that which had enslaved us.

What wisdom can be derived from the military encounters in the Book of Numbers? The answer may be embedded in the expression, "going out to the armed-forces with Israel", so let's try to decode it. We already know that the name "Israel" refers not only to Jacob, but to anyone who proves able to pursue a path of personal and spiritual enlightenment. "Armed" with the Covenant and all that it entails, the Israelites are about to be tested again regarding their readiness to face the personal, communal, and spiritual challenges of the unknown. Using the mountain analogy, the people have started their descent down the slippery slope, shifting attention from physical needs like food and water to their metaphysical yearnings.

"Proving able," however, meant conquering the huge civilization challenge posed by Canaanites, a loose confederation of city- states that prospered economically and culturally due to their proximity to Egypt, Mesopotamia (Sumer, Assyria, and Babylon) and Phoenicia. The Israelites needed to resist the temptations that this advanced polytheistic civilization had to offer or risk returning to where they started: enslaved in a narrow place.

*Why engage in battles for land outside of the Promised Land? The opening three verses of Numbers 21 tell us about the war waged against the Israelites by the King of Arad, a Canaanite king who sat as ruler in the Negev. With YHVH's help, the Israelites captured the Canaanites and vanquished all of their cities. These three verses suggest that the battles being fought at this point were outside of the spiritual boundaries of the Promised Land, but very much inside the physical land of Canaan. Canaan can therefore be viewed like the wilderness (*mid'bar*) -- a set of physical and spiritual challenges that the Israelites must "prove able" to overcome before they are ready to enter the Promised Land.

> The Story of Balak and Bil'am (Numbers 22-24)

Introduction: After more than thirty-nine years of wandering, the Israelites have advanced to the Moab Mountains on the eastern side of the Dead Sea and will soon travel west to cross the Jordan River.[20] Along the way they encounter Balak, the Moabite king, and his pagan prophet, Bil'am. The account of these two non-Hebrews should come as a welcome pause from the stories of rebellion and warfare that preceded it in the Book of Numbers. Included is some comic relief in the form of a talking donkey that outwits the prophet, Bil'am. Also appearing is Satan, who makes his first and only appearance in Torah, but not as the sinister fallen angel that represents him in most literature. The core message in the three-chapter story is that Canaanite city-states are becoming increasingly aware of YHVH's power and the threat posed by the "armed-forces with Israel" to their lifestyle. The armed Israeli forces are serving to awaken their polytheistic neighbors to the narrowness of their ways, just as the ten blows/plagues had done in Egypt.

The Children of Israel marched on and encamped in the Plains of Moab, across from Jordon-Jericho. Balak, King of Moab, son of Tzippor, saw what Israel had done to the Amorites and was fearful before his people. He sent noble Moabite messengers to Bil'am, telling him to curse this people for me, for they are too mighty in numbers. I know that whomever you bless is blessed and whomever you damn is damned. Bil'am replied, "Spend the night here and I will bring back to you whatever word YHVH speaks to me."

---

[20] The Dead Sea is known in Hebrew as *"Yom ha'mel-akh,"* which translates more accurately as "the Salt Sea."

And, YHVH came to Bil'am and said, "Who are these men with you? You are not to go with them, nor damn these Israelite people for they are blessed." Bil'am arose at daybreak and said to Balak's messengers, "Go to your land, for YHVH refuses to give me leave to go with you."

The noble messengers return to Balak with Bil'am's message. Balak sends again other messengers to Bil'am, this time more in number and prestige, with the message: "Do not hold back from going to me; I will honor you with anything that you say, I will do. Only, pray go, revile for me this people." Bil'am answered, "Even if Balak gives me a house full of silver and gold, I would not cross the order of YHVH my God."

Bil'am then said to Balak's nobles: "Pray stay here tonight, that I may know what YHVH will once again speak with me." And YHVH came to Bil'am that night, saying to him, "Go with the men who came for you, but only do that which I speak to you, that alone may you do."

So Bil'am arose at daybreak, saddled his she-ass, and went with the nobles of Moab. This caused YHVH's anger to flare up, so YHVH stationed a messenger in the way as an adversary to him.

Bil'am's donkey saw YHVH's messenger three times, his sword drawn in his hand. Each time the donkey turned aside, each time the messenger blocked more of the pathway, so that finally there was no pathway to turn, no way to go further.

This angered Bil'am, who, not seeing the messenger, repeatedly struck his donkey. YHVH then opened the mouth of the donkey and she said to Bil'am, "What have I done to you that you struck me three times?". Bil'am responded, "I did so because you have acted capriciously with me!" To that, the donkey aid, "Am I not your donkey upon which you have ridden from your past until today?"

Then YHVH uncovered Bil'am's eyes and he saw YHVH's messenger stationed in the way, his sword drawn in his hand. The messenger said, "Why did you strike your donkey on these three occasions? I came here as an adversary – had your donkey not seen me and turned aside from me on three occasions, by now I would have killed you, but her I would have left alive."

Bil'am said to YHVH's messenger, "I did not know that you were stationed to meet me in the way, but now, if it is ill in your eyes, I will head back." The messenger replied, "No, go with your men, but only speak the word that I speak to you."

When Balak heard that Bil'am was coming, he went out to meet him, saying, "Did I not send you to call? Why did you not go to me?" Bil'am replied, "The word of God is put in my mouth and that alone may I speak." At daybreak, Balak took Bil'am up to the heights of Baal, so that he could see from the people.

Bil'am said to Balac, "Build for me here seven alters and prepare for me seven bulls and seven rams." Then the two offered up a bull and a ram on each site. Bil'am then said, "station yourself beside your offering, and I will go; perhaps YHVH will encounter me and the word of whatever he lets me see, I will report to you." And YHVH did encounter Bil'am and told him to return to Balac with the words that bless the Israelites.

Balac hears the words and says, "What have you done to me? If you cannot curse them, then at least do not bless them." Bil'am replies, "It is what YHVH put into my mouth, only those words must I speak."

And, Bil'am saw that it was good in the eyes of YHVH to bless Israel and said, "How goodly are your tents, O Jacob, your dwellings, O *Israel*… The God who brought them out of Egypt, will consume enemy nations; they lie down like a lion, the king of beasts –who will dare to arouse him. Those who bless you are blessed, and those who damn you are damned."

Balak's anger flared up to Bil'am, saying that "I called you to curse them; instead you blessed them three times!" Bil'am replied, "What YHVH speaks, that alone may I speak…for there goes forth a star from Jacob; there arises a meteor from Israel; it smashes the head of Moab, the crown of all the children of Shet! Edom becomes a possession, Amalek's future near oblivion; the Canaanites will be taken captive!"

Discussion questions: Who are Balak, Bil'am, and the Moabites? Why did YHVH's anger flare against Bil'am? Who is the adversary? Does Satan appear elsewhere in the Biblical Hebrew writings? Who is the talking donkey? Why did Bil'am strike the donkey three times on three occasions? What is the number seven symbolizing with regard to the bulls and rams? What is the meaning of Bil'am blessing? Who are the "children of Shet"?

***Who are Balak, Bil'am, and the Moabites?** Balak's name means "devastator"; that is, someone who lays wasted. "Bil'am" translates as "not connected to a people." He is a Canaanite prophet whose awareness of YHVH (whom he knows by name, refers to as "my God," and engages in conversations) has caused him to struggle with his polytheistic beliefs.

It is interesting to note that Bil'am is the first non-Hebrew in the Torah to refer to God as YHVH (meaning the ongoing two-way movement between the distant past and an unbounded, ever-unfolding future; an unknowable force of infinite oneness).

The Moabites are the descendants of Moab, whose name means "from the father" for Moab was one of the two sons that Lot's daughters gave birth to after their father impregnated them (Genesis 13). His descendants became the tribal leaders of one of Israel's great enemies. However, Moabites also hold some positive ties with Israel. For example, the title character in the Book of Ruth, a story said to take place in Moab around the year 1070 B.C.E. (about 130 years after the Hebrews left Sinai and came to the "Promised Land") was a Moabite woman who would become the great-great grandmother of King David. We will also read later that the plains of Moab turn out to be the site of Moses' final resting place (Deuteronomy 34:1-9).

* Why did YHVH's anger flare against Bil'am? Bil'am is a prophet, someone with a direct connection to YHVH and who should therefore understand YHVH's wishes. However, he is not acting on that understanding. Twice YHVH comes to Bil'am at night to tell him to bless the Israelites --first in Numbers 22: 12, and again in Numbers 22: 20 -- and twice Bil'am hesitates. Why? Perhaps he fears the consequences of such a blessing upon Balak's empire and his own esteemed position within it. Remember, Hebrew liturgy does not portray prophets as fortune tellers but rather as people who receive messages from YHVH with instructions to bring them to a community, usually at a time when the community least wants to hear them.

Whatever the reason Bil'am is clearly conflicted, unsure where to place his allegiance. To escape the dilemma he tries to leave with the nobles, having neither blessed the Israelites – as per YHVH's instructions – nor cursed them in accordance with Balak's wishes.

* **Who is the adversary?** The adversary is a messenger from YHVH named Satan! Most of us think of Satan as the Devil or a fallen angel. However, this anti-god imagery is definitely not the Satan that appears in Numbers 22: 22. This Satan is but one of an infinite number of tangible manifestations of YHVH, used for YHVH's own purpose.[21] Specifically, Satan is presented as an adversary not to YHVH, but to Bil'am. (The Hebrew word for "adversary" in the Numbers 22:22 expression, "an adversary to him" is *"la satan"*, which like YHVH is conjugated in Hebrew as a verb, "to satanize".) YHVH is using Satan to try to stop Bil'am from doing what he as a prophet knows to be wrong. That is, YHVH is using this messenger to "satanize Bil'am.

* **Does Satan appear elsewhere in the Tanakh?** While Numbers 22 contains the first and only mention of the name "Satan" in the Torah, the name does appear in two later books: the first Book of Kings (specifically verses 14 and 23 of Chapter 11) and the Book of Job.

21

In addition to Satan, other messengers used by YHVH include the three men who appear at Abraham and Sarah's tent in Genesis 18 to announce the arrival of their son; the messengers of God who were going up and down the ladder in Jacob's dream (Genesis 28); and the mysterious man who wrestled with Jacob until dawn before renaming him "Israel" (Genesis 32).

Kings tells of YHVH's anger with Solomon, who in his later years turned his heart away from YHVH and started to follow other gods. In an attempt to stop Solomon from transgressing any further, endangering not only himself but the future of the nation, YHVH "raised up" two adversaries against him.

While the Satan that appeared before Bil'am was an angelic messenger, the Satan who confronted Solomon took the form of neighboring nations. These two encounters produced vastly different results. While the first Satan was ultimately successful in his mission – i.e., getting Bal'am to choose YHVH over Balak and bless rather than curse the Children of Israel, the two Satans in the first Book of Kings were not successful with Solomon, who failed to recommit to YHVH. . His unfaithfulness is said to have caused the nation to fracture into two separate entities -- the Northern Kingdom and Judah -- once son Rehoboam succeeded him as king.

In the Book of Job, the adversarial role played by Satan was not to prevent Job from doing evil, but instead to test his commitment to doing *tov* (good). Job is someone said to be graciously blessed with all the comforts of life: family, friends, health, respect and wealth. Job is also one of three people in the Tanakh referred to as *tam*, meaning spiritually pure and therefore suitable for being sacrificed to God. (The other two are Noah and the simple son at the Passover Seder.) Satan wonders aloud with God whether Job would continue to maintain his close relationship with God should tragedy befall him. In turn, God encourages Satan to test Job, inflicting any misfortune short of death.

Satan proceeds according to their agreement, initiating a series of terrible blows against Job including the annihilation of his whole family (except his wife); the loss of all of his wealth and possessions; and physical pain. Job initially expresses deep anger at God "who deprived me of justice and embittered my life (Chapter 27: 2). However, he eventually comes to understand the concept of *Ehyeh asher ehyeh,* meaning "God will be what God will be." Job says that he "spoke without understanding of things beyond me, which I did not know" (Chapter 42: 3). Having passed all of Satan's tests, Job dies as a contented old man (Chapter 42: 17).

* **Who is the talking donkey?** The story uses the donkey to illustrate Bil'am's self-absorption. Should he follow Balak or YHVH? Whichever choice he makes, what will be the consequences for himself and his fellow Moabites? He is so preoccupied with his own predicament that he is less aware of his surroundings than is his donkey, an animal not known for its intelligence. While Bil'am, the Canaanite prophet, is unable to see the divine messenger; his donkey not only sees him/Satan but understands why the messenger is blocking their passage.

* **Why did Bil'am strike the donkey three times on three occasions?** The number three has been used in Torah to symbolize clarity of thought, vision, and an impending revelation. For example, in the *Akidah* story (Genesis 22: 4), "On the third day (of journey to Mount Mariah with his son, Isaac) -- Abraham lifted up his eyes and saw the place from afar." In other words, Abraham and Isaac were somewhere between their starting point and destination, which they could see on the third day. [22]   In contrast, Bil'am was so preoccupied that it took three such experiences before he finally "saw YHVH's messenger (Satan) stationed in the way" (Numbers 22: 31).

---

[22] The number three appears many other times in the Torah. It was on the third day of Creation that life first appeared on the dry land, one day before the sun and the moon were formed. Three messengers mysteriously appeared at the tent of Abraham and Sarah, one year before their son Isaac was born. Similarly, it was on the third new moon following the exodus from Egypt that Moses came to Mount Sinai. The Ninth Plague (Darkness) lasted three days. This number also appears throughout the Christian Bible; e.g., the coming of the three wise men to the manger where Jesus was born, and the concept of the Holy Trinity, where the Holy Ghost represents the future, the Father the past, and the Son the present.

* What is the number seven symbolizing? We read in Genesis 1 that the number seven represents the completion of a cycle of creation, involving both the potential to bring forth life and the actualization of that potential. We encountered this number again in the story of Joseph, as it related to a Pharoah's dreams of good and bad years. We read later in Leviticus 23-25 that the Hebrew calendar and its associated holidays are organized around this number. These examples suggest that the number seven represents a concept of time that transcends the physical world. By requesting seven alters, seven bulls, and seven rams, Bil'am – who has gained clarity of thought and vision after experiencing revelation – is now acting to align himself with the spiritual world with the hope that this will promote a third encounter with YHVH.

* What is the meaning of Bil'am's blessing? In speaking only the words that YHVH put into his mouth, he makes the distinction between tents and dwellings. Tents are for sojourners, while dwellings are for residents. Tents refer to Jacob's world, representing sources of physical protection and comfort. In contrast, dwellings are associated with Israel, Jacob's spiritual side. The Hebrew word for "dwelling" shares a three-letter root with the *mish-kan*; -- the tabernacle which was used to house the Covenant (the ten sayings on the two tablets).

When Bil'am says, "Those who bless you are blessed, and those who damn you are damned," he is invoking YHVH's opening blessing to Avram in Genesis 12, verse 3. However, Bil'am is doing more than drawing reference to the distant past by making mention of Avram and Shet. He is also foretelling the distant future by referring to the "star from Jacob; the meteor from Israel" that will conquer Moab, Edom, Amalek, and Cain. That star/meteor is generally thought to refer to David, the second king of Israel.

- **Why refer to Shet?** Why is Bil'am making reference to Adam and Eve's third son? Shet's name (often referred to in English as Seth) means the "Granted-One"; for as Eve said, "God granted another seed in place of Abel." To not be "the children of Shet" would mean that we are all descendants of a murderer, his brother, Cain.

➢ The Final Rebellion: Unfaithfulness and Idolatry (Numbers 25)

Introduction: One of the shortest chapters in the Torah, Numbers 25, which describes the Israelites' last days in the wilderness, consists of only eighteen verses. In Numbers 26, the content shifts to the conquest of Canaan, a discussion that continues through the last ten chapters of the book. While we might expect the end of the wandering to be a time of celebration, that is not the case. Instead, the story ends with the most serious of all the rebellions, in which more than twenty-four thousand Israelites publicly turn away from YHVH in favor of idolatry and the worship of Baal, the Canaanite god of thunder and fertility.

Summary: Israel stayed in Shittim where the people began to whore with the women of Moab and made sacrifices to their god, Baal. YHVH's anger flared up against them, telling Moses to let each man kill those who attached themselves to Baal.

Now, while all were weeping at the entrance to the Tent of Appointment, an Israelite man, Zimri, son of the leader of the Shimonites, came with a Midyanite woman, Kozbi, daughter of the head of the House of Midyan, and stood before the eyes of Moses and the entire community. When Pin'has, son of El'azar and grandson of Aaron saw this, he thrust a spear between the two of them. This put a stop to the plague that already had killed twenty-four thousand. YHVH said to Moses, Pin'has' zealousness has turned away venomous anger from the Children of Israel, so that I did not finish off them in my jealousy. Therefore I give him my Covenant: It shall be for him and his seed after him a covenant of everlasting priesthood.

Discussion questions:

> *** Why is the experience in the wilderness ending on such a somber note, rather than the celebration that might be expected?** Numbers 25 is reminding us that the wilderness years were characterized by struggle -- frightening times when we learn that there is much about our lives that exists outside of our control. This naturally engendered feelings of doubt, insecurity, anxiety, and rebellion. - A core Torah teaching is that understanding these feelings helps us to cope with life's traumas and disappointments; find inner peace and *shalem* (wholeness); and reside in the Promised Land. It is the "chosen" who grasp this teaching. In the words of Exodus 19:5, "If you hearken to My voice and keep My Covenant, you shall be to Me a special treasure from among all

people, a kingdom of priests, a holy nation." Receiving this revelation should by itself be a cause for celebration. However, the merriment is subdued by the realization that while it is we who must do the choosing, our ability to choose is tainted by the seductive allure of polytheism. By "yoking ourselves to Baal," that is, by focusing too much attention on worldly possessions and aspirations, we become the one of the "un-chosen." As an un-chosen, we find it hard to present and engage in life. We lose intimacy with ourselves, others, and the divine. We live a spiritually dead life, filling our days with meaningless and narrow activities. Said differently, by serving other gods, we defy the Second Saying /Commandment ("You are not to have any other gods before My presence") and the Third ("You are not to take up the name of YHVH for emptiness"). There is no greater crime in Torah than polytheism, which represents the antithesis of all of Torah's teachings.

* **What teaching can be learned from the plague?** Verse 9 mentions that by the time that the plague was held back, twenty-four thousand had died. This is reminiscent of the killings that happened just after the episode with the molten calf (Exodus 32). At that time, YHVH ordered the killing of all who strayed from YHVH's covenant. In both cases, YHVH was responding to the people's blatant display of polytheism. However, in contrast to the 24,000 who succumbed to the plague, only 3,000 individuals were said to have died in the calf incident, all of whom were born as slaves in Egypt. Might the Torah be hinting that as we approach the Promised Land the danger of polytheism increases?

Chapter 14: The Last Days in the Wilderness

> ## The Second Census (Numbers 26)

Summary: *YHVH said to Moses and El'azar at the plains of Moav by Jordan/Jericho, "Take up a head-count of the entire community from the age of twenty years and upward, according to their fathers' house, everyone going out to the armed forces with Israel." From the Tribe of Reuven was counted 43,730; Shimon;22,200; Gad, 40,500; Judah, 76,500; Yissakhar, 64,300; Zevulun, 60,500; Menashe, 52,700; Efrayim, 32,500; Benjamin, 45,600; Dan, 64,400; Asher, 53,400; and Naftali, 45,400.*

Among the 601,730 counted, there was not a man who had been counted by Moses and Aaron when they were in the Wilderness of Sinai except for Calev and Joshua.

YHVH then spoke to Moses, saying: "To these shall the land be portioned out as inheritance; to the many you are to give much as their inheritance, to the few, you are to give little as their inheritance, each one according to its count."

As for the accounting of the Levites, there were 23,000 males of at least one month old who descended from Amram and Yokheved, the parents who bore Aaron (the father of Nadav, Avihu, El'azar and Itamar), Moses, and Miriam.

> *** What might the sizes of the twelve tribes represent?** The census taken in Numbers 1 of those who left Egypt revealed a total 603,550 men of fighting age. Nearly forty years later, this second census was taken, that of the children of that slave generation. Their count came to 1,820 less than that of their parent's count, a decrease of less than one percent across the two generations. As it was with the first census, the new total is clearly an exaggeration, but the relative sizes of the tribes might have a deeper meaning: The fulfillment of the Genesis 48 blessings that Jacob/Israel gave to each of his twelve sons while lying on this death bed.
>
> For example, we find that the tribe of Judah (descendants of Leah), which was the largest of the twelve tribes at the time of the first census, remained the largest. Judah's size might be explained by the blessing that this tribe's forefather received from Jacob/Israel's

blessing where he likened Judah to "a lion, the king of beasts; who dares rouse him up? Your brothers will praise you and bow down to you" (Genesis 48:8-9). As we recall, Judah was a deserving recipient of this praise, having transformed himself into a sensitive and generous person -- someone who, like Joseph, acted as his "brother's keeper" while the other sons of Jacob/Israel did not. Also consistent with Jacob/Israel's blessing is the fact that this tribe is now being led by Calev, one of only two individuals from the slave generation (the other being Joshua) who YHVH allowed passage to the Promised Land "because they followed YHVH fully" (Numbers 32:12).

Dan (descendants of Rachel's hand-maid, Bilha) remained the second largest tribe, marginally larger than Yissakhar (descendants of Leah), now the third largest tribe.

The tribe of Shimon (descendants of Leah), which was the third largest tribe in the first census, showed the largest decline in size and rank, having lost more than fifty percent of its members to become the smallest of the tribes. This precipitous decline in size is also consistent with Jacob/Israel's blessing, who said to Shimon and Levi "To their council may my being never come; in their assembly may my person never unite! For in their anger they kill men … damned be their anger, that it is so fierce, their fury so harsh! I will split them up in Jacob and scatter them in Israel" (Genesis 48: 6-7).

Jacob/Israel's condemnation was referring to the time that Shimon and Levi took brutal revenge against the people of Shekhem for abducting their sister, Dina, the daughter of Leah (Genesis 34:30). It was also Zimri, the son of the leader of the Shimonites, who in Numbers 25 audaciously stood before the eyes of Moses and the entire community with Kozbi, daughter of the head of the House of Midyan, the tribe that encouraged many of the Israelites to worship Baal.

Of the three tribes who descended from Rachel (the woman that Jacob loved), Menashe showed the largest increase in size -- about sixty-five percent -- while Ephraim decreased by twenty-eight percent. On the surface, Ephraim's s decline seems inconsistent with Jacob/Israel's blessing, when he said that Menashe "will be a great people, but his younger brother Ephrayim will be greater than he, and his seed will become a full-measure of nations" (Genesis 48: 19). Might it be that Jacob/Israel was defining greatness in terms other than size? Did he foresee that from this small tribe would come Joshua (*Yehoshua*), Moses' successor, "a man in whom the spirit is" (Numbers 27:18), whose name means "Salvation" or "Redemption"?

> Questions about Inheritance (Numbers 27)

Summary: *There came before Moses and El'azar at the Tent of Appointment the five daughters of Tzelofahd, who had died of his own sin in the wilderness and had no sons. They asked, "Why should the name of our father be taken away from the midst of the clan just because he has no son? Give us a holding." Moses conferred with YHVH, who said, "Transfer their father's inheritance to them."*

Say then to the people that "should a man die without having a son, his daughters shall receive his inheritance; should he have no daughters, then his inheritance will go to his brother; should he have no brothers, then the inheritance shall go to his father's brothers; and should he have no such uncles, then the inheritance shall go to the nearest of kin."

YHVH then said to Moses, "Go up the Mountains of Avarim and see the land that I am giving to the Children of Israel… Then gather your kin, even you, as Aaron your brother was gathered, since you had rebelled against my order in the Wilderness of Tzyn." (YHVH is referring to the sixth rebellion which was described in Numbers 20.)

Then Moses said to YHVH, "Designate a man over the community who will go before them, so that the community will not be like a flock without a shepherd."

YHVH replied, "Take Joshua, a man in whom the spirit is, and lean your hand upon him before El'azar and the entire community and commission him." Moses did as YHVH had commanded.

- **What is interesting about Numbers 27?** A key issue in the Book of Genesis concerns the passing of the family's birthright (e.g., from Abraham and Sarah to Isaac; from Isaac and Rebecca to Jacob; and from Jacob and Rachel to Joseph). In each of these inheritance cases, the parents had to decide which son was more deserving.

Recall that Torah draws no link between birthright and a family's material possessions or net worth. Instead, it grants two other treasures: first, the responsibility to live one's life in accordance with the Covenant so that the current and future generations can "move forward" into a closer relationship with each other (our personal challenge) and with YHVH (our spiritual challenge); and second, the choice to accept the offered responsibility.

What makes Numbers 27 noteworthy is that it raises an issue not addressed in Genesis: Who shall inherit if there are no sons, only daughters? Similarly, what would happen in the case of no offspring? Tzelofahd's case affirms the property rights of woman, but is ambiguous as to the all-important spiritual rights. While clearly not up to today's standards of equality, the stated inheritance rules in this chapter were nevertheless progressive by Biblical standards.

Another notable aspect of Numbers 27 is that appearing alongside the inheritance case mentioned above is the question of leadership succession; that is, who will inherit Moses' position? Of course, the close positioning of the succession question, which in the case of Moses has extraordinary spiritual connotations, with the more everyday questions of family inheritance may be purely coincidental. On the other hand, the fact that women's property rights appears almost in the same breath with the question about Moses' successor seems to further legitimize those rights.

> Guarding Sacred Time (Numbers 28-29)

These two chapters largely review material that appeared in Leviticus 23 concerning the development of the Sacred Calendar and the festival offering. The main difference between how the Calendar is depicted in the two books is that Numbers introduces the festival of the New Moon, a holy day on which work is nevertheless permitted. That difference aside, Numbers 28 and 29 contain lists of priestly instructions similar to those in Leviticus 23, presented in a straightforward manner that offers little opportunity for commentary or discussion. Therefore, I will focus on one instruction that is commonly misunderstood: the observance of Yom Kippur.

- **How should we observe Yom Kippur?** Verse 27 of Leviticus 23 states that "On the tenth day after the seventh New-Moon, it is the Day of Atonement; a proclamation of holiness shall there be for you. You are to afflict yourselves and bring near a fire offering to YHVH." Similarly, Numbers 29:7 reads: "And on the tenth day after this seventh New-Moon, a proclamation of holiness there is to be for you and you are to afflict yourselves, any kind of work you are not to do!"

  Notice that nowhere in these two references to Yom Kippur, nor for that matter anywhere else in Torah, is reference made to the practice of fasting. This custom, along with other forms of self-denial, originated from the expression "afflict yourselves." Written in Hebrew as *"v'ah-nee-tem nash na ta'chem,"* it appears in both Leviticus 23 and Numbers 29. While customarily translated as "fasting", a more literal translation of this phrase is to answer, pay attention, or respond to our individual and communal soul;" that is, reflect on the needs of ourselves and our community and how to best fulfill those needs. True, some may increase that awareness through fasting, but many of us fast for the wrong reasons – because we believe either that we are commanded to do so, or that by fasting we can increase our odds of being inscribed in the book of life for another year.

  Isaiah understood this problem about 2,600 years ago, complaining that, "This is not the fast that I desire!" (Isaiah 58, the chapter that is read as the Haftorah on Yom Kippur). He was expressing frustration with his community for performing mindless rituals of self-denial that did nothing to promote the well-being of others. He argued that the holiday is about achieving a sense of communal connectedness by increasing everyone's spiritual and physical fullness - - not about increasing each person's hunger. Put differently, Isaiah understood the essence of Yom Kippur to be companionship and compassion.

Like fasting, there are other expressions that we associate with Yom Kippur – e.g., "inscription in the Book of Life" and "the gates will soon close" – that also have no basis in the Torah or, for that matter, any of the other 32 books that comprise the Tanakh.

> Vows (Numbers 30)

Like the previous two chapters, Numbers 30 contains a list of priestly instructions. The focus in this chapter is on the binding nature of vows (sworn oaths), consistent with Torah's understanding of the power of the spoken word. Specifically, once uttered, words can have effects in the world that are difficult to withdraw. (The Aramaic expression *"abra-ka-dabra"* means "I create as I speak.")

The list of instructions in Numbers 30 differentiates between those vows made between a man and his wife; those between a father and his daughter, and those made by a young woman in the house of her father. The list also distinguishes between those vows that are to be upheld and those that can be annulled; that is, pardoned by YHVH. As with past lists of priestly instructions, the one presented in Numbers 30 does not easily lend itself to discussion or commentary. I will therefore advance to the next chapter, which presents one of the more difficult stories in Torah for us moderns to interpret because of its un-Torah like message.

> Conquest of the Midyanites (Numbers 31)

Summary: *YHVH spoke to Moses, saying "Seek the vengeance of the Children of Israel from the Midyanites. Moses then spoke to the people, saying, "Draft from among you an attack-force, one thousand men from each of the twelve tribes."*

The people did so, and in the attack killed every male, and the five kings of Midyan, along with Bil'am's son. They also captured the Midyanite woman, their children, and all the wealth that the Midyanites had acquired. They also burned all of the Midyanite settlements, while bringing all the booty that they took-as-plunder to the plains of Moab, near Jordan-Jericho, where Moses,

El'azar the priest, and the rest of the community resided. The commanders of each division of the armed-forces then reported to Moses that they took a head-count of their men and "there has not gone unaccounted of us a single man!"

When Moses saw what they had done, he was furious, saying, "You left alive all the females! It was they who caused the Children of Israel to turn away from YHVH, so that a plague came against the community of YHVH! So now kill every male among the children and every woman who has laid with a man, but you can keep for yourselves the younger women who have not lied with a man…As for you, pitch-camp outside the camp for seven days so that everyone who killed a person or touched a corpse can decontaminate themselves on the third day. On the seventh day, you and your captives may do the same."

A count was then taken of those taken captive. It totaled 32,000 young woman, 75,000 sheep, 72,000 cattle, and 61,000 donkeys. YHVH said to Moses that he is to split the loot between those who fought in the battle and those in the community who did not. From the half share of those who went to battle, a levy is to be raised for YHVH. From the half share that went to the community, a levy is to be raised for the Levites.

Moses and El'azar then took all the gained gold, armlets, bracelets, rings, earrings and ornaments, worth 16,750 shekels, from the men of war and brought it to the Tent of Appointment as a reminder for the Children of Israel, before the presence of YHVH.

Discussion Questions: Why did YHVH order vengeance on the Midyanites? Was further brutality against the Midyanites encouraged by Moses? Does the depiction of the Midyanite massacre story defy reason? What is the meaning behind this story? Are the Israelites' forward advances sustainable?

- **Why did YHVH order vengeance on the Midyanites?** It was the Midyanites who, in Numbers 25, enticed more than twenty-four thousand Israelites to publicly turn away from YHVH in favor of polytheism (idolatry) and the worship of Baal, the Canaanite god of thunder and fertility. The Midyanites were also the tribe that allied themselves with Balak (Numbers 22:4). And it was they who, more than four hundred years before, "hauled Joseph out of the pit, and then sold him for twenty pieces of silver to the Ishmaelites, who then brought Joseph to Egypt" (Genesis 37: 28).

- **Was additional brutality against the Midyanites encouraged by Moses?** Apparently, Moses wasn't satisfied that the Israelite attack-forces killed every Midyanite male, destroyed their settlements, and took all their booty. According to the text, he also wanted killed all male children and non-virgin women among the Midyanites, and was furious that they weren't. By ordering the death of every male child, Moses appears even worse than Pharaoh (recall that Pharaoh called for the death of all Hebrew babies, but left untouched their older siblings and parents.)

What should we make of this story? Once again we find ourselves questioning Torah's relevance in today's times and wonder what good can come from a story that glorifies such cold-blooded murder. I say "once again" because the Midyanite massacre is only one in a string of violent sagas conveyed in the Torah. Others include the suffering caused by the Ten Plagues; the drowning of the Egyptian military in the Reed Sea; the call for the extermination of Amalek; and most recently in Numbers 21, where it was written that "Israel struck against the army of Og, king of Bashan, until not a survivor was left" (verse 35).

We will apply the same line of reasoning to Numbers 31 that was used to answer other troubling questions raised in the Torah stories. I am referring to the approach proposed almost a millennium ago by Moses Maimonides, the revered Biblical scholar. He argued that if a literal reading of the scripture suggests something that is clearly contrary to reason, we must interpret what we read as metaphor. As he pointed out, the Torah often speaks "figuratively and allegorically."

- **Does the depiction of the Midyanite massacre defy reason?** There are at least three aspects of this narrative that appear unreasonable, suggesting that the events described in Numbers 31 are unlikely to have occurred as presented. First, a literal reading of this story is entirely void of any philosophical or practical wisdom for living a meaningful and socially conscious life - those lessons we have come to expect from a collection of writings whose name, Torah, means "teachings."

Moreover, the encouragement of vengeance and killing is in direct opposition to the teachings of the Sixth Commandment ("You are not to murder") and the ethical cornerstone of Torah, the commandment to love your neighbor as yourself (Leviticus 19:18). To assert that the Midyanite battles took place in the brutal manner described in Numbers 31 would throw into question the very integrity of the Torah, the consistency of its arguments, and the worthiness of its teaching.

Second, the story contains gross exaggerations which challenge its trustworthiness. For example, the semi-arid plains of Moab near Jordan-Jericho could not have supported the amount of livestock that was said to be captured from the Midyanites (675,000 sheep, 72,000 cattle, and 61,000 donkeys).[23] Consider also that battles in those days were usually fought man-to-man, and the Israelite attack force was outnumbered by a ratio of about three-to-one. It is bewildering to imagine that not a single Hebrew soldier was unaccounted for. [24]

Third, and perhaps most telling, it is inconceivable that Moses (or anyone else for that matter), would have commanded his attack force to kill every Midyanite male regardless of age, as well as all non-virgin women – because in so doing, he would have been signing the death warrant of some of his closest family! Remember, Moses' father-in-law and spiritual mentor is the Midyanite priest Jethro (Re'uel); [25]

---

23 In semi-arid regions of the US, it takes at least two square acres of land to raise one head of cattle, a half- acre to raise one sheep, and another half-acre to raise one donkey. Multiplying these estimates by the number of cattle, sheep and donkeys taken by the attack-force, and then divide that acreage total by 640 (the number of square acres in a square mile), suggests a plot of grazing land in excess of 800 square miles!

24 The size of the conquered Midyan Empire can be imputed by the number of captured young woman (virgins). We can assume that if the empire consisted of 32,000 young women, then it likely had a similar number of married women, and therefore a similar number of men who fought against the Israelite attack force of twelve thousand (one thousand men per tribe).

25 Jethro's fatherly influence on Moses is undeniable. It was Jethro who offered shelter to Moses while the latter was fleeing Pharaoh's wrath. It was Jethro who welcomed Moses into his family by allowing his daughter *Tzippora* to marry Moses without any preconditions. It was Jethro who

Moses' wife, Tzippora, is the daughter of Jethro and therefore a Midyanite woman, making their son, Gershom, a half-Midyanite.

Of course, the fact that the Midyanite massacre story defies reason doesn't necessarily mean that the battle didn't take place. However, it does imply that if it took place, it didn't happen in the manner described in Numbers 31. Rather than debate the authenticity of the story, for which there is no known corroborative evidence, it is more useful to ponder what the writers might have had in mind in claiming such occurrences. Put simply, what is the Numbers 31 story all about?

- **What is the meaning of this tale?** To address this question, we must look deeply into the story in an attempt to identify its figurative and allegorical meanings. For example, perhaps the Torah's intention in describing this battle is not to record an actual historical event, but to proclaim the current spiritual state of the Children of Israel. In other words, could the story be conveying the message that the Israelites, at long last, are ready to embrace their mission to confront the human and divine challenges placed before them without even a hint of rebellion, grumbling, or preconditions? Similarly, maybe the battles are described in this exaggerated, one-sided manner to suggest that the Israelites, after forty years of wandering, are now "proving able" to struggle. As such, the text may be using the battles to symbolically convey that the "armed forces for Israel" that we read about in Numbers 21 are finally ready to live up to their name.

Perhaps the Midyanite battles were not external struggles, but internal conflicts akin to the one we are told of in Exodus 2 when Moses is said to have killed the Egyptian taskmaster. Recall that that slaying could have symbolized Moses' need to "kill" the

---

understandingly replied "Go in peace" when Moses asked "Pray let me return to my brothers that are in Egypt, that I may see whether they are alive." And, it was Jethro who in Exodus 18 advises Moses on how to manage the large number of people who have become increasingly difficult to lead.

Egyptian, or the slave-master, within himself in order to give his life a new and more authentic purpose. Similarly, the Israelites in Numbers 31 needed to "kill" their fascination with the polytheistic ways of the Midyanites in order to enter the Promised Land, as Calev and Joshua had already done; rather than make Canaan their ultimate destination, as was the case with the other ten scouts. By "conquering" all of the physical and material temptations that the text associates with a Midyanite lifestyle, the Israelites may have transformed their consciousness to one focused on YHVH's commandments.

- **Will the Israelites' forward advances be sustainable?** We have witnessed in previous Torah stories that the journey to the Promised Land does not follow a one-way path. Forward movement is often interspersed with backward steps. The question worth asking is, "Will the Israelites build on the momentum achieved in Numbers 31, or will they once again regress to their narrow ways?"

The chapter offers mixed indicators. On the one hand, the people appear preoccupied with their newly acquired loot (I say "preoccupied" because roughly half of the verses in this chapter, specifically verses 25-54, address the distribution of the booty). Will the attention to the Midyanite wealth undermine the Israelites' commitment to monotheism? Will these material possessions prevent them from being present and fully engaged in life? Are they running the risk of violating the Second Commandment by treating the booty like a god and "placing it before YHVH's presence"?

On the other hand, the men of the armed forces appear to understand that their victory was not their own doing, but YHVH's. They therefore offer the gold and jewelry as an "effect-ransom for our lives before the presence of YHVH" (verse 50). This was an expression of deep gratitude, akin to Abel's offering of his "first and his choicest" in Genesis 4. This is to say that these men knowingly gave up control of that which didn't belong to them, regardless of its value.

Which "hand" will win out? We are only up to the thirty-first chapter of the fourth Book of the five that make up the Torah. Twenty-seven additional books, which comprise the Tanakh, will follow; and centuries of time will pass after that. Eventually we will reach the present, where the answer might reside.

> Settling East of the Jordan (Numbers 32)

Summary: *The Sons of Reuven and Gad had many livestock and saw the land of Gil'ad as a place fit for their herds. So they said to Moses and El'azar, "If we have found favor in your eyes, let this land be given to your servants as a holding – do not make us cross the Jordan." Moses replied: "Should your brothers go out to war and you stay here? Why do you constrain the will of the people to cross into the land that YHVH has given to them?"*

So they struck a bargain with Moses: The children, wives and livestock of Reuven and Gad may remain in the land of Gil'ad, while the men from these tribes agree to be drafted before YHVH for war and not return to claim their inheritance in the land east of the Jordan until the land west of the Jordan is subdued and its enemies dispossessed.

So the sons of Reuven and Gad and half the tribe of Menashe conquered the land of Gil'ad and dispossessed the Amorites who had been living there, erected fences for their livestock, and built fortified towns to protect their wives and children.

- **Why did these two- and- a- half tribes willingly forgo their claim to the land that YHVH had promised to them?** The decision made by Reuven, Gad, and half the tribe of Menashe is reminiscent of Lot's decision in Genesis 13. Recall that when given the choice of where to settle, he also chose the land to the east. Like the two- and- a- half tribes, Lot was attracted to the well-watered plains that could amply support his herds. To him, the physical abundance that he saw in the east looked like the spiritually-rich Gardens of YHVH (that is, Eden). Because the preference of these tribes is so similar to that of Lot, we can assume they faced a similar fate. That is, by choosing physical abundance over spiritual richness, they may have put their future at risk by distancing themselves from YHVH's promise. (In later readings, we learn that the Moabites and the Amorites -- two tribes descended from the two illegitimate sons born to Lot's daughters - -will periodically reclaim some of the eastern land.)

> Reviewing the Forty Years of Wandering (Numbers 33)

This chapter's first forty-nine verses list the marching stages taken by the Children of Israel as they moved from the land of Egypt to a spot on the east bank of the Jordan River, opposite to Jericho.

Summary: *Beginning with verse fifty, the Chapter's narrative opens with YHVH speaking to Moses in the Plains of Moav by Jordan-Jericho, saying, "Speak to the Children of Israel, and say "When you cross the Jordan into the land of Canaan, you are to dispose of all the settled-folk... and destroy all their figured-objects, all their molten images, and all high-places, that you may take possession of the land that I have given to you... But, if you don't dispossess the settled-folk, those who will be left behind will be barbs in your eyes, as spines in your sides; they will assault you in the land that you are settling in. As I planned to do to them, so I will do to you!" (Verses 50-56).*

- **Why dispossess the settled- folk?** Few passages in Torah are as politically charged and difficult to interpret as the last six verses of Numbers 33. Some have used them to validate "manifest destiny," a nationalistic philosophy that characterized America's foreign policy in the mid-nineteenth century;[26] while others, in more recent times, have used these words to justify Israel's development on the West Bank. The implied message of these verses is that Israel has the divine right to physically uproot those who made the land of Canaan their home.

---

26 At its core, "manifest destiny" was the belief that America was given the divine obligation to stretch its boundaries to the Pacific Ocean because of its cultural and racial superiority over the resident natives.

The problem with this literal interpretation, however, is that it challenges two of Torah's fundamental tenants. First, it shifts Torah's core philosophy from that of inclusiveness (the belief that it is we who choose to live by YHVH's covenant) to the opposite view that YHVH chooses us to the exclusion of all others. [27] It also poses a conundrum: How can you "love your neighbors as yourself" while at the same time dispossessing them?

Fortunately, we can resolve these interpretive problems by examining the text's usage of the word "dispossess" in Numbers 33. Notice that it is not being used to advocate the killing of every non-Hebrew man, woman and child, as was done in Numbers 31; nor does it encourage the overpowering of an enemy "until not a survivor was left," as in Numbers 21; nor does it necessarily insinuate that the Canaanites - a people who have prospered economically and culturally due to their proximity to Egypt, Mesopotamia, and Phoenicia, and who have yet to physically threaten the Israelites – should be thrown into exile. Rather, the term "dispossess" may refer to the Canaanites' polytheistic influences rather than the people themselves. Specifically, the Israelites are being told to dispossess (or distance, disassociate, or disinherit) those influences that would "assault them on the land that they are about to settle" (verse 55) by making it more difficult for them to live their lives according to the Second and Third Commandments [28] and, therefore, less able to "take possession of the land that I have given to you."

---

[27] Most of Torah reinforces the message of inclusiveness. For example, Exodus 12: 38 describes those who left Egypt as not only Jews, but a "mixed multitude." Inclusiveness also constitutes one of the core teachings of the Jonah story, which is read on Yom Kippur, the most holy day of the Jewish calendar.

[28] The Second Commandment states: "You are not to have any other gods before my presence. You are not to make yourself a carved-image or any other figure that is in the heavens above, earth below, or the waters beneath the earth. You are not to bow down to them nor serve them, for I, YHVH am a zealous God, calling to account the iniquity of the fathers upon the sons, to the third and fourth generations of those who hate me, but showing loyalty to the thousandth of those who love me and keep my commandments"; while the Third Commandment says: "You are not

Bear in mind that the land which YHVH promised to the Israelites in the above quote is not the land of Canaan. Canaan refers to a specific geopolitical locale - the place where the Canaanites live. In contrast, the Promised Land denotes an awakened state of consciousness where we feel a deep sense of oneness and peace with who we are (with no internal conflicts) and where we are (in the world around us). It is a state of mind where we are fully aware of receiving nourishment (symbolized by milk) and pleasure (honey), even during mundane or troubled times.

The point is that the Canaanites may have settled in the land of Canaan, but they have never been present in the Promised Land or even aware of its presence. In this sense, these people were akin to the ten Israelite scouts who thoroughly explored the land of Canaan, but saw nothing promising. Only Calev and Joshua were there – and they knew it.

- **What are the barbs and spines?** The Israelites are about to face a profound challenge once they cross-over into the land of the Canaanites: They will be confronted with powerful earthly temptations offered by this prosperous polytheistic civilization and will have to either resist these temptations or risk returning to where they started - enslaved in a narrow place. Through this lens, the barbs and spines can be viewed as irritants, intended to awaken our senses should they submit to slumber. Like the Ten Plagues in Egypt, these irritants are meant to remind us that our well-being derives not from material possessions but from those moments of *shalem* (wholeness) when we prove able in our spiritual and personal struggles.

That said, it is hard to maintain focus - particularly when living in a prosperous society and reaping its material benefits. Not only do these benefits provide physical comfort and gratify our ego; they can insidiously take control of our lives, causing us

---

to take up the name of YHVH for emptiness, for YHVH will not clear him that takes up his name for emptiness."

to focus more attention on accumulating unessential extras (*chu-matze*) than on building closer relationships with ourselves, our family, and our community (*matzot*). Said in terms of the Second and Third Commandments, they can cause us to place idols before YHVH's presence and take up the name of YHVH for emptiness. In other words prosperity - because it is hard to control - can inflict on us a fate similar to those who have settled in the land of Canaan but remain unaware of land of promise. This is not to say that prosperity is intrinsically bad. The challenge is to control it rather than allow it to control us.

> Identifying Canaan's Borders (Numbers 34)

In the first 13 verses of this chapter, Moses describes what will be Israel's boundaries once they settle in the land of Canaan. While some of the listed locations are recognizable to this day (e.g., the Sea of Salt; the Sea of the Kinneret; the Great Sea [Mediterranean]; and the Jordon River), most of the land markers (e.g., Kadesh; Mount Hill; Hatzar Einan; and Hamat) are not. After listing the boundaries, Moses says to the people, "This is the land for which you are to arrange your inheritance by lot that YHVH commanded to be given to the nine tribes and the half tribe." Then, in the final fourteen verses, Moses names the leaders from each tribe who will decide how the land will be divided.

> Towns of Sanctuary (Numbers 35)

Introduction: How are we to mete out justice in instances of accidental killings or a lack of witnesses? What should be done to protect the accused until and unless sufficient evidence surfaces to warrant a trial? Numbers 35 suggests that the Torah was grappling with these questions and devising innovative solutions that were humane and sensible at a time when honor killings were the norm.

Summary: *YHVH spoke to Moses, saying that once the people cross the Jordan they are to erect six towns under the control of the Levites that are to be places of refuge, intended to protect those* *who have committed an accidental murder from blood vengeance by the family of the deceased. These persons are free to remain in these towns until they can be adequately judged by the community. More than one witness is required to convict, and no person may buy his innocence by paying a ransom. "You are not to corrupt the land that you are in, for the blood – it will corrupt the land... you are not to make tamei the land in which you are settling, in whose midst I dwell, for I am YHVH, Dweller in the midst of Israel!"*

> One Final Detail (Numbers 36)

The Book of Numbers returns to the issue of inheritance discussed in chapter 27 to resolve one final matter: the question of a father who's only offspring are daughters. . The book makes the case that the daughters are the rightful heirs to their father's estate so long as they agree to marry men within their father's tribe. As was mentioned in the commentary to Numbers 27, this ruling is not up to today's standards of gender equality, but is nevertheless progressive for its time.

The expectation is that with this ruling and all the commandments, laws and experiences that preceded it in the Torah's first four books, the Israelites at long last are prepared to leave the wilderness and make an orderly transition to life in the Promised Land.

Chapter 15: Revisiting the First Forty Years

Introduction: The Torah's fifth and final book is sometimes referred to as the *Mishne Torah*, which means "copy of the Torah" or the "second Torah," for it contains many passages that previously appeared in the first four books, most notably a repetition of the Ten Commandments in Deuteronomy 5. As we will soon see, however, Deuteronomy is much more than a copy of the "first Torah."

First, the writer(s) most likely has changed: The book is closer linguistically and stylistically to the books that follow it in the Tanakh – Joshua, Judges, and the two books of Samuel - than to the four books that preceded it. Many biblical scholars have therefore concluded that Deuteronomy was written by a different author(s) than the one(s) who wrote Genesis, Exodus, Leviticus, and Numbers.

Second, the context has changed: The Children of Israel have completed their wandering and, since Numbers 33, are encamped in the Plains of Moab at the border of the Promised Land. Except for Moses, Caleb, and Joshua, all who had left *Mitz'rayim* (Egypt) are presumed dead or too young to remember the enslavements associated with that narrow place. Thus, when Moses speaks to the people in Deuteronomy, he is speaking only to those who were either born or raised in the wilderness and are now about ready to advance beyond it.

Third, Moses has changed: Soon after learning in Numbers 20 that he will not be allowed passage into the Promised Land, he suddenly finds his voice. Gone is the often- repeated phrase, "and YHVH spoke to Moses, saying, speak to the Children of Israel." In its place, this man, self-described in Exodus 4:10 as "a man of few words, heavy of mouth and tongue" speaks in lengthy first-person narrations.

Finally, Moses' message has changed: As he prepares the people to enter the land that was promised to their ancestors, he reviews with them the key events of the past forty years, pointing out Israel's failings and the associated consequences. In so doing, he revises some of the stories and gives them new meaning in the process.

➢ Retelling the Story (Deuteronomy 1-3:22)

Summary: *This section opens with the verse "These are the words that Moses spoke to all Israel." The setting is the wilderness that resides on the east side of the Jordan River, which the people reached after an eleven- day journey from Mount Horev, one day after the eleventh new-moon in the fortieth year since leaving Mitz'rayim. Moses is telling the people of the time when "YHVH your Elohim" spoke to them, saying: "Enough for you, staying at this mountain, march on, to the land that was promised to your fathers, Abraham, Isaac, and Jacob – the land that includes the Amorite Hill-country, the Negev, the land of the Canaanites and Lebanon, the shores of the sea and as far east as the Euphrates river."*

Moses then reminds the people of the many difficulties that he faced as the leader, saying, "I am not able, I alone, to carry you; for YHVH your Elohim has made you many - - How can I carry, I alone, your load, your burden, your quarrelling?" It is here that Moses also tells the people from each tribe to select wise and knowledgeable leaders. "So I took these wise men from your tribes and placed them as heads over you, as rulers of thousands, rulers of hundreds, rulers of fifties, and rulers of ten. I then commanded your judges to hear-out what is between your brothers, judge with equity between each man and his brother or sojourner - - and for any legal matter too hard for you, bring near to me and I will hear it out."

Moses continues: "So we marched on from Horev and came to Kadesh-Barne'a where I said to you, 'See, YHVH your Elohim has given before you this land, go up and take possession of it.' Then you came near to me and said, 'Let us send men before us that they may explore the land for us and return us word about the route that we should use to go up against it and about the towns that we will come to.' So, I took from among you twelve men, one per tribe, and they went up into the hills, as far as the Wadi of Clusters, spied it out, and returned with some fruit and the word: 'Good is the land that YHVH our Elohim is giving us.' However, you were not willing to go up and instead rebelled against YHVH your Elohim's order, saying, 'Because of YHVH's hatred for us, he took us out of the land of Egypt to destroy us.'"

To that, Moses replied: "I tried to tell you, 'Do not shake in fear because YHVH your Elohim goes with you... as YHVH went with you in Egypt and in the wilderness ... places where YHVH carried you as a man carries his child.' But you didn't listen to me - - YHVH became furious upon hearing your words, saying: 'No one from this evil generation will get to see the Land that I swore to their fathers. . . only Calev and Joshua will enter, along with the children who were too young at that time to yet know good or ill.' At me also, YHVH was incensed for your sake, saying 'You also will not enter!'"

You then spoke to me, saying, "We have sinned against YHVH - - we will go up and wage war." But YHVH said to me, "Say to them that they are not to wage war for I am not in your midst." However, you did not listen and were crushed by the Amorites at Se'ir, as far as Horma. When you returned, you wept, but YHVH did not give ear to you.

Moses then retells the encounters with the Children of Esau (the Edomites); the Children of Lot (the Moabites and the Ammonites); and the two kings of the Amorites (Sihon, king of Heshbon, and Og, king of Bashan). This portion of Deuteronomy concludes with Joshua saying to the people, "Your eyes have seen all that YHVH your Elohim did to the two Amorite kings, and thus will YHVH your Elohim do to all the kingdoms into which you are crossing! You are not to be afraid of them, for YHVH your Elohim is the one who wages war for you!"

Discussion questions: Why does the second verse of this chapter refer to the mountain as Horev and not Sinai? Where is the Promised Land? Why does Moses suddenly refer to YHVH's name as YHVH your Elohim? Has Moses become less humble? Has he lost sight as to why he is being denied entry into the Promised Land? Is he engaging in revisionist retelling of history? Is his memory of the past slipping? Is he becoming a less effective leader? Why are there inconsistencies in Moses' retelling of the past forty years?

- **Why does the second verse of this chapter refer to the mountain as Horev and not Sinai?** "Horev," as we learned in the Book of Exodus, translates to "Mountain of Sword and Destruction," while "Sinai" means "Mountain of Revelation." It was at Horev that Moses encountered the Burning Bush and learned of the need to sever those beliefs associated with his Egyptian past that were no longer serving him well, so that new, more meaningful truths could emerge. It was at Sinai that the Israelites were introduced to those truths in the form of the Ten Sayings (Commandments).

   Might it be that the name used for the mountain depends on how far the people have advanced on their spiritual journey? Is the text suggesting that the Israelites are still severing their Egyptian-born beliefs, and have yet to integrate the Commandments into their lives? They may be eleven days beyond Horev, but apparently Sinai (and the Promised Land) remains far from their view.

- **Where is the Promised Land?** The borders of the Promised Land are stated in one verse in Deuteronomy (verse 7), in contrast to the thirteen verses (1-13) devoted to the same topic in Numbers 34 and the four verses (18-21) used in Genesis 15. However, none of these descriptions, whether taken individually or collectively, provide anything more than a very rough approximation of the land's outer boundaries. Perhaps this was done intentionally to remind us that the Promised Land is a state of mind that is not necessarily tied to specific geographical coordinates.

- **Has YHVH's name changed?** In the Book of Genesis, YHVH was known to the patriarchs and matriarchs in Genesis as *El Shaddai* (translated as "Almighty") or *Elohim* (a word conjugated in the plural form which is understood to represent an infinite number of manifestations of YHVH's hidden essence). Only in Exodus does YHVH reveal YHVH's name in its most abstract form: *EHYEH ASHER EHYEH*, or "I will be that which I will be." This name - representing the confluence of the past, present and future, without limits (*ein sof*) and like no other (*ein ode*) - is then used throughout the Books of Exodus, Leviticus, and Numbers.

Beginning with Deuteronomy 1:6, however, Moses introduces a new name, "YHVH your Elohim." Perhaps by invoking the name "*Elohim*" that was used by the patriarchs and matriarchs, Moses was reminding the people of their link with their ancestral roots.

- **Has Moses become less humble?** In Numbers 12 we read that "Moses was exceedingly humble, more than any other human." Indeed, no person in Torah had a closer relationship with YHVH, having spoken with YHVH "face-to-face, as a man speaks to his neighbor"; seen YHVH's "glory" (the "thirteen attributes" named in Exodus 33 and 34); and channeled YHVH's voice. No person has been given greater responsibility than Moses, who was charged with leading the people out of *Mitz'rayim*, through the wilderness, and into the Promised Land. And, no person has been granted more authority. Yet, through it all, Moses remained the reluctant, unpretentious leader who never desired power nor allowed himself to become corrupted by it.

    However, this may be changing. Notice the many "I" statements that Moses uses when reminding the people of the difficulties that he faced as their leader. It is as if he is now trying to take credit for the administrative solution that was entirely the doing of his father-in-law, Jethro. It was he who said to Moses in Exodus 18: 14-27, "Why do you sit alone, while the entire people are stationed around you? You will become worn out. Be there, yourself, for the people in relation to YHVH. But select honest men of caliber to be chiefs of thousands, chiefs of hundreds, chiefs of fifties and chiefs of ten. They will bring every great matter to you, but every small matter they shall judge by themselves."

- **Is Moses engaging in a revisionist telling of history?** YHVH had told Moses in Numbers 20 to draw water from the rock by speaking to it. Instead, he struck the rock with his staff, as he had done thirty-nine years before in Refidim (Exodus 17). For that, YHVH told Moses that he will be denied entry into the Promised Land because "You did not have trust in me" (Numbers 20:12).

This point seems to be lost altogether on Moses just one short year later when, in Deuteronomy 1, he attributed his fate to a very different reason. Specifically, in retelling the story of the scouts, he reminded the people of their unwillingness to enter the Promised Land after hearing the scouts' report, in spite of his efforts to convince them otherwise. For that, he said, not only was YHVH furious with the people, but was also "incensed at me for your sake," saying, "You shall also not enter."

There are various ways to interpret this quote. Moses might be saying that if only the people had listened to him, YHVH would have allowed him entry! Is Moses trying to shift the blame for his fate from his own actions to those of the people; that it is they who made YHVH furious, when, in fact, they were either too young to remember the incident or had yet to be born. Moreover, Moses appears to be confusing the "wilderness generation" with their parents, the now-deceased "slave-generation". Have his "eyes become too dim for seeing," as had Isaac's eyes in Genesis 27:1, when he could not distinguish between his two sons, Jacob and Esau?

Alternatively, he might be implying that the younger generation bears the indelible influence of their parents, such that if put to the same test, they would act as their parents had acted– that for most of us, no matter how many years we wander beyond Horev, we will never quite make it to Sinai? Additionally, when he said "incensed at me for your sake," he might have meant "for your own good," where "your" refers to the community of Israelites who he is leading. Perhaps Moses is recognizing that for the people to reach the Promised Land, they need a new leader, for it is "for their own good."

- **Is Moses' memory slipping?** In Deuteronomy 1:42-44, Moses tells the people of how the Amorites "pursued you as bees do" and crushed you because you did not listen to YHVH. Moses was referring back to the Third Rebellion, mentioned in Numbers 13 and 14, when the people were punished for trusting the report made by ten of the twelve scouts more than YHVH's word. In so doing, however, Moses seems to have confused the Amorites with the Amalekites and Canaanites.

It was the Amalekites and the Canaanites who crushed the Israelites after the Israelites were warned by Moses not to wage war against them "for YHVH is not in your midst" (Numbers 14: 42). As for the Amorites, they did not overwhelm the Israelites, as Moses had said; rather, it was the Israelites who soundly defeated the Amorites before settling in all their towns and dispossessing their residents (Numbers 21: 21-31).

- **Why are there inconsistencies in Moses' retelling of the past forty years?** This question is particularly interesting because Moses had previously retold the story just a few chapters before, in the first thirteen verses of Numbers 33. As we have just witnessed, there are subtle and not-so-subtle inconsistencies between the two retellings and the original story.

Were they inserted into the text to reinforce the message that the Torah is not a static document, but rather one that invites active interpretation? This is to say that what may have appeared to be true for one generation is not necessarily self-evident for the next. If so, the Torah teaching is clear: It is the responsibility of each generation to decide what in Torah is inalienable and what is subject to context.

Another possible explanation is that the inconsistencies might exist to remind us, once again, that the Torah is not a history book. It is first and foremost a theological document primarily concerned with conveying spiritual and ethical teachings, not necessarily historical happenings. The implication is that many battles described in the Torah may never have taken place, at least not in the brutal way depicted in the text. After all, what would have logically motivated the Israelites to fight over territory lying outside the physical land of Canaan and the spiritual borders of the Promised Land?

"The thing to remember about the Bible," said Professor Yair Zakovitch, Dean of Humanities at the Hebrew University, "is that the events and characters are just there to convey messages…not so much to tell us what really happened."[29] My sense is that the described battles are to be seen as metaphors - each representing a test for assessing the people's readiness to accept YHVH's teaching no matter what barriers lay in their path. Just as Jacob had his name changed to Israel when he "proved himself able" by struggling with the mysterious man, the Children of Israel are now proving themselves able through the many battles they've faced along their journey to enter the Promised Land.

- **Is Moses becoming a less effective leader?** In this first section of Deuteronomy, we raised the possibility that he was becoming less humble, in that he tried to shift the blame for his fate from his own actions to those of the people. We also read that he seemed to have confused the "wilderness generation" with that of their parents; and the Amorites with the Amalekites and the Canaanites.

  In Numbers 20 we witnessed other evidence. I am referring to the episode where the wilderness generation was expressing very different culinary cravings than their parents had experienced. Whereas their parents wanted the foods that they had back in *Mitz'rayim*, this generation desired the foods from the Promised Land, yet Moses (and Aaron) appeared to have missed the meaning of this shift. Instead of interpreting the new cravings as evidence that the people longed for the Promised Land, Moses and Aaron "flung themselves upon their faces" (Numbers 20: 6) and accused the wilderness generation of "rebelling" (Numbers 20: 10).

  The bottom line is that Moses, like the patriarchs and matriarchs before him and Joshua, David, and Solomon after him, is not presented as faultless. Indeed, everyone that appears in the Torah and the later books makes mistakes. The question, therefore, might be asked, "Why would the Bible seemingly go out of its way to present its main characters as imperfect characters?" The answer put forth by many is that the

---

29 Professor Zakovitch's quote appears on page 85 of Bruce Fieler's 2005 book, "Where God was Born."

Bible doesn't present perfect people because there is little that we could learn from them.

> Moses' Impassioned Plea (Deuteronomy 3: 23-28)

Summary: *Moses told of how he pleaded with YHVH, saying: "Pray let me cross over that I might see the good land that is across the Jordan. But, YHVH was cross with me on your account and said, 'Enough for you! Do not speak to me anymore again about this matter! Go to the top of the Pisga Range and lift up your eyes –towards the sea, the north, the south and the sunrise … see it with your own eyes for you will not cross this Jordan! But command Joshua, make him strong for he will cross-over before this people and will cause them to inherit the land that you see.'"*

Discussion questions: Is YHVH losing patience with Moses? What does "crossing-over" refer to? What did Moses see on Mount Pisga when he looked in four directions?

- **Is YHVH losing patience with Moses?** The passage opens with Moses saying that he pleaded with YHVH. The Hebrew word for "plead" is *kha'nan,* which has the same root as the word *ha'nah,* meaning "grace." Used in verse 23 in the reflexive tense, this verse can be translated as Moses asking YHVH to grace YHVH's self on Moses' behalf. On the surface, this seems like a perfectly reasonable request, given that Moses dedicated his life in service to YHVH.

Grace in Torah, however, is viewed as a gift from YHVH, something that is beyond the control of humans. No one, not even Moses, can do anything to earn or hasten it. Like the meaning of YHVH's name ("I will be whatever I will be"), grace "will come whenever it will come." By not granting Moses grace, YHVH is telling him in no uncertain terms that the journey to the Promised Land is not about him or any other individual – it is about the community.

Has Moses learned this lesson? Perhaps not: In Deuteronomy 1: 37, Moses remarked to the people that he will not be allowed entry into the Promised Land because YHVH was "incensed at me for your sakes." Now, in Deuteronomy 3: 26, Moses appears to once again blame the people for his fate when he says that "YHVH was cross with me on your account." This is not to say that Moses' time has passed. He still has the rest of the Book of Deuteronomy to prepare the wilderness generation – those who did not witness the exodus from Egypt nor the revelation at Sinai - for their crossing into the Promised Land and to empower their new leader, Joshua, to take them.

* **What does "crossing -over" mean?** As we learned in Genesis 17, the root of the Biblical word for cross-over is "*ah-ber,*" which is used to construct the word "Hebrew." In other words, a Hebrew is defined as someone who crosses-over into a closer relationship with self, community and YHVH.

- **What did Moses see on Mount Pisga?** We won't be told what Moses saw at that moment until Deuteronomy 34. However, in preparing ourselves for this 34th chapter, we might refer back to Genesis 13. There, YHVH told Avram to "lift up your eyes and everything that you see to the *Tzafona* (the north, or "towards the hidden"), the *Negba* (the south, or "the parched dry"), the *Kedem* (east, or "towards the beginning"), and the *Yama* (west, or "towards the sea"), I give to you and your descendants for the ages." (Note that when speaking to Moses, the word YHVH used for the south is *tminah*, which means to the right or to the south.)

Did Moses see the same thing? Probably not. Like Avram before him, he was told by YHVH to look at the land in four directions (recall from Genesis 13 that the number "four" in Torah represents the components of spiritual wholeness and is a portal into the infinite). However, when the two of them looked at the land, they were doing so from starkly different vantage points. Avram was already inside the land, but had yet to have the letter '*hey*' added to his name by YHVH, meaning that he was still in the early stages of his spiritual development and therefore wasn't fully aware of being in it. (Avram's name was later transformed in Genesis 17 into Abraham after he willingly entered into a Covenant with YHVH.)

Moses, by contrast, is viewing the land from a position east of the Jordan River and was thus looking at it from the outside. He did so, however, through spiritually elevated eyes, suggesting that most of what Avram saw was the physical borders of the land of Canaan, while Moses was primarily seeing the metaphysical borders of the Promised Land.

> Moses' Sermons: (Deuteronomy 4- 11)

Introduction: Having completed the retelling of Israel's wilderness travels, Moses begins a series of talks to remind the people of the laws and regulations that they are to follow. I will organize my comments using a more traditional format because most of what is written in these eight chapters does not invite as many questions as the material in previous chapters did.

Summary: Deuteronomy 4:1 to 4:14: *This chapter opens with Moses instructing the people that only by adhering to the commandments, laws and regulations will they be able to enter and take possession of the land that YHVH is giving them. He also tells them: "Neither add nor subtract from that which YHVH commanded... rather, keep the commandments and observe them, for that will be the wisdom for you... Make them known to your children and to your children's children of the day when YHVH spoke to you from the midst of the fire... announcing the covenant, the Ten Sayings that YHVH wrote on two tablets of stone."*

Commentary: When the people heard Moses say "Neither add nor subtract from what YHVH commanded you," it should have reminded them of the Leviticus 10 story about Nadav and Avihu. Recall that after these two sons of Aaron put incense on the alien fire (*aysh ze'rah*), "Fire went out from the presence of YHVH and consumed them." The message is clear: It is not for us to tamper with or try to improve upon that which YHVH tells us to do.

Moses is also reminding the people in this Deuteronomy chapter that the essence of the Promised Land is not the physical land, but how we choose to live on it. What makes the Land a land of promise, able to provide milk (sustenance) and honey (sweetness and joy) even during mundane or troubled times, is the willingness of the people to live by YHVH's teachings.

At their core, these teachings all pertain to becoming more human, appreciating life before death, and participating in the ongoing process of creation. They make no reference to what we believe, how fervently we believe, or our religious affiliation. Instead, they provide guidance about how to transform our consciousness to more life-enhancing levels of awareness.

In other words, Moses is telling the Israelites that their journey will not end when they cross-over to the Land of Canaan. Therefore, think of Canaan as a metaphor representing one in a long line of milestones on the pathway to becoming a virtuous community- - a continuation of the marching stages that were listed in the first forty-nine verses of Numbers 33.

Summary: Deuteronomy 4:15 to 4:24: *Moses continues his sermon by retelling the story at Horev when YHVH spoke to the people and they heard only a voice, but saw no form. The Voice told them to take care not to make a carved form of any figure, lest they wreak ruin onto themselves, for YHVH will scatter them among the people where they will serve gods made by human hands... which cannot see, nor hear, eat, smell. Take care not to forget the covenant, for YHVH your Elohim is a consuming fire, a jealous Elohim!*

Commentary: Without mentioning it by name, Moses reminds the people of the second Saying/Commandment ("You are not to have any other gods before my presence"), when he tells them that they will never know YHVH, nor ever see YHVH, nor should they even imagine what YHVH might look like. However, they can experience YHVH and gain wisdom from that experience by listening to the "Voice" - that same Voice that spoke the world into existence in Genesis 1 and later spoke to the patriarchs, and to Hagar, Joseph, and Moses.

Moses then warns the people that YHVH will appear as a consuming fire to those who do not heed the Voice. That is to say that unlike Moses at the burning bush, spiritually deaf people will never see the extraordinary in the ordinary; never partake in, nor appreciate the richness that is all around them; never inhabit the present with enough clarity and mindfulness to perceive a new and more authentic purpose to their lives.

Moreover, those who do not listen will be scattered. We learned in the Genesis 11 "Tower of Babel" story that being scattered means being in exile, vulnerable, and disconnected from YHVH, the land, community, family, and our authentic self. Said differently, it means to be cursed. The Hebrew word for "curse" is *clah-la;* that is, being so light as to be easily blown away without leaving a trace. To live a cursed life, therefore, is to live a life that does not matter to anyone, such that when we are gone, no one will remember us or our names.

Summary: Deuteronomy 4: 25 to 4:43: *Moses sermon ends with a message of compassion: Even during times of distress when you feel disconnected, you can still find your way back and be forgiven, if you seek YHVH with all you heart and being. This is because YHVH your Elohim will not bring ruin on you nor forget the covenant with your fathers. Moses concludes this portion of his sermon by saying, "You are to keep the laws and commandments that it may go well with you and your children after you in order that you may prolong days on the soil that YHVH is giving you all the days to come."*

Commentary: The message is similar to the Leviticus 26 teaching, namely that humans have the capacity to influence their own fate. We can choose to move either forward or backward and face the resulting consequences. Moreover, our choice need not be permanent. No matter how far we may have regressed back to *Mitz'rayim*, we still have the opportunity to reverse course, be redeemed, and start over. Thus, while YHVH is sometimes presented in the Book of Deuteronomy as zealous, jealous, and short-tempered; from the perspective of Torah, YHVH ultimately represents compassion, forgiveness, and - as we read in the opening verse of Genesis 1 ("In a beginning") - the opportunity for a fresh start.

Summary: Deuteronomy 5: *Moses urges the people to follow God's rules and warns them against violating the covenant. He then restates the Ten Sayings (Commandments) in verses 6 through 18. The only difference from the original version that appeared in Exodus 20 lies in the Fourth Saying, which originally stated, "You are to remember the Sabbath day"; while Moses more emphatically says in Deuteronomy, "YHVH your Elohim commands you to observe the day of the Sabbath."*

Commentary: By saying "commands you to observe," Moses is suggesting that the Israelites have advanced far enough on their spiritual and personal journeys to actively participate in all of the Sabbath practices; something they were unable to do while wandering in the wilderness. The best that they could realistically do there was to "remember" the Sabbath.

This revision to the fourth Saying, therefore, implies causality: If we are observing the Sabbath, then we must already be in the land which YHVH promised to us. The closing verse of Deuteronomy 5 makes a similar point. There, Moses tells the people that they are to observe the commandments "so that you may prolong your days in the land that you are possessing." Notice that while some translate this verse using the future tense - that is, "you shall possess"- it is more correctly translated in the present tense (see Everett Fox's translation). Deuteronomy 5 is thus not about enduring the hardships of the wilderness, nor the distance traveled, nor the time it takes to get there. Instead, it is about coming to the realization that the Promised Land is within our reach if we willingly observe the rules of conduct that YHVH has laid out for us.

What has made this realization so difficult to grasp, however, is that ever since leaving Egypt, we have assumed the Promised Land to be a specific geographical location; a physical border which we can see and touch but have yet to enter. More specifically, we have been expecting a kind of Pleasure Island where, once we set foot on it, we will be magically transformed, showered with milk and honey, and forevermore care- and worry-free. However, Torah depicts the Promised Land as none of these. Rather, the "Promised Land" is an enlightened presence of mind and an awakened state of being.

Summary: Deuteronomy 6: 1 to 6:9: *Moses then urges the people to follow YHVH's rules and warns them against violating the Covenant. What makes this chapter in Deuteronomy unique is that it contains the liturgy's most sacred affirmation: the Shema (verse 4) followed immediately by the V'yahavta (verses 5-9).*

Commentary: The Shema ("Hear O Israel, YHVH is our Elohim, YHVH is One") represents the Hebrew mantra for monotheism. To this day it is repeated throughout the morning, afternoon and evening prayer services on Shabbat and all other holidays.

Let's decompose this short prayer into its basic components. "Hearing" connotes the importance of ridding ourselves of distractions so as to better focus our attention on the Voice that spoke the world into creation. As Hanna experienced (her story appears in the Book of Samuel), the Voice can be an internal voice that may be heard during times of meditation, silent prayer, and introspection. By listening intensely to our inner voice, we can become more aware of who we are and what we need to do. Alternatively, as Elijah learned in I Kings 19:11-12, the Voice can also be external and present everywhere - even in the smallest of actions, objects, and situations, and in the "smallest of still voices."

"O Israel" is defined in Genesis 32, the story about Jacob wrestling with the mysterious man (*eesh*). However, "Israel" refers to more than a person or a place. As the mysterious man said, one becomes Israel by struggling with God and men and prevailing. Put another way, to be "Israel" is to show a willingness and ability to live by the precepts of the Covenant and commit ourselves to a lifetime of struggle with things both divine and human.

"YHVH" means "I will be what I will be." The name implies that we cannot claim to understand YHVH, know what YHVH wants, speak on YHVH's behalf, nor try to improve upon that which YHVH tells us to do.

"YHVH is our Elohim" asserts that "I will be what I will be" will be known to us as "Elohim," a name for the divine that is conjugated in the plural form to represent an infinite number of manifestations. For example, in Torah, Elohim appears as a voice

(Genesis 1), a messenger (Genesis 18), an "eesh" (Genesis 32), the messenger that asks Joseph "who do you seek" (Genesis 37); and holy ground (Exodus 2). However, Elohim represents a small aspect of YHVH's hidden essence because YHVH is without limits (*ein sof*) across time and space.

"YHVH is One." In Torah, Oneness is where the infinite (*ein sof*) collides with singularity (everything in creation is connected with everything else). To say "I will be what I will be is One" is to say that YHVH is like no other (*ein ode*).

Putting these pieces back together, we can read the *Shema* as "You who are willing and able to struggle with things both divine and human, listen intensely to the Voice that comes to you from within and without; for "I will be what I will be" is the unifying force that is without limits and is like no other."

Commentary: The *V'yahavta* represents a continuation of the *Shema*, rather than being separate from it. Like the *Shema*, it too can be broken down into its basic elements. In its opening verse, Moses states that "You are to love YHVH your Elohim, with all your heart, with all your being, with all your substance!" (The more familiar translation of this verse is "- -with all your heart, with all your mind, and with all your might.") This verse is about love; indeed, the word *V'yahavta* is rooted in "*ahava*," meaning "love" in Hebrew. Mindfulness is another key message of this verse, which suggests that YHVH's ubiquitous nature makes YHVH's presence difficult to perceive and therefore to love, unless we awaken all of our senses to that which we are experiencing in the very moment we are experiencing it.

Moses continues with Verse 6: "These words, which I myself command you today, are to be open upon your heart." In Biblical times, the heart was understood to be the center of wisdom. Only with an open heart - that is, one that is devoid of such heart-closing emotions as pride, anger, envy, jealousy and hatred – can we experience things that bring us closer to YHVH's presence like compassion, kindness, empathy, love, and life.

Everett Fox takes exception to the translation "I command you" which, he argues, comes across as unnecessarily authoritarian. His point is that when our hearts are open, we do not require an external force to "command" us to follow for the force will naturally come from within. We will then be drawn to YHVH's words and follow of our own choosing. Rabbi Harold Kushner makes a similar point in his book, "When Bad Things Happen to Good People." There he argues that the goal of the Torah is not to make us feel guilty, but rather to make us feel good about ourselves.

In verse 7, Moses says, "You are to repeat these words to your children and are to speak of them when sitting in your house and when walking on your way; when lying down and when rising up." Moses recognizes that it is the parents' responsibility to educate their children on the Covenant's practices and values. Doing so, however, requires that parents fully recognize any activity performed with the child as a teaching moment; for that which is learned in our formative years greatly influence the way in which we will later behave.

Moses concludes with verses 8 ("You are to tie them as a sign upon your hand, and they are to be for bands between your eyes") and 9 ("You are to write them upon the doorposts of your house and on your gates"). He was emphasizing the need for frequent reminders to live in accordance with Covenant. Verse 8 mentions the daily morning ritual of putting on *tefillin,* while verse 9 refers to placing a *mezuzah* on each doorpost in the home.

Summary: Deuteronomy 6: 10 to 6:25: *Having just affirmed the people's orientation to monotheism and love, Moses reminds them that keeping the commandments, precepts and laws given by "YHVH your Elohim" will allow them to take possession of the good land that was promised to their fathers, a land flowing with milk and honey, where they can eat and be satisfied. However, he also tells them that the land is filled with good things that they did not fill, towns that they did not build, cisterns hewn that they did not hew, and vineyards and olive-groves that they did not plant. Finally, Moses recaps the hardships that will befall them if they "walk with other gods."*

Commentary: Moses' message in the final 26 verses of Deuteronomy 6 is largely a repetition of what he said in Deuteronomy 4, with one exception: The people are now warned not to attribute the land's goodness to their own doing. This point is later repeated in Deuteronomy 8.

Summary: Deuteronomy 7: *Moses continues his sermon: YHVH will bring you to the land that you are entering to possess, a land where seven great nations currently exist (the Hittites, Girgashites, Amorites, Canaanites, Perizzites, Hivvites and Yevusites), each one more numerous and mightier in number than you. Do not be afraid for YHVH your Elohim is among you. Remember what YHVH your Elohim did to Pharaoh and to all of Egypt. Strike down these seven nations, devoting them to destruction! Do not cut with them a covenant, nor show them mercy, nor marry with them, for they will lead you astray and have you serve other gods. Should you do so, the anger of YHVH would flare up against you and quickly destroy you. Instead, observe the commandments, laws and regulations that were given to you. If you do, YHVH your Elohim will keep for you the covenant of loyalty, love and blessings that was sworn to your fathers; YHVH will choose you as a treasured people. Blessed shall you be among all people.*

Commentary: Using data from the second census, detailed in Numbers 26, the story would have us believe there are approximately two million Israelites encamped at this time on the Plains of Moab at the border of the Promised Land, of which about 600,000 are men of fighting age. Unrealistically large as these numbers are, Moses states that the seven nations currently residing in the land are each "more numerous and mightier than you."

Clearly Moses is either exaggerating or is ill-informed, for the land, about the size of the current state of Israel, could not possibly have supported in excess of fourteen million people. Bear also in mind that most of those living during biblical times were shepherds who resided in tents, not in high-rise, high density urban dwellings. Might this inaccuracy be presented in the text to remind the readers that the Torah is again speaking figuratively and allegorically, conveying a symbolic message rather than a historical account?

There are other clues in this chapter which suggest that literal interpretation is unreasonable. For example, are we to conclude from the chapter that Moses, a man who once spoke face-to-face with YHVH, told his followers to commit genocide by wiping out such a large population? Similarly, are we to believe that Moses called for a holy war, such that all occupants of the Promised Land who are not embracing YHVH as their Elohim are infidels and therefore should be put to death? Are we to presume that Moses, who once led a "mixed multitude" out of bondage in Egypt, is now making the case that the Children of Israel belong to a divine members-only club that excludes all others?

Most will agree that such conclusions about Moses are not only entirely inconsistent with his character, but also imply values and behaviors that are antithetical to the commandments, laws and regulations that, we are told, are prerequisites to entering the Promised Land. So, what might be the chapter's true metaphorical message? The answer that I like is that the message pertains to the struggles that still lay ahead for the people as they journey toward the Promised Land. I am referring not to their upcoming battles with the seven mighty nations, but instead to the fact that the number of nations that they are said to be facing is "seven". As you will recall, this number holds special meaning in Torah. It is used in Genesis 1 to represent the completion of a cycle of creation and the start of a Sabbath (*Shabbat*), which means "to stop." The number seven is also central to the structure of the Hebrew calendar, as is described in Numbers 23. The message in that chapter is that if we practice the art of "stopping" on a regular basis, as the calendar prescribes, we can move closer to YHVH and thereby begin to see the extraordinary in the ordinary.

How do we practice this art? Torah teaches that we do so through the ongoing process of separating the pure from the impure and keeping them "set-apart." As such, the process of creation is one of purification by which we drain out our impurities (*chu'matze*) in order to become more awakened to our essential or authentic selves, symbolically referred to at the Passover Seder as the *matzot*. With the completion of each "seven-day-cycle" of creation, we move closer to the Promised Land.

When viewed in this light, Chapter 7's message becomes clearer: As in Numbers 31 (when the Israelites proved able to confront the human and divine struggles placed before them without the hint of rebellion, grumbling, or preconditions), the Israelites are again being tested. This time, however, the focus of the test is on the process of separation. Will they prove able in separating themselves from the polytheistic influences of each of the seven residing nations? [30] Will they successfully complete the creation cycle placed before them, and in so doing move forward on their journey to a more awakened state? These questions are left unanswered in this early Deuteronomy chapter. However, the reason for the repeated testing of the people is explained in Deuteronomy 8.

Summary: Deuteronomy 8: *Moses continues: You are to bear in mind that the route that YHVH had you pursue for these forty years in the wilderness was done to test you – to know what was in your heart and whether you would keep the commandments – so YHVH afflicted you, made you hungry, had you eat manna in order that you know that it is not by bread alone that you are kept alive, but by YHVH's orders. You are to know in your heart that just as a man disciplines his child, so YHVH disciplines you. When YHVH your Elohim brings you to the good land - a land of streams, wheat and barley, fruits, olives and honey; a land where you never eat bread of poverty; a land where you will not lack for anything; a land where you will eat and be satisfied – you are to bless YHVH for all that was given to you.*

Take care, lest you forget YHVH by not keeping his commandments, regulations and laws and attribute the goodness that you reap from the land as due to your own doing, and walk after other gods, you will perish, like the nations that YHVH is causing to perish before you.

> **Commentary**: Moses' message in this chapter is largely similar to that mentioned in a number of places in Torah, most recently in Deuteronomy 6. Specifically, if the people keep the commandments, regulations and laws, they will be rewarded with milk (sustenance) and honey (sweetness and joy), but failing to do so will bring dire consequences. This "if/then" message is then extended in Chapter 8 by likening

---

30   As brief review, Torah defines polytheists as those who choose to live their lives in narrow places where they focus more on *material* than *spiritual* pursuits. Said differently, polytheists are those who define their lives in terms of pursuits other than the seeking of *shalem* (wholeness) by trying to be like *Israel* (both willing and able to struggle with personal and spiritual matters).

YHVH's relationship with the people to that of a parent and child ("Just as a man disciplines his child, so YHVH your Elohim disciplines you").

As Rabbi Harold Kushner writes, this parent/child image of YHVH has unfortunately caused many to picture YHVH as an all-wise parent figure that rewards us when we do right and punishes us if we don't, almost as if YHVH is a kind of "cosmic vending machine." Consequently, some will blame themselves for the tragedies that befall them, causing them to suffer twice: once from the tragedy itself, and again from the guilt brought on by believing they were responsible. Others will blame the victim (e.g., "If he had only worked harder, he wouldn't be poor" or "There must be a reason why he was afflicted rather than me"). Some will hold the belief that everything happens for a higher purpose (e.g., "God must have wanted our child sooner rather than later"). Others will feel anger toward God for not rewarding their prayers. Some may feel envy toward those whose prayers seem to be answered, while others incur a loss of self-esteem by believing that they were somehow not deserving enough.

Kushner's point is that we do not live in a deterministic world of "if's and thens." Some things just happen simply by chance: A stray bullet fired by a deranged person strikes a loved one; a flight that your son was supposed to be on crashed shortly after takeoff; a relative wins the weekly jackpot. Said simply, if prayer worked (at least in ways that we would like it to), there would be no suffering, poverty, unhappiness, or death in the world.

From the perspective of Torah, however, no one - not even Moses - can control "I will be whatever I will be." This is not to say that we shouldn't keep the commandments, laws and regulations, but we should do so because it is the right thing to do for ourselves. They help us to advance on our journey to a more awakened state of *shalem* (wholeness), which we defined in the commentary to Genesis 11 as a deep sense of oneness and peace with *who* we are (with no internal conflicts) and *where* we are (in the world around us). During *shalem* moments, our heart opens and all of our senses come alive. We become more able to inhabit the present without distractions, while holding a memory of the past and a vision of the future. In short, during these moments, there is no need to journey any further because we are already in the "Promised Land."

Summary: Deuteronomy 9: *The chapter opens with: Hear, O Israel, today you are to cross the Jordan and dispose nations greater and mightier in numbers than you. You are to know today that YHVH your Elohim is the one who is crossing before you, in the form of a consuming fire that will cause those living there to perish quickly. Do not say that YHVH is doing this because you are righteous, for you are a hard-necked people, rebellious against YHVH. Do not forget how you infuriated YHVH your Elohim in the wilderness from the day that you were taken out of Egypt until coming to this place. Know that YHVH chose you above all others because of the wickedness of the other nations, in order that YHVH might uphold the word that YHVH swore to your fathers, Abraham, Isaac, and Jacob, for "Only to your fathers was YHVH attached, to love them, so he chose their seed after them, you above all other people."*

Moses then proceeds to retell the story of Horev: Do not forget how you infuriated YHVH at Horev while I went to the top of the mountain to receive the two stone tablets of the covenant and stayed there for forty days and forty nights without food or drink, while you made a molten calf. YHVH was furious with you, but with Aaron YHVH was exceedingly incensed, but I interceded on behalf of both you and Aaron, for you are YHVH's people.

Commentary: By retelling the story of the Golden Calf (Exodus 32-34), Moses is reminding the people not to regard themselves as anything special - for doing so will cause them to meet the same fate as the seven nations that they will soon be dispossessing. Moreover, by invoking the names of the three patriarchs along with reference to the Land, Moses is showing an appreciation for how his actions in the present serve to connect the past (the Covenant) with the future (the Land).

Interestingly, Moses' retelling of the Calf story departs from the original in that the Exodus chapters made no mention of YHVH being "exceedingly incensed" with Aaron or of the need for Moses to intercede on Aaron's behalf. Indeed, in the original telling, neither YHVH nor Moses seemed particularly disturbed by Aaron's behavior. Instead, they readily accepted his excuse that the fault lies with the people rather than himself: "You yourself know this people and how set-on-evil it is."

Summary: Deuteronomy 10: *Moses retells the story about his second trip up the mountain carrying the two new tablets onto which YHVH would write the same Ten Sayings that had appeared on the first pair that Moses had smashed. He also reiterates the story of Aaron's death and of El'azar taking over Aaron's responsibilities as high priest. Moses then asks, "What does YHVH your Elohim ask of you, except to hold YHVH your Elohim in awe, to walk in all his ways, and to love and serve YHVH with all your heart and with all of your being, to keep the commandments and YHVH's laws?" So, circumcise the foreskin of your heart; your neck you are not to keep hard anymore, for YHVH your Elohim is powerful and awe-inspiring. Love also the sojourner by giving him food, clothing, and shelter, for you were so in the land of Mitz'rayim. As seventy persons from your forefathers went down into Egypt (Gen 46:27), you are now like the multitude of stars in the heavens! (Gen 15:5 God's promise to Abraham).*

Commentary: The heart is often portrayed in Torah as a metaphor, representing the center of our awareness; the source of our insights; and the place where we can listen intently to our inner voice. To have a circumcised heart is to have an open heart. Solomon understood this. In I Kings 3, shortly before ascending to the throne, he wished to be an understanding leader, a leader with a "hearing heart." In contrast, Pharaoh's heart was described in Exodus 4 and 7 as being "strong-willed" or closed and unable to listen to reason. Metaphorically put, the foreskin of his heart – its thick, outer layer - remained uncircumcised and thus unable to perceive reality as it was presented to him.

When Moses said, "Love the sojourner" in Deuteronomy 10:19, he was extending YHVH's instruction in Exodus 22:20-22 and 23:9 to not "afflict" the sojourners, and instead treat the sojourner (i.e., stranger) as a neighbor ("You shall love your neighbor as yourself," which appears in Leviticus 19:18). Of course, "love" connotes a very special relationship - one that we would not think would apply to someone we barely know. We infer from Rabbi Hillel, a contemporary of Jesus, a more realistic interpretation, when he said, "Do not do to others as you would not have done to you." In other words, treat the sojourner in the same ways that we would want to be treated, regardless of your true feelings towards them.

Summary: Deuteronomy 11: *Moses opens this chapter with "So you are to love YHVH your Elohim and keep his laws, regulations and commandments, all the days to come." He then again reminds them of what YHVH did to Pharaoh and to his army in the Reed Sea, and to Datan and Aviram, how "the earth opened up its mouth and swallowed them, their households, and their tents." Keep all the commandments that I command you today in order that you may have the strength to enter and take possession of the land that you are crossing into so that you may prolong your days on the soil that YHVH swore to your fathers, a land flowing with milk and honey; a land that drinks water from the rain of the heavens.*

In verses 13 through 21, Moses repeats almost verbatim the V'yahavta, which first appeared in Deuteronomy 6 as an accompanying statement to the Shema. He then concludes the chapter with "See, I place before you today a blessing or a curse, the blessing is to keep YHVH's commandments, the curse is if you do not and instead walk

Chapter 16: Extending and Clarifying the Covenant Code

Everett Fox notes on page 903 of his book "The Five Books of Moses" that the laws and regulations conveyed in Exodus chapters 19-24 pertain mostly to property and damages, whereas those in Deuteronomy 12-26 are more about criminal and moral issues, intended to protect the individual, particularly the powerless (like the sojourner, widow, and orphan), while also introducing a more humanistic tone to the other aspects of Israel's legal system. In reviewing these Deuteronomic laws and regulations, I will follow Nelson's four-level classification scheme: Purity of Worship (Deuteronomy 12:1 – 14:21); Life in the New Land (14:22-16:17); The Structure of Society (16:18- 20:20); and Interpreting Traditional Laws ((21:1- 26:19).[31]

Before doing so, however, I want to point out a subtle yet profound shift in the lead narrators as the text advances from the Book of Numbers, to the first eleven chapters of Deuteronomy, to Deuteronomy's next fifteen chapters (that is, chapters twelve through twenty-six), to Deuteronomy chapters 27 and 28. In Numbers, Moses is the principle narrator, though the text makes it clear (by its frequent use of the expression: "YHVH spoke to Moses, saying, speak to the Children of Israel, and say to them") that his words are coming directly from YHVH. As such, Moses' role in Numbers - as it is in the Books of Exodus and Leviticus- is that of mediating the relationship between YHVH and the people.

This ceases to be the case beginning with the first chapter of Deuteronomy, for nowhere in this chapter, nor in any of the Deuteronomy chapters that follow, does the above-mentioned expression appear. Instead, Moses speaks entirely in the first person - with repeated references to the personal pronouns "I" and "me"– and does so presumably on behalf of YHVH.

Some might say that by doing so Moses is being presumptuous; that by speaking on behalf of YHVH he is taking liberties with the Third Saying. Recall that this Commandment is telling us not to claim that we understand YHVH, know what YHVH wants, or speak on YHVH's behalf. Others might conclude that his speaking in the first person suggests that Moses is not the same humble person that he once was described to be in Numbers 12. Still others might interpret

---

[31] Richard Nelson classification scheme appears in a 1988 "Harper's Bible Commentary."

Moses' persona shift in a more positive light, as providing additional evidence that he is a true prophet, someone able to channel YHVH's voice and bring YHVH's message to the community.

The persona of the focal speaker appears to shift again with the beginning of Deuteronomy 12. I say "appears to shift" because the speaker is neither identified in this chapter nor in any of the next fourteen chapters. However, we can infer from the text that the speaker is not Moses, for his name is conspicuously absent in these chapters, in stark contrast to the many times his name appeared in previous chapters. It therefore follows that the speaker in Deuteronomy 12 through 26 is YHVH; that -for the first time in Torah- YHVH is speaking directly to the full assembly of spiritual seekers.

Might this mean that the people have advanced far enough on their journey to hear YHVH without quaking in fear and without requiring a mediator? Might this also mean that the people are finally able to see Mount Horeb, the "mountain of destruction," not as a consuming fire, but as Sinai, the "mountain of revelation"; that the people have transformed their consciousness to one focused away from material and personal gain and towards YHVH's commandments? From the perspective of Torah, might this mean that the people have entered the Promise Land, at least for the moment?

On the other hand, the text gives us reason to believe that their transformation is not yet complete; that the people may have momentarily entered the Promise Land, but they give no indication that they know it. If they did, we could question the purpose served by Chapters 12 through 26, for as we will soon read, most of what these fifteen chapters cover has been covered before. On the other hand, if the speaker of these chapters is YHVH, it might suggest that the particular rules and regulations included in these chapters are to be given more weight than those which are not reviewed.

In the first verse of Deuteronomy 27, the principle narrator is once again Moses ("Moses and the elders of Israel commanded the people, saying"). This final shift in narration is reinforced in verse 9 of the twenty-seventh chapter ("Moses and the Levite priests spoke to all Israel, saying") and again in verse 11 ("And Moses commanded the people at that time, saying"). What is interesting about these three verses is how the focal speakers narrow, beginning with Moses and all the elders, then to Moses and those from the tribe of Levites, and finally to Moses alone, who remains the center of our attention for the rest of the Book of Deuteronomy.

Having introduced the subject of narration as the background context for all that will follow in Deuteronomy, we are now ready to discuss each of Nelson's four-level classifications, starting with "Purity of Worship".

➢ Purity of Worship (12:1 – 14:21)

This section begins with the statement: "These are the laws and regulations that you are to take-care to observe - - - all the days that you live on the soil that YHVH your Elohim gave to your fathers to possess." Following this opening, "separation," a core theme of the Book of Leviticus, is reviewed. Recall that separation involves the set of rules to distinguish the holy from the profane, the pure from the impure, and the boundary between life and death. From the perspective of Torah, these rules are to be followed to create a society set-apart from others by its ethical values – a society worthy of entering the Promised Land.

For example, we are told in Deuteronomy 12 to demolish all the sacred places where the nations that we dispossessed served their gods… for everything they do, including the burning of their sons and daughters, is abominable to YHVH. Instead, we are to use the slaughter sites that YHVH our Elohim chooses, bring to them our offerings, tithing, contributions, and freewill-offerings of the firstborn of our flock.

- **Commentary:** We are once again reminded of the insidious nature of polytheism (i.e., the tendency to choose to live our lives in narrow places where we focus more on *material* than *spiritual* pursuits), and the importance of distancing ourselves from their many psychological and physical manifestations so that we can prolong our days in the Promised Land. It is interesting to note the many times in Torah that we've been reminded of this, suggesting that the writers understood that our attraction for pagan pursuits is as much a part of our DNA as are our spiritual pursuits. (Spiritual pursuits were previously defined as the seeking knowledge of good/*tov*, evil/*rah*, and life; as well as answers to personal questions such as "Who am I?", "Who am I not?", "Why am I?", and "What is my real purpose?")

The text then reminds us not eat the blood along with the meat, for blood symbolizes life while meat represents that which is dead. We are also not to eat animals that do not have hooves or a cleft in their hooves, nor those that bring-up cud. We are not to eat fish that lack fins and scales, nor birds of prey, nor swarming things that fly, nor from any carcass. And, we are not to boil a kid in the milk of its mother.

- **Commentary:** The above Covenantal codes about eating meat, fish, fowl, and insects were previously mentioned in the eleventh chapter of Leviticus, in the section "Rules of Pollution and Purification," while the milk and meat restriction appeared earlier in Exodus 23: 19 and Exodus 34: 26. Why repeat these dietary laws? Might it be that their first mentioning took place about thirty-nine years ago, and therefore was only spoken to those who had recently left Egypt? It is a very different audience that is listening to the Deuteronomy retelling.

We are told that if a prophet or a dreamer of dreams invites us to walk after other gods, we are not listen to them, for YHVH is only testing us to know if we truly love YHVH our Elohim with all our heart and our being. We are to show the false prophets and dreamers no mercy, but rather to stone them until they die, for they sought to drive us away from YHVH our Elohim who took us from the land of Egypt. Similarly, should settlers from one of our towns serve other gods, strike them down with a sword, destroy the town, gather all of the town's booty and burn it all with a fire; it should be a mound for the ages that we are not to build on again.

- **Commentary**: We have confronted troublesome passages like the above, in Leviticus 20 and Numbers 15:32. In those two passages, a litany of capital offenses were presented, like insulting ones' parents, bestiality, incest, adultery, and homosexuality, which left many of us in a quandary about the Torah in general and specifically about YHVH, for as moderns we tend to prefer a more compassionate, forgiving, and loving God over one that evokes fear.

As I previously noted in the commentary to Leviticus 20, some try to defend what was written by arguing that the understanding of justice that is expressed in this ancient document should not be held up to today's standards. Others note that the apparent inconsistency in YHVH's nature is due to the fact that the Torah was likely written by different writers at different times and with different points of view.

That said, there is scant evidence that anyone was put to death by public stoning, regardless of how heinous the crime. Only a few such instances are mentioned in the Tanakh: Leviticus 24: 23, which deals with blasphemy, a violation of the Third Commandment; Numbers 15: 36, which deals with gathering wood on the Sabbath, a violation of the Fourth Commandment; Joshua 7: 25, which deals with stealing, a violation of the Eighth Commandment; and I Kings 12: 18, which deals with an abuse of power. The last of these four examples occurred around the time of King Solomon, or about three thousand years ago, Moreover, the Mishnah (also known as the "Oral Torah") points out that leading rabbinic scholars from around the second century CE imposed so many restrictions on the implementation of capital punishment in general and specifically stoning as to effectively ban it. As I mentioned in the commentary to Leviticus 20, what makes this point particularly salient is that these rabbis were some of the most ardent of believers – those who regard the Torah as flowing directly from the mouth of YHVH. Apparently even they are willing to question YHVH's words when questioning is called for - and by doing so, they passed YHVH's test.

The passages about "purity of worship" state: "Take care to hearken to these words that I command you, by doing what is right in the eyes of YHVH – we are not to add to it, nor diminish from it - in order that it may go well for us and with our children after us, into the ages."

- **Commentary:** This quote, like the one that appeared in Deuteronomy 4 should remind us of the lesson that we drew in Deuteronomy 4 from the Leviticus 10 story of Nadav and Avihu, the two eldest sons of Aaron, who were punished for putting incense on alien fire -- meaning fire that is not "set-apart," i.e., not "separated." In brief, the moral from that story is that YHVH dictated a set of detailed priestly guidelines for a reason. It is not for us to claim that we know the reason, but only to know that individual initiatives like the one committed by Nadav and Avihu will be neither appreciated nor tolerated.

➢ Life in the New Land (14:22-16:17)

The second of Nelson's four classifications of Deuteronomy's laws and regulations is "Life in the New Land." This section begins by telling us to "tithe all the produce of your seed-sowing, of what comes forth from the field, year after year-the tithe from your grain, new wine, shining oil, and from the firstlings of your flock and herd -- so that you may learn to hold YHVH our Elohim in awe." Should the task of carrying our offerings to the sanctuary be too much of a burden, however, we are advised to first convert the produce into silver and then bring the silver to the place that was chosen by YHVH.

- **Commentary:** The concept of tithing, also known as the ten percent tax, was first introduced in Leviticus 27, a chapter that also details a tax schedule that differentiates based upon each person's gender, age, and financial well-being.

At the end of three years, we are to bring out all the tithing of our produce from that year and deposit it within our gates, making it available for the Levites who might be passing through, as well as for sojourners, orphans, and widows so that they can eat and be satisfied. We are then reminded not to oppress the debtors, but instead to release them at the end of seven years (the "Sabbatical" year). Bear also in mind that we are not to set them free empty-handed in the seventh year, but rather adorn them from our flock and threshing-floor. Remember that we were once serfs in Egypt until YHVH redeemed us. Therefore, there should not be any needy persons among us. Rather, we are to open our hands and our hearts to the afflicted, for YHVH blesses those who care for the needy.

- **Commentary**: Consistent with Covenant's themes of social-justice and charity (*tza'da-ka*), which were first made explicit in Leviticus 25, this portion of Deuteronomy reiterates the message that we are to care for the powerless members of society (sojourner, widow, orphan) and the needy. Curiously, the text reminds us to observe the Sabbatical Year, the details of which appeared in Leviticus 25, but it overlooks the Jubilee Year, a related practice mentioned in that Leviticus chapter. The Jubilee Year is to come the year after seven cycles of seven years, to remind us that the Land does not belong to us – we are only sojourners and resident settlers.

Might the reason why the Jubilee Year was never put into practice was because it was *overlooked* in this portion of Deuteronomy? Or, might it have been overlooked in Deuteronomy primarily because the writers understood that the concept is *too idealistic* a concept to be put into practice. For more discussion on this point, refer to the commentary that corresponds to Leviticus 25.

We are told not to use the male firstling that are born in our flock for serving tasks, nor sheer the firstling of our sheep; instead hallow them to YHVH. We are not to slaughter to YHVH any animal with a defect.

- **Commentary:** The text is saying that we are to show our appreciation for the bounty in our lives by willingly offering up our "first and our choicest." We were first told this message in the Cain and Abel story of Genesis 4. Recall from that story that it wasn't so much what Abel gave that caught YHVH's attention, but the sincere intentionality in which he gave it. This message was then revisited in Genesis 22 when YHVH asks Abraham to sacrifice his son Isaac; in Genesis 37: 12-14 when *Israel* tells his son Joseph, the one whom he loves, to tend to the wholeness of his brothers; and in I Samuel 2 when Hanna makes good on her promise by giving up her first born, Samuel, to the priesthood.

The Deuteronomy section, "Life in the New Land," ends with mention of the three harvest pilgrimage festivals (Matzoth/Passover, Weeks/Shavuot, and Huts/Sukkot) and how we are to observe them.

- **Commentary:** The core messages are that these holidays are to be observed exclusively "in a place that YHVH chooses to have his name dwell"; and that no one is to be seen in the presence of YHVH empty-handed, but rather, each man is to give according to his giving capacity. Most of what is said in these passages is review, having already been addressed in Exodus 23:14-17; Exodus 34:18; 22-24; and Leviticus 23.

- ➢ **The Structure of Society (16:18- 20:20)**

This third section of Deuteronomy's laws and regulations opens with the impassioned plea that judges not give preferential treatment to anyone, nor take a bribe – for this can bias the eyes of the wise and twist the words of the equitable. Instead, they are to pursue each case with equity "in order that we may live and possess the land that YHVH our Elohim is giving us." For example, a person cannot be judged on the basis of one witness. And, should a case involve legal matters that are too difficult for the local judge to decide, then the case should be brought to the attention of the Levite priests and they shall decide.

- **Commentary**: As with the previous two sections, "Purity of Worship" and "Life in the New Land," most of what appears in "The Structure of Society" was previously presented in Exodus 20-23. Recall that these chapters dealt with the regulations for creating a system of justice, based on being fair (providing guidance for doling out punishments that fit the offense); flexible (recognizing that extenuating circumstances are often involved); and compassionate (offering protection for the powerless). As such, these regulations served to lay the groundwork for translating the visions and values expressed in the Ten Commandments into a body of civil law. That which is stated in Deuteronomy seems to offer a modest extension of that groundwork.

We are then told that if, upon entering the land that YHVH our Elohim is giving us, we should say "I will set over me a king like all the nations that are around me," we are to select one whom YHVH our Elohim chooses. That person must be from our own people and not a foreigner. Moreover, he shall not keep many horses nor send people back to Egypt since YHVH has warned "You must not go back that way again." Moreover, this king shall not have many wives, lest his heart goes astray, nor shall he amass silver and gold in excess. When he is seated on his throne, he shall have a copy of this teaching. It shall remain with him and he should read it all of the days of his life, so that he may learn to revere YHVH, to observe every word of this teaching as well as these laws. Thus he will not act haughtily towards his fellow nor deviate from what is written so that he may prolong his days over the kingdom.

- **Commentary**: Fox notes on page 928 the ambivalent attitude that ancient Israel had toward a monarchy. On the one hand, it viewed YHVH as the sole king (see Judges 8: 22-23), while on the other, it yearned for a human king, particularly during times when the nation felt threated.

By placing clear restrictions on the authority of kings, this section of Deuteronomy (and, later in I Samuel 8:10 -18) recognized the corrupting potential of power. Interestingly, almost three thousand years later, Lord Acton, a British historian and moralist, in the late 1800s picked up on this recognition when he wrote the now-familiar quote, "Absolute power corrupts absolutely."

We see this happening during the reigns of David and his son, Solomon, both of whom failed to live up to their potential. Regarding David, the longer he stayed in power, the more arrogant and self-serving he became, even to the point of ordering the death of those who got in his way. Solomon turned out to be even greater disappointment, doing exactly what this portion of Deuteronomy says not to do: Revered in his early adulthood for his "hearing heart" (1 Kings 3), in his later years he essentially traded it for seven hundred wives, three hundred concubines, a huge stable of horses, and a sizeable bounty of silver and gold – and funded these excesses with an oppressively high tax that he imposed on the people.

We read in later books of the Tanakh that YHVH grew increasingly disenchanted with monarchies, and eventually shifted power from kings to prophets - those who speak YHVH's words. These would include Elijah, Isaiah, Jeremiah, Ezekiel, and Amos.

We are then told not to engage in sorcery, speak for the dead, nor claim to be a prophet, for doing so are abominations. You might ask, "How can we know it is the word that YHVH did not speak?" The answer is that if the word that the person spoke did not happen nor come about, then that is the word that YHVH *not* speak.

- **Commentary:** The text is reminding us of what we first read in Exodus 22: 17; that is, it is not for us to claim YHVH-like powers, for in so doing, we trivialize YHVH. As such, magical practices represent a clear violation of the Third Commandment, which is "We are not to take up the name of YHVH for emptiness, for YHVH will not clear him that takes up his name for emptiness."

When we settle in the towns of the Promised Land, divide the territory into thirds, one portion for those who are fleeing for their lives from an accidental murder. This portion shall be a safe haven, lest the blood redeemer pursue the murderer and the blood of the innocent be shed amid your land. . These murders include the striking down of a neighbor with no foreknowledge or hatred born towards the victim, neither on the day before or the day before that. These murders also include those by mishap, such as when in the act of chopping wood, the iron part of the axe accidently slips off the wood part and strikes another.

- **Commentary:** We are reminded of the role played by towns of asylum which was previously addressed in Numbers 35.

Should the murder be *intentional* and the murderer flees to an asylum town, the elders of that town are to have him removed and handed over to the blood redeemer. Your eye is not to take pity on him – rather it shall be a life for a life, an eye for an eye, a tooth for a tooth, a hand for a hand, a foot for a foot. You shall burn out the innocent blood from Israel.

- **Commentary:** This same call for equity previously appeared in Exodus 21:24-25: where it detailed punishments that cause personal injuries.

One witness shall not condemn a man – to establish a legal matter, at least two witnesses are required. Should the witnesses disagree, then it will be up to the priests or the judges to decide who is telling the truth and who is bearing false witness. And if a witness falsely testifies against another that which he schemed against the other is to be done to the accuser.

- **Commentary:** How are we to mete out justice in instances of accidental killings or a lack of witnesses? What should be done to protect the accused until sufficient evidence surfaces to warrant a trial? Numbers 35 suggests that the Torah was grappling with these questions and devising innovative solutions that were humane and sensible at a time when honor killings were the norm. Meanwhile, Exodus 20's Ninth Saying/Commandment ("You are not to testify falsely against your fellow witness") touched upon the importance of bearing true witness. While Deuteronomy reviews those solutions and values, it offers little in the way of extensions to them.

When you go out to war against your enemies and see their horses, chariots, and fighting people many more than you, do not be afraid, for YHVH our Elohim, is with us.

- **Commentary**: The opening lines of this verse are very similar to what appeared in the seventh chapter of Deuteronomy, where Moses tells the people that as they enter the Promised Land, they will face seven great nations, each one more numerous and mightier than it, but not to be afraid, for YHVH will be fighting on their behalf.

Officials are to speak to the people who are assembling for war, saying "who is the man who built a new house, but has not yet dedicated it; or planted a new vineyard, but has not yet made use of it; or engaged to a woman but has not yet married her; or is afraid and soft of the heart – let these people return to their homes, lest they die in the war."

- **Commentary**: Departing from the practice of saying what already has been said, the above passage offers something original. Put in the words of a later writing, that from the Book of Ecclesiastes, "A season is set for everyone, a time for every experience under heaven - A time for being born, a time for dying- A time for war and a time for peace." This passage advances the thought that it is the wise and fair community who knows what time it is for its members and therefore not to treat them as the same, for only by having this awareness can we fully participate in the seasons of our lives.

When we draw near a town that is far from the land that YHVH has given as our inheritance, before waging war against its inhabitants, call out the terms of peace; allow them the choice of becoming forced laborers. But if they do not make peace, we are to strike down all males, keeping alive the women, children, and the animals – YHVH gives us everything that is within the town as booty.

- **Commentary:** This passage is difficult to understand on at least three levels. Why would the people want to wage war against others who live far from the Promised Land? Isn't it hypocritical to say that we are to "structure a society" based on a fair, flexible, and compassionate system of justice, but then give others the ultimatum of death or forced labor when they committed no apparent wrong other than being in the wrong place at the wrong time? And, regarding the choice of forced labor, have we learned nothing from the time when we were serfs in the land of Egypt? That is to say, is our foreign policy to be guided by the first Saying/Commandment *("I am YHVH your God, who brought you out from the land of Mitz'rayim, and from the house of serfs")* or by Pharaoh's inhumane practices?

But in those towns that YHVH gives to us as an inheritance, we are not to leave anyone alive – but cause the destruction of the Hittite, Amorite, Canaanite, Perizzite, Hivvite and Yevusite, lest they lead us astray into abominable practices by which they serve their gods and sin against YHVH our Elohim. When you besiege a town for many days, do not bring ruin to the trees that grow food, for from them you are to eat.

- **Commentary:** This order to destroy these nations comes directly from the same morally troubling order that was originally mentioned in Deuteronomy 7. Recall from the discussion of that chapter that we deemed its literal interpretation to be unreasonable and therefore rejected it. In its place, we suggested that the story was conveying a test: Would the Children of Israel prove able to separate themselves from the polytheistic influences of each of the seven residing nations?

In other words, the Torah is not advocating genocide in the Book of Deuteronomy any more than it did in Exodus 17: 14 when it called for Amalek's extinction. Rather, it is using these stories to teach us the importance of struggling with, and ultimately conquering, our non-covenantal urges.

Similarly, the Torah is not telling us to destroy the people while showing compassion to the trees, for such a message is inconsistent with the Torah's core values. Rather, it may be telling us not to focus on that which is life-destroying (*ra*) about the adversarial nations, but instead to look for that which is *tov* (life-sustaining) and to preserve those qualities.

What I find mystifying in the retelling of this story is that one of the seven mighty nations mentioned in Deuteronomy 7, the Girgashites, is inexplicably missing from the list of nations mentioned in the above passage; that is, in Deuteronomy 20: 17.

> **Interpreting Traditional Laws (21:1- 26:19).**

Most of what is addressed in Deuteronomy's fourth set of laws represents addenda to, or extensions of, what has already been addressed in the Books of Leviticus and Numbers, and therefore do not require additional comment. Presented in no particular order, these include such wide ranging topics as the rights of a woman who is captured in battle (Deuteronomy 21: 10-14); how to divvy up one's estate to the next generation in cases where the man has children from two or more wives (Deuteronomy 21: 15-17); the burial protocol for a man sentenced to death for a capital offense (Deuteronomy 21: 22-23); how to handle the situation where a neighbor's animal wanders onto your property (Deuteronomy 22: 1-4); how to build a roof that won't collapse when someone walk on it (Deuteronomy 22: 8); what to do should either a husband or wife put out capricious charges against the other (Deuteronomy 22: 13- 21); the rights of the husband and wife in cases where the man wants a divorce (Deuteronomy 22: 13-21); how to handle instances of adultery, rape

(Deuteronomy 22), and prostitution (Deuteronomy 23: 18-19); when to charge interest and when not to (Deuteronomy 23:20-21); how to determine a reasonable boundary between two neighbors' farms (Deuteronomy 23: 25-26); protocols for remarrying so as to avoid ritual pollution (Deuteronomy 24: 1-4); the length of military leave for a recently married man (Deuteronomy 24: 5); a reminder regarding skin disease (Deuteronomy 24: 10-13). This listing of Covenantal codes continues through Deuteronomy 26: 19).

There are, however, four codes in this fourth set of Deuteronomy's regulations that can benefit from some additional interpretation: The Unsolved Murder (Deuteronomy 21: 1-9); The Rebellious Son (Deuteronomy 21: 18-21); The Bird's Nest (Deuteronomy 22: 6-7); and Those Who Qualify for Entry into the Community (Deuteronomy 23: 2-9).

Regarding the "unsolved murder," the text states that if there is found a corpse on the soil that YHVH our Elohim is giving us but no one knows who struck the person down, the elders from the closest town are to sacrifice an unblemished calf, as a way to symbolically atone for the death of the murder victim. While sacrificing the animal, the elders are to say: "Our hands did not shed this blood, our eyes did not see! Oh, YHVH, do not put innocent blood amid your people Israel."

- **Commentary:** As true today as it was during biblical times, unsolved murders are particularly unnerving, for they imply that the culprit may be residing near-by, lying in wait to strike again without warning. The consequences to the community can be toxic, engendering a flow of false accusations, unsubstantiated suspicions, feuds and honor killings that can undermine the community's social structure. Apparently the writers of Deuteronomy 21 understood this. While we moderns likely judge the recommended resolution as superstitious nonsense (not to say that we have better solutions today), most would not find fault with its intended purpose: to bring closure to the victim's family as quickly as possible before things get out of control.

Regarding the Rebellious Son (Deuteronomy 21: 18-21), the passage tells of the situation where a child does not listen to his parents, even after being disciplined by them. The parents are to proclaim to the elders of their town that their child is a glutton and a drunkard, after which the town's men are to pelt the boy with stones, so that he dies.

- **Commentary:** As previously mentioned in the commentary to Leviticus 20, citations like that of the "Rebellious Son" leave many of us in a quandary about the Torah in general and specifically about YHVH, for as moderns we tend to prefer a more compassionate, forgiving, and loving God over one that evokes fear. Moreover, in that the word "Torah" means "teaching," the question must be asked: "What can we learn from this citation?" Is it to "love your neighbor as yourself" (Leviticus 19:18), or to behave with the same self-righteous intolerance and barbaric cruelty as do today's Taliban? These kinds of questions have troubled readers of the Torah for thousands of years.

    My position is that if we interpret the above-mentioned passages in the context of another teaching in Torah - the one that encourages us to actively question YHVH's words when these words pose rulings that challenge our sensibilities – then we will not find these passages troubling, nor conclude that YHVH is capricious and inconsistent. For more on this issue, I encourage the reader to refer back to this book's commentary about the "Rebellious Son" that appeared in Leviticus 20.

Regarding the "Bird's Nest," we read in Deuteronomy 22: 6-7 that should we encounter by chance a bird's nest with a mother crouching upon either fledglings or eggs, we are to set the mother free, but fledglings or eggs we can take for ourselves, in order that it may go-well with us and prolong our days.

- **Commentary**: Everett Fox points on page 946 the obvious parallels between the expressions used in these two verses; specifically, "prolonging days" and "going well" - and that of the Fifth Commandment (honoring parents). Recall that this Saying literally translates as "give weight, or close attention to" your parents. This is another way of saying, "bear true witness" on your parents (the Ninth Saying). However, "how do we bear true witness on an animal?"

An answer implied by the text is that we do so by viewing the mother bird for what it is: the potential to bring forth life that is embedded in creation by YHVH. It follows that the children are the actualization of that potential –something which the Creation Story in Genesis1 deemed as being *tov*, or "good." Just as we would not chop down a tree to get to its fruits, so too we would not take the mother bird to get to its children. Doing so is tantamount to destroying life's potential; that is, destroying something which never belonged to us, nor did we ever have a hand in creating it. This is to say that the taking of the mother bird serves to destroy that which is embedded in the creation by YHVH, or what the Torah defines as being *rah*, or "evil". On the other hand, taking the children in this context represents the showing of appreciation for, or giving weight to, that which is given to us by the creation. As such, this particular regulation is reminiscent of what Abel did when he offered up to YHVH the choicest parts of the first born of his flock in Genesis 4.

Regarding the decision as to who qualifies for entry into the "the assembly of YHVH" and who does not, the text instructs us in Deuteronomy 23: 2-9 not to allow entry to an Ammonite or a Moabite, not even to the tenth generation, for those from these two tribes did not greet us with food and water on our way out of Egypt; and because they hired Bil'am to curse us. However, we are to allow entry to an Edomite, for he is our brother, and to an Egyptian, for we were once sojourners in his land.

Commentary: The five verses that comprise these instructions are fraught with inconsistencies. For example, while we are told that even a tenth generation Moabite is disqualified from the community of spiritual seekers, (the number "ten" is often used in Torah to represent an amount sufficiently large to capture our attention and affect our behavior), the Book of Ruth tells us that Ruth, a Moabite, was King David's great-great grandmother.

In turn, the Edomites were anything but gracious hosts. When asked by the Children of Israel to "let us cross through your land – we will not cross through your fields or through your orchards, nor drink water from your wells," they responded by saying "You shall not cross through me, lest with the sword I come out to meet you!" (Numbers 20: 14-19.)

As for the Egyptians, Exodus 12 leads us to believe that some of the Egyptians have already qualified, being among the "mixed multitude of others" that left Ra'amses for Sukkot during the mass exodus from Egypt.

➢ Concluding Remarks: (Deuteronomy 27-30)

Deuteronomy 27 begins with Moses and the elders of Israel commanding the people to keep all of the commandments as we cross the Jordan and enter into the land that YHVH our Elohim is giving us. In verse 9 it is Moses and the Levite priests who state the same message. Finally, in verse 10, Moses speaks, telling the people that when we have crossed the Jordan, we are to bless Shimon, Levi, Judah, Yissakhar, Joseph and Benjamin, while cursing Reuven, Gad, Asher, Zevulun, Dan, and Naftali. The chapter ends with the Levites instructing us to damn those who commit twelve specific offenses, including the making of a carved image; insulting our parents; leading astray a blind person; casting aside a sojourner, an orphan, or a widow; having sex with an animal, sibling, or mother-in-law; taking a bribe; and striking down a neighbor in secret.

Deuteronomy 28 continues the theme of blessings and curses by listing fourteen rewards for observing all of the laws and regulations that comprise the Covenantal Code, and fifty-five curses if we do not observe them. Each curse depicts in gruesome detail something that the land of milk and honey is not - a future where parents will consume the flesh of their sons and daughters because they have nothing else to eat (Deuteronomy 28: 53); a future where YHVH will scatter us (Deuteronomy 28: 64); a future where YHVH will return us to Egypt (Deuteronomy 28: 68).

Discussion Questions: The content of these two chapters raises a few baffling questions.

- **Why are we told to bless the tribes of Shimon, Levi, Judah, Yissakhar, Joseph and Benjamin, while cursing the tribes of Reuven, Gad, Asher, Zevulun, Dan, and Naftali?** I will address this question when we read Deuteronomy 33 where Moses offers a second and final round of blessings, some of which will inform those that he mentions in Deuteronomy 27.

- **Why damn the twelve offenses listed in Deuteronomy 27?** Why single out these twelve and not the many other offenses that have already been stated in various locations of Torah including Leviticus 27 or are about to appear in chapter 28 of Deuteronomy? The Deuteronomy 27 list would make sense if it was closely tied to the Ten Commandments or the so-called "Golden Rule" from Leviticus 19: 18 ("You shall love your neighbor as yourself"), but its tie to either is both faint and inconsistent.

- **Why does Deuteronomy 28 list far more curses than blessings?** And why are some of the curses so graphically described? Perhaps the writer(s) understood that the very threat of these curses (e.g., consuming the flesh of your sons and daughters) would be enough to maintain social order by deterring those who are inclined to stray.

In Deuteronomy 29 Moses again offers a brief retelling of the past forty years and a final reminder of the many painful consequences that will befall us if we abandon the covenant and serve other gods. In contrast, Moses offers a more upbeat message in Deuteronomy 30. He states that no matter how severe our transgressions, we have the opportunity to be forgiven and "return" (*tshu'vah*). Specifically, should we return to YHVH our Elohim and listen to the Voice with all our heart and with all our being (soul), YHVH will restore our fortunes; circumcise our hearts; show us compassion; collect us from where we have been scattered; and bring us back to the land that YHVH swore to our fathers, Abraham, Isaac, and Jacob. Moreover, we have it within us to observe the commandments. As Moses said, we don't have to go up to the heavens to hear the Voice, nor cross the sea. Instead, the Voice resides within our reach, as near to us as are the words in our mouths and as close to us as our hearts.

- **Commentary:** As we have read before, words can either create or destroy, and once uttered, they are nearly impossible to withdraw. (Or, as the Aramaic phrase *abra-ka-dabra* tells us, "I create as I speak"). In turn, a circumcised heart – a heart that is fully alert to our surroundings - symbolizes the source of compassion, kindness, empathy, love, and life – all that brings us closer to YHVH's presence. Thus, Moses seems to be saying that we are best able to observe the commandments if we draw on our inner wisdom before engaging in speaking and doing.

  As an aside, the Hebrew word for "compassion," *rakh'man-ee-oot*, shares the same three letter root (*shoresh*) as does the word *ra'khem*, which means "womb." Showing compassion, therefore, is understood in Torah to be a born-again experience; it is like returning a person to an unblemished place, a place of innocence, a place of starting over.

Moses concludes his sermon with the following: I set before you today life and good, and death and ill. Choose life: Love YHVH your Elohim, walk in YHVH's ways and keep the commandments, laws and regulations, so that we may stay alive and become many.

Closing thoughts: All of the many above-listed instructions address ways to minimize the kinds of disruptions that can tear at a community's social fabric and shorten our days as a spiritual community; that is, a community that can appreciate life before death, participate in the ongoing process of creation, and attain an awakened state of being where we find both milk (symbolic of nourishment) and honey (symbolic of sweetness and joy), even during mundane or troubled times. The question is, "Will the people be able to follow this long list of instructions?" Bear in mind that they have just spent the last forty years of their lives wandering in the wilderness, and therefore have no experience in inhabiting a home base, let alone a place of such promise.

Chapter 17: The On-Going Journey

Summary: *Moses said to all of Israel, "I am today a hundred and twenty years old and am no longer able to go out and come in. YHVH has said to me: You are not to cross over this Jordan!" But, YHVH your Elohim will cross-over before you and destroy those nations from before you, so that you may dispossess them. So, "be strong, be courageous, for YHVH your Elohim will not abandon you." Moses called for Joshua and said to him that Joshua will enter with the people into the land that was sworn to their fathers, to allot to them their inheritance (Deuteronomy 31: 1-7).*

YHVH then said to Moses: "Your days are drawing near to die… you are about to lie besides your fathers… Know that when I bring the people to the land that I swore to their fathers, a land flowing with milk and honey, they will eat and grow fat, and proceed to violate my covenant and go whoring after the gods of the foreigner living in the land. My anger will flare up against them and I will conceal My face to them. Yes, I know the plans that they are making today, even before I bring them into the land about which I swore!" (Deuteronomy 31:16-18).

YHVH then commanded Moses to write down a song to remind the people one last time of their unfaithful tendencies. That song, the subject of Deuteronomy 32, is sixty-nine verses long. It contrasts YHVH's caring parental nature with that of Israel's ingratitude. Once Moses spoke all the words of the song to the people, he said to them to "set your hearts towards all these words. Indeed, no empty words is it for you…the words speak of your life, for through them you shall prolong your days on the soil that you are crossing over the Jordan to possess" (Deuteronomy 32: 44-47).

YHVH spoke to Moses on the same day, telling him to go up to the heights of Mount Nevo, in the land of Moav, that faces Jericho and see the land of Canaan that I am giving to the Children of Israel for a holding… indeed, at a distance you shall see the land, but not enter it. Instead, you are to die on that mountain – "because you broke faith with me in the midst of the Children of Israel at the waters of Merivat Kadesh, in the Wilderness of Tzyn, because you did not treat me as holy (Deuteronomy 32: 48-52).

Moses then proceeds in Deuteronomy 33 to bless the tribes of Reuven, Judah, Levi, Benjamin, Joseph, Efrayim, Menashe, Zevulun, Yissakhar, Gad, Dan, Naftali, and Asher.

In Deuteronomy 34, Moses went up from the Plain of Moav to Mount Nevo, at the top of the Pisga Range that faces Jericho. There YHVH let him see all the land: Gilad as far as Dan, all Naftali, and the land of Efrayim and Menashe, and all the land of Judah, as far as the Hindmost Sea, the Negev, the round-plain, and the cleft of Jericho as far as Tzo'ar. And YHVH said to him: "This is the land that I swore to Abraham, Isaac, and Jacob, saying: To your seed I give it! I have let you see it with your eyes, but there you shall not cross! So there died Moses, a servant to YHVH, in the land of Moav, at the mouth of YHVH (Deuteronomy 34: 4, 5).

YHVH buried him in the valley in the land of Moav… and no man has knowledge of the site of his burial until this day. Now, Moses was a hundred and twenty years old at his death, but his eyes had not grown dim and his vigor had not fled. The Children of Israel wept for Moses for thirty days. [32]

Now, Joshua was filled with the spirit of wisdom, for Moses had laid his hands upon him, and so the people listened to him as they had to Moses. But, there arose no further prophet in Israel like Moses, whom YHVH knew face-to-face, in all the awe-inspiring acts that Moses did before the eyes of all Israel.

Discussion Questions: Was Moses really a hundred and twenty years? Is the Torah suggesting that we don't have free will? Why did Moses in Deuteronomy 27 bless some tribes and curse the others? How did those blessings and curses compare to the blessings that Moses made in Deuteronomy 33? What did Moses see at Mount Nevo? Was Moses denied entry into the Promised Land? Did Moses exist?

- **Was Moses really a hundred and twenty years?** A like-question was previously addressed in connection with the Exodus 3 story at the time when the eighty year old Moses was encountering YHVH at the burning bush. In my commentary to that story, I noted that recent archeological evidence suggests that during biblical times people

---

[32] The tradition of mourning for thirty days, referred to as *shlo-shim*, was first observed in the Torah for Aaron after his death, in Numbers 20.

viewed two holidays, Rosh Hashanah and Passover, as New Year celebrations. As such, each twelve-month year, as we measure time today, may have represented two years to them. If so, then Moses was a much more realistic age of about forty when he encountered YHVH at the Burning Bush and was sixty (not a hundred and twenty) when he died – at an age "when his eyes had not grown dim and his vigor had not fled" (Deuteronomy 34: 6).

I also mentioned that we need not try to explain Moses' age literally, but rather metaphorically, built around the number "40". As you will recall, the number "40" is repeatedly used in the Torah to symbolize the birth of a fundamentally new understanding about the meaning of life, and therefore the death of what we once held to be true. Put another way, when the text associates an event with the number "forty," it usually means that a revelation has taken place that allows the protagonist to cross-over into a closer relationship with himself/herself, with others, and with the divine.

Staying with this "40" metaphor, we can say that Moses was forty when, in Exodus 2, he "killed" the Egyptian inside of himself, and in so doing separated himself from his princely past and all the wealth, comfort and power that came with being a part of the royal family, for a life predicated around serving YHVH.

Then, at the age of seventy-nine, he was about to have a second "forty" experience when he came upon the Burning Bush and saw something extraordinary in the ordinary - a bush that was burning, but not being consumed. Understanding the profoundness of that moment, he uttered the phrase, "here I am" (*hee-ney-nee*), symbolizing that once again his life would be changed.

He had one last transformational "forty" experience, in Exodus 20 when, after camping out for forty days and forty nights at the top of Mount Sinai, he received the Ten Sayings, each Commandments intended to help us along our personal and spiritual journeys as we struggle with questions about good, evil, and the meaning of life.

Might this explain why Moses was said to be a hundred and twenty years old at the time of his death? While the text doesn't tell us, we can assume that Moses has remained at this spiritual age for the next forty calendar years that followed, as he led the people in the wilderness, for those years of wandering were not transformational for Moses; he had already been transformed (enlightened) by the Sinai experience. However, those forty years were transformational for those whom he led. It was during those years of wandering in the *mid'bar* "where they could hear YHVH speak" that they readied themselves to enter the Promised Land. [33]

- **Is the Torah suggesting that we don't have free will?** YHVH shares with Moses a vision of the not-so-distant future when the Israelites will cross-over into the land of the Canaanites, be confronted with powerful material earthly temptations offered by this prosperous polytheistic civilization, and give into these temptations. This foretelling the future, however, raises the question as to whether, from the perspective of Torah, we are imbued with free will, for how can there be free will if YHVH can foretell the future?

We first asked this question in the commentary to Genesis 16. There I pointed out that free will is a fundamental Torah tenet, first introduced in the Garden Story, when we are given the freedom to choose between good and evil. Without this freedom there would be no need for us to struggle (that is, to be like "Israel") and, consequently, no opportunities for personal and spiritual growth. Without this

---

[33] Recall from the commentary of Genesis 14 that the Hebrew word for wilderness, *mid'bar*, is rooted in the verb, *da'ber,* which means "speak." Thus, in Torah, the wilderness is more than a desert; rather it is a spiritual place where one can hear God speak. That is to say that through the forty years of wandering in the *mid'bar,* the people purged themselves of the slave values that they once held to be true, and gave birth to a fundamentally new, more "promising" understanding about the meaning of life.

freedom, Adam and Eve would never have left the Garden, which would have caused Creation to have ceased on the sixth day, instead of being an ongoing process. And, without free will, we would not be "created according to YHVH's likeness and name" because we would never be able "to be what we will be."

Since Genesis 16 we have been introduced to many other references that support the existence of free will. For example, in Deuteronomy 6 we are told that if we keep the commandments, regulations and laws, we will be rewarded with milk and honey, but face dire consequences if we fail to keep them. Accordingly, we have the capacity to influence our own fate. By the actions that we choose, we can either move ourselves forward or backward in our relationships with ourselves, our community, and the divine.

Moreover, our choices need not be permanent. No matter how far we have regressed back to Mitz'rayim, we still have the opportunity to reverse course, seek forgiveness, be redeemed, and start afresh- if we so will it. In other words, set-backs are to be the expected norm as we journey to the land that is promised to us, but so are forgiveness and the promise of returning.

The question remains, however: Can there be free will if our future is predetermined? Some might favor an explanation that claims that both conditions are simultaneously possible because YHVH exists outside of our linear understanding of time. Specifically, YHVH can predict our future because YHVH resides in some uncharted dimension where the past, present, and future converge.

I prefer a less metaphysical explanation: The Torah isn't suggesting that YHVH can predict the future, but rather that some of our behaviors are predictable. The simple fact is that we are all prone to choosing poorly, particularly in the face of material temptation. It is as if this inherent weakness is programmed into our DNA, but so is the ability to learn from our set-backs. It is these set-backs and the struggles that they pose that give us the opportunity for growth and advancement. Without the struggles, we will be unable to live up to the name, "Israel" (recall that this name means "someone who is able to struggle with things both divine and human). Without struggles, we let complacency set in; we "eat and grow fat."

- **Why did Moses in Deuteronomy 27 bless some tribes and curse the others and how did those blessings and curses compare to the blessings that Moses makes in Deuteronomy 33?** Recall that in Deuteronomy 27, Moses blessed the tribes of Shimon, Levi, Judah, Yissakhar, Joseph and Benjamin, and cursed the tribes of Reuven, Gad, Asher, Zevulun, Dan, and Naftali. As we will read, the distribution of blessings and curses bears little resemblance to that metered out by Jacob/Israel shortly before his death (see Genesis 48 and 49); nor is it patterned by the relative sizes of the tribes at the time of the second census (Numbers 26); nor does it correlate with Moses' parting blessings in Deuteronomy 33:1 through 33:27. The one possible exception is the half-hearted deathbed blessing that Moses made to the tribe of Reuven in Deuteronomy 33:6: "May Reuven live and not die, but let his menfolk be few in number." While not exactly a curse, Moses' blessing of Reuven is hardly a strong endorsement.

Couple this "blessing" with Reuven's past, however, and the curse that Moses placed on Reuven and his descendants in Deuteronomy 27 makes more sense. For example, it was Reuven, the first born of Jacob's twelve sons, who naturally expected to inherit the family birthright. It went instead to his younger brother, Joseph, a person whom Reuven resented. It was Reuven who, when seeing Joseph approaching him from afar, suggested to his brothers that they "strip him of his ornamented coat and drop him into a dry pit" (Genesis 37: 22-24). It was Reuven who further eroded his relationship with his father by having sex with Bilha, his father's concubine. For this act his father cursed him and --by inference -- his descendants (see Genesis 35:22 and Genesis 49: 3). It was Reuven who, along with the Tribe of Gad and half the tribe of Menasha, willingly relinquished his inheritance rights to the Promised Land for the grazing pastures east of the Jordan. And, it was two of Reuven's descendants, Datan and Aviram who - along with Korah, a Levite- rose up against Moses and Aaron, in what is known as the "Korah Rebellion" in Numbers 16, exclaiming, "Too much is yours!

Indeed, the entire community is holy… why then do you exalt yourselves over the assembly?"

Of course, the above explanation about Reuven and the Levites offers no insight as to why the Levites weren't similarly cursed, but instead were blessed by Moses in Deuteronomy 27. If the Levites' behavior in the Korah Rebellion wasn't enough, it was the patriarch of that tribe who, along with his brother Shimon, was cursed by Jacob when on his death bed Jacob said: "Damn be their anger … I will scatter them in Israel" (Genesis 49: 7). On the other hand, Moses and Aaron came from the tribe of Levi. Moreover, YHVH assigned this tribe with priestly roles in perpetuity (Exodus 28:1) as well as giving them the responsibility for overseeing the well-being of the Tabernacle (Numbers 1:51), all suggesting that the tribe redeemed itself, though the text is vague as to how and when it did so.

Also perplexing is the blessing that the Tribe of Shimon received from Moses in Deuteronomy 27 : given the curse that Shimon, the tribe's patriarch, received from Jacob for the brutal revenge that Shimon took on the inhabitants of Shekhem for abducting his sister, Dina in Genesis 34: 30; given its small size relative to that of the other tribes at the time of the second census in Numbers 26; given that it was also Zimri, the son of the leader of the Shimonites who, in Numbers 25, audaciously stood before the eyes of Moses and the entire community with Kozbi, daughter of the head of the House of Midyan, the tribe that encouraged many of the Israelites to worship Baal; and given that Moses conspicuously overlooked Shimon in his parting words to the other tribes (Deuteronomy 33).

Regarding the curses made to the tribes of Asher, Dan, and Naftali, what these three tribes have in common with that of Gad, a fourth cursed tribe, is that they were all born from Leah's and Rachel's handmaids, Bilha and Zilpa. By cursing their offspring, might the Torah be making a similar statement to that which it made about Ishmael, son of Sarah's handmaid, Hagar, when the two were sent out to the wilderness, presumably to die? That is, is the Torah making a strong statement against the use of handmaids, that no good will come of their use, for in using them, we are over-reaching: Trying to control that which we cannot control? Are the curses to remind us that there is much about our lives that we are not in control of, and the sooner we understand this, the sooner we can deal with life's traumas and disappointments, and find inner peace and wholeness? Are Moses's curses to the offspring of handmaids a way of saying that like Hagar, are destined to become "enslaved strangers from a narrow place"? (see Genesis 16 for the derivation of Hagar's name).

As for the blessings that Moses made to the tribes of Judah, Joseph, Benjamin, and Yissakhar, explaining the first three is relatively easy. Regarding Judah, recall Jacob/Israel's deathbed blessing to him, when he likened Judah to "a lion, the king of beasts; who dares rouse him up? Your brothers will praise you and bow down to you" (Genesis 48:8-9). As we recall, Judah was a deserving recipient of this praise, having transformed himself into a sensitive and generous person -- someone who, like Joseph, acted as his "brother's keeper" while the other sons of Jacob/Israel did not. Also consistent with Jacob/Israel's blessing is the fact that this tribe is now being led by Calev, one of only two individuals from the slave generation (the other being Joshua) who YHVH allowed passage to the Promised Land "because they followed YHVH fully" (Numbers 32:12). Finally, the descendants of Judah will be one of the two tribes that end up inhabiting the Southern Kingdom, also known as "Judah."

[As an aside, the Southern Kingdom and the ill-fated Northern Kingdom were formed around the ninth century (900 BCE), soon after Solomon's reign as king ended. Contributing to the breakup of the United Kingdom of Israel was the fact that only the tribes of Judah and Benjamin accepted Rehoboam, the son and successor of Solomon, as their king. The Northern Kingdom was subsequently conquered by the Assyrian Empire around 720 BCE, and its population scattered into what some refer to as the "Ten Lost Tribes." Did Moses foretell this outcome in that six tribes of the tribes that he cursed were among those "ten", while he blessed only two of the ten tribes (i.e., Shimon and Yissakhar). The remaining two tribes from that infamous list were Ephraim and Manasseh, two tribes that Moses neither blessed nor cursed in Deuteronomy 27.]

Regarding Joseph, whose name means "God has added," and his younger brother Benjamin, they were the only two off-spring of Jacob/Israel's marriage with Rachel, the woman whom he loved. That said, the Torah tells us little else about the life of Benjamin, while it devotes almost half of the fifty chapters of the Book of Genesis to the life of Joseph. However, we learn later that the tribe of Benjamin is one of the two tribes to other tribe to inhabit the Southern Kingdom, the other being the tribe of Judah.

As to why Moses blesses Yissakhar and curses Zevulum, about all that we know about these two tribes is that they both descended from Leah; are similar in size and are large relative to most of the other tribes; and, as we will later read in Deuteronomy 33:18, are mentioned almost in the same breath by Moses, as if they are close allies ("Rejoice, O Zevulum, in your going out and Yissakhar, in your tents").

Not mentioned in Deuteronomy 27, but cited in the thirty-third chapter are the tribes of Ephraim and Manasseh, both of whom descended from Rachel, the woman that Joseph loved. We know from Genesis 48: 19 that each was blessed by their grandfather, Jacob/Israel, who acknowledged that Manasseh was the older of the two, "but that his younger brother, Ephraim will be greater than he, and his seed will become a full measure of nations!" In making this prediction, was Jacob/Israel peering into the distant future? Might it be that he foresaw that from this small tribe would come Joshua (*Yehoshua*), Moses' successor, "a man in whom the spirit is" (Numbers 27:18), whose name means "Salvation" or "Redemption"? Could he have known that in about four hundred and forty years, half of the tribe of Menasha (along with the tribes of Reuven and Gad) would willingly relinquish its inheritance rights to the Promised Land for the grazing pastures east of the Jordan (Numbers 32)? On the other hand, his blessings displayed no awareness that both tribes would eventually disappear with the fall of the Northern Kingdom.

Regarding Yissakhar, this tribe is mentioned in Moses' list almost as an afterthought, along with its brother tribe, Zevulun.

- **What did Moses see at Mount Nevo?** Standing east of the Jordan River, with the mountains of Judea and Samaria blocking his view, Moses nevertheless looks to the west. What he sees is the distant future, a time when the tribes have settled in the land. What he is then reminded of is the distant past, when YHVH first promised the land to his forefathers. At that moment, in which the past and the present converged, he may have realized that his life has been like a vessel connecting the past with the future. At that moment, he may have perceived that which is possible should the covenant ever be completed and its potential realized. In other words, what Moses may have been seeing is the completion of the journey that began over six hundred years before by Abraham.

- **What land is Moses being denied entry into?** Moses is being reminded in Deuteronomy 32: 49-52 of the time when YHVH instructed him to speak to the rock, but instead he struck it twice. For this, YHVH told Moses that he will be denied entry into "the land that I am giving you" because "you did not have trust in me" (Numbers 20: 11, 12). (For thoughts about "Why is Moses, along with Aaron, being denied entry into the land?" refer to the commentary associated with Numbers 20.) Left ambiguous in the Numbers' telling of the story is: Which land is YHVH giving, the land of Canaan or the Promised Land?

I bring this detail to your attention because it is easy to conclude from a surface reading of the Torah that the lands of Canaan and Promise are one and the same. They are not. As I previously discussed in the commentary associated with Numbers 13 and 14, the two lands encompass very different world views - one human and physical; the other Divine and spiritual. We should note that this two-level view of reality permeates much of the writings of Torah. (Consider the meaning of *Israel* that was revealed in Genesis 35: "those who show the willingness and ability to struggle with things both *Divine* and *human*.").

This means that depending on where individuals are in their personal and spiritual journey, some will experience Egypt as a place rich in material comforts and food, while for others it is *mitz'rayim* - a spiritually narrow place where more attention is given to our physical needs than to questions of good, evil, and life. Similarly, for some the wilderness is the land of parched dryness and desolation, while for others it is the *mid'bar*, a place to go to hear YHVH speak. We can thus say that Canaan is to the Promised Land as Egypt is to Mitz'rayim, and as the wilderness is to the *Mid'bar*.

Put another way, Canaan refers to a specific geopolitical locale – the place where the Canaanites live. They may have settled in the land of Canaan, but they have never been present in the Promised Land or even aware of its presence. In this sense, the Canaanites are akin to the ten Israelite scouts who thoroughly explored the land of Canaan but saw nothing promising. As you will recall from Numbers 13 and 14, only Calev and Joshua knew that they were "there".

Alternatively, the Promised Land is not about a specific locale, but how we choose to live on it. Specifically, it represents an awakened state of consciousness wherein we feel a deep sense of oneness and peace with *who* we are (with no internal conflicts) and *where* we are (in the world around us). It is not a Pleasure Island where we are magically transformed, showered with milk and honey, and forevermore carefree and worry free.

The point is that in Deuteronomy we read about how YHVH brings us to the land of Canaan and with a strong arm will displace the seven mighty nations that inhabit this land. What we don't read is YHVH bringing us to the Promised Land. I suspect that we don't read about it because the responsibility for advancing to this enlightened state resides entirely within us. Whether we enter the Promised Land - and how long we stay – will be determined by our ability to live by the commandments, rules and regulations that YHVH gave to us. We have been given what we need to advance ourselves on our journey, but will we prove able?

Returning to the question at hand, "What land is Moses being denied entry into?" we are told in Deuteronomy 32: 49-52 that he was denied entry into the land of Canaan. The text does not mention that he was also denied entry into the Promised Land. All that is said is that he gets to see the land that YHVH swore to his ancestors and will be given to his descendants. We are also told that "Moses died at the mouth of YHVH, a servant to YHVH" (Deuteronomy 34: 4, 5) and was buried at a site that no one to this day has any knowledge of.

What a beautiful and touching way to bring closure to the Torah! With the last chapter of Deuteronomy, the personal and spiritual journey, which began more than six hundred years before with Avram, is nearing completion. Moses gets to see the fulfillment of the promise first made to Avram when YHVH said, "I give this land to your seed" (Genesis 14: 7). Moreover, just as Adam was born at the mouth of YHVH when YHVH "blew into Adam's nostrils the breath of life" (Genesis 2:7), so too does Moses die at the mouth of YHVH (often interpreted as a divine kiss in which YHVH withdraws Moses' breath).

About the phrase "no man has the knowledge of Moses' burial site until this day," the Torah recognizes the iconic status of a person who was the central character in four of the five books of Torah, the one exception being the book of Genesis. To make the location of his burial known would risk transforming an unassuming plot of land into something of idol-like proportions, in clear violation of the Second Saying/Commandment, which reads: "You are not to have any other gods before my presence. You are not to make yourself a carved-image or any other figure that is in the heavens above, earth below, or the waters beneath the earth. You are not to bow down to them nor serve them, for I, YHVH am a zealous Elohim."

About the phrase "died a servant to YHVH," consider its meaning in the context of Moses' life: He was born a slave in Egypt and died a servant to YHVH. From the perspective of Torah, this phrase suggests that Moses completed the journey. Might this mean that while he was denied entry into the land of Canaan, he was allowed entry into the Promised Land? Few questions have elicited more opinions and discussion.

- **Did Moses exist?** Like the patriarchs and matriarchs before him, nobody knows, and quite likely will never know. If he had once lived, it would have been about 3,500 years ago, or at least 500 years before the oral stories about all of them were believed to have been written. (Some biblical scholars estimate that the Torah was written down around the time of Solomon's Temple, or 1,000 B.C.E.) Thus, even if Moses was a historical person, the stories about him were likely embellished over time into folklore, as tends to be the case with oral traditions. Any lack of historical accuracy, however, should not diminish the value of these stories, for the Torah, in the opinion of many, was never intended to be read as a book of history, but as a collection of mythologies and metaphors, all of which convey practical and spiritual meaning.

Made in the USA
Columbia, SC
09 May 2022